Born, raised, and educated in the United States, Mario Lazo went to Cuba after receiving his law degree from Cornell and serving as a Captain in the U.S. Army in World War I. He took a law degree from the University of Havana and later founded and headed one of Latin America's most prestigious law firms. Through the years his firm represented the U.S. Government, major corporations, and a distinguished Cuban clientele.

After the fall of Batista, Dr. Lazo valiantly continued his law practice in Havana. Imprisoned and threatened with execution by the Castro regime, his wife, Carmen, saved his life and helped him escape to the United States. For the next seven years Dr. Lazo set himself the task of writing what even *The New Republic* has called "the best account to date of Castro's victory," bringing to the undertaking the investigative skills of a great lawyer, and a reputation that permitted him to reach into the highest official circles in Washington.

★ ★ ★

"*Dagger in the Heart* had to be written and no one was better qualified to write it."—HARRY F. GUGGENHEIM, *former Ambassador to Cuba*

"Wherever I had first-hand knowledge in my position as U.S. Ambassador in Cuba during that period . . . the facts are accurate."—EARL E. T. SMITH, *former Ambassador to Cuba during Castro's rise to power*

"The Lazo book is superb. . . . The depth of the research is astonishing."—W. L. WHITE, *Emporia Gazette*

"By far the most authoritative book which has been written about Cuba. . . ."—ELLIS O. BRIGGS, *former U.S. Ambassador to seven countries*

1.45

DAGGER

IN

THE HEART

American Policy Failures in Cuba

BY

MARIO LAZO

TWIN CIRCLE PUBLISHING COMPANY
86 Riverside Drive
New York, N.Y. 10024

This book is dedicated to the Cuban people,
in the firm conviction that they will soon again
be free

"The Castro regime is a thorn in the flesh;
but it is not a dagger in the heart."

—SENATOR J. WILLIAM FULBRIGHT,
in Memorandum to President Kennedy,
March 30, 1961

Contents

A Foreword

How did Communism succeed in establishing an outpost in Cuba, at the very threshold of the world's most powerful capitalist nation, posing a threat to the entire Western Hemisphere? In attempts to answer this question, many books have been written by Cubans and non-Cubans.

Some of these, written by people who suffered grievously at Castro's hands, naturally reflect their hatred of the dictator and those who lifted him to power; others, treated well by Castro or charmed by his magnetic appeal, portray him sympathetically, sometimes in heroic dimensions.

This book will be different, if only because I have been quite literally a man of two countries, as much an American as a Cuban, long and well acquainted with key actors in the drama on both sides of the ninety-mile water strip between the countries.

Of Latin American parentage, I was born, raised, and educated in the United States and during forty years of residence in Cuba, I constantly visited the land of my birth, maintaining old friendships and making new ones.

In this unique position it was essential that I understand the traditions, customs, and laws of both countries, that I think in Cuban as well as American terms. Over the years I came to know many of the men in both countries destined to play important roles in the Caribbean tragedy of the last decade. To protect clients and friends I remained in Cuba in the initial

Castro years. After the Bay of Pigs debacle I was arrested and threatened with execution by a firing squad.

I write as one who was in a position to see what was taking place from close-up, and to appraise it from the vantage point of both Cuba and the United States. By providing this extra dimension I hope to give the reader a more rounded picture of the events that led to Cuba's betrayal to Castro and Communism.

My law partner of several decades, Jorge E. de Cubas, who became one of the most respected lawyers of our generation, contributed a great deal to my understanding of Latin America. I first met Jorge de Cubas in 1927, just after I had obtained my law degree from the University of Havana. He was twenty-two years old and had spent his life in Cuba, whereas I had lived for thirty years in the United States. It seemed to me that if he and I combined the experience of our different backgrounds and our respective knowledge of the traditions and psychology of each country, the partnership might well prove effective. Jorge agreed, and soon we rented a small office and installed second-hand desks, a typewriter, and a filing cabinet.

From that time until the firm of Lazo & Cubas was destroyed by Castro a few days after the Bay of Pigs invasion, our partnership prospered. With every year its clientele and income grew and its staff expanded. At the end we numbered twenty-two lawyers and seventy-five employees altogether, all Cubans. The primary reason for such progress in a relatively short period was the exceptional talent, excellent judgment, and far-ranging cultural and intellectual interests of my partner. A second reason perhaps was that we adopted and adhered to the highest American professional standards of organization and responsibility, which I had learned from a brief but intensive experience with one of New York's outstanding law firms.

On countless occasions Jorge and I discussed the customs and traditions which prevailed in Cuba and Latin America, in contrast to those of the United States. Our conversations covered a wide range of social, political, economic, and legal problems. My erudite partner explained the Latin American attitudes, while I presented the American point of view. These discussions, which have continued to the present day, have always been a source of delight and wisdom.

We quickly reached the conclusion that it was impossible to understand the American and Latin American people without an understanding of the historical background of the peoples and areas from which they emerged. This would teach us why nations are what they are and cannot, in fact, be anything different. A recognition of the reasons for the inherent dissimilarities, we agreed, would provide the only true basis for friendship between the nations of the western hemisphere, and this simple conclusion interested us very much indeed.

The Iberian peninsula, which now embraces Spain and Portugal, was overrun through the centuries by a series of invaders, including the Romans, who gave the natives their Latin language. The Arabs arrived in A.D. 711, and dominated the area for about seven centuries. During this long period Jews also were present in great numbers, and there was a blending of Christian, Moslem, and Hebrew cultures. Side by side in Iberia, the Jews worshiped Jehovah, the Moors Muhammad, and the Christians Christ.

The Jews were the intermediaries between the Christians and the Arabs. With their renowned intellectual alertness they had a gift for languages, and excelled also in the monetary field, although their principal contribution to Spanish culture was in literature. Many famous Spanish authors were Jews or partly Jewish. Significant also is the fact that the Jews intermarried with the Christians to a far greater extent than did the Moslems.

The Arabs made tremendous contributions to science. They originated algebra and developed general and pharmaceutical chemistry. Their influence was great in agriculture—they built irrigation systems and introduced many new crops, including sugar cane, cotton, lemons, and oranges. They established new enterprises such as the leather and ceramics industries, and they organized a system of weights and measures and a customs service. A vast number of words in the Spanish vocabulary are of Arabic origin, as is much of Spanish cooking.

The most indelible Arabic influence on Spanish civilization, however, was political in nature. The caliphs were the absolute rulers on all matters, both civil and religious, and the people came to regard them as all-powerful and all-wise. When the Arabs were eventually defeated by the Christians and expelled, this universal "messianic" concept of the caliphate was transferred to the king. For the people, conditioned by centuries of Arab rule, he became the final all-powerful authority on whom they depended with child-like faith for the solution of all their problems.

The Jews were expelled in 1492 and the Arabs driven out a little more than a century later. Since virtually all professions and trades, and all kinds of governmental, scientific, intellectual, and business enterprises had been in the hands of these practical and intelligent members of society, the effect on the economic and cultural life of the region was catastrophic. The set-back was made worse by the tendency of the natives, who considered themselves Christians first and then Spaniards, to regard themselves as far superior to the other two races, and to disdain their occupations and trades. Craftsmanship and commerce dried up. The splendid farms of the Moors fell into ruins.

In a spirit of racial purification called *limpieza de sangre,* the Spaniards would do nothing that the banished castes had previously done. With the exception of the farming needed for survival, they regarded manual work as beneath them. Their means of earning a livelihood, therefore, became circumscribed. They could enter the priesthood, join the military and bear arms for their king, or go to sea and seek gold in newly discovered America. In the name of racial purity the Spaniard became a super-Christian, more Catholic than the semi-pagan Popes, and this in turn explained the Inquisition and Counter-Reformation. Religious intolerance became a national trait that persists to this day.

The Spaniards were the first people in Europe to embrace the doctrine of racial purity, which later was espoused by the Nazis in Germany. They were indeed the master race of the world in the sixteenth and seventeenth centuries, when they founded the first great empire since Rome.

The Spaniards call the fall of Granada and the final defeat of the Moors the "Reconquest" of their country. Yet they retained the Moorish pattern of government, under which the caliphs had wielded absolute power in every field. They continued to regard their king as the all-powerful and all-knowing authority, in effect a messiah. This complete and blind trust in the monarch proved decisive in shaping the political structure of Spain and of its colonies in America, even after their independence. It prevented the ordinary Spaniard from developing a sense of responsibility in public affairs. To this day he lives with little feeling of social responsibility to individuals or to his community. He has little concept of the teamwork and cooperation which are so characteristic of the Anglo-Saxon societies.

In 1559 Philip II took a step that greatly affected the history of Spain and Latin America: He shut the frontiers of Spain against the ideas of the Reformation. Spaniards were not allowed to leave and study outside of Spain, so that the country became insulated from the cultural and political progress being made elsewhere in Europe. Spain ignored not only the Reformation but the Industrial Revolution and the new political ideas of the eighteenth and nineteenth centuries as well, and its isolation continued virtually until the twentieth century.

These then were the salient characteristics of the Spaniard as he emerged from the crucible of the Reconquest, and it was in this era that the *conquistador* set forth to discover, conquer, and colonize Latin America.

The fabled *conquistador's* trinity was "gold, glory, and God," but he scorned ordinary labor to accomplish these ends. He was the knight of the purified faith, but he was also quite unfitted for the task of civilizing a new continent. He was incapable of methodical, patient, continuous effort. He was a bad politician and a worse administrator and he arrived in Latin America in a spirit of adventure *and without his women.* These virile young men mixed their blood with the natives and produced the mestizo, or half-breed. Later, when Negroes were brought from Africa, the Spaniard mixed his blood with theirs too and produced the first mulattoes.

In contrast, the settlers of the North American colonies arrived in the new world from the land of the Reformation, *with their families,* bringing with them the great traditions of democracy developed under the common law of England. They did not intermarry with the Indians, whom they defrauded, debased, and almost exterminated. (At the time of the Battle of Little Big Horn—Custer's famous Last Stand—the Indian population of what is now the United States of America numbered only about 300,000.) Later, when the colonists imported slaves from Africa, they did not openly mix with them either. This is one reason why the United States is faced today with such serious racial problems, whereas Latin America is virtually exempt from racial intolerance and tensions. (Brazil, for instance, is thought by many to be the best adjusted society in the world; it has never had a race riot.)

There were other striking differences between the colonization of North America and that of Latin America. The civilization and culture of Latin America were fairly well advanced when North America was still a wilderness inhabited by savages. Hence the English and the Dutch had the experience and example of Spain and Portugal—to emulate or to avoid. Holland was a small country with a middle class interested in expanding its commerce and trade. The English settlers accepted few restrictions imposed upon them by the mother country. They did not come merely in a spirit of adventure but for new and permanent homes. Some came to the new world in search of religious freedom. Others came to avoid the provision of English law that only the oldest son could inherit land. All brought with them a way of life similar to that which they had known in the mother countries.

They were not motivated by the lure of gold or silver, since these had not been reported to exist in quantity in North America. They had no interest in converting the Indians to their faith, understanding their religion as a guide for their private consciences. They were prepared to engage in all kinds of work, no matter how menial. They were frugal, they planned ahead, and their willingness to tackle manual tasks set a salutary example for the succeeding generations. Their ties to the mother country were loose, their commercial activities virtually unrestricted. They had a strong sense of public and community responsibility and strove to develop a relatively democratic form of government.

The civilization of Latin America developed along entirely different lines. The new territories were ruled and strictly regulated by the needs of the mother country, with which the colonies were not permitted to compete. The new colonies, therefore, were little more than a source of precious metals and raw materials for Spain and Portugal. The most to which they could aspire was cultivation of the agricultural products needed for survival. Furthermore, in order to protect its ships against pirates Spain regulated its trade with the colonies in such a way that only two of its own ports, Cádiz and Sevilla, were permitted to trade by sea with the colonies; by the same logic, products of the overseas territories could be exported to Spain only from certain designated points. For many years the only ports authorized to carry on this trade were Havana, Vera Cruz in Mexico, Porto Bello in Panama, and Cartagena in Colombia. Thus, great areas of the continent located far from the authorized ports, in many cases with virtually no means of communication to them, were left undeveloped. Not until the eighteenth century was England permitted a limited maritime trade with some of the Latin colonies. Portugal's attitude toward Brazil was similar to that of Spain toward its own colonies.

The Christianity which the Spaniards brought to the new world was strongly apostolic in nature. Exploration and missionary work went hand in hand, the colonizers considering it their obligation to convert the Indians. This explains the magnificent cathedrals of Latin America and its numerous churches and convents, its religious schools and universities. In contrast, there are few notable cathedrals and missions in North America, with the exception of those in former Spanish and French territories. The English settlers built churches in every town and hamlet, but they were small and modest.

The conqueror and colonizer of Latin America came to the new world to enrich himself quickly, not to undertake enterprises that required patient effort. Foresight is not a characteristic of the Spaniard. He utilized the Indians and then the Negroes to do the work he would not do himself. Until very recently, in consequence, the youth of Latin America for the most part chose university studies leading to degrees in the field of letters and the humanities. There is a great lack of engineers and technicians in Latin America, but an overabundance of lawyers, many of whom are idle. Fidel Castro was a lawyer—without clients— one of many political activists with legal training.

In the millennial tradition of their forefathers, who looked to the caliphs and kings for leadership, the Latin Americans seek and admire strong political figures. This has produced what is commonly known as the *caudillo,* or leader, who is followed less for his ideas than because of his charismatic personality. This has been a serious deterrent to civic development, of course, but the concept is deeply rooted in history. It will disappear, but slowly—very slowly.

Democracy has been emerging in Latin America but also very slowly. It could not be otherwise. For many centuries Spain and Portugal deliberately cut off their colonies from the new political, social, and philosophical ideas burgeoning in the progressive areas of the world. True, in the early nineteenth century the ideals of the American and French revolutions did reach Latin America through the leaders of the independence movements there, but the masses lived in a political vacuum and were completely unprepared for political freedom. The South American countries have had constitutions for well over a century and a half, but constitutional government and democracy are not the same thing. For many years, let us remember, the Constitution of the United States protected slavery, and part of the national economy rested upon that system.

No free and stable political institutions can be imported. Democracy can be achieved only through a long and slow process during which the people realize from personal experience that it is for them the best form of government. It has to grow out of the soil, out of the traditions and psychology of the masses. Most of the Latin American countries, for inescapable reasons of history, do not yet have this tradition and spirit. In fact, many well-educated and intelligent Latin Americans are still far from convinced that democracy is the best form of government for their nations at their present stage of political and economic development. Some of them feel that for them it is a weak and costly form of government, one that does not necessarily guarantee progress. Although the Latin Americans and the Spaniards are strongly individualistic and resent being deprived of their fundamental personal rights, most of them believe that constitutionalism and democracy, as well as economic growth, cannot be maintained and cannot flourish *except on a foundation of order and stability*. Communism, anarchy, and totalitarian regimes are intolerable to the Latin Americans, who prefer military rule to any of these. Military regimes come and go, but Communism is feared to be permanent.

It is a mistake for Americans and Latin Americans to compare their countries to one another to the disadvantage of either. It is a mistake, for instance, for Latin Americans to argue that their countries are more democratic in the personal sense than the United States because of their spirit of racial tolerance or because their mode of private living may be more advanced. The racial problems in the United States derive from history, as do the Latin American political problems.

Again, we must try to understand why we are what we are. We must learn to live with the facts of life because we will not be

able to change them in any short space of time. It was the failure
on the part of the Washington policy-makers to recognize these
simple truths that in time delivered Cuba to Communism, and
the cost has been very high, so high that it cannot yet be measured.

CHAPTER ONE

Darkness Descends

In the early morning hours of the third night following the Bay of Pigs invasion in April 1961, I was summoned from a Cuban prison and told I was about to be executed.

During the next forty-odd minutes, while seated alone on a bench, I looked back on my life as a Cuban lawyer, crowded with colorful events. There was no reason for the slightest hope that I would live to record my experience, and I had none. The Castro firing squad, I thought morosely, would blot out any chance of recounting personal experiences which might help explain why and how the happy Cubans of a few short years ago had been plunged into darkness.

I had been arrested at our Varadero beach house, eighty miles east of Havana on the north coast, on the morning of the invasion. Three G-2 Agents, with Czech Tommy guns slung over their shoulders, had taken me in a patrol car to the town jail, where my cell was soon packed with other prisoners. Varadero is a vacation resort, but many of the natives live the hard life of professional fishermen, and a number of them greeted me as they were brought in. Carmen, my wife, had followed the patrol car to G-2 headquarters in Varadero, where the police officials lied to her. I was wanted only for questioning, they said, and would be released shortly.

During the next three days we were moved three times, on foot and in trucks and buses. We spent two days and nights in the baseball park of the city of Matanzas, twenty miles west toward Havana. It was an improvised concentration camp. On platforms over the high wall which enclosed it, machine guns had been mounted at locations which permitted their crews to sweep the field. Gradually the park filled with other prisoners from the surrounding countryside until about thirty-five hundred men were massed together there. The small grandstand along the first-base line, the only partly covered structure, had been roped off, and guards prevented the prisoners from approaching it. Four hundred women prisoners were herded beneath the grand-stand.

Almost all the men were laborers and unskilled workers, including many cane cutters. A few were priests. When soldiers escorted into the camp the first of these, a smiling mulatto in his cream-colored robe and red sash, the prisoners applauded and cheered. The machine gunners on the walls opened fire, and all of us dropped flat, not knowing whether the shots were passing overhead. No food was served, and the shooting was repeated several times when small groups began shouting *"hambre, hambre!*—We are hungry!"* Water came from a single hose, with a line of men a block long awaiting their turn. There was no protection from the rain, nor shade protection from the burning midday sun. Like myself, most of the prisoners were in their shirtsleeves, and at night we huddled or stretched out together on the ground for warmth in the chill air.

At times we watched tanks, mounted on flatbed trucks, move slowly past on the adjoining Havana-Cárdenas road, the gun turrets visible over the walls. Two or three men rode on the turret of each tank. Their black leather hoods, laced under the chin, gave them a sinister appearance in the poorly lighted street, especially when the men themselves were black. Some, apparently not realizing that we were prisoners and expecting a friendly response, raised their arms in the clenched-fist Communist greeting. The prisoners, as they stood in small groups watching the tanks, were totally, eloquently silent.

Most of my fellow prisoners were inured to physical hardship, but on the second day they began to drop. We carried more than a hundred to the main portal, where we lowered them to the ground in the meager shade. Eventually they were taken away on stretchers. Curiously, many of those who fainted were youngsters. We thought they would revive, but were not so sure of the elderly men.

Gusanos (worms) is what Castro called us. Weeks later I would learn that approximately a hundred thousand had been rounded up and imprisoned throughout the island on the day of the invasion. The lists had been compiled by secret street-corner "Vigilance Committees" of fanatical Castroites, in preparation for the expected invasion. Our immobilization was managed very effectively from Castro's point of view. In the prisons and concentration camps many died. Men were crowded into underground pits for more than a week, without food, water, or sanitary facilities. Women had miscarriages, and some went insane. My cousin, Dr. Enrique Guiral, a gentle and scholarly Havana lawyer, died in a damp cell in La Cabaña fortress. One of his cellmates, the grandson of a former Cuban president, later brought me the sad news. It had been evident that Enrique was developing pneumonia, he told me, and for five days his fellow prisoners had vainly pleaded for a doctor. Then the guards removed the body, and the government bulletin reported heart failure. Pedro Menocal said, "Your cousin was a wonderful person. Because he had seen us shivering from the cold, he wouldn't let us wrap him in our clothes so long as he had the strength to resist."

I know that a permanent bond was forged among the Matanzas prisoners during those April days, when we received from one another only unaffected kindness. From the first moment a spirit of fellowship prevailed. The term "lower class" was never used in Cuba; there were few class distinctions. At first, naturally, we spoke freely only with those whom we knew well, but before long everyone was a friend.

Though we could not know what was happening at the Bay of Pigs, we had no doubt that the invasion would succeed. It was common knowledge that the liberation forces had been trained and equipped by the United States government, and the thought that the action could fail did not occur to any of us. That possibility was never even mentioned—it seemed outside the bounds of reason. American troops would be there if needed, we assumed, and there would of course be overwhelming air coverage. It would all be over in a week at most, we agreed.

By the second day we had established friendly relations with the machine-gun crews on the walls. The word went around that they would come over to our side when the first attacking planes appeared. I used to speak jokingly of Cuba as a country of "organized disorganization"—provinces, municipalities, ministries, and bureaus, with little discipline below these levels. The Cubans are notoriously individualistic. I was all the more struck, therefore, by the plans for a mass break to take over the city of Matanzas that quickly took shape within the ball park walls.

Almost at once, out of the seeming confusion, leaders emerged who organized the prisoners into groups, assigned to converge on specific military posts and police stations where arms were deposited, and on radio facilities. We were elated at the thought of contributing to Castro's defeat by capturing Matanzas, where the only two good highways connecting Havana with the four eastern provinces merged into one. In view of the temper of the people at the time, we were certain that this could be accomplished with little bloodshed. A report circulated that Santiago had fallen and that a provisional government had been installed there. It evoked joy, but not surprise.

Subsequently certain Americans claimed that Castro had little popular opposition and that the invasion could not have succeeded in any case. This is grotesquely false. Cubans close to the people and their mood at that time believe that the action came close to succeeding *despite* Washington's incredible mistakes. I am thoroughly convinced, in any case, that if any friendly planes had appeared over our concentration camp, we would have broken out and captured the strategic city.

We had our light moments, of course. The bright, quick-witted Cubans are famous for irrepressible and lively humor, even in the most serious situations. One of my devoted friends was a teen-aged boy with whom I had spent many happy hours in my boat. I used to think of him as a Cuban Huckleberry Finn. He was remarkably handsome, bronzed by the sun, barefooted, and always full of good spirits. His long blond sideburns and ready smile were extremely attractive to the girls of his group. At the Matanzas camp he left my side only to forage for things which might bring me some comfort. Once he returned with a half-bottle of Coca Cola given him by a girl friend in militia uniform. Another time it was a crude sandwich of mixed meats and cheese stolen from one of the guards. Late one afternoon this rangy, long-legged kid smilingly brought me a leather jacket. Previously we had covered the field together, picking up scraps of paper to insert under my shirt at night for warmth.

"Where did you get the jacket?" I asked.

"What do you care where I got it," he said. "Wear it, put it on."

He had far more trouble returning the jacket unobserved than he had had in sneaking it away.

(Long afterward word reached us that this fine youngster was shot, but we have no details other than that there were no charges and no trial.)

One of the prisoners, in his early thirties, had the blackest skin and the whitest teeth I had ever seen. He must have been born with a smile on his thin, happy face because it never left him. He was extremely popular and was known to everyone as "El Americano." I walked over to him and asked if he could speak English. *"No, Señor Gusano,"* smiling broadly. Had he ever been to the United States? "No, but I would like to be there *right now."* Did he smile when he was angry, while cursing someone, for instance? *"Si, amigo Gusano,* that is my problem. No one will ever believe I am angry." Later I learned that he was known generally in the Matanzas area as "the American" only because he was so well liked.

During the second night it was announced over loudspeakers that the prisoners were to be moved from the ball park, and lines began to form. I stood observing the scene. A tall, slender, somewhat stooped sugar farmer was beside me, and I asked him where he thought we would be taken. He was in his late sixties, about my age. We had become friends when I learned that for many years he had cultivated cane for a nearby mill owned by George Walker, a modest, soft-spoken, handsome ex-Marine who, until his recent death, was one of the most respected figures in the Cuban sugar industry. My new friend had lived a hard and simple life; I liked the economy of his speech, the manner in which he thoughtfully weighed his answers, and his serenity. He responded in this instance by turning his haggard face with its bloodshot eyes toward me and slowly drawing his forefinger across his throat.

Up and down the column the rumor now sped that, once on the open road, the buses packed with prisoners would be locked and set on fire. Those who fought their way out would be machine-gunned. Another rumor was that the signal for our mass execution would be the cheers following an announcement that the Castro government had fallen. Someone remarked wryly that the Castro boys had picked an appropriate place for the *matanza*. The name of the city, Matanzas, also means "massacres," and although it no longer has that connotation in ordinary speech, it derives from a dark page of colonial history: Near Matanzas the Spaniards had herded the last of the native Siboney Indians into a beautiful valley and had exterminated them.

No reports reached us that the invasion, a short distance away on the south coast, had begun to collapse. I am certain that even our guards would not have believed such a report. Our faith in the power, efficiency, and determination of the United States government was simply too deep to encompass the thought of its failure, despite two years of Castro's hysterical "anti-imperialist" campaign against the United States through his controlled press and broadcasting facilities.

It should be recalled that no American publications were permitted to reach the Cuban public. The Voice of America spoke feebly to only an insignificant part of it. In his own language, moreover, Fidel Castro has oratorical talents which sway unthinking masses. He had been telling the Cubans that in 1898, with the war against Spain already won, the United States had "intervened" in order to exploit the Cuban people and resources through the imperialist system of capitalism.

The indoctrination of Cuban youth along these lines was well under way. But the thousands of Matanzas prisoners of April 1961 were mostly of the older generation, untouched by the anti-American avalanche of lies. Their confidence in the American people and Government was especially heartwarming to a man like myself, born and educated in the United States, who for so many years had enjoyed the dual nationality of both countries.

Lined up in double columns, we were transported in buses to some unoccupied school buildings on the outskirts of Matanzas. I found myself with thirty other prisoners stuffed into a dormitory room intended for two students. The window had been nailed shut and there was no ventilation. We sat or stretched across one another on the floor, hungry and exhausted. The sanitary conditions were appalling, the stench suffocating. It was night, and quiet. My farmer friend sat propped in a corner at the far end from the door, and I was dozing against his shoulder when someone nudged me.

From far down the hall I could hear, "Let prisoner Mario Lazo present himself," and the men began to shuffle and move to open a path for me. The farmer reached for my hand, clasped and held it, but we did not speak. I looked at an old friend from Varadero seated nearby; he was slowly moving a fist as if to pound the tile floor, but he did not look up. As I picked my way toward the door someone said, "Lazo, wait." I stopped and turned. It was "El Americano." He had begun to move toward me, steadying himself on shoulders and heads. Most of the men were awake now; there was a light in the hall just beyond our door, and the scene was dimly visible. For once "El Americano" was not smiling. I stood motionless, and when he reached me he kissed me on the cheek and turned back without a word. As I made my way down the hall other prisoners patted or touched me, and several kissed my hand.

The young man who called me out was a sergeant militiaman. He must have been of mixed Chinese and Negro parentage, and I could not fail to identify him again. He spoke only once as we moved off: "Bad news for you. We have a Revolutionary Court Decision ordering you to the *paredón.*" The word had not been known to most Cubans before the Castro era. It is derived from *pared,* meaning wall, and was occasionally used to describe the crumbling thick wall of an ancient building. But by then every Cuban knew that *paredón* meant the execution wall. They had heard the screaming mobs at the organized mass rallies chanting, *"Pa-re-dón!*—To the wall!"—in cadence when Castro denounced those who had the courage to disagree with him. Already several thousand Cubans, and some Americans, had fallen at the *paredón* without the semblance of a fair trial or, as in my case, any trial at all.

Thus was my death sentence announced to me, casually, quietly, without a hint of drama or a tremor of feeling. Yet the sergeant's words did not shock me. We prisoners had been steeped in thoughts of death for only a few days, but already it seemed routine.

"May I speak to someone in authority for three or four minutes?" I asked.

There was no answer. We walked toward the main entrance of the adjoining school building, about a block away. I wondered why I had been singled out from all the Matanzas prisoners. Was it perhaps because the law firm of which I was senior partner had rendered many thousands of hours of service to various departments and agencies of the American government? Some of my friends had warned me that I was regarded as an American spy. In fact, I had been using the diplomatic pouch of a European country to get reports to the FBI, and it now occurred to me that the pouch might have been violated. Was it perhaps because the British Ambassador and his family had been our guests at Varadero during the weekend before the invasion? I had walked down the beach with the Ambassador one night, carrying a bug light. In view of the invasion which followed two days later, might this innocent pastime have been regarded with suspicion by the G-2 agents who, I knew, had me under surveillance?

I was ordered to sit on a bench, where I began to observe my surroundings. The grounds were lighted. There were three long school buildings, and one or two small administration buildings. The main building, in front of which I was sitting, was a two-story structure, and those on either side were of one story. The whole area, comprising eight or nine acres, was surrounded by a grilled fence built into a masonry wall. The bench on which I sat, trembling, cold, and frightened, was one of several along both sides of the walk leading to the main entrance of the center building. A machine gun mounted to my right pointed toward the entrance on my left, and its crew sat on a nearby bench. Armed guards paced the walks and the exterior wall, which was about the distance of a football field away. I was in the very center of the enclosure, the only person not in uniform.

Across the walk from me, but nearer the building, sat an army captain whom I took to be the officer in charge. He was talking to another officer standing at his side. I strained to hear their conversation, but could catch only an occasional word. The windows on the ground floor of the main building were barred shut, as ours had been, but the second-story windows were open and prisoners leaned over the ledges. Someone there shouted my name. I raised an arm in response, without discovering who had called. It did not occur to me to try a break—I would have been shot down after the first few steps. Here I sat for the better part of an hour, resolved that my life would end with dignity, even among strangers and with no one to record the scene.

Resting an arm on the back of the bench, I lowered my head into the palm of my hand, closed and covered my eyes. I thought of Carmen, who would be working tirelessly to obtain my release. Though she knew there was not an ounce of compassion in the Communist-controlled G-2 Secret Police, she would work on anyway. I thought of my children, Sandy, Chips, and Don, and of my sister Blanche and my brother Carlos.

All of them knew that two months earlier I had been in the United States on business, and had chosen to return out of a conviction that where there is despondency and danger among one's friends, that is where a lawyer belongs. They thought well of me for having returned, and this was a source of deep satisfaction as I sat alone on the prison bench that night.

I reviewed again the circumstances that had brought Castro to power and were responsible for my personal plight. I thought to myself: How shocked the American people would be if they knew and understood the full story. More keenly than before, in what I took to be my last hour of life, I resented the conduct of a number of Americans—two in particular, a journalist and a diplomat—whom I considered the principal architects of the Cuban tragedy, also a tragedy for their own country. How utterly catastrophic that a firing squad was soon to cancel out the intention I had cherished of some day recording the facts as I knew them.

Today I am able to say with Virgil, "These things I saw and part of them I was." I have little mysticism in my makeup, but I have wondered whether I was spared by fate in order to fulfill that intention.

CHAPTER TWO

Fragments of the Past

I am sure that man's most precious possession is his memory, and now I know that under conditions of intense stimulation the power of recall is remarkably sharpened. This was in some measure my experience as I sat in the prison yard awaiting execution in April 1961.

The panorama of the years seemed to unwind before my mind's eye. Episodes that had stretched over days and months were reenacted completely and in detail in fractions of a second. The facial expressions of an affectionate father as he related, more than fifty years ago, incidents of my childhood, came clearly into focus. As though they had taken place only moments before, I recalled events of my school and college years, adventures in World War I. Long forgotten episodes and even conversations seemed to surface from the depths.

* * * * * *

The years spent at a well-known preparatory school in a Philadelphia suburb were the unhappiest of my life. Students in American private schools are more sophisticated and tolerant nowadays, but back in 1909 Latin Americans were regarded as outsiders by most of their classmates. But the college years were quite another story.

Half a century ago, as today, Cornell University was one of the world's most democratic educational institutions. In a setting of great natural beauty, the campus high above the small college town and the lake in the valley below, students of every race and color took part in the wholesome community life with an equal and fair chance in all campus activities. The rugged, competitive life, the bitter cold winter months, the heavy class schedules, and the high scholastic standards combined to develop character, stamina, and self-confidence. What counted were the simple virtues that have been cherished through the centuries, with social and economic position meaning little. My law degree is among the lesser benefits of the good Cornell years.

I was halfway through college when Germany started the First World War by hurling her armies through neutral Belgium. My roommate and I began marking the positions of the retreating Allies with small colored pins on a large wall map. The British were overwhelmed and decimated by the tremendous numerical superiority of the Germans, but they fought delaying actions at Mons and Le Chateau, permitting the French to assemble for the "Miracle of the Marne," when it seemed Paris would fall within a week. Finally, the western front settled into trench warfare waged from the English Channel to the Swiss border; the line swayed backward and forward without breaking, while more than a million lives were poured into the conflict.

Possibly there were pacifists on the Cornell campus at that time, but I do not recall any. In 1915 and early 1916 many of my classmates debated whether we should complete our courses or enlist in the Allied armies. The vast majority of the students yearned for American intervention. Then, on April 6, 1917, the United States entered the war.

At the end of our Officers' Training Course at Plattsburg, New York, I was commissioned a Captain of Infantry. A small group from our camp volunteered to report to the New York Port of Embarkation in the belief that we were on our way to France, but we got to the Port and no further. I was assigned as Assistant to the Chief of Staff there.

The embarkation work in New York harbor involved the colossal task of coordinating the movements of troop ships—

mainly British and American, and seized German liners—with the arrival of troop trains from all parts of the United States. There were only two embarkation camps in the New York area to cushion the inevitable schedule dislocations, but we managed to dispatch the constantly arriving regiments of eager young Americans at the rate of one-third of a million each month. Often we worked around the clock.

One day a General Staff Officer who had just landed from France told us of the shocking report he was carrying to Washington. The Allied cause seemed on the verge of collapse. The French offensive at Chemin des Dames had been a disastrous failure. Firing squads had been used against men who broke and ran, and there was talk of revolution. England was in danger of starvation because of the strangulating German U-boat campaign, and Russia, too, was suffering frightful defeats in the field. The question, the General said, was whether the weary veterans in the trenches of Europe could sustain their fearful burden until enough fresh American troops arrived to turn the tide of battle.

That night I left a note on my superior's desk, saying that I wished to resign my commission and be attached as a private to any combat unit moving through the port. Despite his firm refusal, he must have made some moves in my behalf because the following week I was summoned by the General in command of our Embarkation Port. Washington wanted a captain for a special mission to General Pershing's headquarters in Chaumont, France. The purpose of the mission would be explained on arrival, and I would have to return quickly to the United States. Did I want this assignment? I certainly did, feeling that once in France I could find a way to remain there.

I set some kind of a record in reaching the headquarters of the American Expeditionary Force, where General Pershing and members of his staff received me almost at once. Pershing was reputed to be a stern taskmaster and disciplinarian, but he spoke to me, a young captain, with cordial informality.

Later, alone with Pershing and his American Chief of Staff,

I learned of the long and hard struggle they had waged to achieve and maintain an independent American Army. Because it was related to my mission, I was shown the battle plans for the St. Mihiel offensive, the first major action in which the American Army was to fight under its own flag. Pershing gave me letters addressed to President Woodrow Wilson and to his father-in-law, Senator F. E. Warren, suggesting that I keep them fastened to my chest with adhesive tape. I also carried back to the United States nine small boxes of hand grenades and other French ordnance, to be duplicated and mass-produced in the United States.

On completing my mission in Washington, I was able to join a line division training in California, but just as we were about to start east on our way to France, the war ended.

Naturally, I had watched the reports of the St. Mihiel offensive with intense interest. Launched along a 25-mile front in mid-September of 1918, we had liberated more than 70 villages, taking nearly 16,000 prisoners and capturing 450 enemy guns. Probably more than any other single operation, this one imbued the war-weary Allies with the conviction that they could drive forward to victory. Within a month the German Chancellor requested a general armistice, and full triumph came to the Allies on November 11, 1918.

Details of these great events swarmed through my mind as I sat on the prison bench. The American fighting man and his professional leaders have no superiors in the world. In my travels I have talked about them to men of many nationalities—British, French, German, Russian, Japanese—and I have never heard them deprecated. It was not until after the Bay of Pigs fiasco that I first heard American military leadership disparaged, when criticism of the Chiefs of Staff was leaked from the White House to the press in an effort to shift blame for the failure to the Pentagon, in order to shield the President's reputation for the resolute leadership he had failed to demonstrate in this instance.[1]

[1] Arthur Krock, *In the Nation: 1932–1966* (New York: McGraw-Hill Book Company, 1966), p. 323.

*   *   *   *   *   *

There were also good memories of the Second World War, when my Cuban law firm was entrusted with a great mass of work for various departments and agencies of the U.S. Government. The Florida Straits and lower Atlantic seaboard were then alive with German submarines, and airports from which bombers could hunt down the intruders had to be either expanded or built from scratch. A great nickel-producing war plant would rise out of the jungles of eastern Cuba. All these enterprises involved negotiations with the Cuban Government, and they kept our increasingly large staff of lawyers working late into the nights.

Early in its career my firm had adopted the policy of offering its services *gratis* to any American citizen who was in serious trouble in Cuba and was unable to pay a lawyer. Now, during World War II, we decided to handle the work for the American Government without profit, as an expression of respect and affection and as a contribution to the common war effort.

The practice of law in Cuba for over a third of a century had been a rewarding experience, until the courts were purged by a Communist police state. Respect for the integrity and independence of the judiciary had mounted notably before the advent of Castro. All this progress was destroyed in less than a year in the name of "proletarian revolution."

While I was still brooding, engrossed in such memories of a life that seemed about to be cut short, someone nudged me. It was the sergeant. He said that the captain wanted to see me.

CHAPTER THREE

Reprieve and Escape

When I approached the captain, he asked for my name.

In the Latin countries, one's name is customarily a composite of the paternal and maternal surnames, joined by the letter "y," meaning "and." It is a custom firmly imbedded in filial devotion, in that it permits one to retain the mother's name for a generation, but because of the length of the composite name, the second part is usually dropped in everyday conversation.

"Mario Lazo," I said.

"Mario Lazo what?"

"Mario Lazo y Guiral."

"Yes," said the captain, "you're the one. Go back and sit down." He turned again to the officer standing at his side.

"Sir, may I speak to you for two or three minutes?" I asked. But he neither responded nor looked in my direction. I went back slowly to my bench, realizing he simply wanted to make sure they were going to shoot the right man. Other G-2 prisoners with whom I have talked have all observed the arrogance of the Communist Secret Police. Sometimes, when one asks a question, they may glance at you for an instant and then turn away as if they had not heard or even seen you. Their attitude, especially toward those who do not work with their hands, is one of total contempt.

Once more I returned to my thoughts, but soon the sergeant was nudging me again. This time the captain was motioning to me to come along. We walked back toward the building from which I had come and we reached a place where a patrol car was parked. As we approached, three soldiers got out, armed with Tommy guns. The captain motioned me into the front seat and he got into the driver's seat, the three soldiers climbing in behind.

As we began to move toward the main portal, I remembered the manner in which my close friend, Dr. Pelayo Cuervo, had been murdered following an attempt to assassinate Batista and his family in the Presidential Palace. The chauffeur of the death-ride had given the details later. In the emotional aftermath of the assassination attempt, in which members of the Palace guard and of the police corps had been killed, Pelayo, an honorable and courageous Havana lawyer, had been taken from his home and driven out to Country Club Park; while sitting in the front seat he had been shot through the back of the head and dumped beside the road. I imagined that I would be taken to some isolated spot and told to get out and run, whereupon I would be shot down "trying to escape." Now, out of the corner of my eye, I began observing how the soldiers in the rear were handling their guns. They were holding them in their laps.

The heavy grilled doors of the main entrance were swung open by guards; the car moved through and pulled up on the outside, and I was told to get out. It was a moonless night and dark. At that moment, from the deep shadow of the wall, out stepped my wife, Carmen, and two of my most devoted friends, Eugene Desvernine and Ernesto de Zaldo, junior partners of my law firm. They were smiling. I stood motionless for a moment, wavering, unbelieving. Then the captain told me I had been released, I could go.

I will not attempt to describe the scene, the embraces, the tears, the almost paralyzing sense of relief. Our car was parked in the shadows down the street, and we quickly got into it and drove to Varadero.

The reason for my reprieve? Several circumstances had combined to bring it about. On the previous day Carmen had driven to Havana and had returned with a medical certificate attesting that I was under insulin treatment that, if withheld for even a short time, would induce coma and death. The G-2 officials paid little attention to such certificates, but Carmen was reaching for any straw. In truth the statement was not accurate, but the doctor was an old friend; great loyalty to family and friends is one of the marks of the Cuban character. That night Gene and Ernesto had completed a four-hour trip back to Havana from a Revolutionary Court trial in Pinar del Rio, and they continued east with Carmen to Matanzas. There the three sat on the curb outside G-2 Headquarters for six hours, trying to get to the officer in charge.

The break came when Carmen was able to push into the office of the G-2 chief. At that moment he had received the news that the Bay of Pigs invasion had been crushed. Also the G-2 had decided to move the Matanzas prisoners again, this time to an abandoned chicken farm, as the school buildings were needed for the wounded in the invasion battle. The officer in charge read the medical certificate and heard Carmen's tearful plea while waiting to be connected with the school prison.

In this atmosphere of jubilation, confusion, and feverish activity, with armed agents excitedly shoving their way into and out of the crowded office, the chief completed his call and at the end, with Carmen's hand gripping his arm, added as an afterthought: "And by the way, you have a prisoner who is an old man and sick and whose name is Mario Lazo y Guiral. If he is able to walk, release him."

That was it! Except that those in charge at the other end of the line had thought it would be amusing to act out the execution threat. The young sergeant who gave me the *paredón* news, I feel sure, did not doubt its accuracy. The Castro regime once claimed that it did not resort to physical torture. This has been disproved long since, but in any case I can testify to the mental torments.

On our way back to Varadero my rescuers informed me that the invasion had been crushed. The news left me momentarily stunned and speechless. Could it really be possible? I finally asked. Were they absolutely positive about it? Yes, the report had been confirmed by radio from Miami. There was a long silence. I tried to collect my thoughts while watching without seeing the passing landmarks.

Then I asked how the Howard Anderson case was going. Andy, a respected member of the American community in Havana, was the commander of the only American Legion Post in Cuba, a director of the American Chamber of Commerce, and owner of the three best automobile service stations in the capital. Each of the three charges against him was of itself inconsequential. One, for instance, was that at the request of a Cuban friend Andy had introduced the friend to a member of the American Embassy staff who was a neighbor. But to the Secret Police these charges, taken together, marked him as a CIA or FBI agent.

For several weeks after his arrest we and the Swiss Embassy, which represented the United States in Cuba, were unable to learn where Andy was being held. During this period he was repeatedly told he would be put on the next plane to Miami if he would sign a simple statement that he had been a CIA or FBI agent. The police wanted the "confession" for political purposes only, they said, but Andy was one of those who believed that the greatest homage one can pay to truth is to adhere to it. Also, he felt it would be unpatriotic to give a statement that could be used against his country. Eventually he signed a truthful statement covering the activities on which he had been questioned, after which we were permitted to see our client. Six of our lawyers studied the case and were in agreement that under Castro's own Revolutionary Code the maximum penalty that could be imposed was a prison term of nine years. When I asked Gene and Ernesto what the outlook was, I wondered whether we had had a favorable break in the case.

After a moment's hesitation Gene said, "I am terribly sorry to tell you this, Mario, but Andy was executed at dawn this morning. When the invasion came they moved the trial up a week."

Again I was shocked into silence. One thought that came to mind was that this atrocity might well return to plague Castro. Howard Anderson was an important man in the American Legion, and I could not believe that this influential organization of more than two million members would accept with equanimity the news that Andy had been murdered.

"How did they get away with it under the law?"

Gene said, "Mario, the law had nothing to do with it."

He explained that all the arguments for the defense had been offered. The decision itself had quoted the article of Castro's own Penal Code, which called for a nine-year prison term, but had gone on notwithstanding to impose the death penalty. The prosecuting attorney had closed his delirious demand for execuiton with a monstrous lie. If Andy had been a Cuban, he shouted, and were charged with the same offense in the United States, he would have been executed without a trial or tortured for twelve years first, as Caryl Chessman had been tortured in California. He ended by saying the happiest moment of his life would come at dawn the following morning, as he watched the bullets penetrate the body of Howard Anderson and saw "rotten American blood fertilize the soil of Cuba." Perhaps, he added, some plant would grow there and Cuba would receive a benefit, after all, from having been placed by God only ninety miles from the United States.

"That was what the man said," Gene concluded. "We have a date with him when Castro falls."

We drove in silence along the winding coast road.

Then he said, "I imagine that we are the last four Cubans who still admire the United States."

We were approaching Varadero, which was in darkness. When we reached our house, at the far end of the beach, we did not turn on any lights. Carmen brought some Scotch to the northern terrace overlooking the Florida Straits, and we drew our chairs around a small table. It was tremendously comforting to have Gene and Ernesto with us. We had worked together in complete harmony for many years. Their devotion, courage, and intellectual capacity had fashioned a bond between us that had taught me to count my age by friendships such as theirs rather than by years. They were both Phi Beta Kappa graduates of American universities, as well as graduates of the University of Havana, and I did not know any Cubans more familiar with the great traditions of the United States.

No other houses shared our particular stretch of beach. The servants were in Havana; we were isolated and alone. It must have been three o'clock in the morning. The sea was calm and the waves barely rippled as they washed ashore. Far off to the east, in the moonless night, the lighthouse on Cayo Piedra flashed long and short, marking the entrance to Cárdenas Bay. We were too wrought up to think of sleep, so we talked until the first streaks of dawn colored the sky.

We could not understand why nothing had been heard from the Cuban underground. We had assumed that when the invasion came the underground would sabotage power plants and knock out broadcasting stations, water facilities, road and railroad bridges in the invasion area. This had not occurred. During the preceding three days Castro propagandists had been on the air constantly, and tanks had moved freely along the highways, unmolested in any way.

We all knew boys who were in the underground. Some of them were as close to us as sons or brothers. It had been a stirring experience to talk to them, especially to members of the Catholic Action group. Their courage, zeal, devotion to one another, and hatred for Castro were superb. Unhesitatingly they had risked their lives again and again to help a friend. There was nothing they would not do for one another or for their cause, yet they had been modest and almost casual in relating their fascinating, often heroic experiences. Many had died at the *paredón*.

Catholic Action is a church organization of volunteers who desire to help their fellow faithful be better Christians in the Catholic manner. As a means of identification the activists in Cuba used a simple drawing of a fish. This was copied from early Christian art on the frescoes of the Roman catacombs, dating from the persecutions under Nero. The fish was chosen by early Christians because the Greek word for it, Ιχσυε, formed the initials of the phrase "Jesus Christ, Son of God, Savior." Carmen and I had often seen this symbol painted or scratched on walls, or stroked in sweeping curves in the Varadero sand.

A discussion arose about the Monroe Doctrine. It isn't strange that the educated Latin American should be better informed on the history and significance of the Monroe Doctrine than his American counterpart. For 138 years it had been a bulwark protecting the independence of the former Spanish colonies. And it had been effective from the start because, although the United States was still a small and struggling republic in 1823, when President Monroe had warned Russia, Prussia, and Austria to keep hands off the American continent, England had co-operated. She did so with good reason, seeing in the Doctrine a solution to the restrictions Spain had imposed for almost 300 years on her trade with the Spanish colonies. Without England's consent the nations comprising the Holy Alliance could not cross the Atlantic. By 1895 the United States had grown in strength and stature. When the Doctrine was invoked against Britain itself that year, in a boundary dispute involving British Guiana and Venezuela, the British had bowed, accepting arbitration. It was then that President Cleveland wrote, "The Doctrine cannot become obsolete while our Republic endures."

On one point we were all solidly in agreement as we talked that night—the Latin Americans have known power and they respect power. What they deride is hesitation, weakness, and failure.

What, then, had brought about the incredible invasion failure? Why had the United States been unable to act as a first-class power in the Caribbean, which the whole world regarded as an American lake? Someone remarked that the Soviet Communist leaders must have been fascinated by this revelation. I vowed that *if it took me the rest of my life I would find the answers to these questions.*

Day had come. It was time to start back to Havana. As we arose and stood looking out over the Florida Straits, we were comforted even then by the thought that the American people, our friends, lived only a few miles beyond the horizon. The fight would be ours, and we would carry on alone if necessary, but the Americans had helped us in our struggle for independence and we could at least count on their understanding and sympathy. Thus we started back to Havana, eighty miles to the west, reassuring one another on the way to restore our spirits. When we reached the outskirts of the city Gene and Ernesto went ahead to learn of any overnight developments. The news they relayed to us was both bad and good. The G-2 had seen through Carmen's ruse and were after me again. One of their jeeps had left our house only minutes before, after searching every room. The good news was a message that we were expected at the Italian Embassy. A guest room was being held for us. We drove there at once.

The Cuba of tomorrow will owe a debt of gratitude to the Marquis and Marchioness de Teódoli, the Italian Ambassador and his wonderful Hungarian wife. Valorous, able, experienced, and devoted to their friends, they gave asylum to members of the underground who were able to reach their Embassy. Unlike the Latin American countries, Italy did not have a treaty right to protect political refugees, but in the aftermath of the invasion collapse, when access to the Latin American Embassies was under strict surveillance, the high, grilled portal of the Italian Embassy garden was opened and relocked, again and again, to admit men and boys who would have been shot had they been captured. It was all accomplished with quiet, hospitable efficiency. The experience was not a new one for the Marchioness, who had saved more than fifty lives in Budapest when the Soviets smashed the rebellion of 1956.

Among the political refugees we found a young man who had commanded the underground group in the area where the invasion took place. He was a soft-spoken lad, in his early twenties, and extremely attractive. He had a smile that appeared and faded very slowly, while the expression of his eyes remained unchanged. In impressive detail he explained how his group had been prepared to destroy the power plants and bridges in the whole province of Matanzas, "in less than two hours, and to create the worst panic imaginable." He and his group had been trained and supplied with explosives by the CIA, he said, and they had infiltrated into Cuba from Central America. His men were in constant contact with one another and always ready for action, but, unbelievably, they had never received the agreed-upon signal from the United States. Hence, when the time came they had not moved, thinking the invasion report a Castro trap.

Castro had every reason to fear such freedom fighters. Day after day the Cuban cities had resounded to explosions as government buildings and plants had been sabotaged. The guerrilla activities had far surpassed those of the anti-Batista underground in 1958. The night skies often reflected flames of burning cane fields, all eloquent testimony of the mounting opposition to Castro and Communism.

While Carmen and I listened, absorbed and astonished, to the young man's almost fantastic tale, one of the other saboteurs spoke to us, motioning with his head to an adjoining room, where an improvised altar had been set up. About sixteen boys had gathered there. My wife moved close to the altar as they knelt in prayer. I am not a practicing Catholic, and I withdrew to a corner to observe the inspiring scene. I watched a boy who a few days earlier had helped set the fire which, without loss of life, had totally destroyed the El Encanto department store and who was now on his knees. While they were immersed in the service the thought crossed my mind that I was witnessing one of the bright moments in the history of the Church.

The service ended and the boys arose slowly, one by one, and then began joking and roughhousing. One of them approached me and said, "Sir, don't look so serious; we will bring Castro down." He turned to leave, but came back and repeated,

"Never doubt it for a moment, Dr. Lazo. You may be absolutely certain that, eventually, we will bring him down."

That night two of our closest American friends, Louise and Gilbert Smith, also took refuge at the Italian Embassy. Louise, beloved everywhere in Cuba for her untiring social work, had more recently shifted her energy to dangerous activities, joining us in helping underground fighters. Now she tried to raise our spirits by telling us of a speech President Kennedy had made that day, April 20, to a group of newspaper editors, that had been broadcast from Miami.

The Cuban Freedom Fighters gathered around as Louise began speaking. It had been a very strong statement, she said, to the effect that the United States would not hesitate to meet its own obligations to prevent alien intrusion if the inter-American commitment proved ineffective. "And President Kennedy made the definite statement," she added proudly, "that the United States did not intend to abandon Cuba to Communism."

The small group listened intently and somberly, and remained silent. Finally, someone asked me what I thought of the President's speech. "Just words?" I didn't think so, but it was too early—coming events would tell. Later, while alone with the Smiths, Louise recalled that the President had also said that any unilateral intervention by the United States would have been contrary to American tradition. But, we reasoned, if non-intervention is a moral doctrine, the U.S.S.R. also must be bound by it. "Unless it is," Carmen declared, "you end up with the sorry wreckage which surrounds us today." Was Kennedy saying that the wrong side may help the wrong, but the right must not help the right? What about the massive Soviet intervention that had already taken place in Cuba? And had not the United States intervened by mounting the invasion?

It was too early, I repeated; we did not know what had happened, or why. But I would find out, *even if it took me the rest of my life.*

It was in the Italian Embassy that we watched Castro on

national television explain, with a pointer and large maps, how the Bay of Pigs battle had been won. He gave credit to his air force for having turned the tide and excoriated militia units for having joined the invaders. They were in need of discipline, he said. The chosen landing site, he admitted, had caught him by surprise, and he called the invasion plan "masterful." He also conceded that if the invaders had been able to consolidate their beachhead, they could not have been driven out. It was clear to all of us, as we watched and listened in silent grief, that America's failure had raised Castro to the pinnacle of his power and prestige.

After a week the Embassy became so jammed that Carmen and I decided to give up our room to others who, we felt, were in greater danger than we were. So, under assumed names, we moved to a hospital owned by a friend.

We made our escape from Cuba, where I had lived for thirty-six years, several weeks later, in late May 1961. Our last individual client had been murdered, the properties of virtually all our corporate clients, both Cuban and foreign, had been confiscated. Our beautiful law offices, occupying the top floor of Havana's most modern office building, had been demolished, although technically they had become our property under Castro's Urban Reform Law (the rentals paid to the State were regarded legally as purchase price instalments). The government had notified us that it wanted the space for its own use; the paneling had been ripped from the walls and the partitions and doors removed. Our cherished Varadero house, with its treasure of family records and art objects lovingly chosen and personally brought from Central and South America, had been confiscated the day following our departure for Havana. No explanation or receipt was ever given. The Havana house had been left temporarily free in the hope that I could be trapped there.

There was drama in our escape from Cuba but some of the people who helped us are still subject to reprisal, and that story must be left for another day.

When we arrived in the United States we had not wholly lost

confidence in its greatness, but as a result of our experience our enthusiasm had been dimmed. I felt that a trip across the continent, to immerse ourselves in the expansive beauty of the land and its civilization, would refresh us. Carmen had never been on the Pacific Coast, and my own acquaintance with California was limited to the brief period I had spent at an army camp there during World War I. We drove to Seattle, then down the coast of Oregon and California, and came east through the National Parks.

No one can make that journey without being overwhelmed by the grandeur of the nation, but even more impressive to us were the people we met. We made it a point to talk to as many as we could—hotel clerks, shop people, filling station attendants, and others. And the therapy was effective—our faith in America was restored. Invariably, when they learned that we were Cubans, their response was the same: "We have to get rid of Castro." The American people, we saw clearly, were single-minded in their desire to take whatever action was necessary to rid the Western Hemisphere of Communist penetration.

To these people in particular I address myself. The more they know about the way in which Cuba was turned into the first Soviet beachhead in the Americas, the greater will be their resolve to eliminate it.

CHAPTER FOUR

The Brightest Pages

While still young, I learned that the historian tends to write from the point of view of his own nation. Usually it is not his conscious intent to distort events but simply to emphasize the aspects with the greatest appeal to his readers. Few Americans, for example, are aware that at the decisive battle of Yorktown in their own Revolution, more Frenchmen were engaged in the assault than were American patriots, or that the French suffered more than twice as many casualties. School children in France, however, read this in their histories; they learn more than American youngsters about the brilliant achievements of the carrot-headed young Marquis de Lafayette and about the vital part played in the Yorktown victory by French Admiral de Grasse's blockading fleet.

Similarly, Americans and Cubans received divergent accounts of the Spanish-American War and of the final Cuban War of Independence. Americans think of their war in terms of the blowing up of the battleship *Maine,* Teddy Roosevelt's charge at San Juan Hill, the sinking of the Spanish fleet as it attempted to run the blockade of Santiago harbor, and Admiral Dewey's victory at Manila. The Cubans, on the other hand, regard the Spanish-American War, which lasted less than four months and involved 385 American battle deaths and a total of 4,108 casualties altogether, as merely the final chapter of their own three and a half year struggle, in which about 200,000 people died. Both accounts are correct. The disparity is one of emphasis rather than of distortion.

But with the advent of Castro an element of planned distortion entered the picture. Since 1959 all Cuban history books have been rewritten. Cuban children are now being taught that in 1898, with the Cubans on the verge of victory, the Americans "intervened" imperialistically in order to dominate and exploit their country. Castro has expounded this theme in television broadcasts on many occasions.

In any case, it is not possible to evaluate the events of the misnamed "Castro" Revolution of 1957–1958 without at least a summary knowledge of Cuban history. Having lived in both the United States and Cuba, I believe that I am able to outline the salient record objectively.

The Cuban War of Independence, which began on February 24, 1895, was a vicious and brutal conflict that in some respects resembled the American Revolutionary War. Although there were numerous sharp encounters, in neither was there any one decisive battle in which the rebels gambled everything. In both cases raw rebel troops faced numerically superior and well trained regulars. The population of Cuba at that time was approximately 1,500,000, and Spain sent more than 200,000 soldiers to subdue the country.

The chief blunder of the Spaniards was that despite an overwhelming superiority in numbers they fought defensively, fortifying the cities and, at great expense, building long defensive lines of entrenchments the entire width of the island, from north to south. These entrenchments proved no barrier to guerrillas under Generals Máximo Gómez and Antonio Maceo. The latter was a mulatto and probably the greatest Negro military genius. His exploits, in which he defeated superior Spanish forces almost at will, made him a legendary figure. At West Point, so long as the cavalry remained an important military element, his brilliant campaigns were taught in lectures. (Maceo's mother bore her first husband four sons. On his death she married Marcos Maceo, to whom she bore seven sons. Nine of the eleven sons, together with the elder Maceo, died in Cuba's struggle against Spain.)

Another hero of the War of Independence, General Calixto García, achieved fame through the book by Elbert Hubbard, *A Message to Garcia.* In dramatic rhetoric it told of a determined American, Lieutenant Andrew S. Rowan, whose mission was to find General García in order to coordinate military plans when the Americans entered the war. Rowan got to García, but he never thought he had performed a heroic deed and disliked the publicity he received from the estimated four million copies of the book disseminated.

As Gómez and Maceo continued to inflict defeats on the Spaniards, command of the Spanish forces was turned over to Valeriano Weyler, known in Cuba as "The Butcher." He immediately launched a reign of terror. His plan was to suffocate the rebellion by exterminating the population, old and young, women and children. Inhabitants of country districts were ordered into concentration camps and those who refused were treated as rebels. Executions became a daily occurrence, anticipating the Castro era. The *reconcentrados* died of hunger and disease by the thousands. It is estimated that more than 300,000 unfortunates, a fifth of the population, were thrown into concentration camps, and that less than half of them survived.

When accounts of these atrocities were published in the American press, popular American sympathy swung solidly to the side of the Cubans. In fact, a joint belligerency resolution was overwhelmingly approved by Congress, but the President held back, influenced by strong pressure groups favoring suppression of the rebellion.

The War of Independence reached a turning point on February 15, 1898, when the U.S. battleship *Maine,* dispatched to Cuba to protect American citizens, was mysteriously blown up in Havana harbor with a loss of 266 of her officers and crew. The disaster provoked investigations and endless discussions as to who was responsible. (Although the *Maine* was raised to the surface and studied in detail in 1911, the mystery of her sinking was never solved.) But the American people now clamored for an end to Spanish rule in Cuba.

Joining in the outcry was the colorful Under Secretary of the Navy, Theodore Roosevelt. On March 27 President McKinley sent an ultimatum to Spain, which accepted most but not all its conditions. On April 11 McKinley asked for a declaration of war, and Congress authorized him to send an American force to Cuba. The Congressional Resolution provided that after pacification the United States would "leave the government and control of the island to its people."

The Cubans exulted over the American declaration of war but not all of them welcomed an invasion. General Máximo Gómez, for instance, said frankly that he would prefer that not a single American soldier set foot in Cuba. He asked only for arms and ammunition and a blockade against Spain. He wanted to retain for the Cubans credit for winning their own independence, and he also feared that invasion and occupation would mean annexation. Many Americans, in fact, ridiculed the promise that the United States would withdraw from Cuba after Spain capitulated.[1]

From now on events moved rapidly.

The major part of the Spanish fleet was blockaded in the Bay of Santiago de Cuba, and toward the end of June an American army was landed near that city. Best known of the troops were a regiment of "Rough Riders," made up of western cowboys. To many of his countrymen Roosevelt, who was second in command of this regiment under his friend Colonel Leonard Wood, came to personify the Spanish-American War.

When the Spanish fleet tried to run the blockade early in July, it was completely destroyed. Puerto Rico was occupied and Admiral Dewey's naval victory at Manila Bay had been followed by American occupation of the Philippines. The Spanish army in Cuba surrendered two weeks after the annihilation of the fleet,

---

[1] Willis Fletcher Johnson, *The History of Cuba* (New York: B. F. Buck & Company, Inc., 1920), Vol. Four, p. 109.

and Spain was ready for peace less than four months after the Americans entered the war. Commissioners from the United States and Spain met in Paris to draw up a treaty, the non-Cuban features of which proved to be the acquisition by the United States of Puerto Rico, Guam, and the Philippines.

What is not generally remembered—and is a circumstance that Castro never mentions—is that one of the first steps taken by the chief of the Spanish peace mission was formally to request that the United States annex Cuba.[2] The "Pearl of the Antilles," the exquisite gem of Spain's island possessions, where Columbus had touched the New World, had bestowed many rich gifts on the mother country. More Spaniards resided there than in any other distant area; more Spanish capital was invested there. Now, in Paris, the vanquished were asking their conquerors to protect by annexation Spanish citizens and investments in Cuba.

The United States refused to annex Cuba. There are few brighter pages in American history than those which tell of the unselfish and constructive policy pursued by its government at that time and during the difficult years that followed the signing of the Treaty of Paris. The story is in marked contrast to what had happened in other times and at other places, notably in Mexico.

The Treaty of Paris provided that the United States should act as a trustee of the island, assuming responsibility "for the protection of life and property," and that on the termination of American occupancy the new government should assume the same obligations.

Historians linger lovingly over the drama of battles and campaigns. Usually they have little to say of the dreary years of political adjustment and economic organization that always follow the termination of hostilities. Yet no nation was ever born without such a period of trial. Fighting had ceased on July 16, 1898,

[2] *Ibid.*, p. 119.

but it was not until May 20, 1902, almost four years later, that the American flag was lowered over Morro Castle and the new Cuban flag raised.

Patriot soldiers drifted home, ragged and penniless, often to find that their very houses had disappeared. Family after family, stripped of everything by years of war, set valiantly to work, tilling the soil with home-made wooden plows, often with teams of men tugging in harness. What would be the relationship between Cuba and the United States? The question was a source of anxiety for the Cubans and equally perplexing to the United States. The atmosphere was explosive. What might have happened had already been demonstrated in the Philippines, where, under similar conditions, an accidental fight between sentries had touched off two years of cruel and bloody warfare.

Happily, no such event occurred in Cuba, and the American military occupation marked the beginning of a half-century of political and economic progress in Cuba that perhaps has never before been equaled in modern history. The manner in which the relationship between the two countries was defined profoundly influenced Cuban political developments during the first half of the twentieth century, indeed until the day Castro was brought to power on January 1, 1959.

The first important steps for the creation of a Cuban Government were taken under the military administration of General Leonard Wood. An elected Constituent Assembly convened in November 1900 to draw up a constitution similar to that of the United States, with an executive branch and an independent judiciary and a bicameral legislature. The resulting 1901 Constitution reflected American influence not only in its content but even in its phrasing.

The aspect of Cuban-American relations that aroused most controversy was the so-called Platt Amendment. Congress was about to end its session in 1901 when Senator Orville H. Platt submitted an amendment to the army appropriation bill consisting of seven brief articles designed to provide the basis for the future relationship between the two countries. It was part of an Army bill because Cuba was then being administered by the War Department.

Of the seven articles, only two aroused opposition in Cuba. One, Article III, provided that Cuba "consents that the United States may exercise the right to intervene for the preservation of Cuban independence, the maintenance of a government adequate for the protection of life, property and individual liberty. . . ." The other, Article VIII, provided that Cuba would "sell or lease to the United States lands necessary for coaling or naval stations at certain specified points . . ." The delegates to the Constitutional Assembly were told that inclusion of these provisions, as an appendix to their Constitution and later in a permanent treaty between the two countries, was the price of independence. The American demands were acceptable to conservative Cuban elements but provoked opposition by some politicians.

On June 12, 1901 the Convention adopted the Platt Amendment, and in due course it was added as an "appendix" to the Constitution. Later, in 1903, its provisions were incorporated into a treaty between the two countries.

The considerations that inspired the Platt Amendment were realistic and in keeping with the principles of the Monroe Doctrine. Cuba's privileged geographical position made it the key to the Gulf of Mexico, and the United States did not wish to have a situation develop in Cuba that would invite non-American intervention. As early as 1562 King Phillip II of Spain had underlined the importance of Cuba. "He who owns the island of Cuba," he said, "has the key to the new world."

Over the years the Platt Amendment proved to be of inestimable value to the young republic. It induced the flow of American capital to Cuba, contributing enormously to its economic development. It was the sole reason why Cuban bonds sold in the market at a better price than those of such countries as France, Brazil, Argentina, and Chile. After its adoption, however, the American diplomatic representative in Havana would exert, on occasion, greater influence in the political life of the country than the Cuban President himself. Political opponents of the established Cuban Government would at times look to him as the final arbiter among contending forces.

Cuban political leaders thus became accustomed to relying on American political tutelage. Even after the Platt Amendment was abrogated in 1934, during the first administration of Franklin D. Roosevelt, they often looked to the American Ambassador for solutions to major problems. That the significance of this is not well understood by Americans who lack a knowledge of Cuban history is suggested by a remark which Arthur M. Schlesinger, Jr., attributes to President John F. Kennedy. Referring to the former American Ambassador to Cuba, the President commented, "Earl Smith once said to me that the American Ambassador was the second most important man in Cuba. What a hell of a note that is!"[3]

Smith was right, of course. He might have added that on occasion the Ambassador was the *most* important man. That is why in 1958, only twenty-four years after Cuba had attained full sovereignty, many Cubans believed that Washington knew what it was doing when it ousted Batista and cleared the path for Castro to come to power.

After the adoption of the Constitution of 1901, with the Platt Amendment as a rider, Cuba went on to choose its Congress and President. The chief of the triumphant revolution, General Máximo Gómez, was offered the presidency but declined. "Men of war for war," he said, "men of peace for peace." Gómez suggested Don Tomás Estrada Palma, who was elected without opposition.

Meanwhile General Wood had done an excellent job as military governor. With inflexible integrity and great rapidity he created new institutions based on U.S. models. A public school system was established, and fifteen hundred Cubans were sent to Harvard for a summer of teacher training. Roads, hospitals,

---

[3] Arthur M. Schlesinger, Jr., *A Thousand Days* (Boston: Houghton Mifflin Company, 1965), p. 224.

a postal service, and port customs were put in order. The judicial system was reorganized. Many of the men who had served in the revolutionary army were incorporated into a system of rural guards. Not the least of the achievements was a medical miracle. Yellow fever, long a scourge of Cuba, was virtually wiped out within a year after General Wood had assigned Dr. Walter Reed to conduct the experiments which eventually proved the validity of Dr. Carlos Finlay's theory that mosquitoes transmit the dread disease.

Cuba's first President was a man of dignity and integrity. The years of his first administration, 1902 to 1906, are generally regarded by Cubans as the best of their Republic. Don Tomás Estrada Palma carried on General Wood's program of public works, education, and sanitation, and by 1905 there were approximately twenty-five million dollars in the National Treasury. This, however, is said to have excited opposing political ambitions, and there were charges that the President's reelection that year was fraudulent. In August 1906, facing open rebellion, Don Tomás requested American intervention under the Platt Amendment, and this took place in September 1906 when William Howard Taft, who had headed that mission, became provisional governor of the island. He was soon replaced by Charles E. Magoon. Although the Magoon administration was later criticized, it introduced the merit system into government service earlier than in any other Latin American country.

These and subsequent events illustrate the fact that the democratic process cannot be implanted merely by changing the form of institutions. *Democracy must evolve slowly and painfully through trial and error, as demanded by an increasingly enlightened public.*

Government became the second biggest "industry" after sugar. Thousands of government jobs were designated as "confidential" or "political" in order to remove them from the merit system. As civil service salaries often were inadequate, many government employees held other jobs or profited extra-legally. These practices became a form of "social security," but the greater evil was the patronage aspect of government. Until the advent of Batista there were six national elections. In every case the victor had the support of the outgoing administration and each of the six administrations was marked by growing corruption.

Politicians seeking high office often looked upon the Platt Amendment as the ultimate weapon in their arsenal. Thus in 1917, when General Mario Menocal was elected to a second term, the Liberals revolted on the assumption that the United States would intervene as it had done in 1906, provoking new elections. World War I was approaching, however, and the United States made it clear that it opposed revolution. Marines were landed at Guantanamo, and although they took no part in the fighting their presence had a quieting effect and the rebellion soon ended.

When Alfredo Zayas was elected President in 1920, the opposition succeeded in obtaining a form of American intervention. President Harding sent General Enoch Crowder to Havana, where he remained as financial adviser until 1923, forcing Zayas to appoint what became known as "Crowder's honest cabinet." It was in 1923 that I first went to Cuba, and General Crowder was the first American diplomatic representative with whom I dealt. Until the ascent of Castro it was my privilege to deal with all the American Ambassadors, although the degree of intimacy varied in accordance with the personalities involved.

In considering the circumstances that led to Batista and later to Castro, the administration of General Gerardo Machado deserves attention. Machado won the 1924 elections by promising honest elections and a single term of office. Despite his campaign promises and in disregard of the advice of Ambassador Harry F. Guggenheim,[4] Machado in 1927–1928 obtained constitutional amendments extending the presidential term to six years, and in 1928 he was reelected without opposition.

[4] Thirty years later Guggenheim would offer the same counsel to Batista. Through a Cuban cabinet official the former Ambassador pleaded with Batista to relinquish office after presiding over honest elections. Had this advice been followed, Castro would not have come to power.

Machado's second administration coincided with the world depression and a collapse in the price of sugar, aggravated by the enactment of a higher United States tariff. Economic chaos provoked political unrest, which led Machado to adopt suppressive measures. As terrorist activities were stepped up, reprisal begot reprisal, and by 1933 Cuba was again on the verge of civil war. Machado's strong-arm methods stamped him as a dictator, and with the election of Franklin D. Roosevelt the United States sent Sumner Welles to Havana as its Ambassador, with instructions to attempt mediation.

During this period, as guerrilla warfare developed in the countryside and terrorism spread in the cities, I was in almost daily contact with Welles. On occasion I would drive to appointments with him in a suburb of Havana at night, when the only lights were the headlights of my car, and with bomb explosions and machine-gun or rifle fire punctuating the stillness. Only the police force stood between the civilian population and complete anarchy, and even here there was a certain amount of turmoil. Havana's police chief had been replaced on many occasions and there came a time when about a third of the police force was composed of men with criminal records. Reports reached us of plots to assassinate the Ambassador in order to provoke intervention, and I conveyed these to Welles. Nevertheless, he always rode through the streets of Havana unguarded, and we came to have the highest regard for his courage. Welles was later replaced by Jefferson Caffery, who moved through Havana preceded and followed by patrol cars of heavily armed men, as Castro does at the present time.

The Welles mediation attempt failed, and when a general strike developed he concluded that Machado must go. But a spontaneous revolt occurred during the first days of August and the Cuban army took charge of events, forcing Machado to flee the country on August 12, 1933. The government that replaced him proved to be vacillating and indecisive, and political intrigue continued under conditions of near-chaos.

It was under these circumstances that Batista rose to power—

not, as in the case of Castro, with the help of the American State Department, but on his own. He offered the only hope for stability in Cuba. Much of the country's history between 1934 and December 1958, when the United States once again intervened, forcing Batista to leave the country, revolves around his figure.

CHAPTER FIVE

The Rise of Batista

Close friends of Fulgencio Batista y Zaldívar, some of whom are men of great integrity, speak of him as having been sincerely devoted to democratic ideals. There are those among them, in fact, who believe that his principal weakness was a reluctance to be sufficiently ruthless under conditions of extreme provocation, out of an excessive desire to achieve and hold popularity with the masses.

They point to the fact that although he was the most powerful man in Cuba during the seven-year period following the Sergeants' Revolt of September 4, 1933, he did not take over the Presidency until he had been constitutionally elected in July 1940; that capital punishment was ruled out during the seventeen years he held power; that in May 1955 he sponsored a sweeping amnesty of all political prisoners (including the Castro brothers, who had served only a year and a half of a fifteen-year prison term for leading an assault on an army post).

Batista's bitterest enemies and critics, on the other hand, paint him as a monstrous dictator. Castro has accused him, repeating the charge over and over again in Hitler fashion, of having murdered twenty thousand Cubans. Herbert L. Matthews, commanding the immense influence of *The New York Times,* generally supports Castro's charges, depicting Batista as a beast of the jungle, of tigerish ferocity, "as ruthless and predatory as any dictator in Latin American history." [1]

[1] Herbert L. Matthews, *The Cuban Story* (New York: George Braziller, 1962), p. 58.

Between the two extremes were the hundreds of thousands like myself who attempted to assess Batista's strengths and weaknesses objectively. I became disillusioned with him on March 10, 1952, when he interrupted the democratic process and took over the Palace by a *coup d'état*. I viewed the event with dark foreboding. It seemed to me at the time that the clock had been turned back, that the slow progress Cuba had been making over the years toward free government had been dealt a crushing blow. Although my law firm had supervision over a number of important industrial construction projects, including the two largest in Cuban history, all requiring constant dealings with the Havana Government, I never spoke to Batista again while he remained in power and have had no contact with him, directly or indirectly, to this day.

By training and experience, a lawyer learns to distinguish fact from fancy, and now with the perspective of retrospect, I believe I am able to relate the events which ultimately will determine Batista's place in Cuban history.

From 1934 to 1940 Batista was in command of the Army and stronger than the president. From 1940 to 1944 he served as a constitutionally elected president. After a lapse of eight years, he returned to power illegally and held it illegally until constitutionally elected in 1954 and then until he was replaced by Castro on January 1, 1959.

On May 7, 1933, American Ambassador Sumner Welles had arrived in Havana and three months later a general strike developed against President Machado. The streets of Havana became deserted. In the interior, commercial and industrial activities also ground to a halt; stores closed, people stayed at home. On the highways private cars were fired upon. Amid these critical conditions Machado fled the country in August 1933, and was succeeded by Carlos Manuel de Céspedes.

The army post which dominates Havana is Camp Columbia on its outskirts, originally laid out by the Americans, during the first occupation, in typical American style, with the parade ground in the center. The Cuban officers did not live in Camp

Columbia, and this facilitated a revolt by the non-commissioned officers in charge. During the remaining days of August conditions deteriorated. The capital was flooded with reports of conspiracies, including a rumor that Communists were planning a soldier-worker government. A group of non-commissioned officers under the leadership of Batista were the first to take decisive action.

Batista called military posts throughout the island during the early hours of September 4 and told the sergeants that they were in command. These in turn sent word to the officers not to return to their posts. Realizing that the Cuban people would not support a military government headed by sergeants, Batista summoned to Camp Columbia the *Directorio Estudiantil* of the University of Havana and members of its faculty. The sergeants then began broadcasting over the radio that they had taken over. A five-man commission, headed by Dr. Ramón Grau San Martín, a member of the University faculty, was appointed to form a new government.

Batista, then thirty-two years of age, had been born of poor parents in the easternmost province of Cuba in 1901. He received some education in a local school and, after working at odd jobs, joined the army in 1921. He learned typing and shorthand and in 1928 was promoted to sergeant-stenographer and assigned as a court reporter. He had a natural gift of oratory and an attractive personality. Although deficient in education and culture, his mind worked like lightning and he thought and acted logically.

President de Céspedes was away from Havana on the morning of September 4, when the revolt occurred. He returned about noon. His advisers urged him to declare the army in rebellion and to ask the United States to land Marines. De Céspedes vacillated and in the end did nothing.

On September 8 several hundred army officers moved into the National Hotel, where Ambassador Sumner Welles was then residing, but Welles moved out shortly after the officers moved in. Batista threw a cordon around the hotel and the staff walked out; the officers began to do their own cooking, dish-washing, and cleaning up. The aviators were assigned to running the elevators, the officer in charge telling them jokingly, "You are accustomed to going up and down."

On September 10 Dr. Grau San Martín, a tall, thin, anemic-looking physician, installed himself at the Palace as Provisional President amid scenes of wild disorder. With the students in control, other political groups withdrew. Grau appointed a young Communist, Dr. Antonio Guiteras, as Secretary of Interior, the most powerful cabinet position, since that department had jurisdiction over the national police.

Although his mother was an American, Guiteras, who did not look like a Cuban, was strongly anti-American. Tall, very thin, and slightly stooped, he had reddish-brown hair, talked little, and made decisions swiftly. He dominated the cabinet and was responsible for considerable radical labor legislation. Soon after taking office he ordered the seizure of two of Cuba's finest American-owned sugar mills. Replacing Grau as the leader of the radical student group, he and Batista became bitter enemies. Eventually, when Batista decided to break the power of the students, Guiteras attempted to escape from Cuba, but he was trapped by the army in a small Spanish fort near Matanzas and killed in a spectacular gun battle. Twelve of his followers, including two women, were captured.

With Dr. Grau in the Palace, anti-American sentiments surfaced in Cuba for the first time in my experience, coupled with reports that in the interior Communist agitators were inciting workers to seize sugar mills and loot their commissaries. Ragged and belligerent mobs rioted through the streets of Havana. As they approached, the alarmed merchants would hurriedly pull down the big iron shutters used instead of doors on most small establishments. In Cuba, everyone, including Batista and the student government, believed American intervention might occur momentarily. U.S. warships were known to be close at hand, to protect American lives and property. An elaborate plan was devised for evacuating the Americans from Cuba in case of complete chaos. Havana was divided into districts and in each a key man was given a list of telephone numbers so that at a signal from the American Consulate he could form groups, after which trucks guarded by marines would take the Americans to the ships.

At six o'clock in the morning on October 2, 1933, the Cuban army attacked the National Hotel, more troops moving in from Camp Columbia. The officers were the best shots in the army, many having trained at American military schools. During the action two hundred Cubans, most of them enlisted men, were killed, and hundreds more were wounded. When the ammunition of the officers ran out, they raised the white flag. After they had been gathered together outside the hotel, unarmed, to be taken as prisoners, sixteen of them were shot down and killed.

Two days later, on October 4, Batista called on Ambassador Welles to express his regret over the killing of an American who had been hit by a stray bullet, the assistant manager of Swift & Company, one of our clients. Batista and Welles had a long talk, and in reporting this conversation to Washington Welles said that Batista had asked for his opinion and that Welles had told him that he believed Batista himself was the only individual in Cuba who then represented authority. Welles complained to Batista of the actions of the Grau government, blaming a small group of students and a few individuals who had joined them for selfish motives.

Terrorists continued their depredations. In Havana bombs continually exploded. The Santiago-Havana express was blown off the track. On November 8 there was a major attempt to oust the Grau-Batista government. In Havana people ran for cover when planes stolen from the Camp Columbia air base, and flown by rebel pilots, sprayed machine-gun bullets into the streets. Revolutionists raced through the streets in automobiles, firing rifles and machine guns. News of similar terrorism came from all over the island. Batista crushed the revolt, but more than five hundred had been killed on both sides, a toll greater than in any uprising in Cuba since the country had gained independence.

Batista realized that, as the United States would not recognize the Grau government, there would have to be a major change.

In late November 1933 Welles was recalled to Washington, and on December 18 Jefferson Caffery arrived in Havana as the special representative of President Roosevelt.

As conditions grew worse and Grau lost support among the Cuban people, he became increasingly anti-American. All this strengthened Batista's hand, and Caffery threw his support solidly behind him.

I had first met Batista at a luncheon given by H. Freeman Matthews, the First Secretary of the American Embassy, at the Matthews residence in Country Club Park in January 1934. It was a very small group. In addition to our host and hostess, my wife and myself, there were Sergeant Batista and his wife and two of his closest army associates and their ladies, ten or twelve in all. One of those present was José Pedraza, who would later serve as Army Chief of Staff and be arrested in February 1941 on charges that he was planning to depose "President" Batista. Still later he would be charged with a plot to assassinate "President" Grau and sentenced to a short prison term. Eventually he would again join forces with Batista in the fight against the Castro rebels. His son would be detained by a group of Castro followers and murdered in cold blood when his identity was established. Jaime Mariné, another of the sergeants at the Matthews home that day, would eventually become a Lieutenant Colonel and President Batista's spokesman in extra-legal transactions during his first administration.

Naturally we were tremendously interested in the man who for the first time in modern history had deposed the officers of a national army and become, almost overnight, the most powerful man in Cuba. Batista was a good-looking fellow, of medium but muscular build, and thoroughly *simpatico* (an untranslatable Spanish word which implies charm and personableness). He weighed about 180 pounds and appeared to be imbued with self-confidence, although he spoke rather slowly for a Latin, in a modulated voice. With a ready smile he gave his undivided attention to anyone who addressed him, grasping a question so quickly that at times he would answer before it had been completed. Later my wife's sister told us that before the Sergeants' Revolt Batista had been giving private typing instruction in his free time to a next-door friend and that the teenaged girls in the neighborhood thought him unusually attractive. They would be on the lookout for him. "Look," they would say, "here comes *el profesor.*"

Batista's determination to obtain American recognition provoked a conflict with the Student Directorate. After a tenure of less than two days by Carlos Hevia, following Grau's forced resignation, Batista's original choice for the Presidency, Colonel Carlos Mendieta, was made Provisional President. His inauguration on January 18, 1934, reflected the real temper of the Cuban people. Great crowds surrounded the Palace for blocks and cheered themselves hoarse. They cheered President Roosevelt, Ambassador Caffery, and Sumner Welles, who was now Assistant Secretary of State. The United States recognized the Mendieta government six days after it took office. The elimination of the Grau student government had been received in Washington with much enthusiasm. Batista and the American government were now in accord.

During March 1935 the political opposition attempted a general strike, with Communist support, and the struggle became a direct one between the radicals and Batista, who used the army to break the strike and jailed hundreds of terrorists. Although communications were largely disrupted, reports were reaching Havana from population centers in the interior that sugar mills and industrial plants were being seized by the workers under the leadership of Communist agitators and that local councils or "soviets" of manual workers were replacing management. The United Fruit Company, one of our clients, had its own radio facilities, and one day its General Manager, Walter W. Schuyler, was informed that the main water pipeline serving the great Preston sugar mill in the eastern province of Oriente (not far from the Guantanamo Naval Base) had been cut and a group of workers was about to take over.

In Cuba there were two kinds of urban settlements, the ordinary city or town, and the industrial *bateyes* of the sugar mills, consisting of unionized industrial workers and administrators permanently employed by the mill and housed near it. The agricultural field workers lived near the outlying cane fields, known as *colonias,* which were linked to the mill by railroad. Our report was that a small group of men who had never been employed by the company was already in control of the Preston *batey.*

The United Fruit Company, which has contributed so notably to the industrial and agricultural development of various Caribbean countries, had its principal office in Boston. In Cuba its activities consisted of a passenger and freight steamship service connecting New York and New Orleans with Havana, and the operation of two of Cuba's finest sugar mills in Oriente province, on Nipe Bay. On a clear day one could see from Preston the smoke of the smaller mill located at Banes in the far distance, across many square miles of silver-green cane fields. When originally purchased by the United Fruit Company, the lands had been a virtually uninhabited jungle, except for the town of Banes. Springs were tapped in the nearby mountains to supply water for the mills and *bateyes.* Close to 280,000 acres were converted into cane lands and fields for cattle grazing. In 1935 the United Fruit sugar properties in Cuba were valued at close to $40 million. Their annual Cuban payroll was approximately $10 million and 40,000 people depended on the two mills for their livelihood.

The company's relations with its workers had always been cordial. Its hospitals at Preston and Banes were among the best in Cuba; their medical and nursing staffs met the highest American standards. Its excellent housing facilities, schools, dairies, and stores had attracted thousands of Cuban workers to the two mills. They were provided with free electricity and water services and encouraged to plant vegetable gardens, the company furnishing seeds, tractors for plowing, and technical supervision, all without charge. Pasteurized milk was available to the workers at considerably less than cost.

The wide *batey* streets were lined with shade trees and well-kept lawns, and there were moving picture theaters, clubs, and sport facilities. When technical workers wished to send a son or daughter to an American college, the company contributed to the educational expenses. Unlike other sugar mills, those of the United Fruit Company gave most of their labor force year-round employment, in field cultivation, research, and other activities. In 1934 the Preston mill produced more sugar than any mill in the world, and as early as 1935 there were only thirty or forty Americans employed.

Now the owners had lost control of this magnificent property, and we requested an interview with Batista to lay the problem before him. Walter Schuyler, a powerfully built engineer and former football star, is the best executive I have ever known. He was regarded by Cubans and Americans alike as one of the leading figures in the Cuban sugar industry. Stern and tough, but always fair with the few Americans on his staff, he was silky-smooth in dealing with the Cubans, who often spoke of him affectionately as a *criollo,* a word used to denote anyone who identifies himself with Cuba in nationality and outlook. Now Schuyler wanted to regain control of the sugar properties which had been his dream and achievement and to which he had given the best years of his life.

At the appointed time, nine o'clock one evening, Schuyler and I were on hand at Camp Columbia. More than a hundred persons were crowded into a large anteroom, awaiting an audience. Seated beside me was Pincho Gutiérrez, the manager of the famous pugilist Kid Chocolate, who hoped one day to stage a prizefight in Havana for his protégé. This was the problem *he* would lay before Batista! I remember asking Pincho whether he thought Chocolate could regain his crown. "Yes, for two reasons," he said. "The first is that I am broke and the second is that Chocolate is broke."

Batista received us at three A.M., six hours later. The conversation was brief and to the point. Since he had been born in Banes, he was thoroughly familiar with the extraordinary development of the Preston-Banes area, and no time was wasted on preliminaries. How many soldiers did Schuyler believe were needed? "Fifty or sixty." Smiling, Batista commented that Cuba should have an army half the size of its population; "one soldier for each civilian," he said. He assured us he would order a trusted sergeant to proceed with an army detail from Santiago to Preston that same day.

Within seventy-two hours order was restored in both Preston and Banes without bloodshed or violence. During the following weeks this experience was repeated over and over throughout the country. As a consequence, business and industry and the conservative elements of Cuban society rallied behind Batista. He was on the way to becoming the *jefe supremo,* expected to be the final arbiter on all major questions. However, he never became the all-powerful absolute dictator commonly believed, as he had to rely on army support and to deal with organized labor, the political parties, university students, professional associations, major business interests, the Catholic Church to some extent, and the American Embassy to a very large extent.

The stocky figure of President Mendieta, always dressed in white linen suits, was also a symbol of returning normalcy. He was honest and conservative, although somewhat indecisive.

One of Batista's first popular successes was the negotiation by the Mendieta government of the abrogation of the Platt Amendment, which occurred on May 29, 1934. Relations between the United States and Cuba were further improved in August with the signing of a new Reciprocity Treaty covering mutual tariff reductions. The economy began to improve.

Mendieta tried hard to conciliate the warring political groups before the elections slated for January 10, 1936, and when he failed, discouraged and saddened, he resigned. The Secretary of State, José A. Barnet, became Provisional President, the fifth since the fall of Machado. Batista, now a Colonel, repeated that the army would remain neutral and act impartially in the coming election, the first in which women would be permitted to vote. It resulted in a victory for Miguel Mariano Gómez, son of an earlier president and a popular political personality. With Laredo Brú as Vice President, he took office in May 1936.

At Camp Columbia, Batista built a modern hospital and masonry barracks for officers and enlisted men, to replace the wooden barracks originally built by the Americans. He conducted a publicity campaign condemning radicalism and eulogizing the military. He advocated public works to provide employment, and a number of social benefits such as old-age pensions. His favorite project was the establishment of civic-military rural schools in remote country districts where educational facilities were non-existent. These areas could be reached only by the mounted rural guards stationed throughout the country, who would be the teachers. He opened seven hundred of these schools and planned to establish twenty-three hundred more. Revenue for carrying out this program was to be provided by a nine-cent tax on each bag of sugar produced in Cuba. Farmers and workers throughout the country staged demonstrations in favor of the program, and sugar producers themselves supported it. The House of Representatives passed the tax bill by a vote of 106 to 43.

President Gómez had quickly come into conflict with Batista when he dismissed from government office several thousand military reservists. Now, in a further effort to restore civilian supremacy, he vetoed the nine-cent sugar tax law, claiming that it aimed at the "militarization of the nation's childhood." Lacking the support of the people, the press, and Congress, however, he was impeached at a Senate trial, which ended on December 24, 1936 with the decision that he had transgressed against the free functioning of the legislative power. The Vice President, Federico Laredo Brú, took office. Thus, by the late 1930s, as Batista's popularity steadily increased, he had consolidated his control of the island.

Shortly after the impeachment I had occasion to call on

Batista at his headquarters in Camp Columbia. I no longer remember the purpose of the interview, but at its close I raised the question of the impeachment. Many of us, I told him, although aware of the friction between himself and Gómez, had been stunned. We had not expected an elected President to be ousted so soon and in such a fashion. Batista replied that as he enjoyed little, if any, patronage influence, the legislative impeachment had been a genuinely democratic move, reflecting the wishes of the population.

The Cuban people, especially the children, needed education but also had to be taught discipline, he argued. He spoke of his son Papito, who was in the habit of interrupting him while at work alone in his office, ruffling the papers on his desk and running his fingers through his father's hair. Recently the boy had picked up an open inkwell and hurled it across the room. "What is the future of a country," he asked, "whose Army Chief cannot control his own son?" But he planned to sponsor elections for a Constituent Assembly which would formulate an up-to-date constitution, he informed me, to be followed by free and honest elections.

The conversation left me uneasy. I had no doubt that he had engineered the removal of Gómez. His plan to have mounted sergeant-teachers reach into remote rural areas to give instruction certainly had popular support, but why had this not been accomplished through the constitutional process of having Congress override the President's veto? My American training had taught me that there was nothing more important than respect for the law.

Almost all my Cuban friends had a different order of values, however. To them the essential thing was that Batista had brought order out of chaos, had given the country the stability it so greatly needed, and the issue of military versus civil rule was secondary. By instinct they were attracted to the young new leader who had met with so much success and was already regarded by many as a *caudillo*.

My partner, Jorge de Cubas, was more analytical. He also

regretted the impeachment but pointed out that it was merely the culminating incident in a relationship which had become wholly incompatible. The Cuban people still had a long way to go along the road to viable democracy, said Jorge. Democracy cannot be imported from the United States or anywhere else and great world areas are totally unsuited to democracy—parts of Asia, Africa, and the Middle East, where the god-king or tribal chief rules. Stability is the essential requirement, said Jorge, and in many countries it is the monarch alone who provides it. Without a monarch these countries would be torn apart by personal ambitions and the new social forces. He mentioned the chairman-of-the-board type of European king, who presides over his country without being its chief executive officer. He thought that, after Franco, Spain would probably restore its royal house in order to assure political stability.

The qualities which the Latins look for in a leader are at times likely to conflict with the democratic restrictions imposed upon him, said Jorge. Expected to be responsive to public pressures, he is also, as *jefe supremo,* expected to be resolute and skillful in putting an end to controversy. His duty, as the people see it, is to get things done, bureaucracy notwithstanding. The Latins admire firmness, power, and success. As an example of leader-worship, my associate cited the fact that in Cuba it is customary to refer to political groupings as Batistianos, Machadistas, or Fidelistas, instead of naming the political parties which the leaders head, and this is true of every Latin American country. In any case, he concluded, "we are what we are, so you will have to be patient, Mario."

Jefferson Caffery left Havana in January 1937, and in June Ambassador J. Butler Wright arrived to replace him. I had not been close to Caffery and his staff, with the exception of Walter J. Donnelly, the Commercial attaché, who went on to a distinguished career as Ambassador to Venezuela and High Commissioner in Austria and West Germany. In Havana he already displayed qualities that marked him as a Foreign Service officer of exceptional qualifications.

Caffery, it seemed to me, was disloyal to Welles, who, as an Assistant Secretary of State, had become his superior. As an intermediary between himself and President Mendieta, Caffery used a notorious Cuban rascal, smart, witty and completely unscrupulous. He and the Ambassador had code names for well-known personalities in Cuba. On one occasion I heard him telephone the Ambassador and refer to Welles as *"el caido,"* the fallen one. When, as Caffery's spokesman at the Palace, the emissary was instrumental in rendering a service to a company, including American clients of our firm, there would often be a subsequent shake-down. The party approached, on occasion, would consult a member of the Embassy staff and, as the result of a nod or silence, assume that a payment to the intermediary had the Embassy's approval.

Prominent Cubans came to me to inquire whether the Ambassador was aware of his intermediary's record and reputation, which of course he was. Eventually these incidents attained scandalous proportions, and Caffery arranged to have the man go to Europe. Shortly before his departure, this character phoned me at home one Saturday morning and reviled me from the Embassy. "I am sitting at the Ambassador's desk," he said, "and I will soon be on my way out to shoot you." He was under the mistaken impression that I had been responsible for his impending exile. That afternoon our chauffeur, armed, followed our golf foursome at a distance as we played. The same evening I received a not altogether comforting apology from the Embassy.

Caffery served in Havana during a period of great tension and crisis. More than any other American, he was responsible for restoring order in Cuba, lending Batista the immense influence of his office, at times even accompanying him on horseback on visits to rural guard posts. This achievement therefore overshadowed any shortcomings, and he is entitled to recognition for a great service rendered to Cuba.

When Ambassador J. Butler Wright arrived in Havana, he told me at our first meeting that the State Department had instructed him to deal with the Cuban President in normal fashion, through the Cuban Foreign Office. "We will not be cutting corners," he said, "there will be no repetition of the past." Shortly after this I was entrusted with negotiating the purchase for the State Department of the land on which a new residence for the American Ambassador would be constructed. The irreproachable attitude of Ambassador Wright, popular and respected by Cubans and Americans alike, restored prestige to the U.S. diplomatic mission.

In late 1938 Colonel Batista was invited to attend the Armistice Day ceremonies in Washington as a guest of the War Department. There he saw snow for the first time and, with President Roosevelt, reviewed West Point cadets at Arlington. When he returned to Havana, entering the harbor on the gunboat *Cuba*, he received a tumultuous popular welcome. Banks and commercial establishments closed in his honor and, as the guns of Cabaña Fortress fired a salute, almost a hundred thousand people lined the waterfront. Disembarking at Caballería Wharf, he walked almost a mile to the Presidential Palace between cheering crowds held back by police, soldiers, and marines.

President Laredo Brú, the cabinet, and other high officials were waiting to welcome him. From the Palace balcony he assured the cheering throng that as long as he had any influence with the Cuban Government there would be a cordial relationship between Cuba and the United States. Whatever military or economic cooperation Cuba could give the United States, he said, would always be available to it.

CHAPTER SIX

Toward Democracy

Batista's decision to hold elections for a constitutional convention in November 1939 greatly enhanced his popularity. For the first time all political groups, including the recently legalized Communist Party, could openly debate methods to eliminate the political abuses of almost forty years of republican life. One of the main objectives now would be to limit the dominance of the executive power built into the original 1901 Constitution and adopted under American pressure. The major opposition party, headed by Grau San Martín, would be strongly represented in an arena where political decisions of the utmost importance were to be made. The delegates would work in an atmosphere of idealism, free from any outside pressure. The country's best brains would engage in an effort to create a more desirable society.

Dr. Grau San Martín presided over the Assembly's first sessions and was followed by my cousin, Dr. Carlos Márquez Sterling; they were both political opponents of Batista. Out of the deliberations, extending over a period of several months, came the now-famous Constitution of 1940, which Castro, while in the mountains in 1957–1958, repeatedly vowed to respect. Its importance today lies in the certainty that when the Communist regime falls, the first succeeding government will restore it, for the Cuban people attach great importance to this fundamental law.

It provided for a system of semiparliamentary government

and took the form, in part, of statements of national goals, requiring subsequent implementation by legislation. Thus an autonomous Superior Electoral Court was to have final authority in deciding electoral disputes, with power to instruct the armed forces and police during elections. A Board of Public Offices would regulate the Civil Service, the Constitution carefully defining and limiting the types of positions that could be considered "political" and hence outside the civil service merit system. A third autonomous agency, the Tribunal of Accounts, was to be responsible for auditing all government accounts in order to eliminate graft. The Constitution called for the organization of a national bank of issue and rediscount. The size of large landholdings, by both Cubans and foreigners, was to be reduced and limited by law.

Of the 286 articles, 61 dealt with social and economic issues, including the government's obligations to provide obligatory and free education and to eradicate illiteracy. The section on labor specifically incorporated much advanced legislation that had been enacted between 1933 and 1940, including minimum wages, a maximum day of 8 hours, a maximum week of 44 hours, and a month of paid vacations every year. Employers, when hiring, were required to favor Cubans over aliens and, when dismissing workers, to lay off foreigners first. They were prohibited from dismissing workers except through government-controlled procedures and for a limited number of specified causes, a provision which later created the most acute problem faced by employers and came to be known as *inamovilidad* (immobility). In 1959 the Castro regime went even further by freezing all workers in their jobs, prohibiting all dismissals for whatever cause, and taking over enterprises that planned a reduction of personnel. (Once Castro had confiscated the enterprises, however, workers were fired and wages cut indiscriminately.)

The three branches of government—executive, legislative, and judicial—were maintained as in the American-imposed 1901 Constitution, with provisions designed to guarantee the independence of the judiciary. Executive power was vested in a president elected for a four-year period; he could serve a second such term only after a lapse of eight years. To further limit executive domination, the cabinet was made responsible to Congress.

The individual rights granted by the new Constitution, such as free speech and assembly and provisions against arbitrary arrest, were similar to those guaranteed in 1901 but spelled out in greater detail to prevent earlier abuses. To protect the citizen from arbitrary police action, an arrested person had to be presented to a judicial authority within seventy-two hours, and if this was not done a writ of *habeas corpus* could be filed in his behalf. The independent courts usually ordered such a person released, and in times of public disturbance, when terrorists were thus set free, the authority of the executive branch was weakened.

One of the important provisions restricted the president's right to suspend these constitutional guarantees to cases of invasion or serious public disturbances, and even then, this could be done for only forty-five days, and the Congress was required to meet within forty-eight hours to approve or reject the suspension. Confiscation of property without adequate compensation fixed by judicial authority was prohibited. So was the death penalty, except in cases of treason or in the military establishment.

The 1940 Constitution, one of the most advanced documents of its kind, marked a step of great significance in Cuba's progress toward democracy, even though in practice it was never fully applied or implemented. The government remained highly centralized, with political appointment the most common source of corruption. It continued to be difficult for an individual to become a civil servant, a teacher, or a policeman without political patronage. Each of the three presidents between 1940 and 1952 (Batista, Grau San Martín, and Prío Socarrás) violated constitutional provisions. Grau especially (1944–1948) openly flaunted his disregard of constitutional restrictions. The government that came closest to conforming, providing by legislation four of the autonomous institutions called for in the Constitution, was that of Carlos Prío Socarrás (1948–1952).

The next election date, July 1940, approached, and the candidates were Batista and Grau San Martín. Both conducted an intense campaign, touring the country and addressing large rallies everywhere. Slogans were coined, campaign songs composed, and posters exhibited in every town and village. At midnight before the election, troops were ordered into quarters, and the police took over the task of maintaining order. The polling was orderly, and the election was regarded by impartial observers as having been fair and virtually free from the usual abuse of vote-buying. Colonel Batista won a sweeping triumph, carrying his entire party to victory in both the Senate and the House of Representatives. He had achieved his ambition to rule as a constitutional president. There could be no doubt of his popularity.

Yet within a few months there was a plot to overthrow him, fomented by Colonel José Pedraza, Chief of Staff of the Army, and Colonel Angel A. González, Chief of Staff of the Navy. On the night of February 3, 1941, Batista, dressed in a leather jacket, dark trousers, and a white shirt open at the throat, went to Camp Columbia, called together the colonels, and demanded and received from them a pledge of loyalty. The two Chiefs of Staff were arrested but permitted to leave Havana for Miami the next day.

Two days after Pearl Harbor the Cuban Congress, at Batista's request, joined the United States in the war against the Axis powers. Ten days later, as an emergency war measure, Congress made a sweeping delegation to the President of its own powers, including authority to impose taxes, regulate trade, industry, and labor, and make military pacts with the United States and its allies. Batista thereby became the most powerful President in Cuba's history and was in a position to extend to the United States complete cooperation in the war effort. Within a few days he raised all existing taxes and created new ones, including the country's first income tax.

Following the lead of the United States, a concentration camp was established, and the government began rounding up thousands of Japanese, Germans, and Italians. The entire 1942 sugar crop, except for a small amount needed for local consumption, was sold to the American Government at a price considerably lower than what it would have brought in the open world market. Authority to control prices was given to Carlos Hevia, who later became Minister of State, known by all to be honest and upright. A former Minister of Agriculture, Amadeo López Castro, also widely respected for his probity, was appointed as liaison with the American Embassy on sugar matters, and Dr. Carlos Saladrigas, the Prime Minister, who also enjoyed a good reputation, as liaison on an airport development program.

With the signing of the Nazi-Soviet pact the Cuban Communists directed their attacks against the United States and its allies, but after Germany invaded Russia in June 1941, they shifted their position to a popular-front program and refrained from criticizing the United States. Batista permitted them to operate openly on the understanding that they would forego violence in favor of peaceful tactics. In January 1943 they adopted the name *Partido Socialista Popular* (PSP) and in April 1943, with the Soviet Union an ally of the United States, the Batista Government renewed diplomatic relations with the U.S.S.R. The President appointed two well-known Communist leaders to his cabinet. He gave official status to the powerful Communist-controlled Confederation of Cuban Workers (CTC), which dominated labor throughout the country. Only later was it learned that the PSP, during this period of its legal activity, had kept an underground organization intact for use in insurrectional or infiltrating activities in case its legal status was withdrawn.

I met with Batista frequently during his first administration. My firm was handling the government relations, labor, and legal work connected with war projects for the U.S. Government, including the fifteen-million-dollar San Antonio de los

Baños Air Base twenty-five miles south of Havana, with its mile-long concrete runways. American heavy bombers made training flights from northwestern United States to this base prior to undertaking operations in the Pacific. To cope with German U-boats, which had sunk hundreds of vessels in waters within striking distance of Cuba, airports were expanded and new ones constructed from which U.S. bombers could hunt down their prey. A multi-million-dollar nickel plant, financed and owned by the United States Government, was to be constructed in a jungle area of Eastern Cuba.

To carry out these emergency projects without delay, it was essential that the normal labor law restrictions on daily and weekly working hours be lifted, as the workers themselves desired, and that the thousands of necessary government permits and licenses be processed with great rapidity. I asked Batista to designate competent government officials who would be available to us and have authority to solve with dispatch the myriad problems requiring government action. This was done.

We requested tax exemptions of millions, representing savings to the United States and a loss to Cuba, and they were granted. When the problem arose as to how the United States should hold title to the peninsula in Eastern Cuba on which the great Nicaro Nickel plant would be built, Batista readily accepted my proposal that the property be acquired by a Cuban corporation, the stock of which would be owned by an agency of the Washington Government. In every instance my firm received from the President immediate and cordial cooperation.

It was during this period that the accusation of dictatorship was first raised, and Batista often spoke to me of democracy. On one occasion, when a liberal American newspaper branded him as a dictator, he remarked, smilingly, that at least he was trying to be a "pro-American democratic dictator." I would recall these experiences when, in 1958, the liberal Washington policy-makers decided to oust the conservative, pro-American Batista in favor of Fidel Castro.

As the constitution required the lapse of eight years before a president could seek a second term, Batista did not run for reelection in 1944. He backed Dr. Carlos Saladrigas, a tall, slender, attractive, conservative lawyer who was devoid of rabble-rousing talents. His opponent was Batista's old political enemy, Dr. Grau San Martín. In the campaign Grau promised a redistribution of wealth and the restoration of civil authority. My wife voted for Grau, believing him to be honest and well-intentioned; my partner and I supported and worked hard for Saladrigas. The election was honest and the leftist Grau won by a handsome majority. Batista was commended on all sides for having permitted his political opponent to be swept into office. It was the first time in Cuban history that a government-supported candidate had been defeated. Batista relinquished the presidency amid praise and good wishes from the vast majority of the public.

With the exception of Estrada Palma's administration, Cuba's first, and generally regarded as the golden era of public administration, there has always been some corruption in Cuban public life. The first years of Batista were certainly no exception. Paradoxically, however, while the war projects with which we were so intimately associated, involving a disbursement of $125 million, were totally free of graft so long as Batista remained in power, there was corruption in Washington in connection with one of these projects, corruption reaching into the White House itself, although the American President was not personally involved.[1]

In the meantime, in May 1942 Ambassador Spruille Braden had arrived on the scene. Vigorous, tough, forthright to the point of bluntness, and a man of the highest principles, Braden proved to be the antithesis of his predecessor. From the outset he made it clear that shady or undercover transactions involving American interests would not be countenanced. As the 1944 elections approached, he sternly and publicly warned Americans

---

[1] Herbert Solow, "Who's Going to Clean up Nicaro?" *Fortune*, June, 1953, p. 108.

to keep clear of political involvement and to avoid campaign contributions. Cuban politicians who sought to enrich themselves in transactions involving American companies came into conflict with Braden, and there were palace intrigues designed to discredit the Ambassador. Relations between Batista and Braden, however, remained of mutual respect.

There were high expectations when Grau took office, but disillusionment followed within a few months. With the exception of the Castro regime, which helped itself to virtually all privately owned property, all Cubans agree that the administration of leftist Professor Grau (1944-1948) was the most incompetent and corrupt in Cuban history.

This—and the digression seems in order here—should have been a lesson for Washington policy-makers committed to the doctrine that the so-called "non-Communist democratic Left" is the cure for the political ills of Latin America. The lesson has been ignored. Whenever a leftist professor in Latin America shuffles from the lecture platform into the presidency of a country, no matter how incompetent he may be, he receives the support of the U.S. State Department and the open purse of the monetary agencies under U.S. control. But right-wing military men, no matter how able, who step in to save their country are branded as dictators and, at best, given belated recognition, along with oceans of abuse from the liberal press. Reliance on Leftism as the best defense against Communism is the policy line that dictated support of Sukarno, Nasser, Nkrumah, Bosch —and Castro.

Grau began a shakeup of the army almost immediately, removing the commander of Camp Columbia and military chiefs throughout the country, especially those who had been close to Batista. Within a few months most of the officers who had supported Batista were no longer members of the armed forces. Grau fully exploited the tremendous patronage power at his disposal. He gave the Communist-dominated Confederation of Cuban Workers (CTC) $750,000 to build a Workers' Palace. Revolutionary groups which had long been secret organizations

surfaced and moved in on the government ministries. Labor unrest was intensified by struggles for union control between Communist and non-Communist leadership, and there was a decline
in public order.

Communists began gaining control of teacher associations in
order to spread their doctrine. Cuba became one of the focal
points of Communist propaganda in the Western Hemisphere.
Although there were few Russians residing in Cuba and no
Russian business or trade interests, the Soviets established an
oversized diplomatic mission in Havana, taking over a beautiful
mansion as a Legation, which entertained lavishly and at which
Moscow emissaries met with Latin American Communist leaders. Coining the word *Cubanidad* to denote a nationalistic
stance, with the close of World War II in 1945 Grau permitted
anti-American propaganda to get underway.

Under Grau the Ministry of Education became a prime
source of graft and patronage; the Minister, José Alemán,
ended up a multi-millionaire. It was under Grau's direction that
the Cayo Confites expedition was mounted against Trujillo and
the Dominican Republic. Fifteen hundred youths were recruited,
trained, and sent to a tiny, sandy island off eastern Cuba, from
which they were to embark. Some $2 million worth of ships,
planes, arms, and equipment had been accumulated there. When
the United States urged Grau to break up the expedition he ordered the army and navy into action. They surrounded Cayo
Confites and captured 850 members of the expedition, confiscating their ships, weapons, ammunition and 11 bombers. Fidel
Castro, then a student at Havana University, was in this group
but escaped by swimming to the Cuban mainland.

When the expedition failed, the Cuban Senate approved a
motion expressing lack of confidence in Alemán, who was in
Miami. He was reported to have stolen $60 million in bills
from the Treasury. When asked how he had taken the money
his answer was, "in suitcases." He died a few years later, leaving a huge fortune invested in Miami real estate. Grau himself
was later charged with misappropriating $174 million of gov-

ernment funds. On July 4, 1949, during the succeeding administration of Carlos Prío Socarrás, who had been elected with
Grau's support, a group of gunmen invaded the court and stole
the entire record of the proceedings against Grau. The case
never came to trial; no one ever was arrested; and none of
the documents ever was found. Grau died in Havana in July
1969. Less than a hundred persons attended his funeral.

I had first met Prío, who was a lawyer, when he came to our
office in his shirtsleeves one day in 1943, representing a group
of laborers who had worked at the San Antonio de los Baños
Air Base, constructed in 1942–1943. The base had been built
by a New York contractor under a cost-plus wartime contract
for the U.S. Army and represented an investment of between
$15 and $20 million. The contractor had employed about 600
Americans and 11,000 Cubans. Article 62 of the 1940 Constitution called for "equal pay for the same kind of work," and
Prío argued that his clients had done the same kind of work
as Americans but received a lower wage. They had been carried
on the payroll under the same classifications as the Americans,
i.e. "carpenters," "truckdrivers," "foremen," "timekeepers,"
"crane operators," "assistant paymasters," etc. Prío, thirty-nine
or forty years of age, attractive and intelligent, presented his
case courteously and forcefully. It was interesting to talk to
him. He had spent several years in prison for revolutionary
activities against Machado and he had helped write the 1940
Constitution.

Our subsequent study disclosed Prío's claim to be of considerable importance, involving a possible liability of close to
$19 million, apart from the precedent that would be set in other
Latin American countries where war projects had been carried
out by the U.S. Government. At our second meeting with Prío
we rejected his claim.

This case was eventually tried before Chief Justice Byrnes of
the New York City Court, since the defendant was a New York
corporation, but it was defended by the U.S. Government,

which would have been liable for any recovery. My firm was retained to work under the direction of the U.S. Attorney in New York.

As our study developed we found it increasingly difficult to enlist serious and intelligent collaboration on the part of the United States Attorney's office in New York. Young men recently out of law school were assigned to the case and constantly changed. Several came to Havana on junkets without giving more than passing attention to what should have been the purpose of their visit. Finally we decided to resign as associate counsel, not wishing to be associated with a needless failure.

Our resignation created a stir, and I was asked by Ellis O. Briggs, an old friend, to come to Washington. Briggs had served on the Braden staff in Havana as Counselor of Embassy and was now an Assistant Secretary of State in Washington. One of the best qualified Foreign Service officers of our generation, he was later ambassador to seven nations by appointment of three presidents. He grasped the problem instantly. Would we continue our collaboration if jurisdiction of the case were transferred to the Department of Justice, which would designate an experienced and highly qualified lawyer to work with us? We would; and under the direction of Marvin C. Taylor, a Harvard lawyer of great capacity, the case was eventually tried in New York in September 1949. The decision was in favor of the United States Government.

President Grau appointed Prío Socarrás as Minister of Labor on April 30, 1947, and almost at once Prío moved to break the hold of the Communists on the labor organizations. He ordered them evicted from the Labor Palace, contending that the building belonged to the Confederation of Cuban Workers. Eventually he based his bid for the presidency largely on having destroyed Communist influence in Cuba. "We must remove their masks and expose their aims of world domination," he said.

In 1946 the disillusionment of the Cuban people in their

government seemed to have found an outlet in a new leader, Senator Eduardo Chibás, who organized the Ortodoxo Party (Party of the Cuban People). His personal popularity stemmed largely from weekly radio broadcasts in which he spared no one implicated in graft. In the 1948 campaign he used a broom as an electoral symbol and made a good showing, polling about 16 percent of the popular vote, nearly twice the party's registration figure. But Carlos Prío Socarrás was elected President on June 1, 1948, and *in absentia,* as he was then living in Daytona Beach, Batista was elected a Senator.

Batista returned to Cuba on November 20, 1948, and established himself and his family at his country estate, known as Kuquine, where soldiers were detailed to maintain a twenty-four-hour guard. It was from this beautiful estate that Batista was to run for president again and eventually to stage the military coup which would once more put him in control of the island.

Prío's government (1948–1952) enacted several constructive laws setting up institutions called for by the 1940 Constitution; but the Cubans were to judge him harshly, since public disorders continued and there were financial scandals. The brightest period of the administration was the ten months during which José M. (Pepín) Bosch served as Minister of Finance. Bosch, one of Cuba's most successful and respected industrialists, had headed the renowned Bacardi Company. His reputation for integrity was such that when he called on the Cuban people to pay their taxes fully and promptly, there was an astonishing response, unprecedented in Cuban history.

During this period the chief of the American diplomatic mission in Cuba was perhaps the worst ambassador the United States had ever had—anywhere. He has passed on now and a veil may charitably be drawn over his shameful record. But his appointment illustrates one of the weaknesses of the American

Foreign Service—the fact that about a third of the ambassa-
dorial posts still go to non-professionals.

The diplomat who is an amateur works in an atmosphere that
is strange to him, with new and oddly shaped tools. The career
diplomat has a feel for his job and a skill which is acquired by
experience and cannot be acquired in any other way. Most of
the problems the career diplomat faces are of a pattern that has
been met and repeatedly solved in the past. Political appointments are usually made for the good of the nominee. Appointments of career diplomats, with the exception to be noted, are
made for the good of the United States. The incumbent ambassador whom the politically influential outsider "bumps" is
usually a competent career man.

This was what happened in Havana in 1948 when Ambassador R. Henry Norweb was abruptly replaced by a grossly
incompetent amateur whose sole qualification was that he had
rendered a political service to President Truman. Harry Norweb's performance throughout a long career had been impeccable. He and his wife, Emery May, a lady of culture and quality,
were loved by the entire Embassy staff and respected by Cubans
and Americans alike.

But experience in the career service is not the sole requisite
for a diplomat. As long as the cold war continues, in fact if not
in name, he should be of a conservative persuasion. R. Henry
Norweb was a conservative as well as a skilled professional. The
Cuban experience teaches, as will be explained in later chapters, that liberals are unable to assess and counter the Communist threat. They only see enemies on the right. Late in the
Batista administration and early in the Castro regime the performance of a conservative non-professional ambassador proved
to be infinitely superior of that of a liberal career ambassador.

In the closing days of July 1951, I was visited at my home
late one night by Eduardo Chibás, known affectionately throughout the country as "Eddie," the most popular political figure in

Cuba at the time. His weekly Sunday evening radio broadcasts were rated as having by far the highest audience of any program. Eddie had been reared in a wealthy family but had given away his inheritance little by little to friends in need. This generosity had endeared him to the masses. His courage and eloquence electrified the working class. Every Sunday evening at eight o'clock a very large proportion of the Cuban population gathered around radios in cities, villages, and isolated farms to hear the familiar voice denounce the corruption of the Grau and Prío administrations. The wealthy and more conservative people regarded Chibás as a demagogue, a rabble-rouser. Some held him to be mentally unbalanced because he had "squandered" his wealth. By mid-1951 it was generally believed that he would walk away with the presidency in the 1952 elections. I admired him for his incorruptibility and unrelenting crusade for clean government.

Shortly before coming to see me, Eddie had publicly accused President Prío's Minister of Education of hiding stolen millions in Guatemala, and he had been challenged to produce the evidence. During his weekly harangue two days earlier he had promised to produce it the following Sunday. Now, having heard in some way that I had knowledge of a secret trip President Prío had made to Guatemala in a military plane, without the constitutionally required consent of the Cuban Senate, he had come to me for this vital information.

An attractive smile came over his tired face as we sat alone in my living room that night. He had a fair complexion, was short and stocky and scholarly in appearance. His glasses had very thick lenses. Chibás began by saying that there were only two ways that one could become president of Cuba. The first was with money, to assure press support and to perfect a political machine in every town and hamlet. He had no money, however; his followers were the poor. He had not even been able to pay for his Sunday evening radio time; the greatly respected Mestre brothers, owners of the broadcasting facilities, had never pressed him for payment. The second way to reach the palace, he explained, was by demagoguery and that was his only choice. But he wanted to assure me that once he became president he would follow a middle-of-the-road and pro-American policy. He had never hidden his contempt for Communism. "Tell me about Prío's trip to Guatemala," he then said, and, gesturing as if to lift an armful of bundles from his lap and place them in mine, "If I had a million dollars, Mario, I would give them to you for this information. I am facing the greatest crisis of my life."

Eddie's information was correct. Prío had made a secret and unauthorized trip to Guatemala, but not in connection with public funds stolen by his Minister of Education. The FBI had spotted his arrival at the Guatemala airport and had reported to the State Department in Washington that he was at the moment closeted with the President of Guatemala. I told Eddie I could not discuss the subject without violating a professional confidence and that he himself would think less of me if I did. He lowered his head in dismay, slowly nodding affirmatively, and said, "Yes, you are right, you are right."

But I also knew that Prío had been seen at the Guatemala airport by persons whom former United States Ambassador Braden described as "unimpeachable witnesses" and that Braden had so reported to one of my neighbors. I offered to accompany Eddie to that neighbor's home, and it must have been about three o'clock in the morning as we walked over. On the way we talked. I asked Chibás what he thought of the behavior of American private capital in Cuba. "If the Cubans did as well," he said, "there would be no budgetary problem; this country would be a paradise." The Americans obeyed the laws, he said, including the rigid social and labor laws.

When we arrived, my neighbor, a respected American industrialist, joined us on his terrace. He had been one of Ambassador Braden's closest friends and agreed to telephone him in New York. The next morning he called to say that Braden was writing to one of Chibás' political associates and would close his letter with, "By the way, I talked to friends in Guatemala, who saw your Chief of State there," giving the date and place.

When I passed this news to Eddie, he was elated. He was certain that this word from a former American Ambassador would be all he needed, that Prío would be subject to impeachment. My interest mounted as the time for the next Sunday broadcast approached. When it started, however, it was at once evident that the tone was entirely different from any previous one. Absent were the denunciations of specific instances of corruption. Instead, Eddie spoke calmly and in generalities, imploring the Cuban people to insist upon a high moral code of political conduct. Nothing was said about Prío. Eddie closed his broadcast with, "This is my last plea; I am knocking at the door for the last time, listen." And at that point he shot himself through the stomach.

A great curtain of sorrow descended on the nation. Eddie lingered for several days while hundreds prayed in the street below his hospital window. He died on August 16, 1951, and his funeral was one of the greatest mass demonstrations of sympathy in Cuban history.

There was an ironical touch to the dramatic way he ended his life. His broadcast had gone over the time limit and he was off the air at the time he pulled the trigger. To this story, which has been told repeatedly, I can add a footnote, a story that is not known. The Braden letter that Eddie so desperately wanted had been sent to Dr. Herminio Portel Vilá, a close political associate of Chibás. Unfortunately, it was addressed to him at the Cuban-American Cultural Association, which had recently moved its offices, and the letter remained undelivered. Had it reached Portel Vilá, Eddie Chibás probably would have become President of Cuba in 1952. In that case Castro might never have been heard of. He had joined Eddie Chibás' Ortodoxo Party but got little encouragement there because Chibás considered him to be a gangster, under Communist influence, and not to be trusted.

As the 1952 elections approached, the new Constitution had been in effect for twelve years. Many of the institutions for enforcing government responsibility had been created, and Cuba was still prospering from the Korean War. The government's pro-labor policy had produced strong labor support. Its point of vulnerability was the widespread gangsterism, violence, and corruption. There were three candidates for the presidency— Carlos Hevia, an Annapolis graduate, an honest man who had Prío's support; Roberto Agramonte, who succeeded Eddie Chibás as leader of the Ortodoxos; and Batista. Agramonte was the strong favorite and Batista the least likely to win.

On March 10, 1952, an important date in Cuban history, Batista, convinced that he would lose the election, engineered a successful and almost bloodless *coup d'état*. Having confided in only a handful of supporters who were sworn to secrecy on pain of death, and with army support, he seized Camp Columbia. One of his collaborators appeared at Cabaña Fortress, across the entrance of the harbor from Havana, and was immediately accepted as commander. In the interior other, younger elements of the army took command. Prío resigned as ordered, and he left the country, making little effort to arouse his followers. Within two hours Batista had again made himself the ruler of Cuba. Displaying his usual political skill, he responded to the widespread discontent with gangsterism and graft by promising order and an honest administration until elections could be held. He temporarily suspended constitutional guarantees, dissolved the political parties and Congress, prohibited strikes, raised the pay of the army, and kept Congressmen on salary.

I received news of the coup at about four in the morning, barely an hour after it had occurred, from the wife of one of my lawyers. Depressed and disheartened, I remember saying, "This is a black day for Cuba. Batista is destroying the Constitution he himself created, and he is certain to regret it." Although the experience under Grau had been much worse than under Batista, it appeared to me at the time that it was a tragedy to interrupt the democratic process.

In retrospect, it is clear that Cuba had not achieved democracy in 1952. The system had not worked, either in the American form under the 1901 Constitution nor in a semiparliamentary form under the Constitution of 1940. To be elected a Senator during the Grau and Prío administrations, a candidate had to spend approximately $250,000 and the salary for the term was $96,000. A seat as Representative cost about $125,000 and the salary during the four-year term was $48,000. The difference had to come from somewhere, and since Congressmen enjoyed parliamentary immunity they did not fear investigation. The prevailing idea, with many honorable exceptions of course, was that politics was a spoils system. Few politicians regarded public office as a public trust.

It should be remembered, however, that in 1952 Cuba as a fully sovereign nation was only eighteen years old. In the town where my wife and I now live there is a house that was once occupied by Mark Twain. He once set down some words about an all-American group of politicians who lived eighty years after the American Constitution became effective. In referring to Tammany Hall, Samuel Clemens said, "It had but one principal, one policy, one moving spring of action—avarice, money-lust. So that it got money it cared not a rap about the means and methods. It was always ready to lie, forge, betray, steal, swindle, cheat, rob; and no promise, no engagement, no contract, no treaty made by its Boss was worth the paper it was written on or the polluted breath that uttered it."

One of my most respected friends is Robert L. James, at present Washington representative of the Bank of America. Dr. James was one of our clients in Havana and formerly lived in Chicago.

"My fellow Americans," he recently wrote me, "should realize that there was a striking similarity between the way Batista ran Cuba and the manner in which, for many decades, the City of Chicago was run by political bosses. Decent people in Chicago tolerated a corrupt government in the same way that the people of Cuba tolerated the Batista government. In both cases they were left alone to pursue their private lives and their business activities as they chose. The only Cubans who came into conflict with the Batista government were the few who engaged in acts of terrorism. . . . Those of us who lived and worked in Cuba in 1958 never had the feeling that we were oppressed, and I never heard any Cuban express that sentiment."

Many Cubans came to regard democracy as a weak and expensive form of government that did not necessarily produce either stability or progress. While some of us strove and hoped for a "real" democracy, others advocated increasing the power of the central government as the best means of achieving large-scale socio-economic reforms. They justified concentration of power as essential in order to bring about stability and a structure in which democracy eventually could function. Some argued that the most successful form of government in Latin America was that of Mexico, which is a compromise between democracy and dictatorship. The President of Mexico is elected under a one-party system and rules as a dictator for six years, after which he can never again be elected. He can do virtually anything he wants while in office. Of course, the single large party contains elements of democracy.

In any case, on March 10, 1952 a large portion of the population welcomed the return to power of Batista. It welcomed his announcement that, if the United States became involved in a war with the U.S.S.R., Cuba would fight on the side of the Americans. Business and industry were encouraged by his assurance that he would keep order and his hint that he would accede to its principal demand—a modification of labor regulations to permit an employer to dismiss a worker with severance pay, a change never consummated because of opposition from organized labor. Those most bitterly disappointed over the coup, of course, were the candidates running on the Ortodoxo ticket, including the young radical, Fidel Castro, who aspired to membership in the House of Representatives.

During the following two and a half years Batista governed as "Provisional President" under a fundamental decree that incorporated most of the 1940 Constitution but omitted the sections providing for representative government. The functions of Congress were vested in the Cabinet, with an eighty-member Advisory Council created to make suggestions on legislation.

On March 27, 1952, two weeks after the coup, the United States recognized the Batista administration.

A week earlier two Soviet diplomats arriving in Cuba were subjected to regular customs procedures, and the Soviet Union, in protest, broke diplomatic relations with Cuba. During 1952 and 1953 Batista gradually moved against the Communists, and on October 21, 1953, their party (PSP) was declared illegal. Most of the known Communist leaders were arrested or went into exile. The PSP, which then numbered approximately 150,000, was ordered by Moscow to go underground, reduce its membership to a hard core of the faithful, and await future instructions.[2]

The major achievements of Batista's second period of rule included the building of a good water system for Havana (something which political leaders had promised the people for generations) and other public works. He created a Sugar Stabilization Fund to prevent economic collapse after the end of the Korean War. The early 1950s were relatively prosperous years, and once again, in 1954, Batista attempted to legalize his position by holding popular elections. Grau San Martín was again the opposition candidate but he withdrew before the election, claiming that Batista would prevent a fair vote. Under these circumstances Batista was unanimously elected. He was inaugurated on February 25, 1955, before a packed assembly of diplo-

[2] R. Hart Phillips, *Cuba: Island of Paradox* (New York: McDowell, Obolensky, Inc., 1964), p. 263.

mats, congressmen, government officials, and high-ranking military officers, while a huge crowd cheered outside the Palace.

In May 1955 Batista felt sufficiently secure to declare a broad amnesty of political prisoners, releasing hundreds of his enemies, while others, including Prío Socarrás, returned from exile. Among those amnestied were Fidel and Raúl Castro.

CHAPTER SEVEN

Facts and Fallacies

The day before President Kennedy was assassinated, Fidel Castro spent several hours in a Havana hotel room being interviewed by French journalist Jean Daniel. This, however, was no ordinary interview. Less than a month before, Daniel had met with President Kennedy in Washington and the President had given him an "off-the-record" message for Castro. Much of the discussion in the hotel room concerned that message.

"I think," the President had said for Castro's benefit, "that there is not a country in the world, including all the regions of Africa and including any country under colonial domination, where the economic colonization, the humiliation, the exploitation have been worse than those which ravaged Cuba, the result, in part, of the policy of my country, during the regime of Batista. I think that we spawned, constructed, entirely fabricated without knowing it, the Castro movement. I think that the accumulation of such errors has endangered all of Latin America . . . I will tell you something else: In a certain sense, it is as though Batista were the incarnation of some of the sins committed by the United States. Now, we must pay for those sins. . . ." [1]

Castro listened to this statement with nervous amazement. Daniel reports that he twisted his beard, pulled at his beret, and

---

[1] *The New York Times,* December 11, 1963, p. 16. Substantially the same account of President Kennedy's statement to Jean Daniel appeared in *Eye on Cuba,* by Edwin Tetlow (New York: Harcourt, Brace & World, Inc., 1966), pp. 199, 200.

kept adjusting his jacket as it was read. Then, unbelieving, he asked the journalist to read it again. And again a third time.

Later in the interview Castro paid a glowing tribute to President Kennedy: "He still has the possibility of becoming the greatest President of the United States." [2]

After the tragedy in Dallas on November 22 Jean Daniel decided that the death of the President voided the confidential nature of his interview at the White House. *The New York Times* published the story of the private message on December 11, 1963, and a detailed account appeared in the *New Republic,* December 14, 1963. Thus it became known that the President had held the astonishing belief that Cuba before Castro not only was the victim of the most ruthless colonial exploitation in all history but that the United States was to blame and must atone for these "sins."

This shocking disclosure once more reminded me and others close to Cuban affairs of the abysmal ignorance in the United States with respect to Cuba, even in the highest official circles.

I was in Cuba in 1960 when the new regime confiscated almost a billion dollars in American-owned property. I either heard or read all of Castro's pronouncements attempting to justify that outrage. His tirades were no stronger, and no more warranted, than was President Kennedy's confidential message to him in 1963. Small wonder that on hearing it Castro excitedly voiced his gratification, exclaiming that Kennedy might become "an even greater President than Lincoln," [3] and that "anyone else would be worse"—for Castro, of course.

Perhaps the President's views on the supposed American sins in relation to Cuba were more extreme than those of most Americans. Unfortunately, however, I have found these woeful misconceptions about social and economic conditions on the island just before the Castro take-over, and of American responsibility for the evils, widespread. This is particuarly

[2] *The New York Times,* December 11, 1963, p. 16.
[3] *Ibid.,* p. 16.

true in liberal circles, where pre-Castro Cuba is depicted in blackest hues as a country in which a wealthy few exploited illiterate and poverty-stricken masses; where large farms were becoming larger, with the little farmer on the way out; where American corporations helped drain the economy they dominated for the benefit of their stockholders at home; and where a bestial dictator ruled this complex of social injustice.

I once encountered the same stereotyped thinking about Cuba in talking to Eleanor Roosevelt, who felt that the Cubans were so hopelessly mired in poverty that "perhaps a Socialist government would be the best solution for them." The liberal Columbia University professor C. Wright Mills, after visiting Cuba in 1959–1960, concluded that the revolution had been a "peasant uprising," provoked by unbearable poverty and despair in a miserably underdeveloped country.

Myths of this sort, of course, have been so massively reinforced by Havana's propaganda since the takeover that they are treated uncritically as fact even by some self-styled experts and journalists who should know better. They are exploited to the limit to put Americans on the psychological defensive.

What are the realities behind the myths?

Although Cuba lived under the blight of Spanish colonial rule seventy-six years longer than any other country in Latin America, by the 1950s, in the incredibly short span of half a century, *it had attained the highest standard of living of any semi-tropical or tropical country in the world, except possibly for Venezuela.* According to a U.S. Department of Commerce report, Cuban national income in 1956 had reached levels which gave the Cuban people "one of the highest standards of living in Latin America." [4] The Economic and Technical Mission of the International Bank for Reconstruction and Development stated in its Report on Cuba, 1951: "The general im-

---

[4] U. S. Department of Commerce, *Investment in Cuba* (Washington, D. C.: Government Printing Office, 1956), p. 184.

pression of members of the Mission, from observations in travel all over Cuba, is that living levels of the farmers, agricultural laborers, industrial workers, storekeepers, and others are higher all along the line than for corresponding groups in other tropical countries and in nearly all other Latin American countries. This does not mean that there is no dire poverty in Cuba, but simply that in comparative terms Cubans are better off, on the average, than people of these other areas." This statement, written in 1951, summarizes equally well the situation in 1956.[5] Cuba's transportation system and domestic markets were the most highly developed in Latin America.[6] In 1956 Cuba had three times the U.S. railway mileage per square mile of area.[7]

In 1958 even unskilled labor received as much as six and seven dollars a day. Cuban labor laws, rigidly enforced, were more advanced in almost every respect than those prevailing in the United States. They included, for instance, one month of paid vacation for every worker, minimum wages, an 8-hour day with time-and-a-half pay for overtime, a 44-hour week with 48 hours of pay, social security, maternity and accident benefits, and the provision that no worker could be dismissed from his job except for a limited number of proven causes. The Cuban Confederation of Workers, according to the American CIO, had attained a much higher numerical degree of organization in proportion to population than the labor movement in the United States.[8]

Agricultural workers, too, were well paid. According to statistics published in 1960 by the International Labor Organization

[5] *Ibid.*, p. 184.

[6] Wyatt MacGaffey and Clifford R. Barnett, *Twentieth Century Cuba,* prepared under the auspices of The American University (New York: Doubleday and Company, Inc., 1965), pp. 101, 103.

[7] U. S. Department of Commerce, *Investment in Cuba,* p. 22.

[8] Ernest Schwartz, "Some Observations on Labor Organization in the Caribbean" in *The Caribbean: Its Economy* (Gainesville, Florida: University of Florida Press, 1954), p. 167. In 1954 Ernest Schwartz was the Executive Secretary of the Committee on Latin American Affairs of the CIO.

in Geneva, the average wage in 1958 for an 8-hour day was $3. When adjusted to compensate for the differences in purchasing power, this compared with $2.70 for Belgium, $2.86 for Denmark, $1.74 for France, $2.73 for West Germany and $4.06 for the United States. The same ILO statistics showed that the Cuban workers received 66.6% of the gross national income, compared to 57.2% for Argentina, 47.9% for Brazil, and 70.1% for the United States.

During the 1960 presidential campaign Senator John F. Kennedy stated in a Cincinnati speech that American companies dominated the Cuban economy. Here too, as in his subsequent interview with Daniel, he was repeating a widely held misconception. The fact is that in 1958 only 5% of the invested capital in Cuba was American,[9] and out of a working force of about two million, only seventy-odd thousand were full-time employees of American companies.[10]

What about the common belief that Cuba was a country of mammoth land holdings, with the landowners a privileged class virtually above the law?

In the first place, it is a good logic that agrarian reform should be related to the problem of food production, especially in areas such as Latin America that are experiencing one of the world's highest population increases. The growing of food is clearly a most important enterprise in any country. If small land holdings produce more food, the laws should aim at a break-up of latifundia (large land holdings). But small farms do not always produce more food. This has been demonstrated, for example, in the Belgian Congo, where the natives seized the splendid farms slowly developed through the years by the toil,

[9] José R. Alvarez Díaz, *Trayectoria de Castro: encumbramiento y derrumbe* (Miami: Editorial A.I.P., 1964), p. 11.

[10] U. S. Department of Commerce, *U. S. Investments in the Latin American Economy* (Washington, D. C.: Government Printing Office, 1957), p. 75.

knowledge, and capital of Europeans and broke them up into scraggly plots for the raising of yams, scarcely able to sustain human life.

In the United States the trend nowadays is toward fewer, larger, and more mechanized farms. Most Cubans, by contrast, felt that smaller farms were desirable, and the Cuban laws strongly favored the small sugar cane farmer. Although statistics of this kind can be misleading, the U.S. Department of Commerce reported that in 1946 the average size of Cuban farms was 140 acres,[11] as against 195 in the United States in 1945.[12] While the average size of the Cuban farm decreased during the fifteen-year period 1931–1946 from 188 to 140 acres, that is, by 25.5%,[13] it *increased* during the nineteen-year period 1940–1959 in the United States by 73.5%.[14] At the same time there was a marked trend in Cuba away from American ownership and toward Cuban ownership of sugar mills. In 1958, for instance, Cuban-owned mills accounted for about 62% of the total sugar output, compared to only 22% in 1939.[15] U.S. control of the Cuban sugar industry declined from about 70% in 1928 to about 35% in 1958.[16]

Most of the cane in Cuba was grown by *colonos,* individuals who either rented from the sugar mills or depended upon the mill to buy their cane. The rest of the cane, called "administration cane," was produced by the mill itself with hired labor. In 1944 only 10 percent of the crop was administration cane. This low proportion was the result of a sugar quota law in 1937 that allotted larger quotas to *colonos,* favoring the small farmer.

[11] U. S. Department of Commerce, *Investment in Cuba,* p. 32.

[12] U. S. Department of Commerce, *Statistical Abstract of the United States, 1962* (Washington, D. C.: U. S. Government Printing Office, 1962), p. 610.

[13] U. S. Department of Commerce, *Investment in Cuba,* p. 32.

[14] *Statistical Abstract of the United States, 1962.*

[15] U. S. Department of Commerce, *Investment in Cuba,* p. 37.

[16] Theodore Draper, *Castroism: Theory and Practice* (New York: Frederick A. Praeger, 1965), p. 109.

Many mills thereupon gave up producing their cane and leased all their lands to farmers at low rents, tied by law to the price of sugar.

The task of cutting cane during the annual crop is entirely manual. Cane-cutting machinery has been tried but none has been found to be as efficient as hand labor. Experimental machines built for the Castro regime by the U.S.S.R. have been a failure.

The 1937 Law for Sugar Coordination, which remained in effect through 1958, established minimum wages, production quotas, prices for grinding cane, and, as explained, low rent ceilings based on the value of sugar. The quotas given to the small farmers were taken away from the large growers and the small farmers were guaranteed against eviction so long as they produced their quota of cane. The 1940 Constitution went even further, calling for the breakup of the remaining large land holdings and the elimination of foreign influence in agricultural affairs.

Batista's final period in power lasted almost seven years, from March 10, 1952 until December 31, 1958. The first five were peaceful and the sixth relatively so. They were years of expanding prosperity, culminating, in 1957, with the most prosperous year in Cuban history. As rebel activities mounted toward the end of 1958 the economy deteriorated sharply, and Batista contributed to the decline of the economy and his own downfall by failing to hold free and honest elections in 1958.

On the positive side, however, in 1954 Batista instituted a long-range Economic and Social Development Plan, by far the most ambitious ever formulated in Cuba. It called for an expenditure of $350 million over an initial four-year period. In its agricultural sector it called for immediate improvements in storage and refrigeration facilities, increased mechanization, fertilization and irrigation, and intensified research by agricultural experimental stations.

To reduce further the perils of a one-crop economy, it proposed more production of meat, milk, fowl, eggs, fish, rice, beans, fruit, vegetables, and coffee. On the social side the program called for agrarian reform, including technical economic assistance to small farmers through agricultural cooperatives and trade and credit organizations. This ambitious program had counterparts in industry and trade, offering tax incentives and credits to private investors. Although it never had a chance to prove itself completely, since many of the measures were of a long-term nature and the Castro rebellion disrupted their operation, the early results were spectacular.

Per capita income figures, although considerably lower than in the United States, rose to the second highest level in Latin America in 1957.[17] The middle-income group expanded until it also became one of the largest in Latin America, estimated at between one-fifth and one-third of the population—a remarkable achievement.[18] Between mid-1952 and mid-1957 savings and fixed-term deposits in banks jumped from $140 million to $385.5 million.[19]

Real estate had always been the preferred form of investment in Cuba, and in 1953 a vast and astonishing building boom got under way. It spread throughout the island. In Havana new hotels and scores of apartment houses changed the skyline. New streets were paved, old streets were patched, and all the famous Havana restaurants were redecorated and air-conditioned. At the Plaza Civica, surrounding the monument of José Martí, a huge wheel of beautiful government buildings, projected and initiated by Prío Socarrás, were completed. When Batista took over in 1952, private construction totaled $53 million annually and public construction $76 million. By 1957 the corresponding figures were $77 million and $195 million.[20] A tunnel was built under the entrance of Havana harbor, leading to the magnificent scenic highway to Matanzas along the north coast.

---

[17] *Ibid.*, p. 98.
[18] *Ibid.*, p. 78.
[19] MacGaffey and Barnett, *Twentieth Century Cuba*, p. 225.
[20] *Ibid.*, p. 100.

The expansion in the industrial sector during this period was phenomenal. Three new refineries for processing imported crude oil were constructed, giving Cuba an export balance of gasoline for the first time. Two new tire installations and the expansion of a third more than doubled the 1956 production of automobile tires. A new copper-wire drawing mill was built, capable almost by itself of filling the country's copper wire needs. A cast-iron water pipe factory placed Cuba in an export position for this product. In 1957 five new paper and paperboard manufacturing plants using baggase (a byproduct of sugar) as a raw material were either being built or in the planning stage. Owens-Illinois built a plant with sufficient capacity to provide Cuba with all the glass containers it needed. Reynolds Aluminum erected a plant to produce aluminum foil and packaging. Water works were provided for several cities, roads and highways were built, and exploration for oil was undertaken.

It was during this period that my firm undertook the legal and government-relations work involved in the construction of a second nickel and cobalt plant in Eastern Cuba that, when completed, was to be the largest producer of nickel in the free world and the largest producer of cobalt in the Western Hemisphere. This project represented an investment of $115 million. When Castro came to power the plant was dismantled and cannibalized. As in the case of the United States Government-owned Nicaro Nickel project this great installation had advanced almost to the point of completion without a trace of graft in Cuba, not a dollar having been either demanded or paid.

These were only a few of the more important construction projects, which provided jobs for scores of thousands of unskilled and skilled workers during the boom years of 1954–1957. When Castro seized power in 1959 the building industry collapsed overnight; all the construction workers were thrown out of work.

The funds to carry out Batista's Economic and Social Development Plan came from private Cuban sources, from several government banks, and from private American interests. American investments had been chiefly responsible for making Cuban industry the most heavily capitalized (relative to population) in Latin America. From 1938 to 1958 the Cuban record for servicing its foreign debt was spotless, and by 1950 Cuban currency had become among the hardest in the world.[21]

According to the U.S. Department of Commerce, the Cuban Government's revenues for the fiscal year ending June 30, 1957, reached an all-time high of $370.8 million, showing a budgetary surplus of $12.9 million. For the fiscal year ending June 30, 1958, according to the same source, although revenues had dropped to $359.9 million, the budgetary surplus stood at $29.8 million.

I believed for many years that the development of tourist travel to Cuba would benefit the country in every way, and, in fact, my partner and I were responsible for the construction of the 32-story $24 million Havana-Hilton Hotel, the finest structure of its kind in Latin America at the time. But later I came to change my mind about this. Although tourism helped to some extent to maintain a favorable international balance of payments, it directly benefited only an infinitesimally small segment of the population, mainly hotel and restaurant workers, taxi drivers, and entertainers, and it hurt Cuba in almost every other way. The tourist facilities were not of the healthful, recreational kind, such as public beaches and golf courses, that attract the most desirable visitor; some were plainly tourist "traps."

Very few of our visitors ever saw the real Cuba. Even those who had Cuban friends seldom saw the inside of a Cuban home, because social visiting in the home is limited by custom chiefly to relatives and intimate friends. I am sure it did not occur to many of them that, as Thomas Merton, the Trappist monk, has

[21] *Ibid.*, p. 228.

written in *Emblems of a Season of Fury,* we might have a life, a spirit and a culture of our own, something irreplaceable that cannot be bought with money. They probably imagined, said Merton, that all Latin Americans live for the siesta and spend their days and nights playing the guitar and making love. "How could they possibly know," he asked, "that Latin America is by and large culturally superior to the United States, not only on the level of the wealthy minority which has absorbed most of the sophistication of Europe, but also among the desperately poor indigenous cultures [those of the Inca and Maya Indians], some of which are rooted in a past that has never been surpassed on this continent."

The typical visitor had little rapport with the human beings on the island. He arrived with his camera, exposure meter, and sunglasses and gazed in every direction without seeing what was there. *In some cases he saw things that were not there.* Can anything be more spurious than the cosmopolitanism of Professor Arthur M. Schlesinger, Jr., who left Havana after a brief visit in 1950 with the preposterous notion that the city "was being debased into a giant casino and brothel for American businessmen over for a big weekend from Miami"? [22]

Again, what are the facts?

In 1950 Greater Havana, with a population of close to one million, had three gambling casinos, which were adjuncts of restaurants offering dancing and entertainment facilities. When the new tourist hotels were erected during the great building boom of the late 1950s, four or five additional casinos were authorized. Few of the Cubans who patronized the night clubs or hotels entered the gambling rooms. On the few occasions that I visited the casinos with American tourists during the nearly forty years of my residence in Cuba, I do not recall ever having run into any member of my large office staff there. Casinos were an American institution, alien to Cuban life, operated by

[22] Arthur M. Schlesinger, Jr., *A Thousand Days* (Boston: Houghton Mifflin Company, 1965), p. 173.

Americans for Americans. And, of course, there was no more prostitution in Havana than in any American city of comparable size.

Although education for all had been one of the slogans of the leaders of the War of Independence in 1898 and the principle of free and compulsory schooling had been established as early as the 1901 Constitution, the number of persons aged ten or older able to read and write was only a little over 70 percent in 1933 when Batista first came to power.[23] It was lower than this in rural areas and higher in urban areas. Batista's original program called for use of the army to extend education to remote rural districts, where schools were constructed and teachers given the rank of sergeant. At that time there were few public vocational schools but their number had increased enormously by mid-century, especially the polytechnic schools, which supplied tuition, lodging, food, and sometimes even clothing to the pupils, free of charge.[24] The number of general secondary schools more than tripled during the Batista era. They included agricultural schools in every one of the six provinces; these owned their own land and livestock and were adequately equipped. Admission was by competition but limited to children of farm families.[25] The three-year program led to a certificate of Master Farmer.

At the time of the Sergeants' Revolt in 1933 the strongest advocates of educational reform were the student and intellectual followers of Professor Grau San Martín, but shortly after Grau had become President in 1944 the Ministry of Education became a center of wholesale graft that, by the end of his term, had become a national scandal. During the Grau administration the sale of teaching appointments became a common practice and teachers, who were civil servants and had a life tenure, were

[23] MacGaffey and Barnett, *Twentieth Century Cuba*, p. 190 .
[24] *Ibid.*, p. 193.
[25] *Ibid.*, p. 194.

paid whether they taught or not. Professor Grau's Minister of Education made a fortune of several millions.

By the mid-1950s, however, these conditions had been virtually eliminated. There were 25,000 teachers in the public school system and 3,500 in the nearly 900 officially recognized private schools. There were three state-controlled universities, with a total enrollment of about 20,000. The private schools alone, including three private universities, had an enrollment of more than 100,000. *In education and literacy Cuba ranked at or near the top among Latin American countries.* It ranked first in the percentage of national income invested in education.[26] American and Cuban authorities in the education field agree that it was less expensive and easier to obtain a college education in Cuba than in the United States.

In the welfare field Cuba was notably advanced. It had huge *centros,* or clubs, with memberships ranging from 10,000 to as high as 90,000; these maintained schools, homes for the aged, and some of the finest hospitals in the country. For a monthly fee of three dollars a member was entitled to free medical treatment for himself and his family, as well as the use of the clubs' educational and recreational facilities. Also, there were a great number and variety of pension and retirement funds (social security) affording protection against old age and disability. By 1950 they covered approximately half the working population. In addition to the benefits provided for the insured, pensions were usually provided for widows, unmarried daughters, and underage dependents of those who died. These funds were financed by the insured, the employers, and the state. During the Grau and Prío administrations, however, many of the retirement funds met with financial difficulty and had to cut back al-

---

[26] Article 52 of the 1940 Constitution attested to the importance attached to popular education. It provided that the Ministry of Education budget should not be less than the ordinary budget of any other Ministry and that a teacher's monthly salary should not be less than one-millionth of the annual national budget.

lowances and pensions when the government "borrowed" millions from the trusts without ever publicly acknowledging the fact or obtaining the consent of the fund administrators.

In the field of public health Cuba surpassed the United States in some respects. It had almost twice as many physicians and surgeons in relation to population (and twice as many teachers) [27] and it had a lower mortality index, among both adults and infants. Its annual death rate of only 15 per 1,000 persons was unusually low. Before Castro assumed power its food supply was abundant, and a United States Government report described the Cubans as "among the better fed people of the world." [28] The country was relatively disease-free. Malarial infection, for example, had fallen to 2.1 cases per 100,000 of population, and there had been no epidemics of any sort since the influenza experience during World War I. Cuba had a higher proportion of doctors and dentists, including some of the world's best, than any other country in the Caribbean area.

Until Castro came on the scene the people of Cuba had all the necessities of life and they were getting an increasing measure of luxuries. Cuba had one radio for every 5 inhabitants, one television set for every 20, one automobile for every 27, and one telephone for every 28.

Ironically, one element of Cuba's former prosperity inherited by Castro helps him retain his hold on the people. No other nation except the United States had as many television sets *per capita* as Cuba. By comparison, Soviet Russia has one set per thousand inhabitants and China has only one set per ten thousand. For a person with Castro's talents for acting and oratory, the medium is made to order, and he has used it with the utmost effectiveness.

[27] U. S. Department of Commerce, *Investment in Cuba,* p. 183.
[28] Economic Research Service of the U. S. Department of Agriculture, *Agriculture and Food Situation in Cuba* (Washington, D. C.: U. S. Government Printing Office, 1926), p. 2.

Such then was the extraordinary progress made by Cuba during the pre-Kennedy and pre-Castro era. Far from having been "exploited" or "humiliated" by the United States, the exact opposite had been the case. Following the Spanish-American War, the United States rejected Spain's suggestion that the U.S. annex Cuba. For many years it bought Cuban sugar at considerably above world market prices. And, most important of all, except for the native intelligence and industry of the Cuban people themselves, American private capital and American know-how were the principal contributing factors in making Cuba the most industrialized country of Latin America in ratio to population, and in raising its living standard to one of the highest.

I believe I am in as good a position as any living man to evaluate the performance of American business and industry in Cuba, as my firm represented almost a third of the American investment there. With strikingly rare exceptions American participation was benevolent and highly beneficial. During the last ten years of my residence there I obtained jobs for more than a thousand Cubans and in virtually every case the applicant sought employment with an American company. Why? Because the Americans treated their employees generously and fairly, adhered to the rigid labor and social laws, paid their taxes, and didn't cut corners. The contribution of American private capital to the Cuban economy was enormous.

I know of no "sin" that can be ascribed to the United States in its treatment of Cuba prior to 1958. But I know of grievous sins that came later, especially during the thousand days of the Kennedy administration, when all the progress of the previous sixty years was wiped out.

CHAPTER EIGHT

Castro's Early Days

The Civil Code of Napoleon Bonaparte, which is the basic law of Cuba, says that children are obligated to respect and aid their parents, and parents are obligated to support and educate their children, even if they were not married when the children were conceived. Every Cuban family abides by these rules as a matter of course. The family is by far Cuba's most important institution, and these mutual obligations have been ingrained in the Latin character through the centuries.

So great is the degree of filial and parental devotion that at times it becomes a weakness. Unworthy parents retain the affection of children, who, in turn, are pampered. But, in general, strong family unity and devotion adds a warmth to Cuban life that is rarely equaled elsewhere.

The Castros were no exception to this basic rule. While far from an ideal family, they were closely knit and got along well enough together, although there are many published reports to the contrary. Some of the stories that purport to tell of the relations between Fidel Castro and his father border on the fantastic. They tell of a smoldering hatred between them that occasionally erupted into violence. According to one account, when Fidel was only nine or ten years old he set fire to a cane field owned by the family and his father threatened to shoot him. Supposedly his mother intervened and got him out of harm's way by sending him to *Colegio Dolores,* a Jesuit School in Santiago de Cuba. Another tale has it that he once publicly denounced his father for employing Haitians to cut cane and that once again the father threatened to kill the boy.

These stories are not true and others concerning Angel Castro, the father, are equally false. It has been claimed that he came to Cuba with the Spanish army in or shortly before 1898 and developed a passionate hatred of Americans while fighting against them and the Cuban Army of Independence. It has been said that his violent diatribes against the Americans instilled in Fidel the hatred he later showed for the United States. Angel Castro did indeed come to Cuba shortly before the turn of the century and, like most Spaniards at the time, may well have had no love for Americans, but friends of mine who knew Angel Castro well scoff at the idea that he participated in the fighting.

However, the elder Castro was anything but an admirable character, one indication of which is that Fidel is an illegitimate child, born in his father's house in Birán, in the Eastern Province of Oriente, on August 13, 1926. Cubans attach little stigma to common law marriages, but they condemn bigamy, and Fidel was the product of a bigamous union between Angel and a servant in his household.

Angel Castro was an illiterate, stolid Galician peasant. He came to Cuba with nothing and left an estate that was worth more than a half-million dollars when he died in 1956 at the age of eighty-six. He built the base of this fortune honestly enough, working on the properties of my client, the United Fruit Company, from 1904 to 1918. He was first a pick-and-shovel laborer, working on railroad construction, then digging drainage ditches for the cane areas. Finally he helped build small, low bridges across creeks and streams. Physically he was a good specimen, hardy and strong, and, like most *Gallegos,* he saved his money. Usually he went about barefooted, and when he wore shoes they were made of canvas.

One of the legends about Angel Castro, widely circulated by an American columnist, was that he had been fired by the United Fruit Company for theft of sugar from the company over a period of years.[1] According to this account, the company started legal proceedings against him but the suit was dropped for lack of witnesses. This, the columnist surmised, was why Fidel had such a phobia against Americans. The truth is that the United Fruit Company never had any trouble with Angel. He and the company's overseers often hunted guineas and other game together, and sometimes the young, barefoot Fidel would be taken along to carry the birds.

Angel Castro did get into serious trouble with another company, which may have been the origin of the columnist's distorted version that appeared in many American newspapers. In the mid-1920s Angel was in business as an oxcart contractor, hauling sugar in Alto Cedro, where large warehouses of the West Indies Sugar Company were located. In league with one of the night watchmen, a plan was devised to steal bags of sugar, and these were systematically carted off to Castro's farm in Birán by one of his *carreteros,* a man named Francisco Calderín, alias Virulilla. The company learned about the thefts and Virulilla was caught and took the blame. He was sentenced to several years in jail. Angel Castro spent considerable money on Virulilla's defense and after his "fall guy" had been imprisoned for some time he was able to get him pardoned.

This story is in character. Cubans who knew Angel personally considered him a scoundrel who had no qualms about cheating if he thought he could get away with it. His cane scales were always way off in his own favor. His boundary fences would frequently be moved out over a neighbor's land, and cattle and other property belonging to a neighbor would often end up on Angel's side of the fences—if the old man thought he was not likely to be caught.

These sharp practices certainly helped build the fortune he left when he died, but most of his money was made legitimately. With what he earned working for the United Fruit Company

---

[1] Drew Pearson, "Washington Merry-Go-Round," February 28, 1961.

he built a few shacks and bought a restaurant in the small town of Guaro, and these he sold to the Company in 1920 for five thousand dollars. The Company also bought wood from Castro, logged from the hills and delivered to its cane switches, but these purchases were discontinued when it discovered that Castro was cutting timber illegally in government forests adjacent to his farm.

Angel Castro was only one of thousands of men employed by sugar mills in the area where he lived, and it is difficult to obtain a precise record of his activities over the years. However, it is known that in the main his fortune came from growing sugar cane during a period when it commanded very high prices.

He married a former schoolteacher, María Argeta, from Banes, around 1907. She was a *mulata* with whom he had two children, Pedro Emilio and Lidia. As he prospered, the Castros brought to their house a Cuban servant girl named Lina Ruz Gonzáles, and within a short time Angel seduced her. This broke up the marriage; there was a separation and María took the two children with her to Santiago. At last report Angel's first wife was still alive, in her eighties, occupying an apartment in Nuevo Vedado, Havana, near the homes of her two children.

Lina Ruz bore Angel seven children: Angela, Ramón, Fidel, Raúl, Juana,[2] Emma, and Agustina. The oldest, Angela, is now in her early fifties. Fidel was third and Raúl fourth. Sometime between 1940 and 1942, after all the children were born, at the urging of a neighbor and close friend, one del Pino, Angel divorced María and married Lina.

An American overseer of the United Fruit Birán Farm, which adjoined Castro's property, became well acquainted with Angel and his family. In his opinion Lina Ruz's mixed ancestry included Chinese blood. This, he said, was evident not only in her own facial features but in those of some of her children, Raúl especially, who has unmistakable mongoloid character-

---

[2] "Juanita" Castro later defected and came to the United States, where she denounced her brother's regime.

istics. One of these, his inability to grow a beard, was a source of amusement to Raúl's bearded comrades in the hills. Instead of a beard he cultivated long hair, wearing it in a bun over his neck and thereby emphasizing his somewhat effeminate appearance. Later, stung by derision, he cut off the bun and wore his hair as other men do.

Cuba never had a racial problem until Fidel Castro himself invented the issue when he came to power many years later. About 21 percent of the population is believed to have some Negro ancestry but, unlike the attitude which prevails in the United States, a person of predominantly white ancestry is not regarded as a Negro. During the many years I resided in Cuba I never heard the racial issue discussed as such. In Havana the better hotels, some beaches and places of entertainment were patronized mainly by whites, but for reasons which were largely economic. Some of the social clubs were exclusively white, and there were some that were exclusively for Negroes.

After the Bay of Pigs misadventure I heard Castro ask a Negro prisoner whether it was not true that he had been excluded from white officers' clubs of the Batista army. The answer was, "I do not know, Comandante, it never occurred to me to inquire." During the Machado administration in the late 1920s, when my office was handling the heavy initial work for Pan American Airways, I dealt almost exclusively with the full-blooded Negro who was then Minister of Communications, an honorable and competent public official. The color of his skin was meaningless to us and was never mentioned.

The physical environment in which Fidel Castro was raised was in no sense typical of Cuba, where the humblest homes are kept clean. The Castro home was a large, rambling wooden structure elevated on wooden piles that raised it about seven feet off the ground; under it the horses were tied and sheltered.

The Cuban people, like the Japanese, are among the cleanest in the world, but the men in the Castro family were an exception in this respect. Neighbors who were familiar with the Castro home say that in the early days it was indescribably filthy.

Although there was a stream nearby, the Castros seldom washed or bathed. In Fidel's youth the house had no running water or toilets, although these facilities were installed in later years. Visitors reported that chickens had the run of the dirty interior, sometimes roosting on the foot of beds.

One of my intimate friends, Gustavo Hevia, relates that on a visit he once made there, a garden sprinkling can had been hung up for him in a corner of an alcove near his bedroom, to serve as a shower. A cord was attached to its spout so it could be tilted downward, making a contraption that greatly amused the entire Castro clan. The only bed in the house which had sheets and a pillow case was his own. The respected Hevia family owned properties adjoining the Castro farm and had many business dealings with Angel Castro.

The Castros had little family life. In farm families women usually served meals to the men but did not eat with them, and the Castros seldom sat down to a meal together. Whoever was hungry would find some food and eat it on the spot or while walking around.

Fidel's mother, the servant-cook, was hard and resourceful, as was her husband. When the family acquired a general store, she ran it. She usually carried a pistol in a holster when she went about her chores, within the house as well as outdoors. She was the dominant force in the family. Although there were no books in the house and Angel could scarcely sign his name, she believed in education for her brood.

Students of the Cuban scene who have searched for the origin of Fidel Castro's antisocial attitude refer to his stigma of illegitimacy. His birth was not the consequence of a common law marriage, which involved little stigma. In some rural areas such unions were almost as numerous as formal marriages and produced the same legal obligations. A sharp distinction was drawn, however, between bigamous or casual unions and common law marriages, and Fidel's birth came from a bigamous relationship. Others attribute his antisocial sentiments to the fact that when he entered *Colegio Dolores* in Santiago de Cuba, his personal hygiene was such that he soon acquired the nickname of *bola de churre,* roughly "greaseball." This nickname followed him to the excellent *Colegio de Belén* in Havana, also run by Jesuits.

All those who knew Castro in his youth agree on two traits of his character: his tendency toward self-dramatization and his insatiable craving for conversation, which invariably became monologues. This may have convinced his mother that he was destined to be a lawyer, a career which she ordained for him. Lina's anxiety to give all her children an education was not wholly shared by the tight-fisted Angel. He frequently complained that he worked like a slave to make money while his children squandered it in Santiago and Havana getting educated.

Among the stories which purport to explain Fidel Castro's pathological hatred of the United States is one with a romantic flavor. He started courting an attractive girl in Banes, one Mirta Díaz Balart. Mirta was a great favorite of Cubans and Americans alike there, but the *bola de churre* was not accepted by the American colony. How much this rejection had to do with his attitude toward America is a matter of conjecture. Mirta's father, a respected and honorable country lawyer, represented our firm in the Banes area. Fidel married Mirta but before long the marriage ended in divorce.

An attempt to determine the origin of Fidel Castro's anti-Americanism is a fascinating exercise, and I have spent very considerable time trying to pinpoint it. It is particularly intriguing because of the fact that there was probably no country in the world where Americans were generally held in higher esteem than in Cuba, partly for reasons of history but especially because of the conduct of the large American colony engaged in business and industry. Such anti-Americanism as existed is said to have been found in intellectual circles, where Communist tendencies were also apparent at times, but it was never evident to me or to my partner. Our staff eventually grew to almost eighty men and women, all Cubans, yet we do not recall ever having heard a seriously critical remark among them directed against either Americans or the United States, which the great majority of Cubans regarded as their second country.

All indications are that Fidel Castro's anti-Americanism originated during his formative years at the University of Havana. He aspired unsuccessfully to leadership in the small, leftist, radical student organizations that, with the Communists, made a fetish of anti-Americanism. His classmates looked upon him as a firebrand, a terrorist, and a gangster-type individual, and they were the first to become aware of his anti-American sentiments.

It remains incredible that Castro could have believed the monstrous charges he hurled against the United States shortly after coming to power. But it is likely that as he came under increasing Communist influence and repeated those charges again and again, he came to believe part of what he was saying. This process of self-deception must surely have been accelerated when he learned that his accusations were being taken seriously by the liberal segment of the American public and even by President Kennedy himself, who believed that the Cuban people had been subjected to unprecedented exploitation and humiliation by the United States.

On July 26, 1953 a serious incident brought Castro to public attention. His Movement later took its name (26th of July Movement) from this; in Latin America it is customary to name a political movement after the date of a historical event.

As it turned out, this was the first of several occasions on which Castro was to misjudge the temper of the Cuban people. With 150 youthful followers, including two girls, he attacked the Moncada Army Post and its garrison of a thousand soldiers at Santiago. Castro expected that the garrison would not fight but come over to his side, and that the attack would touch off a general uprising in Santiago. Taken by surprise, the garrison did relinquish a section of the post and for a few moments the attackers occupied and held the nearby Palace of Justice. Then the troops recovered. Within an hour the battle was virtually over. Most of the rebels fled to the hills outside Santiago and were captured. No official figures of dead and wounded were issued but the best estimate was that approximately a hundred had been killed on both sides.

Rumors of the Moncada battle reached Havana the following day, but in spite of the censorship which was imposed for a few hours, it soon became evident that the government troops had been victorious. Within a few days it ceased to be a topic of conversation.

Detailed reports of the Moncada incident vary according to their source. The Castro version, as related later by Herbert L. Matthews, emphasizes the cruelty of the Cuban Army. Matthews says that only ten of Castro's followers were killed in the attack—that the others were slaughtered in cold blood after surrendering, some after torture. Orders went out, according to Matthews, to kill Castro on sight, but the lieutenant who captured him disobeyed and brought him in alive.[3]

Castro's detractors give a quite different account. They claim that the brothers Fidel and Raúl were cowardly and that neither actually participated in the fighting.

The version eventually accepted by the Cuban people, drawn from participants on both sides, was that in the heat of battle there was some wanton cruelty on the part of both the attackers and defenders. According to this version, the Archbishop of Santiago, Enrique Pérez Servantes, arranged for the surrender of the remaining rebels who were in the hills and hiding in Santiago, including Fidel Castro. The men surrendered under the auspices of the Archbishop with the understanding that they would not be maltreated and would be accorded a fair trial. In any case, on October 16, 1953 Castro was brought to trial before the *Tribunal de Urgencia* in Santiago. Reporters were present and took down stenographically his impassioned defense

[3] Herbert L. Matthews, *The Cuban Story* (New York: George Braziller, 1962), p. 145.

plea, which eventually, after considerable editing, became one of the major Revolutionary documents, under the title of his concluding words: *History Will Absolve Me.*

The Castro brothers and some other survivors were sentenced to fifteen years of imprisonment and sent off to the Isle of Pines prison. In May 1955 Batista decreed amnesty to all political prisoners, the Castros included. Their apologists, unwilling to picture Batista as anything other than a dictator and killer, contend that this act lacked any element of compassion. Matthews wrote that it was "a curious process of reasoning" to argue that Batista was "more civilized and merciful" than Castro because he spared the latter's life.[4]

November 1956 found Castro in Mexico; from there he launched his second military adventure—an "invasion" of Cuba in an 82-foot launch, the *Granma.* He purchased the boat with funds furnished by ex-President Prío, who had been deposed by Batista in 1952. This leaky old launch, which would normally accommodate from twelve to fifteen persons, took seven days to cross the Gulf of Mexico to the landing site on the southeastern coast. The whole operation was badly planned, and from the start everything went wrong. Eighty-three rebels were jammed into the *Granma* and its departure was hastened by the fact that the Mexican authorities were closing in. All but six or seven of the group became desperately seasick during the crossing.[5]

The plan was to coordinate a landing near Niquero with an uprising in Santiago. Once in Oriente Province, where reinforcements were expected, the group planned to attack Niquero and then move north for an assault on the larger city at Manzanillo. Again Castro misjudged the Cuban people. He thought that a campaign of sabotage and rebellion would sweep the country and culminate in a general strike. It did not occur to him that he might have to take refuge in the Sierra Maestra Mountains; he had made no study of that region.

[4] *Ibid.,* p. 145.
[5] Ernesto "Che" Guevara, *Reminiscences of the Cuban Revolutionary War* (New York: The Monthly Review Press, 1968), p. 40.

Castro had boastfully announced in Mexico that he would be back in his homeland before the end of the year, and the Cuban Army was on the lookout for him. The crew of the *Granma,* fearing that it had been spotted, made a hasty landing in a swampy area where the men landed safely but lost virtually all their equipment. As the government troops closed in, all but twelve of the rebels were killed or captured. The twelve survivors made their way into the mountains. Among them were the two Castro brothers and the Argentine firebrand Ernesto "Che" Guevara, who had joined the group in Mexico.

The expedition had landed on December 2, 1956. The following day, when news of the adventure reached Havana, it caused scarcely a ripple of interest. Castro was still an unknown personality to the Cubans, who went about their business as usual. An official report was issued to the effect that the expedition had been annihilated by the Cuban Air Force and that Fidel Castro had been killed. The related disturbance in Santiago three days before the landing had been immediately squelched; the timing was bad, because at that moment Castro was still far at sea in the *Granma.* Thus Castro and a handful of survivors backed into a guerrilla operation on which they had not counted and for which they were not prepared. Nothing more was heard from them for nearly three months. In the meantime, Edmund Chester, Batista's publicity man, assured the American Embassy with complete confidence that Castro was dead. Anyone who saw Castro, he said, would have to bend over.

The United Press Bureau in Havana also reported that Castro had been killed, and *The New York Times* front-paged his death.

CHAPTER NINE

The Build-Up

Hugging the southern coast of Cuba's eastern province, from the Guantanamo valley to Cabo Cruz, some 140 miles distant, rises the magnificent cordillera of the Sierra Maestra, or Master Range, the highest chain of Cuban mountains. The ridge line, set back from the coast from 7 to 10 miles, has an average elevation of 3,000 feet but Turquino Peak, the highest in Cuba, rises to about 6,500 feet. The views from its summit in good weather are superb. Jamaica, which is 90 miles away, can be seen on a clear day across thousands of square miles of the blue Caribbean. To the north stretch palm-flecked plains. From the cordillera ridge many small rivers wind down the valleys to the rolling shore line indented by small bays. The foothills for the most part are a jungle wilderness, and the whole area is covered by pine and many forms of Cuban flora; parrots and other birds of exotic plumage abound.

In the late 1920s, when I was negotiating the purchase of lands for Pan American airstrips, I flew over the Sierra many times. Often it is partly hidden by a bluish mist, but on the slopes of the shimmering peaks one spots from the air occasional *bohíos,* the typical peasant houses constructed by nailing or tying planks of tough royal palm bark to a skeleton of poles, which supports a canopy of royal palm leaves.

In the Sierra Maestra area, comprising 1,500 square miles, lived approximately 50,000 of Cuba's poorest peasants, many of them squatters. They were notoriously the most illiterate and backward of the Cuban farmers, and they knew little or nothing of the modern era. They had no radios, newspapers, or electricity, no means of transportation other than mules, and there were no roads except in the foothills themselves, where most of them lived.

It was in this area that Castro and eleven followers, those who remained of the eighty-three who had "invaded" Cuba on December 2, 1956, took refuge. The army general staff had reported to Batista that the group had been wiped out or had given up the struggle. Army units did not attempt the hopeless task of pursuing what may have been left of it into the mountains. Army planes flew over the area, however, urging them through loudspeakers to give up and promising them freedom, but without result. The government put planes at the disposal of reporters who, with army officers, made a broad reconnaisance of the Sierra, but they observed no trace of the rebels. The troops were then withdrawn from the area.

During the first month and a half after the twelve men who had arrived on the *Granma* reached the mountains a few peasants joined them, feigning loyalty for self-protection, and then promptly deserted. One of the original twelve also deserted. The scores of *montunos,* mountain people, whom they approached with great caution, were either hostile or totally disinterested. They wished only to continue living their own lives in their own way. On balance, after seven weeks the group had been augmented by only six, so that by late January the Castro "rebel army" was composed of eighteen men altogether. Thus, as Herbert L. Matthews of *The New York Times* subsequently wrote, "Without a press Fidel Castro was a hunted outlaw, leading a small band of youths in a remote jungle area of eastern Cuba, isolated and ineffectual." [1] He must have been saying to himself, added Matthews, that "without a press we shall get nowhere." [2]

This was, in fact, exactly what Castro had decided after six

[1] Herbert L. Matthews, *The Cuban Story* (New York: George Braziller, 1962), p. 16.
[2] *Ibid.,* p. 18.

weeks of near-futile recruiting. In mid-January, 1957, he made the smartest decision of his life, from his own point of view. He sent a member of his group to Havana to try to arrange an interview with a journalist—and only a foreigner, because no Cuban journalist, even among the many who were hostile to Batista, could be expected to swallow the audacious lie he planned to put over, namely that he had mastery of the Sierra Maestra![3] A Cuban reporter misinformed and credulous to that extent would be impossible to find, or even to imagine. He could have brought out photographs proving that Castro was alive, but he would have had to debase his profession to do the kind of reporting Castro had in mind. Moreover, the audience Castro hoped to reach in his strategy for winning press attention was in the United States.

Probably Castro's luckiest single break was the circumstance that the journalist chosen by fate to conduct the crucial interview was the Latin American specialist of *The New York Times,* Herbert L. Matthews.

Then fifty-seven years old, Matthews had been on the *Times* staff for thirty-five years. His thinking, sympathies, and preconceptions were strongly "liberal." Repeatedly he had shown himself highly susceptible to personal contacts and influences on the "revolutionary" fringes. In reporting the Spanish Civil War he had been an outspoken partisan of the Communist-infiltrated Loyalist forces, disdainful of concepts of objectivity, to the point of having made the Loyalist situation appear much brighter than it was and having been reproached on this score by the *Times* publisher.[4]

Whenever Matthews had visited Latin American countries, including Cuba, the more conservative elements and the business community—on the basis of past experience—had stirred uneasily. Strongly and openly anti-Batista, he often wrote of "thousands of Cubans slaughtered, often after torture." [5] Opin-

---

[3] *Ibid.,* p. 31.
[4] *Time,* July 27, 1959, p. 48.
[5] Matthews, pp. 166, 292.

ionated to the degree of arrogance, politically naïve, a presumed expert on Latin America, he was perfectly conditioned for the disastrous role he was about to play.

When Castro's emissary arrived in Havana, he approached my friend and client, Mrs. Ruby Hart Phillips, resident correspondent of *The New York Times*. Since Castro was believed to be dead, she realized at once that this was a good story. Aware that Matthews was planning one of his periodical trips to Havana, Mrs. Phillips suggested that he come at once.

The meeting between Castro and Matthews took place not long afterward, in mid-February. The journey to the mountains, as the *Times* man told the story, was a highly dangerous venture. Lives of a number of Cubans were in his hands, he wrote, and because of the "fierceness and viciousness" of Batista, those involved were risking death, preceded by torture.

The fact is that there was no danger. Everyone from Batista down believed Castro to be dead. It would not have been possible to convince anyone in Cuba that Matthews was on his way to see Castro.

Matthews and his wife, accompanied by three young Cubans, drove from Havana to Manzanillo, a distance of about five hundred miles, over the Central Highway. The tourist season was at its peak and they planned, if stopped, to say that Matthews was a rich American on his way to look over a sugar plantation which he was considering buying. They were not stopped, however; the few soldiers whom they met on the way merely glanced at them in the friendly manner to which all Americans were accustomed. While passing through Santa Clara after daybreak they circled a policeman standing on a corner several times, asking him where they could stop for coffee and how to get out of town. Mrs. Matthews later declared that they had stopped so often for coffee "that a long trail of people had every chance to examine us in detail." [6] She remained in Manzanillo, a seaport

[6] Mrs. Herbert L. Matthews, in *The New York Times* house organ *Times Talk,* March, 1957.

on the south coast, with a group "you might meet at any Cuban tea party,"[7] while her husband and his companions pushed on in a jeep and then on foot.

Matthews can be forgiven for dramatizing the rendezvous that, as he later said, would "literally alter the course of Cuban history." He wrote of the "two low, soft, toneless whistles" with which his companions made contact with the Castro emissary. All conversations, he recounted, had been carried on in "the lowest possible whispers." Actually it was altogether unlikely that there could have been a Cuban soldier within miles.

What cannot be forgiven, however, is his exaggerated "interpretive" reporting and, especially, certain statements—not quoting Castro, but made in his own name—that were palpably false. The three articles that came out of the Castro-Matthews meeting represent, in my opinion, the most reprehensible act of journalism attributed to a reputable newspaper in my lifetime. They came at the ebb tide of the flood that was to deliver Cuba to Communism. They contained, as Matthews himself boasted, "all the elements out of which the insurrection grew to its ultimate triumph."[8] In effect, a journalist on a reportorial assignment assumed the posture of an insurrectionist. (Guevara, who was not present at the brief interview, later said Castro had told him Matthews "asked concrete questions, none of them tricky" and that "he obviously sympathized with the Revolution.")[9]

Although there had been very little fighting, Matthews wrote that Castro was "fighting hard and successfully" and that "frequent clashes were taking place in which the Government troops were losing heavily." The cream of Batista's army had been "fighting a thus-far losing battle" and Castro *"has mastery of the Sierra Maestra."* (Emphasis added.) And while the rebels

[7] *Ibid.,* pp. 25, 26.
[8] Matthews, p. 39.
[9] Ernesto "Che" Guevara, *Reminiscences of the Cuban Revolutionary War* (New York: Monthly Review Press, Inc., 1968), p. 78.

actually had only nine rifles with telescopic sights, Matthews wrote, "it seems his men have something more than fifty of these." [10]

With respect to the size of the eighteen-man rebel group, Matthews wrote that he had seen about twenty-five rebels and "knew" there were others nearby—perhaps forty in all. He quoted Castro as saying Batista worked in columns of two hundred while he operated in groups of ten to forty. Two years later, in April 1959, at the Hotel Astor in New York, Castro ridiculed Matthews for permitting himself to be bluffed into inflating the strength of his tiny group of eighteen men.[11]

One of Matthews' questions during the interview concerned the anti-imperialistic tone of the Movement, and Castro answered, "You can be sure we have no animosity toward the United States and the American people." I recalled this after Castro had come to power, when we heard him describe the United States as "a vulture feeding upon humanity."

Matthews wrote that the Castro program "amounts to a new deal for Cuba, radical, democratic and therefore anti-Communist." He described Castro as "a man of ideals," who "has

[10] *The New York Times,* February 24, 1957, first of three Matthews articles, beginning on p. 1.

[11] Prior to the Matthews interview the Castro group had engaged in two minor hit-and-run actions that involved little risk and from which they emerged unscathed. On January 17 they swooped down on a small army post and caught the ten guards asleep, with the result that, as Guevara later wrote in *Reminiscences of the Cuban Revolutionary War,* "The soldiers, almost defenseless, were cut to pieces." Five were killed, the others surrendered, and the rebels made a quick escape with the captured weapons. This action later became known in Revolutionary lore as "The Battle of La Plata."

The second adventure occurred five days later and was also devoid of any element of bravery or glory. From a safe distance the rebels ambushed and shot down with telescopic rifles five members of an army patrol. In their scramble to get away they picked up only one Garand rifle. Castro later described this incident as "The Battle of *El Arroyo del Infierno"* (Hell's Creek). After these actions the army pulled its small units out of the mountains.

strong ideas of liberty, democracy, social justice, the need to restore the Constitution and hold elections." [12] Not merely, be it noted, that Castro professed such ideals but that he had them!

For Raúl Castro, the evil younger brother and one of the most sinister figures of the Revolution, Matthews had kind words, describing him as "slight and pleasant." [13] (Shortly after the new regime came to power and before the rudimentary courts had even been set up, Raúl Castro ordered seventy-five men machine-gunned into a common grave.) His brutality far exceeded anything of the kind attributed to Batista by his worst enemies.

On the issue of Communism Matthews emphatically reassured his readers. Although there was a well trained, hard core of Communists in Cuba doing as much mischief as it could, he said, "there is no Communism to speak of in Fidel Castro's 26th of July Movement." [14] More, the Castro program was "anti-Communist." [15]

Matthews reported that as the interview ended Castro said, "I am always in the front line" and the others had confirmed this fact. Then, as the group arose to say good-bye, "You have taken quite a risk in coming here but we have the whole area covered, and we will get you out safely." [16] Castro never would have dared to make this statement to a Cuban journalist, or in fact to any Cuban over ten years of age, and expect it to be swallowed.

The most pernicious and electrifying aspect of the Matthews reporting was that he personally vouched for the large and winning rebel force.

[12] *The New York Times,* February 24, 1957, first of three Matthews articles.

[13] *Ibid.*

[14] *The New York Times,* February 25, 1957, second of three Matthews articles.

[15] *The New York Times,* February 24, 1957, first Matthews article.

[16] *Ibid.*

The New York Times handled the three Matthews articles in a manner designed to obtain maximum publicity. Well advertised in advance, they started on the front page of the Sunday edition of February 24, 1957, because the Sunday circulation is twice that of the daily edition.

Matthews has described the *Times* as "the most powerful journalistic instrument that has ever been forged in the free world." [17] Those who work for it, he says, "use arms that, metaphorically speaking, are the equivalent of nuclear bombs." [18] In this case he did not overstate. The *Times* is without question the most influential newspaper in the world. It profoundly influences politicians, educators, writers, and other newspapers. It has unparalleled access to the corridors and offices of official Washington. It is required reading in other editorial offices, and *Times* copy therefore has a cumulative effect. Teachers and professors read it, quote it, and recommend it to their students. If scholarly papers, magazines, or books are to be written, research invariably calls for *The New York Times* Index, which has a virtual monopoly in its field.

The *Times* has another lever that can exert tremendous pressure on public opinion. Its *News Service* puts most of its foreign coverage on the wire and sends out the *Times* front page makeup to show editors how to play the news. By the end of 1965 the *Times News Service* had 154 client papers, 99 in the United States and 55 abroad.

Any lack of journalistic responsibility, as in this case, is the more indefensible when the power exercised is "equivalent to nuclear bombs." Certainly the Matthews articles on Castro had an explosive impact in the United States and a chain reaction throughout the whole hemisphere.

There was censorship in Havana when the first one appeared and it had been deleted from my copy of the *Times*. However,

---

[17] Matthews, p. 308.
[18] *Ibid.,* p. 308.

tourists brought copies with them, and the story got around. Cubans are great talkers; I cannot imagine any place in the world where news travels faster. The *Times* series became the talk of the town. Within a few days at least ten of my American friends had sent me copies. Since college days back in 1914 I had been a first-to-last-page reader of the *Times*. It carried great weight with me and I was astounded by both the content and the political tenor of the Matthews dispatches.

Batista reacted at once. The Cuban Minister of Defense announced that the government "does not know whether Fidel Castro is alive or dead but takes full responsibility for stating that no such supporting forces as Matthews described actually exist." Then he made the first of his major blunders: He said that "with the same responsibility the government reiterates that at no time did the correspondent have an interview with the man to whom he ascribes so much force and so many non-existent creeds." This played into Matthews' hands and the following day the *Times* published a picture of him with Castro in the mountains. Shortly afterward Batista lifted press censorship and the Cuban press translated and published the full texts of the three articles.

There was much more to come. The *Times* promotion of Castro was only the opening gun of an unprecedented barrage of publicity. A steady flow of journalists, many of them well known as left-wingers, poured into the Sierra Maestra. The first to follow Matthews was a deputy news director of the Columbia Broadcasting System, Robert Taber, with a companion named Wendell Hoffman. Though they hauled with them bulky photographic and sound recording equipment, they had no trouble getting it into the hills. Taber's filmed and taped interview with Castro was broadcast nationally by CBS in the United States on May 17, 1957, and subsequently in various foreign countries.

Almost five years later a Senate Subcommittee uncovered the record of Taber. He had been arrested on various occasions and had served a prison sentence of almost four years in the Ohio State Reformatory for kidnaping, armed robbery, and automobile theft.[19] Following his television-radio interview with Castro, Taber became Executive Secretary of the Castro-financed "Fair Play for Cuba Committee" and traveled behind the Iron Curtain with Castro agents.

American television viewers were subsequently treated to several performances by Fidel Castro on major network programs, where he was accorded what the medium refers to as "prime time." Edward R. Murrow, a promoter of liberal causes, gave him a national forum, and this was followed by an interview with Ed Sullivan that was taped in Cuba. Later on Jack Paar, the popular TV entertainer, met Castro, was captivated by him, and expressed his enthusiasm in a series of telecasts over the NBC network.

As Castro's public relations campaign, sparked and sustained by *The New York Times,* gained momentum, there came a time when a number of American journalists were in the Cuban mountains at the same time, all pounding out the romantic story of Fidel Castro. In fact, when the CIA eventually decided to check on the Castro Movement, at the urgent insistence of U.S. Ambassador Earl E. T. Smith, it sent its agent into the mountains as a journalist. There followed a flood of pro-Castro books and articles by leftist professors and writers such as C. Wright Mills of Columbia University, Kyle Haselden, Carleton Beals, Norman Bailey, Samuel Schapiro, Jean-Paul Sartre, Simone de Beauvoir, and Waldo Frank, all helping to condition public opinion and clear the path for Castro and his Communist henchmen. Waldo Frank, who was subsidized by Castro, called him a "genius" and "less the politician than the poet and the lover." [20] Professor Mills' book, *Listen, Yankee!,* was particularly effective propaganda, presenting the naked, unrelieved Castro line.

During the summer months of 1957 there was an acceleration

---

[19] Senate Subcommittee of the Committee on the Judiciary to Investigate Internal Security, Part 3, April 10, 1962, p. 180.

[20] Waldo Frank, *Cuba: Prophetic Island* (New York: Marzani & Munsell, 1961), p. 141.

of anti-government terrorism in Cuba, although the incidents still occurred only sporadically. On occasions bombs exploded, power lines were cut, communications were interrupted, and fires were started. Nevertheless, there was prosperity in Cuba; business was good, and the tourist season of early 1957 was up to expectations.

Late in August, with the pro-Castro press campaign in full swing, I discussed with my partner the idea of going to New York to see my friend Harry F. Guggenheim in an effort to find some way to induce *The New York Times* to desist from instigating rebellion in Cuba. I knew that Harry was an old friend of Arthur Sulzberger, publisher of the *Times,* and that his sister, Mrs. Roger Strauss, was one of Mrs. Sulzberger's closest friends. We came to the conclusion that I was in as good a position as any Cuban to accomplish this mission.

On arriving in New York I found that one of Batista's cabinet members, Nicolás Arroyo, the young Minister of Public Works, was also there with an aide. Knowing that there were few Americans as well qualified as Guggenheim to counsel a Latin American chief of state facing Batista's problems, I telephoned Harry to ask whether I could bring Arroyo and his friend along. He invited me to do so.

We all had lunch at the Guggenheim estate at Sands Point, Long Island, and Mrs. Strauss came over for the occasion from Greenwich, Connecticut. After lunch the men went to Harry's trophy room, where we sat down to discuss Cuba's problems. I said, "Harry, *The New York Times* is continuing to incite rebellion in our country and I would like to know if there is any way of putting an end to the campaign that was started by Herbert Matthews."

Guggenheim explained that Arthur Sulzberger was very ill, having suffered several strokes, and that it would be impossible for anyone to see him. He added that Sulzberger always displayed great loyalty to his staff and that he thought there was no chance at all of inducing him or anyone else on the *Times* to call off Matthews. I asked whether this would also apply to Louis Loeb, the general counsel of the *Times*. Mr. Loeb was a member of a firm which we represented in Cuba and I could have reached him very easily. Yes, it did, said Harry; and anyway, the Matthews attitude fitted into the liberal ideological pattern of the *Times*. I remember that Harry Guggenheim was much more keenly aware of the danger Castro represented than even his Cuban guests. At one point he said, "Mario, if this man ever comes to power he is going to confiscate the properties of all your clients and introduce a Communist beachhead in our hemisphere." Much later I learned that Guggenheim had warned Vice President Richard Nixon and other officials of the American government precisely along these lines.

Our conversation then turned to Batista. Addressing Arroyo, Guggenheim, in his soft-spoken manner and with his attractive half-smile, expounded his belief that Batista still had the solution of the problem in his own hands. He should at once set the date for a national election. It was not enough that this election be honest—he would have to convince the Cuban people and the Americans as well that it would be conducted on the highest plane of integrity. This, he said, could be done by inviting the United Nations, the OAS, or the American Bar Association to send a delegation to Cuba to witness the conduct of the election, and Batista should announce well beforehand that this was going to be done.

Addressing Arroyo, he said, "Mario can help you with the American Bar Association if that is what you decide upon. If your chief will do this, he can go down in history as one of Cuba's great presidents. He held an honest election once before and his opponent won. That might well happen again; but if it does, Batista can go to Europe for a few months and then return to Cuba a respected citizen, retain and enjoy his properties, and educate his children in his own country. This is what I told Machado when I was Ambassador in Havana, but he did not see it my way. Unless Batista follows this course he is almost certain to be deposed, to lose the respect of his people. I urge you to carry this message to him from one who is a friend of Cuba and who wishes him well."

On returning to New York I called on my old friend C. D. Jackson, then publisher of *Life* magazine, and posed the same question: "How can we stop *The New York Times* from inciting rebellion in our country?" "C.D." was of the same opinion as Guggenheim: It would be impossible to induce the *Times* to call off Matthews or to change its policy. He suggested that Batista might hire an American public relations firm to offset the bad publicity his government was receiving in the United States, and although I did not wish to be involved in this step, I reported the conversation to Arroyo, and later learned that an American public relations firm had, in fact, been employed, but ineffectively.

In Havana some days thereafter, Arroyo told me that upon his return he had given Batista a "blow-by-blow" account of his conversation with Guggenheim. Batista's wife, Marta, was present at the time. They had not been impressed. My mission to the United States had been a failure.

What Dr. Cubas and I most feared in late 1957 was that the American press campaign in favor of the radical, anti-American Castro might eventually have a strong effect on Congress and then on the State Department. We did not, I must admit, have the prescience of Harry Guggenheim and Earl Smith in foreseeing that a Castro regime would mean a Communist takeover. Moreover, we still had confidence that the American State Department could be relied upon to help us achieve the formation of the honest and responsible government the Cuban people so earnestly desired.

We cannot entirely dismiss Matthews at this point, as he continued to play a vital role in the Castro-Communist story. It should be recorded here that when Castro's true colors were on full display, Matthews did not have the grace to correct his original errors. On the contrary, he blamed his journalist colleagues for driving Castro more quickly and deeply into the

Communist embrace. By October 1961, when he was virtually alone in defending Castro, Matthews was writing, "I know good journalistic work when I see it, and I know poor work." The American press coverage of the Cuban situation, he said, was "distorted, unfair, ill-informed and intensely emotional." It lacked "balance and objectivity." And he reconfirmed his "sympathy and, in many respects, admiration for Fidel Castro." If the United States should win the cold war, he said, the Cuban Revolution will nevertheless have played "a great role, and a worthy one." He could never bring himself "to condemn it and to condemn Fidel Castro outright for what he has done, and especially for what he has tried to do." [21]

Even after Castro had announced to the world that he was a Marxist-Leninist and would be one "until the day I die," Matthews told a gathering at the Overseas Press Club in New York that he didn't believe him; that the label didn't fit him. "Today Castro may believe he is a Communist," he said, "but tomorrow he may believe something else." The New York *Herald Tribune* reported these remarks on December 7, 1961. The *Times* remained silent.

Matthews' byline thereafter disappeared from *The New York Times,* but not Matthews. Without fanfare he was elevated to the editorial board of the newspaper, where his opinions became the anonymous expression of the newspaper's opinions. Except when he was away from New York or having his days off, he wrote virtually all the editorials on Latin America, including those on Cuba.[22] When the editorial board met, Matthews was the expert who advised them concerning editorial policy on Latin American affairs. As spokesman for a great newspaper, Matthews called for patience, understanding, and coexistence with the Castro-Communist regime.

Five years after his celebrated Cuban series, Herbert L. Matthews appeared to face up to the calamity he had helped to

[21] Matthews, pp. 277, 284, 299.
[22] *Ibid.*, pp. 115, 206.

˙spark. In the second printing of his book, *The Cuban Story,* in March, 1962, he wrote that if Castro represents a regime "actively playing a role on the side of the Sino-Soviet bloc against the United States and engaging in subverting and stirring up anti-American, Leftist revolutions throughout Latin America . . . then he and his regime will have to be destroyed." He added, "No amount of sympathy for Fidel Castro could lead an American to any other decision." [23]

Since then the "ifs" in the equation have been erased. But Mr. Matthews has scarcely been conspicuous among Americans dedicated to the destruction of the Castro regime.

[23] *Ibid.,* p. 276.

CHAPTER TEN

Cuba at the Crossroads

The glorification of Castro by the American press was deeply demoralizing to the other and more moderate opposition groups. The process moved so swiftly that by the end of 1957, ten months after the Matthews articles appeared, although Castro had been able to recruit only about a hundred men, he felt confident enough to reject with scorn an invitation to join six other anti-Batista elements in a common effort to overthrow the President.

His letter of December 14, 1957 to these six other groups provided indisputable proof of an authoritarian obsession in his thinking. In it he proclaimed himself as the source of law, empowered to designate the Chief of State in a new government, abolish the legislature and judiciary, and do away with political parties other than his own 26th of July Movement. In short, he made clear his intention to create a totalitarian regime. The full text of this extraordinary letter was in the hands of the American Embassy in Havana and of Roy Rubottom and William Wieland at the State Department in Washington by January 1 or 2, 1958.

Despite the eulogies he was receiving in the United States, Castro up to this point had accomplished virtually nothing. As new men joined up others deserted, and the small, half-starved group wandered aimlessly through the mountains. Peasants who were caught and suspected of being informers were ruthlessly executed. On March 16, 1957 a contingent of about fifty men, thirty of whom had arms, arrived from Santiago, recruited by Frank País, a Castro follower. With his "army" thus augmented to about eighty, Castro prepared to mount his most important military adventure.

In late May the rebels descended from the mountains and attacked a small isolated lumber camp on the coast, consisting of two wooden buildings and three small guard posts, each large enough for two or three soldiers. There were fifty-three men in the camp altogether, most of them unarmed workers.

As was his custom, Castro gave the signal to attack by firing his rifle from a distant hill. In the ensuing fight the few defending soldiers fought bravely, killing six and wounding nine of the rebels. Of the lumber camp group fourteen were killed, nineteen wounded, six escaped, and fourteen were taken prisoner. (This is the account of "The Battle of Uvero" given by the candid Guevara.[1] Castro later called it a "battle of extraordinary importance.") The attackers quickly withdrew into the mountains and by the end of the following month more than forty had deserted, "sometimes with our consent, other times without," wrote Guevara, so that by late June 1957 "the troop never had more than twenty-five or thirty effective members." [2]

Elsewhere, however, occasional outbreaks by other revolutionary groups flared up and were as quickly extinguished. The most ambitious of these had been an attempt, on March 13, 1957, to assassinate Batista and his family. Two days earlier Batista had learned that a plot was afoot and used emissaries in an attempt to dissuade suspected leaders. He alerted the Palace guard and kept his older children away from school. His pregnant wife and youngest child, who was sick, remained with him at the Palace.

At about 3 P.M. a group of activists drove up to the rear entrance of the Palace in a truck while the guard was having lunch

---

[1] Ernesto "Che" Guevara, *Reminiscences of the Cuban Revolutionary War* (New York: Monthly Review Press, Inc., 1968), pp. 111 to 119.
[2] *Ibid.*, p. 126.

and rushed the entrance, firing as they entered. They got as far as the second floor, where their progress was stopped by an iron grilled door. The President, his wife, and his child were on the third floor. Had the attackers used a bazooka or explosives to smash the door, their adventure might well have been successful. As it was, forty of the attackers and a number of the Palace guards were killed. Simultaneously a group of students led by a heavyset, handsome young man named José Antonio Echeverría seized the popular CMQ radio station and broadcast reports that the President had been killed and the government overthrown. As they left the station Echeverría was shot down by the police.

This poorly planned but courageous assault had been carried out without Castro's knowledge by followers of ex-President Prío and by the *Directorio Revolucionario* of Havana University students.

That night Batista's military intelligence, known as the SIM *(Servicio de Inteligencia Militar),* began rounding up opposition leaders. They tried to arrest my cousin, Carlos Márquez Sterling, Batista's most formidable political opponent, but he barricaded himself in his home. The incident created such a public disturbance in the neighborhood that the police left without completing the arrest. Carlos had not been implicated in the assault on the Palace.

The SIM did find my friend, Dr. Pelayo Cuervo Navarro, a fifty-eight-year-old lawyer who had always fought for clean government. He was taken to a small lake about four blocks from our home in Country Club Park and shot through the back of the head. His body was dumped close to the lake, where it was found the next morning. Pelayo was a man of great integrity. With little financial backing he had been elected a Senator by one of the highest votes in Cuban history. My partner and I had always given him such support as we could. He used to come to our office about once a month to discuss the political situation, and our talks usually dealt with Washington attitudes and policies with respect to Cuba. Everything about him marked him as a conservative lawyer, and his murder shocked us profoundly and stirred the entire country.

Batista always insisted that this crime was committed without his knowledge in the emotional aftermath of the Palace assault in which army enlisted men and police had been murdered. It was said that a note had been found on Echeverría implicating Pelayo Cuervo as the mastermind of the plot to assassinate Batista. There were other versions, of course. Márquez Sterling, who was certainly as knowledgeable as any of the Cuban politicians of the day, believes the murder was not ordered from the Palace. "Batista will profit personally from his office but he does not kill," he told me. Rightly or wrongly, he felt that Pelayo had been involved in the plot of March 13. The murder of Pelayo left a black stain on Batista's record, however, because those who carried it out were never caught and punished.

Every Cuban knows that Castro's oft-repeated charge that Batista was responsible for the deaths of 20,000 Cubans is a cynical falsehood. The most reliable opinions I have been able to obtain place the total deaths at *not more than 900 on both the government and anti-government sides, including the final revolutionary activities of 1957-1958.* After Castro had come to power the strongly anti-Batista magazine *Bohemia* published a list of those alleged to have been killed on both sides during the last Batista administration; the total came to 869. One of my best informed CIA friends, who worked in Cuba during the closing years of Batista rule and the early months of the Castro regime, put the figure for both sides at definitely less than 1,000. The Latin people are given to exaggeration in matters in which they are emotionally involved, but I believe that virtually all Cubans will agree today that the wide acceptance abroad of Castro's grotesque charge that Batista was responsible for 20,000 deaths was one of his most striking propaganda achievements.

Shortly after the assault on the Palace the Batista regime arranged for a counter-demonstration. Cuban trade, civic, and political groups were called on to visit the Palace to congratulate the President on his escape and express confidence in the government. Telegrams were sent to many of the people specifying the times and dates when they were to appear. The procession went on for several days, and several of those summoned gave impassioned speeches in Batista's presence, condemning the attack and praising the administration.

In the spring of 1957 the State Department began making efforts to remove Ambassador Arthur Gardner, a political appointee, but was unable to induce him to offer his resignation.[3] He worked hard to retain his post, which he greatly enjoyed. Havana, so close to home and among the attractive and friendly Cuban people, was one of the more valued diplomatic posts. Gardner argued that his departure would be interpreted as lack of confidence in Batista—the least convincing argument he could have advanced to the State Department, since that was what was developing in Washington. An ardent admirer of Batista, he seldom missed an opportunity to praise him.

When the appointment of Earl E. T. Smith to succeed Gardner was announced in May 1957, I received a letter from Charles Hallenborg of New York, a close and highly regarded friend. He had known Smith as a colleague on the War Production Board and described him as wealthy, socially prominent, conservative, and intelligent. "I don't know how much he knows about Cuba," Hallenborg wrote, "but you can be sure no one will pull the wool over his eyes."

Earl Smith arrived in Havana in mid-July. Our home was directly across from the Embassy residence, but before we could make the customary neighborly call the Ambassador telephoned, and we lunched together downtown. Our first meeting was strictly social, with no discussion of politics. Smith was a tall man, perhaps six feet five inches, clear-eyed, and possessed of a springy vigor. He had the earmarks of culture and an air of self-

[3] Herbert L. Matthews, *The Cuban Story* (New York: George Braziller, Inc., 1962), p. 68.

confidence. Certainly there was nothing devious about Earl Smith; he said what he thought, and very bluntly. Since his appointment about two months earlier Florence and Earl Smith had been studying Spanish intensively and planned to keep it up. Earl's hobbies were golf and bridge, and although we never engaged in either together, I learned that he excelled at both. I asked if it were true that he had been the intercollegiate boxing champion while at Yale in 1926. No, this exaggeration derived from the fact that Earl, who was the heavyweight champion at Yale, had knocked out the heavyweight champion of Annapolis in the Yale-Navy boxing meet of 1924.

I remember telling the Ambassador that I thought he was lucky to have a competent staff, several of whom were my intimate friends. He knew that to be the case, he said, but would look to my partner and me for the strictly Cuban point of view on the problems ahead.

Socially our relationship proved to be neither warm nor distant. My wife was never invited by Florence Smith to participate in the social work she directed. Although we were neighbors, during the year and a half the Smiths were in Havana they dined with us only twice.

Since we did not discuss Cuban politics at our first meeting, I was unaware until much later of significant aspects of the briefing Smith had received at the State Department preparatory to taking up his duties in Havana. One was that the Department had suggested he get together with Herbert L. Matthews! At this meeting, which lasted several hours, Matthews asserted that, as a journalist very knowledgeable on Cuba and Latin America, he believed it would be best for Cuba and the United States to have Batista removed from office.[4] Another even more significant aspect was that in six weeks of briefing in the State Department neither William A. Wieland, Director of the Office of Middle

[4] Senate Subcommittee of the Committee on the Judiciary to Investigate Internal Security, "Testimony of Earl E. T. Smith," August 30, 1960, p. 683.

American Affairs, nor Roy R. Rubottom, Jr., Assistant Secretary of State for Inter-American Affairs, mentioned the Communist uprising in Bogotá, Colombia, nine years earlier, in which Castro had played an active role and during which both these career Foreign Service Officers were present.[5]

We knew Wieland's early record well. He had lived in Havana from 1928 to 1937 and had worked for one of our clients, the *Havana Post,* the best English-language newspaper in Cuba. Its highly regarded publisher, Mrs. Clara Park Pessino, had fired him. Although his salary was only about $35 a week she regarded him as a bad investment. His spotty educational background included one year at Villanova College. Much later I learned that on June 4, 1941, he went from a $3,120-a-year job with the Associated Press to a starting annual salary of $7,000 with the State Department. Eventually his government salary was increased to more than $24,000. Wieland was appointed to his position in the State Department without any security check. He falsified his application by the omission of vital facts and his personal history questionnaire by overt misstatement.[6]

When those of us in Havana who knew Wieland learned that he had become one of the State Department's experts on Latin American and Cuban affairs, in a position where he could exert great influence on his superiors and on American foreign policy, we were astonished. Technically, he was Ambassador Smith's superior. We reasoned that his high position could be explained only by the fact that he spoke Spanish fluently.

To understand Wieland and the part he was to play in Castro's takeover of Cuba, it is necessary to know about the Communist uprising in Bogotá in April 1948, commonly known as the *Bogotazo.*

The Bogotazo occurred on the occasion of the Ninth Inter-

[5] Earl E. T. Smith, *The Fourth Floor* (New York: Random House, 1962), p. 68.
[6] Senate Subcommittee of the Committee on the Judiciary, *The Case of William Wieland,* 1962, p. 3.

national Conference of the American States. The U. S. Ambassador in Bogotá at the time was Willard D. Beaulac, who had previously been stationed in Havana, an able career diplomat. On his staff in 1948 were Rubottom and Wieland, both with the rank of Second Secretary. Wieland was responsible for political reporting. The American delegation that came to Bogotá for the conference was headed by Secretary of State George C. Marshall.

Colombia is rich in democratic traditions. Like the United States, it has only two cohesive political parties, the Conservatives and the Liberals. The President of the republic at that time, Dr. Mariano Ospina Pérez, belonged to the Conservative Party. The "sole leader" of the Liberal Party was a dynamic rabble-rouser named Jorge Eliécer Gaitán, who had been making grave and undocumented charges against Ospina. Political feeling had been running high.

As the opening date of the Conference approached there were strong rumors in the capital that the Communists were planning to disrupt the meeting. Wieland was the staff member whose primary duty it was to gather such information and assist the Ambassador in reporting it to Washington. On March 22, eight days before the first scheduled Conference session, Beaulac telegraphed the State Department a résumé of acts of violence that had already occurred and reported a number of clear indications that Communists intended to wreck the hemisphere gathering.

In the last days of March four Cuban students had arrived in Bogotá from Havana to attend an "anti-imperialist" student congress called to coincide with the Conference of American States. Two of them, Fidel Castro and Rafael del Pino, put up at the Hotel Claridge. The other two, Enrique Ovares Herrera and Alfredo Guevara (no relation to "Che" Guevara) moved into a rooming house. Guevara was a hard-line, disciplined Communist; Ovares had been a founder of an Anti-Imperialist Student Union created in Prague in 1946.

On April 3, shortly after their arrival, Castro and del Pino went to the Teatro Colón and showered anti-American leaflets down on the orchestra from the balcony during a performance. When the police checked on them, quantities of Communist and anti-American propaganda leaflets were found in their room at the Claridge.

On the morning of April 9, 1948, Ovares and Guevara made the rounds of newspaper offices seeking publicity for their coming student congress, while Castro and del Pino planned to visit the leftist Gaitán. Their purpose was to invite Gaitán to speak at the inaugural session of their anti-American congress. Herbert Matthews offers another and milder explanation. "Fidel had a boyish crush on Gaitán," he wrote.[7] Castro, then twenty-one, had been a member of a Cuban terrorist organization and had been arrested, though never convicted, in connection with a murder perpetrated by that group.

It was arranged that if Ovares and Guevara finished in time, they were to join the others at an open-air cafe a block from Gaitán's office. By the time they got there Castro and del Pino had already arrived. They all sat at the cafe and talked for about an hour. Suddenly, at about 1:20 P.M., shots were heard down the block. Jorge Eliécer Gaitán had been gunned down as he left his office by a drifter named Juan Roa Sierra, who had once been an inmate of an insane asylum. Roa Sierra was immediately beaten to death by witnesses of the crime, and a mob dragged his battered body down the street past the cafe where the four Cubans excitedly asked the crowd what was happening.

The murder of Gaitán touched off frenzied killing, burning, and looting that virtually cut off Bogotá from the rest of the world for two days and took the lives of more than a thousand persons. Before the rioting ended 150 buildings had been destroyed by well-organized arson squads carrying sprayers filled with gasoline. Each arson unit had a leader and the leaders had lists of buildings to be set on fire, some typewritten. There were

[7] Matthews, p. 142.

few wooden structures in downtown Bogotá. Buildings were mostly of stone, brick, and stucco, and it called for skill to set them on fire.

Ovares and Guevara decided to get off the street and go back to their boarding house. Castro and del Pino headed for a radio broadcasting station. At about 4 P.M. a street mob swept by the boarding house shouting *"A Palacio!"* Castro was in it, carrying a rifle and yelling hysterically that they were on their way to kill the President. He stopped and tried to persuade Ovares and Guevara to go along. They refused.

In the meantime Secretary of Embassy Rubottom had joined the American Ambassador at the latter's home in a suburb, Wieland remaining with a large group at the Embassy offices downtown. As Beaulac and Rubottom were about to leave the Embassy residence for the chancery, two priests entered the garden, escorting the youngest son of President Ospina. He was given refuge.

The Embassy car in which Beaulac and Rubottom were riding did not make it to the downtown offices. Its occupants abandoned it and tried to get there on foot, but they were blocked by the wild crowds that came surging toward them. They turned and headed for an apartment building about a half-mile away where many members of the American delegation were housed. On the way they passed hardware and liquor stores that were being systematically looted and observed in alarm that uniformed and armed police had joined the rioters. The scene was one of chaos and madness. From the roof of the apartment building the Americans could see fires burning throughout the city.

Earlier in the day, at approximately 2:15 P.M., William D. Pawley, U. S. Ambassador to Brazil and a conference delegate, was riding in an official car when he heard and "remembers as if it were yesterday," he wrote to me, the following broadcast:

This is Fidel Castro from Cuba. This is a Communist revolution. The President has been killed. All the military establishments are now in our hands. The Navy has capitulated to us and this revolution has been a success.

Pawley had previously served as Ambassador to Peru. The name Fidel Castro did not mean anything to him at the time but it caught his attention because Pawley had lived in Cuba for many years, and also because a family photograph taken in Cuba carried the signature of the photographer: Castro. These circumstances impressed the name indelibly on his mind, and he recalled it clearly when Castro broke into the news out of Cuba in 1957–1958.

At the downtown Embassy offices a large American Embassy delegation group had gathered, headed by Norman Armour, Assistant Secretary of State and a conference delegate. The chancery had surprisingly been able to maintain communications with the State Department in Washington over a special system that had been installed for the use of the American delegation. Wieland, the political officer, checked with Beaulac before sending his reports to the Department.

During the first night of the uprising fires in the immediate neighborhood of the Embassy offices increased in violence until the ground floor of the Embassy building itself was ablaze, with flames on the outside licking up to the third floor, where the Embassy offices began. With Communist speakers screaming over the radio that the United States was responsible for Gaitán's murder and that the Foreign Minister of Colombia had taken refuge in the American Embassy, the besieged group was in grave danger. The Avianca airline offices, on the second floor of the building, were entered and sacked, but the rioters were stopped by a grilled door when they reached the third floor. By a near-miracle the Embassy was saved; a paint store on the northwest corner of the building did not catch fire. At 11 A.M. the next morning Colombian army trucks finally reached the Embassy offices. But it was two weeks before the last of the snipers was eliminated.

Castro and del Pino returned to the Hotel Claridge during the first night of rioting with a large quantity of arms and spent many hours talking over the phone. They were holed up there until April 13, when, with the Colombian police closing in, they took refuge in the Cuban Embassy. The head of the Cuban delegation at the Conference, Dr. Guillermo Belt, arranged the escape of Castro and his companions on a Cuban cargo plane.

Both Secretary Marshall and President Ospina placed the blame for the uprising squarely on the Communists, and before breaking up, the Conference of the American States approved an anti-Communist resolution by unanimous vote. A few weeks later Colombia severed diplomatic relations with Soviet Russia. Ambassador Beaulac has written that democracy in Colombia "came within an ace of being destroyed" and that only the Communists could have gained from such an event.

After Castro became prominent in Cuba in 1958–1959, many colorful versions of his participation in the uprising ten years earlier were published. I have restricted myself to the clearly established facts, largely as disclosed by a Scotland Yard investigation requested by the Colombian government shortly after the riots. Its report tells in some detail of the activities of Castro and his student companions. Castro's activities established beyond question his anti-American and pro-Communist convictions as of 1948. They marked him as a gangster-type terrorist and killer.

It was Dr. Belt who informed American Ambassador Earl E. T. Smith, soon after his arrival in Havana in July 1957, of Castro's involvement in the Bogotá massacre. Naturally, Smith was astonished that he had not been filled in on such vital background information by Rubottom or Wieland. In view of Castro's growing notoriety, he urged Dr. Belt to report the facts personally to Secretary of State John Foster Dulles and offered the Embassy plane to fly him to Washington for this purpose. For reasons which he has not been willing or able to disclose to me Dr. Belt refused.

Incidentally, if he is still alive, del Pino, Castro's companion in Bogotá in 1948, is now serving a thirty-year prison sentence in Cuba. In 1959, after Castro came to power, del Pino broke with him and was caught by some of my Cuban friends attempting to escape from the island in a small Cessna plane. Struck by bullets and badly burned when the plane caught fire, he was carried into a "court" on a stretcher and, on Castro's order, given the thirty-year sentence.

What about Wieland and Rubottom in relation to Bogotá?

By an astonishing coincidence, ten years after the Bogotazo the fate of Cuba was largely in the hands of these two men. The important Office of Middle American Affairs, of which Wieland had been appointed Director on May 19, 1957, became the Office of Caribbean and Mexican Affairs, while Rubottom had become Assistant Secretary of State for Latin American Affairs. Wieland's position permitted him to originate, initiate, and recommend American policy. His views carried great weight because, due to an unusual personnel set-up, they reached the White House through only two men, both of whom were sympathetic to his ideas. The first was Rubottom, the highest career officer directly occupied with Latin American affairs. The other was Dr. Milton Eisenhower, Presidential adviser on Latin American affairs. Dr. Eisenhower, who had never seen Cuba, has described Rubottom as "one of the ablest and most forthright men I have ever known." [8] And President Eisenhower has called his brother Milton "the smartest one in the family." Thus, although Rubottom was fourth echelon in the State Department hierarchy, and Wieland sixth (Rubottom's deputy played an insignificant role), they had a short-cut to the White House.

Even if Milton Eisenhower had not been in the picture, the officials above Rubottom would have mattered little so far as Cuba was concerned. Inexperienced in Latin American affairs and intensely preoccupied with other world areas, these officials

[8] Milton Eisenhower, *The Wine Is Bitter* (New York: Doubleday & Co., Inc., 1963), p. 204.

would not normally have been likely to oppose Wieland-Rubottom recommendations. The presence of the President's brother made this even less likely.

In 1961–1962 a Senate Subcommittee on Internal Security conducted a series of hearings which, among other things, delved into the Bogotazo events. When questioned under oath, Wieland was evasive. Asked whether he knew that numerous reports concerning Castro and identifying him as a Communist went either over or around his desk during the Bogotazo, he replied that he could not recall.[9]

> Q: You mean you know there were such reports but you do not recall them?
>
> A: There were such reports but I don't recall them now.
>
> Q: Did you see any reports at that time about Fidel Castro's connections with Communism?
>
> A: I have since learned that there were such reports.
>
> Q: Did you, Mr. Wieland, file any report or reports with the State Department in Bogotá on the youth conference in Bogotá in April of 1948?
>
> A: I would assume so, sir, but I don't remember.
>
> Q: Did you mention Fidel Castro as among the Cuban students who attended?
>
> A: I may well have, again, sir, but I don't recall.[10]

On February 2, 1962, Wieland testified as follows:

> Sir, I knew that Castro had been in Bogotá; yes sir, I knew that he had gone as a member of a Cuban student group to some student gathering down there that I understand was Communist dominated or Communist inspired. I knew that he had been reported active in one way or another in the disorders which took place in Bogotá at the time, but what degree of involvement I don't think I did know.

[9] Senate Subcommittee of the Committee on the Judiciary to Investigate Internal Security, Part 5, Testimony of William Wieland, January 9, February 8, 1961; February 2, 1962, p. 638.

[10] *Ibid.*, pp. 638, 639.

Wieland and Rubottom, of course, did not know, in 1948, the full details of Castro's participation in the Bogotazo. But they learned them later, from a great many intelligence sources. A complete dossier on Castro, the Bogotazo, and the Communists surrounding Castro, prepared by the G-2 of the Cuban Army, was hand-carried to Washington in 1957 and delivered to Allen Dulles, head of the CIA. Although Wieland claimed that he never saw this specific report he admitted under oath that he saw a great many intelligence reports dealing with Castro's Communist connections. *Yet the investigating committee was unable to document a single instance in which he transmitted any of this solid intelligence to his superiors or mentioned it as credible in any report or policy paper.*[11]

As our friendship developed, Ambassador Earl E. T. Smith remarked to me one day that during his six-week briefing period he had never heard a single word in the State Department that was favorable to Batista or unfavorable to Castro. The nearest remark favorable to Batista came from President Eisenhower when Smith was taking his leave to undertake his post as Chief of Mission at Havana. The President asked Smith, on presenting his credentials, to give his regards to the Cuban President and intimated that Smith would find Batista to be a likeable individual in spite of what others may have told him.

But let us go back to the Cuban scene in 1957. Late that year I was retained to negotiate the sale of the largest tract of land in Cuba owned by a single individual. Known as the Hacienda Sevilla, it comprised approximately 425 square miles and included the area of the Sierra Maestra Mountains where Castro and his small rebel force spent a year and a half in hiding. This vast tract had been mismanaged, due to absentee ownership, and was occupied by thousands of squatters. We estimated its value

[11] Senate Subcommittee of the Committee of the Judiciary, *The Case of William Wieland,* 1962, p. 3.

at approximately one million dollars, and that was the asking price.

One day I received a visit from one of the most feared men in Cuba, a gangster known to be a cold-blooded killer. He had been graduated from the University of Havana, where he was a brilliant student, and he had been elected to public office. He was reputed to have a small private army of his own in the eastern area of the country. Murders and atrocities were attributed to his force. When Batista came to power this man became his friend and supporter, but his excesses embarrassed Batista and brought the two men into conflict. I had never met my uninvited visitor before.

He descended on our office without an appointment. He stationed two bodyguards at the outer door, ignored the receptionist, and walked down the long hall toward my office with two more guards, whom he left in the inner reception room. He entered my office unannounced and alone. Removing a pistol from its holster and placing it on the arm of the large leather chair in which he seated himself, he announced that he wished to purchase the Hacienda Sevilla. He planned, he said, to parcel out the entire tract to the farmers and squatters who now occupied it in exchange for their cooperation in running down Castro. He understood that our asking price was one million dollars. I asked him if he was speaking for Batista and he said he was not.

At my age, I told my caller, I did not have too long to live in any case, so before engaging in any conversation I should like to have him replace the pistol in its holster. He did so, explaining with a smile that he had removed it for comfort while seated.

His proposition was that there should be an overpayment and a "kickback." As I remember, the figure he mentioned was $1,400,000, of which we could retain the million we were asking. I replied that his suggestion did not offend me, that we were not saints, but because of the nature of our clientele, which included the governments of the United States and Canada, we had found it to be good business to conduct our affairs on an ethical plane. We would not deviate from that policy, I assured him. There were subsequent meetings and telephone calls that stretched over a period of months, but because of the "kick-back" element the transaction was never consummated. The man's first visit, naturally, had created quite a stir in our office, and of course I reported his conversation to our senior lawyers and our two managers.

I have often reflected on this incident. The plan made political sense, and if carried out it would probably have finished Castro. It was utterly impossible for Batista's army to track the tiny rebel group in the immense expanse of the wooded mountains. With the aid of thousands of *montunos* with a personal stake in the enterprise, Castro undoubtedly could have been brought to bay, but the gangster's venality closed that door.

However, had the plan been accepted and then failed to bring down Castro, there is no doubt that I would have been executed by a Castro firing squad. Although our firm forbade employees to engage in political activities, two members of our staff were in the Castro underground and were aware of my visitor's proposal.

Despite the occasional revolutionary violence, 1957 was a peak year for the Cuban economy. As it drew to a close Havana was busy, gay, and optimistic. Our firm was working at maximum pitch. The Christmas parties at clubs and in private homes throughout the country were marked by the high spirits for which pre-Castro Cubans were famous. The only cloud on the horizon was the pro-Castro press campaign in the United States.

I was especially conscious of this—and of the effect it was having on the State Department—since American Foreign Service officers and FBI and CIA representatives sometimes spent weekends at our Varadero beach house. Probably there were no Cubans with closer and friendlier contacts in the American Embassy than Jorge de Cubas, my partner, and I. We became increasingly aware of a serious and widening cleavage among the members of the large Embassy staff.

Most of them were partial to Castro and his Movement. Others, and particularly the Ambassador himself, distrusted and feared Castro. The staff divided along traditional conservative and liberal lines. The Counsellor of Embassy, Military, Naval, Air, and Commercial Attachés sided with the Ambassador. The Political and CIA officers and most of the lower-echelon personnel seemed favorable to Castro. It was natural that the Commercial Attaché and his assistant should reflect the attitude of the business and industrial community, which hoped for a continuation of Cuban prosperity under strong government control.

An Embassy friend on one occasion told me of having met the Political Officer and a CIA representative emerging from the Ambassador's office. He heard one of them say, white with rage, "This is the first time I've been called a Communist to my face!" Ambassador Smith would sometimes tease staff people who were pro-Castro by asking them, tongue in cheek, whether they were members of the 26th of July Movement. Some of these men complained that his manner was at times abrupt, even rude, and it angered them.

I am sure, looking back on that time, that the division had less to do with facts and logic than with moods and temperament. For his American partisans in Havana, and in Washington as well, Castro was more a symbol than a person. In their minds somehow the Cuban realities were transformed into a morality play in which Batista stood for Evil and Castro for Good. In the Embassy alignment I had a preview of the curiously diffuse American liberalism I have come to know better since then in the United States.

Then, in January 1958, something happened that disturbed my partner and me as a portent of things to come.

William Wieland arrived in Havana. An Embassy friend told me that he had brought a prepared paper describing the Cuban economy as in a state of serious deterioration, predicting that Batista would soon be overthrown, and recommending that the United States apply pressure on the Batista government to hasten its end. The primary purpose of his visit was to obtain a supporting paper from the Embassy along the same lines. In fact, he and the Political Officer, known to be friendly to the Castro Movement, were reported to have already drafted such a report, painting the economy of the island in darkest colors and foreseeing the early fall of the government.[12]

We were somewhat relieved to learn that Ambassador Smith had refused to permit the false assessment to go to Washington from the Embassy. He decided to counteract Wieland's activities in behalf of Castro by flying to Washington to submit an accurate report. When Smith telephoned Rubottom, saying that he wished personally to inform him on the economic and political situation, he was told that the Department did not have the funds to pay for such a trip. Smith countered with an offer to pay his own expenses, and the necessary travel orders were then issued.

In talking to Earl Smith after his return, I sensed that he had lost confidence in Wieland and was worried about the spread of the Castro legend in high places generally. After his resignation he told me of an occasion when, while recording a conference in Washington, Wieland had explained to him that more important than sticking to the facts was that statements should "look good on the record later."

What we did not know at that time, and what the Ambassador himself probably did not realize, was that he was facing insuperable odds at the State Department. But what we did learn a year before the fall of Batista was that a State Department official in a key position in relation to Cuban affairs had pressed the Havana Embassy for a report that Cuba's economy was crumbling—this at a time of exceptional prosperity in the country—to back up his prediction that the regime would soon collapse. It suggested that such a man might go very far to make his prophecy come true.

[12] Smith, pp. 58-59.

Former Ambassador Harry F. Guggenheim has kept a keen eye and an intelligent mind on Cuba and Latin America. He has pointed out that normally the President of the United States, the Secretary of State, and the various Under Secretaries have little time for the problems of Latin America. If a crisis develops, only an Assistant Secretary of State for Inter-American Affairs watches it unfold and makes the necessary judgments.

Yet Latin America is comparable to a great theater of war, Mr. Guggenheim says, and deserves to have a diplomat equivalent to a five-star general in overall command. He should be a statesman of international stature, with financial and economic training and a lifelong experience in the affairs of that great theater. He should have the respect of American Ambassadors to Latin American nations and the judgment and stature to back them. Finally, he should be a firm supporter of the free enterprise system, the great distinguishing characteristic of American democracy, and hence prepared to safeguard private U.S. capital in the area. Unfortunately—still paraphrasing the former Ambassador—the State Department has never had an official directing Latin American affairs who measured up to these demanding specifications.

Certainly it did not have one in Roy R. Rubottom, Jr., when the crisis of 1958 was taking shape. As his assistant on Cuban affairs, moreover, Rubottom had Wieland, appointed to this responsible post largely because he had lived in Cuba and spoke Spanish. In addition, acting as Special Ambassador to Latin America and enjoying the prestige of his relationship to the President there was a liberal theorist and reformer, Dr. Milton Eisenhower. The Department, immersed in other problems, left supervision of the crucial Cuban developments almost entirely to these three men. They were the policy-makers primarily responsible for decisions that helped bring Castro to power.

I remarked earlier that Castro was lucky in making his debut on the stage of American opinion set by Matthews of the *Times*. That luck held in the men chosen by fate to sponsor his cause in the American government. I am not casting doubts on the sincerity or patriotism of these men. Each of them in his fashion was seeking to guide events in line with his honest preferences. But, as former Senator Kenneth B. Keating wrote, "The unfortunate Cuban people are the victims of tragic State Department errors." [13] The fact that such errors were honestly motivated makes them no less calamitous.

[13] Senate Subcommittee of the Committee on the Judiciary, *The Case of William Wieland*, 1962, p. 202.

CHAPTER ELEVEN

American Intervention

From his mountain hideout, on March 17, 1958, Fidel Castro issued a bombastic manifesto. Although he then had fewer than two hundred men under his command, he declared "total war" against the Batista government. He gave army officers and enlisted men until April 5 to resign, on pain of forfeiting their right to remain in the armed forces. He ordered judges of all Cuban courts to resign forthwith. And he called for a "general revolutionary strike," to begin on April 9 and to be backed by military action.

This manifesto seemed to us an absurd display of arrogance, as indeed it was. The strike failed completely. The workers and the middle class, who were doing well under Batista, refused to support it. If any officers or judges resigned, no one heard about it. Even the Communist Party (PSP) rejected and criticized the Sierra Maestra document as a "unilateral call."

The lack of response seemed a setback for Castro, but not for long. On March 14, three days before the manifesto was issued, the United States had taken the first overt step that was to help clear the path to dictatorship for Fidel Castro. On that day, on the recommendation of William A. Wieland,[1] the State Department placed an arms embargo against Batista, suspend-

---

[1] Report of Senate Subcommittee of the Committee on the Judiciary, *The Case of William Wieland* (Washington, D. C.: Government Printing Office, 1962), p. 97.

ing shipment of 1,950 Garand rifles which had been bought and paid for by the Cuban Government and were at shipside ready for delivery. It has now been established that Castro received immediate word of this move by radio from his Washington agent, who was in constant touch with Castro. In all probability this dramatic American signal of policy intentions accounts for Castro's seemingly senseless ultimatum.

To understand the significance of the arms embargo it is necessary to go back seven weeks. Early in January, Ambassador Earl E. T. Smith, with the approval of Rubottom and Wieland, informed Batista that if he would restore constitutional guarantees and lift press censorship, the United States would deliver twenty armored cars which had been on order for nine months. Batista was eager to obtain them, not only because he needed the equipment but even more because it would connote a friendly American attitude.

The State Department offer, however, posed a serious problem for him. Its acceptance would give important advantages to terrorists. If apprehended, they would have to be presented to a court within seventy-two hours and very likely would be released. Saboteurs and terrorists could assemble freely to conspire against him. The lifting of press censorship would magnify every terrorist activity by giving it national publicity. Any Cuban, and any person knowledgeable about Cuba, would have known that restoration of such rights at that delicate juncture would touch off a new round of violence.

Batista therefore made a counter-proposal. He had been greatly concerned over aerial drops of supplies to the Castro rebels and was convinced that ex-President Prío, then in the United States, was organizing and financing this traffic. He felt that if Washington would control Prío, he could readily cope with Castro. Accordingly he asked that, in addition to delivering the armored cars, the United States curtail Prío's activities by enforcing its neutrality laws.

In this connection, Ambassador Smith asked the State Department to arrange for William F. Tompkins, Assistant Attorney General, to visit Havana. Smith and Tompkins met with Batista at his country home, Finca Kuquine. Although the Ambassador made it clear at this conference that there was to be no *formal* quid pro quo arrangement, a gentlemen's understanding was reached.

Batista fulfilled his part by restoring constitutional guarantees on January 25, 1958. But at the American end there was only a meaningless gesture. In mid-January the Department of Justice obtained a Grand Jury indictment against Prío. He was immediately released on bail, the case against him was not pressed, the aerial drops to reinforce Castro continued. As a crowning touch, Rubottom and Wieland reneged on their promise—the armored cars were never delivered.

As Batista had anticipated, terrorist activities were resumed. In the ensuing weeks bombs exploded in theaters, stores, and streets, killing and maiming innocent people. In the countryside the night skies were lighted by the flames of burning sugar cane fields, set afire by tying gasoline-soaked rags to the tails of rats released into the dry undergrowth. Commercial planes were hijacked, and an international automobile race was exploited to get publicity for the anti-Batista movement.

This race, scheduled for February as a tourist attraction, had brought together many world-famous drivers. The night before the event, Juan Manuel Fangio, Argentina's five-time world champion, was kidnaped at pistol point by revolutionists. He was released the next day, unharmed, but the daring stunt hit the front pages all over the world. Even more embarrassing to the authorities was an accident caused by the spraying of oil near a curve on a crowded street; a car skidded into the crowd, killing six and injuring about fifty and Castro was given the "credit."

These incidents brought government retaliation and, as the terror mounted, it became clear that Batista had no choice but again to suspend the guarantees. Even Dr. Márquez Sterling,

Batista's most formidable political opponent, so informed the American Ambassador in my presence.

The interval of seven weeks between the restoration of constitutional rights and their suspension—January 25 to March 12—had been long enough to permit the delivery of the armored cars. Had that American undertaking been carried out, it might in fact have prevented or postponed the suspension. In any case, Batista's action provided a *post-factum* alibi for withholding the equipment and, as a more vigorous reaction, the State Department on March 14 stopped the shipment of the Garand rifles.

The Department did instruct Ambassador Smith to advise the Cuban Government that this action did not indicate a change in basic U.S. policy but had been taken under pressures from the press and Congress. Among the more vocal Congressmen on behalf of Castro was Adam Clayton Powell, of New York, who was urging immediate recognition of a regime headed by Castro and the recall of Earl Smith as Ambassador. Smith complied with Department instructions but he did not believe what he had been told to say. "I knew that after March 12 this was not true," he has written.[2] On March 17, in fact, he called the Embassy staff together and told them there had apparently been a change of United States policy toward Cuba.

The arms embargo marked the second of the main events that brought Castro to power, the first having been the Matthews articles in *The New York Times*. The Cuban Government, of course, recognized its enormous significance. Its ordnance, which included 1903-model rifles and surplus U.S. arms of World War I vintage, was almost entirely obsolete. Batista was planning a drive against the Castro rebels, and as one of the cabinet members told the Ambassador: "Our troops cannot fight with toothpicks." Batista himself told the Ambassador that his government would now be fighting for its life against Com-

[2] Earl E. T. Smith, *The Fourth Floor* (New York: Random House, 1962), p. 88.

munist revolutionaries, and hardly a day passed that the staggering effect of the embargo was not brought to the Ambassador's attention.[3]

Earl Smith strongly urged Washington not to publicize the suspension of arms shipments. He argued that if Batista should fall after such publicity the United States would be blamed for what would follow. *"And the only ones who will benefit,"* he cabled, *"will be the Communists."* [4]

Nevertheless the arms embargo was publicized in *The New York Times* on March 29. Wieland claims that although he had been in the habit of "leaking" information to the press, especially to the *Times,* this particular news did not come from him. In any case, its effect was devastating and its meaning was grasped even by well-informed people in the United States. "When in March 1958," wrote Betty Kirk in *The Nation,* "shipment of military supplies to Batista was canceled . . . this was a signal, understood by all, that the dictator was on his way out and Castro was in." [5] Wieland himself later attested under oath that when it became known in Cuba that the United States was refusing to ship arms to Cuba, the Batista government was "in its last moments." [6]

In addition to the armored cars and Garand rifles, the Cuban Government had bought and paid for a few non-combat training planes and had ordered replacement parts for combat equipment. Ambassador Smith worked hard to obtain shipment clearance for the planes, which were already in Fort Lauderdale, Florida. Finally, over the objection of Wieland, who argued that they would be armed and used against the rebels, Smith obtained authority to notify Batista that the planes would be delivered. Because of its political implications, Batista received the

---

[3] *Ibid.,* p. 107.

[4] *Ibid.,* p. 91.

[5] Report of Senate Subcommittee of the Committee on the Judiciary, *The Case of William Wieland,* p. 140.

[6] Hearings before the last-mentioned Subcommittee, *Testimony of William Wieland,* Part 5, 1962, p. 659.

assurance with great satisfaction. However, although a bill for storage and servicing of the planes was submitted to the Cuban Government, neither the planes nor the spare parts were ever delivered.

During the balance of the year Smith repeatedly recommended that the shipment of arms be renewed, reminding the State Department that he was constantly asking the Cuban Government to protect American property. He spelled it out, listing U.S. plants that had been damaged by Castro supporters. On one occasion, when Smith asked Batista for troops to be sent to the two great American-owned nickel plants, Batista facetiously answered that he would gladly assign a thousand men to each if the United States would send him his rifles. Adequate troops were sent, nevertheless. And Batista continued to cooperate in other ways; whenever Ambassador Smith asked the President for Cuba's vote in the United Nations it was willingly given.

Finally, to save face and, as he said, to avoid further embarrassment to Washington, Batista canceled all orders that had been placed in the United States and turned elsewhere for arms. But when other governments which he approached made inquiries at the State Department, they were bluntly apprised that the United States would look with disfavor on the sale of arms to the Cuban Government. Batista rightly regarded this as intervention in behalf of Castro.[7]

After some delay Cuba did manage to buy some war matériel from the Dominican Republic and a few other countries, but it was an assortment of miscellaneous items that probably did more harm than good. In particular, it emphasized the country's inability to arm itself with the traditional American weapons that had always been used previously.

Further harassment by the State Department was generated through a technicality of the Military Defense Assistance Program (MDAP). Under this program the United States gives

[7] Smith, p. 100.

military aid to Latin American countries, largely in the form of obsolescent weaponry that is gradually discarded to make way for the latest models. Cuba's best military equipment had been obtained under its MDAP agreement with the United States, consummated in 1952 during the Prío administration.

The MDAP agreements with Latin American countries contained unenforceable, window-dressing provisions, theoretically designed to forestall use of these arms in civil conflicts. One was that the equipment should be used only for hemispheric defense. Another was that the United States would have to agree to such use. Wieland and Rubottom saw in these provisions another opportunity to weaken the Batista government.

The State Department suddenly began questioning Cuba on the use being made of MDAP weapons. This came as a complete surprise to Batista, who made discreet inquiries among his staff officers. Rumors as to the reason for this investigation permeated the army with the speed of poisoned arrows, just as its instigators in Washington doubtless had foreseen, with shattering effect on military morale.

Batista answered that the arms had been deployed throughout the army, but the State Department learned that the best Cuban infantry battalion had been equipped with these arms. It called attention to this, pointing out that MDAP arms could be used only for hemispheric defense. Batista replied that this was precisely the use being made of them—to fight Communist intrusion in the hemisphere.

Repeatedly, both through the Cuban Embassy in Washington and the American Embassy in Havana, the State Department continued to charge what it said were violations of the MDAP agreement. It stepped up the harassment by asking Batista to withdraw from his fight against Castro all personnel equipped with MDAP weapons. It demanded that Batista break up and retire from active service in the combat area the crack infantry battalion that it declared was wholly equipped with MDAP arms. Finally it submitted a formal note to the Cuban Government, bringing these matters to its attention and asking for a report.

When Batista delayed answering, Ambassador Smith was instructed to inquire when a reply could be expected. To his credit, Batista did not submit to the American demands. Nevertheless, the Washington pressures hastened the demoralization of the Cuban Army.

These were not the only steps taken by the State Department to topple the Cuban Government. It requested the Department of Justice and the Immigration Service to deal sympathetically with Castro supporters in the United States, who were then engaged in raising funds, propagandizing, and furnishing arms and men to the Castro cause. The leader of these activities, ex-President Prío, had been admitted to the United States on parole status; if he violated the American neutrality laws his right of sojourn in the United States would be automatically revoked. Yet he operated with impunity; the February indictment against him was not pursued. Applications of Cuban exiles sympathetic to Castro to remain in the United States received favorable action.[8]

Rubottom and Wieland maintained cordial contacts with Castro representatives, including his principal spokesman, Ernesto Betancourt, who had once been employed by my firm in a clerical position. They maintained an almost day-to-day contact with Herbert Matthews, who continued to use the influential columns of his newspaper to discredit a friendly government and support the Castro rebels. Despite all these pressures, Batista managed to maintain control.

On the surface he seemed to be experiencing no insurmountable difficulties. During most of 1958 the Cuban people lived their lives and carried on their occupations in an almost completely normal manner, except in the eastern province of Oriente. Incidents that made headlines occurred only spasmodically. The sugar mills, on which Cuba's economy mainly depends, were grinding as usual in the early part of the year, and the crop was in no danger. In Havana business remained good. Our firm was

[8] *Ibid.,* p. 117.

handling several important industrial projects in process of con-struction; on Saturdays and Sundays there were often lawyers in our offices catching up on their work.

There were many rumors, of course. We heard that the num-ber of rebels in the Castro group was growing, that youths from various parts of the island were heading into the mountains. But we learned later, from Castro's own statement, that this was false—that in April 1958 he had only 180 men under his com-mand. We also heard that a group from Havana University's *Directorio Revolucionario* had opened a second front in the Escambray Mountains in Las Villas Province, operating inde-pendently of Castro. The government declared that they posed no threat and reports of their activities attracted little attention.

Castro, who remained in the hills with his little band of fol-lowers, became an object of increasing speculation. At no time, as yet, had he challenged government forces militarily, but the interviews by Americans continued to glorify him. Representa-tives of the U.S. press who visited Cuba briefly were relentless in their condemnation of Batista, unrestrained in eulogizing Castro. Usually they avoided the American Embassy, knowing that Ambassador Smith's views were in conflict with their own preconceptions. Their minds were closed. It was more comfort-able to join the rolling bandwagon by ridiculing Smith without giving him a hearing. One wrote that the State Department should instruct its Ambassadors to contact American corre-spondents and obtain the benefit of their "man-in-the-street savvy." Eventually, after Smith had left Cuba, only one news-man, as far as I know, publicly admitted having been mistaken. Noting in the New York *Daily News* that Smith had not been congratulated for his analysis of Castro "by any of us who rapped him at the time," Ed Sullivan wrote: "But Smith was right and everybody else was wrong." [9]

While the tempo of Cuban life seemed normal in the early part of 1958, news of the arms embargo actually was having a

[9] New York *Daily News,* January 12, 1959.

profound and cumulative impact. Public sentiment began to swing against Batista. I was urged by one of the cabinet ministers to go to Washnigton to try to induce the American Government to change its policy. Knowing that Ambassador Smith had failed in this, it was clear to me that the mission would be hopeless, and I declined. But few of us regarded the overall situation as entirely hopeless, and we worked to find a solution.

There is still a widespread misconception in the United States that Cubans had a choice only between Batista and Castro— that there were no reasonable and practical alternatives. This is untrue. During 1957 and 1958 at least six plans were submitted to Washington, aiming at political solutions that offered alternatives to both Batista and Castro.[10]

The Catholic Church developed a plan providing for a provisional "Government of Unity." The Papal Nuncio had meetings with the Ambassador in hopes of enlisting Washington's "moral support" before approaching Batista and Castro. Despite the impressive sponsorship, the State Department refused even such token cooperation.

Batista had been elected President the last time in 1954 and had been inaugurated February 25, 1955. Now, in 1958, his four-year term of office was drawing to a close, and elections were scheduled for June 1. Under the 1940 Constitution Batista could not succeed himself. Dr. Carlos Márquez Sterling was the leading Presidential candidate in opposition to any government-supported candidate, and everyone believed that in a fair contest under normal conditions he would command the support of the vast majority of the voters. "Carlitos," as he was affectionately known throughout the island, was popular and respected by all classes of Cuban society. In early March 1958 he told me that he would like to meet the American Ambassador, who agreed at once to the interview.

At our meeting we told Smith that we considered it necessary

[10] Smith, p. 175.

for the government again to suspend constitutional guarantees in the interests of stability and to prepare a climate appropriate for the holding of elections. Further, we believed the elections should be postponed until November. I remember Carlitos telling the Ambassador, "I know Castro as I know the palm of my right hand, and I can assure you that, much as I distrust Batista, Castro would be ten times worse." The Ambassador inquired whether he might repeat that statement to his government as coming from him and Carlitos answered, "Of course."

We discussed the plan developed by the Catholic Church. Carlitos said that if the Church obtained the backing of Cuban civic organizations and was able to induce the government to create an atmosphere conducive to free elections, there was a good chance this would be the solution; but it was indispensable that Washington give the program its blessing. Castro would certainly oppose free elections, knowing that even if Batista were defeated, authority would pass to someone other than himself. His strategy was to prevent elections. Dr. Márquez Sterling made it clear to the Ambassador that he was not personally ambitious and would gladly withdraw his candidacy if the political opposition decided on someone else.

We also discussed a plan that called for Batista to leave the country after naming a caretaker government representing all political factions, including the Castro group, with elections to be held under the supervision of the United Nations or the American Bar Association. Its essential feature was that the United States announce a willingness to resume arms shipments timed with Batista's departure, and an intention to recognize any government that resulted from free and honest elections. The Ambassador expressed doubt that Washington would go along with any such plan, and Smith later told me that our various suggestions had been rejected on the principle of "non-intervention." Thus, from a personal experience, it became evident to me, nine months before the fall of Batista, that the Department of State was determined to thwart any action that might obstruct Castro's assumption of power.

Little was asked of the State Department whenever a plan was presented. All that was required was a statement indicating its awareness of the plan and a hope that it would succeed. In every instance Ambassador Smith pleaded for an affirmative reply, stressing the threat of Communism; in every case the minimum support needed was withheld. A negative cable always came back from Rubottom, invoking the principle of "non-intervention." The alibi was plainly fraudulent. The Department had already intervened with the arms embargo and was intervening continuously by its tolerance of Castroite partisan activities in the United States.

Because the coming elections were crucial, Ambassador Smith suggested to Batista that he invite the world press and observers from the United Nations and the Organization of American States to witness them. The two opposition candidates at the time were ex-President Grau San Martín and Dr. Márquez Sterling. Batista accepted the Ambassador's suggestion, asking only that Grau and my cousin join in the request. They agreed with some reluctance, feeling that outside supervision implied an impairment of national sovereignty. The request to the United Nations for observers was subsequently made, but it came late and was never implemented.

The second most influential political force in Cuba, after the army, was organized labor. It had consistently supported Batista because of his pro-labor policies. In March 1958 my partner had a visit from Cuba's most powerful labor leader, Eusebio Mujal, head of the Cuban Confederation of Workers (CTC). Mujal, obviously worried, wanted to know whether the United States had adopted a new attitude toward Batista. If that were the case, he said, he would announce the withdrawal of the support of labor and would leave the country. In that event Batista would have fallen at once.

Although we were by then aware that there had been a policy change, we decided to consult the Ambassador before answering Mujal. Earl Smith thought it best to tell Mujal that the attitude of the United States had not changed—"that the United States did not change its relations with a friendly government simply because that government was facing a serious crisis."[11] It was a tongue-in-cheek reply but this was the message given to Mujal, and Batista continued to have the support of Cuban labor.

In the same month, Ambassador Smith twice received visits from Herbert Matthews. The *Times* man took the position that the United States had already intervened in Cuban internal affairs by trying to obtain free and honest elections. He could not understand why the Batista government had not already fallen and expressed concern on this score.[12]

Postponed from June 1, the general elections were held on November 3, 1958, under conditions that were far from normal. From the mountains Castro called for the assassination of all candidates, whether of the government or the opposition. Citizens who lined up at polling places on election day, he threatened, would be machine-gunned. Nevertheless, it proved to be an extraordinarily quiet election. There were few people on the streets and little traffic.

The government-supported candidate was Dr. Andrés Rivero Agüero and the government announced before midnight that he had won a sweeping victory. The opposition candidates, Dr. Grau San Martín and my cousin, claimed that Batista had rigged the elections through vote buying and the use of patronage. Jobs were promised or threats made that jobs would be taken away, and there had been wholesale ballot fraud, they said. Batista and his supporters denied this. The President had given repeated pledges to Ambassador Smith that the elections would be conducted honestly. Some believed that the combination of a small proportion of the popular vote and the always solid turnout of

[11] *Ibid.*, p. 101.
[12] *Ibid.*, pp. 93, 94.

government employees made it unnecessary for Batista to rig the election.

In Spanish, a diminutive word usually ends with the suffix "ito" and an augmentive with the suffix "azo." Thus the 1948 Communist uprising in Bogotá, Colombia, became known as the *Bogotazo*. In Cuba the Batista opponents dubbed the 1958 election the *cambiazo*, from the verb *cambiar*, meaning to change or alter. But whether the election was honest or fraudulent, it was at this point that hundreds of thousands of disillusioned Cubans turned hopefully toward the little-known rebel in the hills.

In late November my partner and I learned from a responsible and confidential source in the United States that William D. Pawley, the former Ambassador to Peru and Brazil and a personal friend of President Eisenhower, was about to be sent as a secret emissary to negotiate with Batista. Our information was that he would be authorized to offer Batista an opportunity to live with his family in Daytona Beach, Florida, if he would appoint a "caretaker government" composed of five men who were his political opponents. This represented a complete reversal of the policy supported up to that time by Rubottom and Wieland, under which all plans had been arbitrarily ruled out. It was an astonishing but heartening report.

We also learned the State Department intended to call Smith to Washington without advising him of the plan, and we debated whether we should tell him about it. Because we had developed a high regard for the Ambassador, having been impressed by his courage and perseverance in working against great odds for rational solutions, we decided to be forthright with him. On Thanksgiving Day 1958, at the Havana Country Club, I informed him of the decision to send a secret emissary to Cuba to negotiate with Batista. I also gave him the names of the men who were to be suggested for the caretaker government.

Earl Smith was surprised by this news but could make no comment. On December 4 he was summoned to Washington for consultation. Not until December 10 was he informed by Deputy Under Secretary Robert Murphy that Batista had been approached the day before. The Ambassador was not given the name of the emissary or the result of the interview. When Smith disclosed to Rubottom the detailed information I had given him, asking if he could confirm it, Rubottom remained silent.[13] After Smith's return to Havana and prior to an interview he had requested with Batista, he again asked Rubottom by cable if Batista had been approached on the subject of leaving Cuba. He received no reply.

Pawley was the ideal emissary to send to Havana. Sixty-four years of age, he had lived and worked in Latin America most of his life and had actually resided in and out of Cuba more than thirty years. He had known Batista well and had gained his respect. Pawley had had a highly successful business career. He had organized the first Cuban aviation company, built three aircraft factories in China that produced 90 percent of the aircraft used by the Nationalist Government in its struggle against the Communist regime, and built India's first and only aircraft factory, employing 15,000 mechanics. Three years later he built India's first ammonium-sulfate plant. Subsequently he organized an autobus system in Havana that permitted the Cuban Government to beautify the city by removing streetcars, streetcar tracks, posts and wires from its streets. At this writing he is the president of an important Florida sugar company.

In the political field Pawley also had a distinguished career. He organized the legendary Flying Tigers in China, dealt with Chinese leaders such as Chiang Kai-shek, and served as a Special Assistant to Secretary of State Dean Acheson and General Marshall. He became the American Ambassador to Peru and later to Brazil, where he had on his staff as press attaché William Wieland, whom he distrusted. At the request of President Truman he organized the Ninth Inter-American Conference in Bogotá, which was almost wrecked by the bloody Communist-

[13] *Ibid.*, p. 168.

inspired Bogotazo. After that he had successfully carried out important assignments in Europe, including obtaining Franco's approval for the American military bases in Spain.

Conservative and intelligent, Pawley was one of the first prominent Americans to become sensitive to the Communist threat in both China and Latin America. He strongly opposed the policies of Dean Acheson and his advisory group—Lattimore, Vincent, Service, Davies, and others—who regarded the Chinese Communists under Mao Tse-tung as "agrarian reformers." Because he was a political appointee, however, many of the closely-knit group of career officers of the State Department regarded him as an outsider. They also took offense at the candor with which he expressed his convictions.

As a counterweight, Pawley had the advantage of a personal friendship with President Eisenhower. The President offered to appoint him Under Secretary of State for Latin American Affairs, a new post designed to upgrade the importance of the area, but withdrew the offer after strong opposition by the career professionals in the Department.[14]

In late 1958 Pawley was at his home in Miami Beach, increasingly alarmed at the prospect of a Castro-Communist take-over in Cuba. In the publicity buildup for Castro as a democrat and "agrarian reformer," he saw a repetition of the techniques used to impose Communism on China. He knew that planes and ships were leaving Florida with arms for Castro, with Federal agents closing their eyes to the illegal traffic. His views paralleled those of Ambassador Smith in Havana, but while Smith necessarily had to work from the bottom up or be removed from office, Pawley decided to work from the top down. *Both met the same road-block.*

Pawley has written me that he had four or five meetings with President Eisenhower in an effort to persuade him that Castro

[14] Former Ambassador Pawley has certified that all references to him in this chapter are accurate. The chapter was also submitted to the Office of President Dwight D. Eisenhower, in Gettysburg, Pennsylvania, and the references to the President were approved.

was a Communist and should not be permitted to come to power. At about the same time the CIA had finally concluded that a Castro victory might not be in the best interests of the United States. Allen Dulles, Director of the CIA, reported to the President that Communists had penetrated the Castro movement and that "if Castro takes over, they will probably participate in the government." [15]

The President was always sympathetic to Pawley's views and in each case arranged meetings for him with State Department officials. Pawley met with Rubottom, Wieland, Douglas Dillon, and others, and occasionally with Allen Dulles. He reminded Rubottom and Wieland that they had been in Bogotá at the time of the Communist bid for power in 1948, in which Castro had participated, and that regardless of what Castro might now be saying, it would be extremely dangerous to permit him to come to power. To them he did not make any plea for Batista, knowing that it would be useless. But since Batista's term expired in a few weeks, he argued, nothing would be lost by holding out until a new government came in, opening the door for a possible satisfactory political negotiation. Pointing his finger at Wieland, Pawley said, *"If you permit Castro to come to power, you are going to have more trouble than you have ever seen in your life."* [16]

According to Pawley, both Rubottom and Wieland stuck to the myth that Castro was an agrarian reformer and, in their opinion, not a Communist. Having fought a hard but losing fight against such "agrarian reformers" in China, Pawley was unwilling to have his country make the same mistake twice. He was deeply convinced that Cuba was about to be turned over to the Communists by men like Rubottom, Wieland, and Matthews, just as he felt China had been turned over to Mao Tse-tung by

[15] Dwight D. Eisenhower, *The White House Years: Waging Peace* (New York: Doubleday & Co., Inc., 1965), p. 521.

[16] Report of Senate Subcommittee of the Committee on the Judiciary, *The Case of William Wieland*, 1962, p. 109.

confused or ideologically motivated men in the State Department.

The time had come, Pawley decided, to forget the branches and dig at the roots of the Cuban problem. The solution, he felt, was to have Wieland removed from his jurisdiction over Caribbean problems. He therefore returned to President Eisenhower, reporting that his efforts had failed and asking the President to arrange an interview for him with the Under Secretary of State, Douglas Dillon. Fearing that the conversation might be incorrectly recorded by the State Department, he asked Eisenhower to permit him to invite Senator George Smathers of Florida to the meeting. The President agreed.

On arriving for the conference Pawley and Smathers found that Ambassador Leslie Mallory, Rubottom's deputy and Wieland's immediate superior, was present. Pawley presented to the Under Secretary the considerable background information he had on Wieland. Smathers related a supporting experience of his own in which Wieland was involved. Pawley suggested that Wieland be removed from his Caribbean area duties and replaced by someone with less pro-Castro bias.

Secretary Dillon replied that he had no fear of Castro, that the real problem was dictator Trujillo, whom they were about to go after. Time enough to worry about Castro later, he said. Mallory expressed resentment of the "outside pressure." Had he intended to make a change, he said, such interference would cause him to recommend that nothing be done about it. Pawley left the meeting thoroughly convinced that the Rubottom-Wieland policy of promoting Castro to the limit had the full support of the State Department. Discouraged and depressed, he returned to Miami and told his wife that Cuba would soon be lost to Communism.

But he did not give up. Shortly afterward he arranged a meeting at his home with a few high officials of the Latin American Division of the State Department, including former Assistant Secretary of State Henry Holland. A representative of the CIA was present, and they discussed the impasse far into the night. In view of Pawley's close relationship with President Eisenhower, it was decided that he should return to Washington and ask the President to authorize him to go to Havana and try to persuade Batista to capitulate to a provisional government which would be friendly to neither himself nor Castro. Eisenhower agreed and instructed the State Department to work out a program offering inducements to make the proposal attractive to Batista.

For several days Pawley worked with officials of the Department, evolving a plan which included making available $10 million in armaments to the caretaker government as soon as it was constituted. Batista and his family and close friends would be permitted to reside in Florida. No reprisals would be taken in Cuba against Batista followers by the new government and elections would take place within eighteen months. After the elections the courts would be free to prosecute anyone involved in fraud or other crimes during the Batista regime.

The key aspect of the plan was that Pawley would be authorized to speak for President Eisenhower. That would remove the proposal from the category of "suggestions," which Batista was receiving aplenty, and give it the character of a proposal from the highest quarter.

Rubottom requested that before leaving for Cuba, Pawley meet with him once more. At this final meeting, at which a large group was present, including Wieland, Pawley was told that there had been "a modification." *He was not to disclose to Batista that he was speaking in behalf of the President.* He was to advance the plan merely as his own idea, saying that if it was acceptable to Batista, he would then try to persuade the American Government to go along with it.

Rubottom said that the new instructions had been approved by Secretary of State Herter, and Pawley knew from experience that the President would not override a decision of the Secretary of State. He saw at once that this change deprived him of his most persuasive talking point. He would now be only one of the many personal friends who were constantly offering advice to Batista. He argued with some vehemence against the revision. But Rubottom insisted that the change was basic and irreversible, since it was the decision of the Secretary of State. Deeply discouraged once again, Pawley debated whether to undertake the mission at all, but in the end he decided to work on.

In Havana he first reviewed the proposal in a four-hour interview with Gonzalo Güell, Cuba's Foreign Minister, enlisting his support. Then he met with Batista. His interview with the Cuban President lasted three hours. Batista said that he had lost all faith in officials of the American State Department, and felt certain that they would not agree to any constructive plan. He implored Pawley to do his best to persuade them to stop interfering in Cuban affairs and permit the new government to take over in March, after which, he said, any changes the Americans sought could be obtained. Pawley returned to Washington and reported to the President that his mission had failed.

Within a month Batista had capitulated and left Cuba. He telephoned Pawley from the Dominican Republic, inviting him to come over. When he learned for the first time that Pawley's interview with him in Cuba had been authorized by President Eisenhower, he said sadly that if this had been made clear at their Havana conference, he would undoubtedly have agreed to the program. "I believe," Pawley subsequently wrote me, "that the deliberate overthrow of Batista by Wieland and Matthews, assisted by Rubottom, is almost as great a tragedy as the surrendering of China to the Communists by a similar group of Department of State officials fifteen or sixteen years ago and we will not see the end in cost of American lives and American resources for these tragic errors."

The Pawley plan was the last of six or seven submitted to the State Department. Programs developed by the Catholic Church, civic organizations, and others, aiming at political solutions that would eliminate both Batista and Castro, had been rejected. Castro was not the only alternative to Batista, yet in each case the State Department had withheld its support on the principle of "non-intervention."

Yet on December 14, 1958, the State Department did formally intervene to oust Batista and bring in Castro. Ambassador Smith was instructed to advise the President that he no longer had the support of the United States and that he should leave Cuba.[17]

The Ambassador's instructions from Rubottom were crystal-clear. Shorn of meaningless adornment, they were that he tell Batista to get out of his country. He was to say that the United States appreciated Batista's past friendship and cooperation and was aware of his many contributions to Cuban history but that it had now, for humanitarian reasons, reluctantly decided to withdraw its support. The Ambassador was to maintain the fiction that the United States was not intervening in Cuba's internal affairs, although advising Batista to leave. These instructions were not sent through regular channels but in coded wireless, presumably so as not to leave a record in the Department.

The cards were down, and Smith immediately made the decision known to the Foreign Minister, asking for an appointment with the President.

The dramatic interview took place during the night of December 17, 1958. Smith has written that Batista still exuded an air of strength as he sat across the room without the slightest sign of emotion, his piercing dark eyes never leaving the Ambassador's face. He inquired whether he might go with his family to his home in Daytona Beach and was told he should first spend some time in Spain or some other foreign country. He asked how much time he had and was told not to delay his departure unduly. He spoke of the possibility of setting up a military junta and was told that it was too late. Batista repeated what he had often said before. But this time he said *when*—not *if*—Castro took over, the United States would be faced with

17 Smith, pp. 169-174.

Communism in Cuba: "Your country has intervened in behalf of the Castros." [18]

This interview brought about the fall of the Batista government, which Castro could never have accomplished militarily without State Department support.

In his report of the interview to the State Department, Smith said that he was certain Batista would accept any solution. He added that the Catholic Church would go to any lengths to bring about peace and asked for permission to contact the Papal Nuncio. He recommended that the Organization of American States be requested to support mediation by the Church, reiterating once again his conviction that if the United States permitted Castro to take over the Government of Cuba, the only beneficiaries would be the Communists. The State Department remained adamant.

During the following days several proposed solutions were received from the Cuban Government and submitted to Washington. One was that the day after his inauguration the President-elect, Dr. Rivero Agüero, would call for new general elections to take place within four to six months, to fill all elective posts, including the Presidency. Observers from the UN and OAS, as well as the world press, were to be invited to assure a free and honest franchise. The Cuban Government asked only that the United States begin shipping promptly the armament and matériel it had bought and paid for, to permit it to fight Castro and what it considered the Communist threat. This plan was submitted to Washington by Ambassador Smith, with a strong recommendation that it be accepted. It was rejected. The position of the State Department was that there could be no solution so long as Batista remained in Cuba.[19]

According to Smith, "I was not permitted to hold up before him any prospect of appropriate United States backing for a solution which would have the genuine support of the people of

18 *Ibid.*, p. 174.
19 *Ibid.*, p. 181.

his country. . . . I had dealt him a mortal blow. . . . I knew it was now too late to set up a government without Castro . . . if support from the United States was not forthcoming. For twelve months before the ship of state had foundered there were occasions when solutions to the Cuban problem could have been obtained. I recalled the unanimous view expressed by representatives of American business in Havana . . . when they asked me to advise the State Department that the Castro movement was Communist-inspired and dominated. 'It was inconceivable,' they said, 'that the United States could assist Castro by silently standing by and permitting Castro to triumph.' The United States had done more than stand silently by. It had diplomatically, but clearly, told the President of the Republic that he should absent himself from his country." [20]

Batista left Cuba two hours after midnight on the New Year's Eve that ushered in 1959. His ambition to retain power had contributed to his downfall. Yet he was not the ruthless dictator that the American press reported him to be.

During the closing weeks and days of 1958 the activities of the rebels in the eastern and central part of Cuba had expanded enormously. Batista's army was no longer resisting. Terrorism and sabotage were rampant. Thirty to forty railway inspectors in the interior were reporting daily to our client, Consolidated Railways, whose Havana office was located on the floor directly below ours. In this way we were well informed on the rapid collapse of the resistance forces. Each day we prepared a report of railway bridges sabotaged and destroyed and of other acts of terrorism reported by the inspectors. These were given to the American Embassy, which in turn transmitted them to Washington.

In spite of these developments, I have always felt that when Batista fled the island on January 1, 1959, Castro was the most surprised of all the Cubans. Guevara later said the news had

[20] *Ibid.*, pp. 173-176.

been "astonishing." [21] Castro was totally unprepared to take over and his critics say that at first he did not dare even to come to Havana. His defenders claim that the slow march to Havana was deliberate dramatization.

In Havana the crowds were in the streets and there was looting, but far less than we had anticipated. Soon the *barbudos,* as Castro's bearded followers were called, arrived from Oriente and began to restore order. The rebel discipline and the conduct of the young veterans from the East greatly surprised the public. There was no drinking. The *barbudos* accepted only coffee and soft drinks, and they spoke with courtesy and quiet friendliness. They began taking over the police stations and army posts and the radio stations, which constantly called on the people to maintain order. Castro had sent his most impressive men to assume the command posts in Havana while he moved slowly westward through the island. All along the route he was wildly acclaimed, and when he arrived in Havana on January 8, 1959, his ovation was one of the greatest in Cuban history.

One of the peculiarities of Cuban political dynamics has always been that a new chief of state takes office on a wave of extreme jubilation, which soon fades into emotional opposition. Typical was the experience of Estrada Palma, Cuba's "George Washington," a man of irreproachable integrity. It curiously resembled that of Castro fifty-seven years later. When Estrada Palma returned from exile to Santiago in eastern Cuba in 1902, he was received with delirious manifestations. A New York *Tribune* correspondent who was with him wrote, "In my long life as a newspaperman, never have I witnessed a scene which moved me so deeply." In triumphal accompaniment of the people everywhere, he made his way west toward Havana, where tens of thousands came to join in the cheering that engulfed him.

[21] Ernesto "Che" Guevara, *Reminiscences of the Cuban Revolutionary War* (New York: Monthly Review Press, Inc., 1968), p. 253.

Four years later, facing open rebellion, Cuba's first president resigned.

Although some of my Cuban friends do not agree, I have felt that these dramatic shifts in popularity stem in large part from the circumstance that in Cuba government has been one of the largest employers in the country, especially of educated persons; the disillusionment of those who failed to get government jobs found hope in the emergence of a new leader. Since several people coveted each bureaucratic position, the "outs" during any administration greatly outnumbered the "ins" and were by definition anti-government. In 1958 Batista had held political power nearly seventeen years. By that time the "outs" outnumbered the "ins" by a tremendous margin.

One of my friends talked to Batista in the Dominican Republic in January 1959, a few days after he had been deposed by the United States. He said, "Mr. President, the last time I saw you was in Camagüey, two years ago. As you walked down the main street women held their children up above the crowd so they could see you. You were a god to the people. Some wanted only to touch you. What happened?" Batista answered, "What happened was that Castro won and I lost; now everyone is climbing on the bandwagon, as always happens with a change of government. It happened to me in 1940."

Thus in the early days of January 1959, as the rebels rode into Havana on tanks, jeeps, and trucks, they were greeted by hysterical crowds everywhere. A new era had dawned for Cuba, they felt, and the "outs" were now the "ins." The takeover proved to be much more orderly than we had anticipated, and our apprehension diminished considerably during the first days of the new regime.

On the afternoon of January 8, 1959, Ambassaor Smith called Dr. Cubas at our office (I was in the United States at the time), asking if Cubas would come over to see him. He wanted to know whether we felt he should resign as Ambassador to Cuba in view of the change of government.

Almost a year earlier Wieland had arranged a press conference for Smith at the State Department in Washington, without the Ambassador's approval. Smith had been asked, off the record, whether he thought the American Government would be able to do business with Castro. He had answered, specifying that it was off the record, that he did not believe the United States would ever be able to do business with Fidel Castro—he did not think that a Castro government would honor its international obligations. Within two days Castro and his followers in the mountains had received word that Ambassador Smith had stated he was a "Communist,"[22] and from that time on he had conducted a vitriolic campaign against the Ambassador, even accusing him of secret and corrupt dealings with Batista.

Castro and his followers, including ex-President Prío, charged that on one occasion Smith had made a deal with Batista, offering his support in exchange for tax exemptions in favor of an American company. This was a cruel lie. The fact was that my firm had obtained the tax exemptions as a matter of routine procedure under the "new industry" law, without Batista's knowledge and before Smith had even arrived in Cuba to assume his duties. Later, after Castro had come to power, when we began explaining these circumstances to President Prío in Havana, he interrupted to say the Castro people were entirely aware that the accusation was groundless. "We were using every weapon to discredit the Ambassador," he said, "because he was opposing Castro."

Such totally spurious attacks, repeated over and over again in varying forms, made it clear that Smith would be unable to deal with the new regime on cordial terms. My partner told him frankly that in his view this was the case, and Smith said he had reached the same conclusion, after consulting with his staff. He asked Dr. Cubas to so inform the new Prime Minister, Dr. José Miró Cardona, presumably to head off the possibility that the Castro regime might declare Smith *persona non grata* and ask for his recall.

[22] Smith, pp. 59-61.

Cubas put the matter up to the Prime Minister the following morning, but in a slightly different way. He suggested that if the new government felt it could deal more effectively with a new Ambassador, the matter could probably be arranged. The Prime Minister spoke by telephone with the new Minister of State, Dr. Roberto Agramonte, and then told Cubas that the resignation should come within twenty-four hours, as Agramonte intended to have him declared *persona non grata*.

Cubas went at once to the Embassy and found that the Ambassador had already put in motion the steps leading to his resignation, which was to be announced the following day at 5 P.M. The same afternoon my partner reported this development to the Prime Minister, urging him not to submit a request for a recall. The following morning, on January 9, Cubas met alone with Fidel Castro at the Havana Hilton Hotel, where Castro had spent the previous night. He explained the situation to Castro. The resignation would be announced within a few hours, and it would be a mistake, he suggested, for the new government to take any action at that time that would antagonize the United States.

Castro replied in these exact words: "Dr. Cubas, I am in complete agreement with you. Why should we take an unfriendly step when it is not necessary? Let Mr. Smith resign and let us have a new Ambassador; this will assure better relations between the two governments, and also we may eventually need economic assistance from the United States."

My partner said that he was gratified to hear Castro express himself in this way, but that he was concerned over the antagonism of the Foreign Minister, Dr. Agramonte. Castro said, "Don't worry about that at all, Dr. Cubas. Leave it in my hands." As they parted, Castro turned to a telephone, presumably to call the Foreign Office, and Cubas went down to the lobby and telephoned the Ambassador.

I relate this anecdote because of its possible historical significance. It may have been, of course, that Castro already had begun his career as the great dissembler, but at the time, in early January 1959, we believed that he had spoken sincerely and did not intend to break with the United States.

During the same interview, my partner had told Castro frankly that neither he nor I had done anything to assist his coming into power. Castro smiled. He was glad to hear someone tell the truth, he remarked, since he was constantly being given the impression that all Cubans had been members of the 26th of July Movement since its inception. "I know the reputation of your firm," he said, "and I will look to you for help in organizing the new government." Shortly thereafter, I received requests from various government ministries for the loan of lawyers from our staff, principally to go over personal files and eliminate "ghost" employees and grafters from government service. At one time or another, over a period of months, five of our lawyers served in this capacity.

Now that Castro was in power, Cubas and I discussed the situation at considerable length to establish our firm's policy. Ninety percent of our practice was of the corporate variety, which made it necessary that we have good relations with the heads of government departments. This was not in order to court favors to which our clients were not entitled, but simply to expedite the ordinary course of legal business, which at best can be a slow and tedious procedure. Cubans active in the professions or in other fields logically tried to keep on good terms with an existing administration, whether they liked it or not. Under a Communist regime this becomes a matter of self-preservation, even of survival. By late 1960 in Cuba there could be only one answer to the question, "Whose side are you on?"

In view of Castro's apparently reasonable attitude during the interview, particularly his request for our aid, it seemed possible to hope that we might in some degree influence his policies and encourage a friendly relationship with the United States. We knew of his participation in the Bogotazo but we had no positive proof that he was either a Communist or strongly pro-Communist. We did not as yet know that American intelligence reports had shown Castro to be a willing tool of Communist policy. The fact that he was a radical Leftist and strongly anti-American had been sufficient reason for us to oppose him. But now we reasoned that the State Department, with access to intelligence reports from all over the world, may have known what it was doing when it blocked other alternatives in order to bring this man to power.

Castro had issued several statements promising a sound economic policy combined with honest government and free elections; his takeover had been managed with little friction and almost no violence, and his followers thus far had made a fine impression by their earnestness and sobriety. In the flush of his victory, Castro created a favorable impression. His youth and seriousness, his splendid physique and remarkable eloquence, all appealed strongly to the romantic side of the Latin temperament. Cubas and I discounted his charismatic attraction but began to wonder whether possibly the judgment of Ambassador Smith had been too harsh. To the man in the street, who did not share our knowledge of Castro's anti-American attitude, he indeed appeared as a deliverer. Small wonder that acclaim for the new popular hero swept Cuba from end to end!

Meanwhile affairs were moving on the diplomatic front. Earl Smith had resigned as Ambassador. On the day before his departure from Cuba, Carmen and I invited him and his wife to dinner at our home. We invited also the United Press correspondent and his wife. We sat up until four o'clock in the morning discussing recent events. Florence Smith was extremely bitter over the attacks on her husband in both the Cuban and American press. I remember saying something to this effect: "Earl, if Castro turns out to be a Communist, this bitter experience of yours is a blessing in disguise. Your severest critics will be forced to admit that you are one of the few persons who correctly sized up the Communist threat to Cuba. If that occurs, the discredited ones will be the leftists, Matthews, Wieland, and Rubottom." On that note we parted.

Smith left Cuba on January 19, 1959, and with him went

the last hope of averting a Communist takeover. Herbert Matthews exulted in *The New York Times*.

Who was to blame?

Robert C. Hill, the former American Ambassador to Mexico, put the matter succinctly when he subsequently declared under oath, "Individuals in the State Department and individuals in *The New York Times* put Castro in power." [23]

A Senate Subcommittee investigated Wieland and State Department security in 1961–1962, and following the hearing some of its members believed they knew who was to blame. Senator Roman L. Hruska of Nebraska wrote: "The plain truth is that the U.S. State Department was the principal collaborator in creating the vacuum into which Fidel Castro stepped. . . . Our Ambassador, under instructions, told Batista the United States had lost confidence in him, and he had better go. Our hearing record has established . . . that there were those in the State Department who were favorable to Castro, who were suppressing or failing to pass on to their superiors intelligence showing Castro's Communist connections. Trading a non-Communist dictatorship for a Communist dictatorship is no bargain." [24]

Senator Kenneth B. Keating of New York said, "The facts . . . indicate that a breakdown in the process of transmitting vital intelligence to top State Department officials has contributed to serious errors in judging Castro's character and intentions. The unfortunate Cuban people are the victims of these tragic errors." [25]

Nevertheless, in an announcement on July 18, 1965—made

[23] Senate Subcommittee of the Committee on the Judiciary, *Communist Threat to the United States Through the Caribbean* (Washington, D. C.: Government Printing Office, June 12, 1961), Part 12, p. 821.

[24] Report of the Senate Subcommittee of the Committee on the Judiciary, *The Case of William Wieland*, 1962, p. 200.

[25] *Ibid.*, p. 202.

to coincide with the publication of the highly critical Senate Subcommittee report on Wieland—the State Department disclosed that it had cleared him and restored him to full duty. He was given the important post of Supervisory Consul General for Australia.[26]

Intervention *per se* is not necessarily, or even usually, an evil thing. At times non-intervention is the greater evil. Today non-intervention in Cuba means acceptance of unilateral Soviet intervention. It is indisputable that the United States cannot avoid involvement in the affairs of other nations. The great power which it wields by virtue of its prestige, wealth, and strength makes intervention necessary. When it gives economic aid it intervenes. When it withholds such aid, as in the case of the Cuban arms embargo, it also intervenes. The Alliance for Progress is a form of intervention. The question, therefore, is not whether it should or should not intervene *but whether a particular intervention is desirable.*

In 1958 the United States intervened in Cuba with unqualifiedly evil consequences, if not for an evil purpose. Negatively and indirectly at first, and then directly and brazenly, it intervened to bring to power the anti-American Castro, known to some in Washington as a terrorist under Communist influence.

It was the first, and unhappily not the last, of the American decisions for disaster in Cuba.

[26] *The New York Times,* July 19, 1965.

CHAPTER TWELVE

The First Castro Year

On January 1, 1959, the American people could not have known, and most of them still do not know, how Fidel Castro was catapulted to power. Very few Cubans even now are aware of the essential cause of their national affliction. This shroud of ignorance is due in part to the fact that diplomatic maneuvers are normally and properly made in secrecy. Little of what I have recounted in the preceding chapters was public information when it was taking place. Americans and Cubans alike saw the drama on the stage of events but not the plotting and pulling behind the scenes.

More than two years were to elapse before some of the key truths began to emerge, as a result of a U.S. Senate Internal Security Subcommittee investigation. Even when the veils of secrecy were finally penetrated, however, some of the forces behind the Castro takeover were blurred by deceit. Indeed, the Senators themselves were misinformed by the same State Department functionaries who had connived, however highmindedly, in bringing about the catastrophe.

Appearing before the Senate Subcommittee in 1961, William Wieland, who had held the important post of Director of Caribbean-Mexican Affairs, testified that as early as 1957 it had been his belief "that if Castro won he would be far worse than Batista for Cuba and dangerous to the United States." [1] *But the*

[1] Senate Subcommittee of the Committee on the Judiciary, *Testimony of William Wieland* (Washington, D. C.: U. S. Government Printing Office, 1962), Part 5, p. 553.

Senators were denied access to documents which would have disclosed this witness's actual official attitude toward Castro and the specific recommendations that he had made to his State Department superiors.[2] Wieland also swore that he did not realize that Castro controlled the government that had been installed on January 1, 1959. He had not realized it, he said, until six months later, when Castro "threw out" his puppet President Urrutia.[3] Such innocence on the part of a presumptive expert who had played a heavy role in clearing the road to power for Castro was, to say the least, most remarkable.

As the strange facts began to come to the surface, certain journalists anxiously compounded the confusion. In late 1961, for example, the redoubtable Herbert L. Matthews wrote that Rubottom and Wieland could not have prevented the triumph of Castro and that "their policies in 1957 and 1958 *favored Batista and hampered Castro.*" (Emphasis added.) It would be "an astonishing distortion of history to say the opposite," he still insisted.[4]

Castro did not begin to confiscate American-owned properties at once. In the beginning the new regime moved cautiously, feeling its way and testing American responses. No Cuban Chief of State had ever entertained the illusion that he could long hold power if he violently offended the United States, and Castro was too intelligent to entertain any such thought. Shortly after the takeover he made a conciliatory speech stressing that revolutionary reforms would be carried out *poco a poco,* in an evolutionary spirit. This assurance was welcomed by the business community and eagerly accepted by his champions in the American Embassy. Nevertheless, the first aspect of his ideology that came into sharp focus was not his pro-Communist proclivities but his anti-Americanism.

---

[2] The same Subcommittee, *The Case of William Wieland,* p. 150.
[3] *Ibid.,* p. 158.
[4] Herbert L. Matthews, *The Cuban Story* (New York: George Braziller, 1962), pp. 72, 73.

On January 15, only seven days after the triumphal entry into Havana, a reporter mentioned the criticism that the executions were evoking in the United States. Castro exploded in anger: "If the Americans don't like what is happening in Cuba, they can land the Marines and then there will be 200,000 dead gringos." [5] The derogatory word "gringo," used almost exclusively by Mexicans, had not until then been used in Cuba.

The Ambassador appointed to succeed Earl Smith was Philip W. Bonsal. He was, of course, fully aware of the manner in which Castro had been maneuvered into power. A polished career diplomat, tall and slender, soft-spoken and intelligent, he arrived in Havana on January 21. His father, Stephen Bonsal, had covered the Spanish-American War for the New York *Tribune* five years before Philip was born. Philip Bonsal had made a good record in Bolivia and Colombia, where he had been credited with having had a hand in removing the alleged dictator General Gustavo Rojas Pinilla. He spoke Spanish fluently. His first Foreign Service post had been in Havana, as Vice Consul, at which time we had become good friends. He has always been a sincere liberal.

Bonsal never consulted my partner or me on political matters during his twenty-one months in Cuba as Ambassador. This did not surprise us at first, since it conformed to the usual pattern. Upon arrival in Cuba, each new American Ambassador seeks to reverse or undo to some extent what his predecessor had done, if only as proof of his own capacity. Initially he seeks friends and advisers who have not been close to the man he succeeded. It is an understandable human trait, one with which I had long been familiar. Bonsal's tenure, however, marked the first instance in almost forty years when neither my partner nor I—though we represented a large segment of American interests in Cuba—ever entered the Ambassador's office. We were

[5] R. Hart Phillips, *The Cuban Dilemma* (New York: Ivan Obolensky, Inc., 1962), p. 28.

able to follow developments on the diplomatic front closely notwithstanding, through several intimate friends on the Embassy staff.

Sent to Cuba to implement a "soft approach" in line with the Washington commitment to the "democratic Left," Bonsal was by nature as well qualified as any American diplomat to attempt this. Had Castro been the kind of man the State Department wanted him to be, the mission would undoubtedly have been successful. The dictator, however, proved to be of an entirely different breed. Bonsal's failure certainly was not due to lack of zeal in applying that "soft approach." During the ensuing months he established a record for docility and patience as Castro heaped upon the United States indignities and insults as shocking as any suffered by a great power in modern times.

Castro did not even accord the new Ambassador an interview until he had been in Cuba about three months, and he received him only twice during the twenty-one months of his stay there. Eventually Bonsal was reduced to the humiliation of having to deal with a twenty-seven-year-old protocol officer of the Foreign Ministry. His extraordinary forbearance under conditions of extreme provocation should dispel for all time the fairy tale that Castro was "forced" into the Communist camp by an unfriendly attitude on the part of the United States. On the contrary, Bonsal's tolerance unquestionably emboldened Castro to move step by step toward the Left and eventually to line up openly with the Soviets. In early 1959 our office was in close touch with Castro. Our lawyers who had been lent to him to help "sanitize" government ministries, as he expressed it, reported to me that he at first expressed surprise, then astonishment, over the Embassy's indulgence. In due time it convinced him that he could disregard the American presence completely.

During the early months of 1959 a tide of violence swept over the island, directed principally against all who could conceivably be suspected of sympathy with Batista. Because he had been in power for seventeen of the preceding twenty-five years, many Cubans of consequence were tarred in some way by the Batista brush. We heard that Raúl Castro had ordered the execution of seventy-five prisoners in Oriente. He did not wait for his brother to set up even rudimentary procedures for a trial but stood the men up on the edge of a common grave, scooped out by a bulldozer, and had them shot into it with machine guns. It is commonly accepted that the slim, repulsive-looking, twenty-eight-year-old youth, with hawk-like face and hair worn in a pony tail, executed 250 people at Santiago de Cuba in the first few days. Raúl Castro has remained to this day one of the most sinister and hated figures of the Revolution.

I attended a number of trials in Havana and Matanzas. The spectacles filled me with horror. Once I observed that the death sentence had been tacked up even before the trial had ended. The occasional defense witnesses were examined amid loud insults and threats. We reasoned that the purpose of these executions was to terrify the population into acquiescence with the new order. I had never imagined that there could be such ruthlessness among Cubans. The arrests continued day after day, and no one knew when he too might be charged with a "crime." Some of those who witnessed the executions seemed to revel in bloodshed; sometimes at the moment of death there would be cheering and applause. The youths conducting these trials, many of whom were attempting beards, seemed to be convinced that they were doing what was right, but I was certain that the fear and hatred they engendered would some day return to plague Castro.

One of my intimate friends was Edward Scott, the Havana representative of National Broadcasting Company and a columnist for the *Havana Post*. He also attended the kangaroo trials, and now and then we lunched together and compared notes. He had found, as I did, that most of the prisoners died bravely; some had even given orders to the firing squad.

Ted Scott told me once of a young blond Cuban boy who was about to be executed. As the priest moved away and the squad prepared to fire, the prisoner told them that they were shooting an innocent man and that they would suffer for it. He spoke eloquently, saying that when they got home they might find that some of their family had been killed in an accident. When the order to fire was given only one bullet struck the prisoner. Captain Herman Marks, an American with a long criminal record, who supervised the executions at La Cabaña, stepped up and fired two .45-caliber bullets through the prisoner's head. Marks, called "The Butcher," then ordered the arrest of the entire firing squad. Ted told me that one of them could not have been over fifteen.

We learned of a group of Castro followers who cagily spread the rumor that seaworthy boats would leave from a point near our beach house in Varadero at appointed times for the Florida coast. When men and women arrived as instructed, clutching a few valuables and keepsakes, and having paid heavily for the boon of escaping, the women were arrested and the men shot.

This blood-letting shocked the world, but not enough, alas, to puncture "democratic Left" delusions in Washington. If Batista had dealt with the Castro brothers in the same manner that Castro was now dealing with his opponents, Cuba would have been spared its present agony. Let it be remembered that they had assaulted the Moncada Army Post. I received letters from American friends in high office asking me if there was anything I could do to stop the killings. There was nothing. Castro was rarely available, and suggestions from the outside only infuriated him.

During this period my partner and I were visited by black-mailers on several occasions. They charged that we had not paid taxes or duty on imports, but our official receipts and canceled checks were always available and we chose to ignore the extortionist threats.

The first incident that definitely turned a large part of the population against Castro was the trial of forty-three airmen in a revolutionary court in Santiago de Cuba. The accusation was that they had bombed rebel hideouts during the Revolution, but most of those who had engaged in these activities had already escaped from the island. The group on trial included transport pilots and mechanics who had made no effort to get out. Since the prosecutor was unable to find evidence against any of the defendants, they were acquitted.

Castro at once staged a hysterical and inflammatory television broadcast to denounce the acquittal. We gathered around the television set in my partner's office to see and hear him. He branded the three judges as "traitors," called the airmen "the worst criminals of the Batista regime," and accused them of "genocide," comparing their presumed offenses to the mass killings by the Hitler regime. Invoking the Nuremberg trials as a precedent, he declared that it was entirely proper, when legal grounds could not be found, to sentence "war criminals" on the basis of "moral conviction." He announced the appointment of his bearded Defense Minister, Augusto Martínez Sánchez, as the new prosecutor and ordered him to organize a "review" court. (Martínez Sánchez eventually shot himself; I do not know whether he survives.)

Both the Havana and the National Bar Associations protested against the lawless "review." One of the seven defense lawyers stated that "the servility of an entire people was converting Major Fidel Castro into a new and terrible Napoleon of the Caribbean." He was promptly jailed.

At the retrial, twenty-nine of the airmen were given prison terms of from twenty to thirty years at hard labor, twelve received terms of from two to six years, and two mechanics were released. One of the defense lawyers, who had made a particularly impassioned plea for his client, was imprisoned. Shortly after this second trial the presiding judge at the first trial, a twenty-eight-year-old rebel who had fought with Castro in the mountains, was found dead. The authorities claimed that it was a case of suicide.

Such was the background when Castro, in the fourth month of his reign, embarked on his memorable junket to the land of the "gringos." He was received as a hero. His exceptional gifts for play-acting were more than matched by American talents for self-deception. In retrospect it is all too clear that, with some honorable exceptions, the U.S. press and electronic media, the academic community, and officialdom were "taken" by the beguiling tyrant. They played up his promises of free elections and democracy to come; they avoided embarrassing questions about the deepening terror in his country; especially they slurred over his already venomous expressions of hatred for the United States.

When he spoke before the American Society of Newspaper Editors in Washington on April 15, 1959, it was a different Castro whom Americans saw, and naïvely credited, than the one known to intelligent Cubans. This was not the fulminating man of violence who ordered his opponents to the wall or to long terms in prison, but a charming if eccentric character whose friendship was worth cultivating. The editors were impressed and many of their papers sang his praises. The government demonstrated its esteem with a luncheon tendered by Secretary of State Christian A. Herter. At Harvard University Castro was greeted with a thunderous ovation and elsewhere, everywhere, he was loaded with evidences of good will unto adulation.

He tried to convince his audiences that neither he nor his government was Communist, that he wanted nothing but peace and friendship with his good neighbor to the north. Before leaving for the United States he had told his people on television that he was undertaking the trip in order to obtain credits through the World Bank and the Export-Import Bank of Washington. But now, curiously, he asked for nothing. Plans were being prepared by the appropriate U.S. agencies to extend financial aid, when suddenly Castro changed his mind. His advisers were instructed not to initiate negotiations for a loan. Americans in and out of government were surprised and baffled. They could not or would not guess that their lionized visitor had plans for helping himself to far more American wealth than he could have obtained legally.

A preview of what was to come in the way of hemispheric turbulence under the aegis of the new Cuban regime had been provided shortly before Castro's journey to the United States. A group of eighty-seven men, supplied with arms and a fifty-five-foot boat, set off from Cuba to spark a revolution in Panama. Castro denied that he personally had authorized this venture, and in this case he may have been telling the truth. Political exiles from other countries had swarmed into Cuba and "Che" Guevara took a keen personal interest in the pro-Communists among them. The abortive Panamanian expedition undoubtedly had his sponsorship.

A more ambitious project was launched by Castro himself a few weeks later, with the Dominican Republic as its target. The Communist 14th of June Movement, which supported Juan Bosch and has remained militantly active in Dominican politics, takes its name from this venture. By ship and plane 225 rebels landed in the northwestern section of the country. Before they could reach the mountains they were killed or captured by Trujillo's troops. The Dominican Republic complained to the United Nations, but little attention was paid to dictator Trujillo. Castro complained too. He charged Trujillo with an "indescribable violation of human rights."

Meanwhile a noteworthy diplomatic move was made which did not come to light until almost two years later. In April, American ambassadors to the countries in the Caribbean area and Central America met in conference at El Salvador to appraise the Castro problem. One of those present was the energetic and respected diplomat Robert C. Hill.[6] He had served as Ambassador to Mexico since July 1957 and previously as Ambassador to Costa Rica and El Salvador. He knew of Castro's arrest in Mexico in March 1956 and of his plan to "invade" Cuba from there. He also knew that Castro had passed out

[6] Former Ambassador Robert C. Hill has testified that the references to him in this chapter are accurate.

Communist literature in Bogotá in 1948 and that he was closely associated with Guevara, known as a Communist. From the very beginning, therefore, he believed that Castro was oriented toward Communism. His opinions were strongly influenced by intelligence reports that had come to the U.S. Embassy in Mexico.

Because of Mexico's proximity to Cuba, Hill was concerned that the Cuban problem might affect the relations between the United States and Mexico. Agents from Moscow and Red China were going back and forth between the Soviet Embassies in Mexico City and Cuba, and propaganda was flowing freely into Mexico from Cuba. Ambassador Hill had continually reported to Washington on these matters. He had brought the seriousness of the Castro-Communist threat to the attention of every Senator, Congressman, newspaperman, and person of importance who visited Mexico.

Hill was shocked by intelligence reports that the Soviets were amazed at the ease with which they were being permitted to penetrate Cuba. The mounting evidence of Communism in Cuba, he was convinced, should be submitted to the Organization of American States, which could then be convened to take action under the Caracas, Bogotá, and Rio treaties. If the OAS failed to take action, he felt that the United States should act unilaterally, imposing a complete air and sea embargo against Cuba.

The El Salvador meeting in April 1959 brought the liberal Bonsal into open conflict with the conservative Hill. Within five minutes after the conference opened a communiqué was submitted and the conferees were asked to approve it. It was couched in platitudes and recommended patience in dealing with Castro. Ambassador Hill strongly objected, insisting that under normal and correct procedure the communiqué should be considered at the end of the conference, not at its beginning. He took the position that continuing forbearance in dealing with Castro could lead only to disaster, pointing out that Castro had already destroyed the Cuban military forces and the country's bureaucracy. After a heated debate the communiqué was withdrawn. It was resubmitted at the end of the conference with stronger language, and approved over Bonsal's objections.

Hill had argued at the conference that the time to deal firmly with Castro had arrived. Bonsal's position was that the United States should go slowly, in spite of Castro's continuing attacks; that eventually he would see the light and return to the family of Latin American nations; *that Cuba had needed a revolution.* Hill argued that Communism never "sees the light" and that it would be a mistake to issue a communiqué whitewashing Castro. Bonsal, pleading that anything in the communiqué that cast a reflection on Castro would make his job in Cuba more difficult, wanted a statement geared to good will and evading the Communist issue. There were twelve persons present at the conference, including Rubottom and Wieland. Only one, Ambassador Willauer from Costa Rica, supported Hill.

Ambassador Hill has testified that after the El Salvador conference ended, Bonsal approached Ambassador Thomas E. Whelan at his hotel and expressed the hope that he would use his influence with the Republican National Committee to get rid of Hill. He also testified that Bonsal had advised him, "If you cannot be a team player, why not resign?" Hill replied that his resignation was a matter for the President and the Secretary of State.[7] Bonsal has denied to me that he attempted to get Hill fired, explaining that his remark to Hill "may" have been simply to the effect that an American Ambassador who disagrees with his government's policy to the point of expressing his disagreement publicly should resign.

The conference recommended, and two of the highest officials present (Deputy Under Secretary of State Loy Henderson and Assistant Secretary Rubottom) agreed, that all evidence of Communism in Cuba be submitted to the Secretary of State and then to the OAS for appropriate action. There is no

[7] Hearings before Senate Subcommittee of the Committee on the Judiciary, Part 12, 1961, p. 818.

evidence that these steps ever were taken. Ambassador Hill has written me that he believes that this action, which might still have saved Cuba, was torpedoed in the State Department. All that came from the El Salvador meeting was a reaffirmation of American determination to accommodate Castro.

Castro had talked a great deal about an Agrarian Reform Law, and it was published in May 1959. Far more radical than had been expected, it contained provisions clearly designed to strip Cuban and American sugar mills of their immensely valuable cane lands. It provided that no cane plantation could be operated by a stock company unless every stockholder was a Cuban. No foreigner could purchase or inherit Cuban farmland; no one could own more than 1,000 acres except cattlemen and cane planters, who were permitted to retain 3,333 acres.

Excess acreage would be subject to "expropriation," equivalent to eminent domain in the United States. Payment would be made with twenty-year government peso bonds, not convertible into dollars, carrying a 4 percent interest coupon. No such bonds ever were printed. Any farm, no matter how small, could be seized if the government considered it was not being "fully developed." Farmers would have to grow only the crops ordered by the Agrarian Reform Institute, over which Castro would preside, and deliver them at prices fixed by the Institute. The values which Castro announced would be assigned to cane lands for expropriation purposes after the 1960 harvest were approximately a fifth of their real value. Nevertheless, a *New York Times* editorial commented not unfavorably on the confiscatory measure, declaring that "an agrarian reform was overdue in Cuba." [8]

On June 11 the United States presented a note to Cuba conveying "concern" over the manner in which American property owners were to be compensated. Four days after receipt of the toothless legalistic communication, Castro bluntly and scorn-

[8] Phillips, p. 81.

fully rejected it, saying that Cuba would not accept any impairment of its "national sovereignty and dignity." [9]

As if in contemptuous response to the American note, a massive confiscation of cattle lands was immediately begun. For more than two decades Cuba had been self-sufficient in meat, dairy, and poultry products, and it had become an exporter of beef because it possessed natural advantages for cattle raising, including pastures of good native grasses available throughout the year. By 1958 new blood lines had been imported and crossed with native criollo breeds; the quality of beef was excellent, and the price was low, ranging from twenty to forty-five cents a pound. Now this superb industry—livestock was the country's second most important source of agricultural income—was to be stolen and largely destroyed. Although only an insignificant part of the cattle industry was American owned, the experience of these few ranches was typical.

The 3,333-acre area to which the Agrarian Reform Law had restricted these properties was about one-sixteenth the size of the American-owned Pingree Ranch in Oriente Province and one-ninth that owned in part by the King Ranch of Texas in Camagüey Province. These two ranches, valued at close to $10 million, had 22,000 head of cattle.

The Pingree Ranch employed a large force of Cuban cowboys who received eighty-five dollars a month with food, a house, a garden, and equipment. These men were informed by government agents that the ranch would become a "cooperative" and that they would be members, sharing in the profits. Instead it was turned into a state farm; all salaries were reduced and the fringe benefits eliminated. One of my Cuban friends told me he had cried when the soldiers, in seizing his property, slaughtered a twenty-thousand-dollar breeding bull for a barbecue.

During the summer of 1959, ranches comprising an area of

[9] *Ibid.,* p. 85.

about two and a half million acres were taken over. Ranch owners who did not willingly relinquish their property were arrested as "counter-revolutionaries." Seldom were inventories prepared or receipts given to the victims.

Soon the peasantry would fight with the best weapon at its disposal: growing no more than it needed for itself. The flow of meat, fowl, and other foodstuffs from the countryside to cities and towns would slow down with each passing month. Long and dreary queues, chiefly of women, would stretch from shop doors, waiting for food. Eventually this in turn would oblige the government to exert more vigorous pressures on the peasants.

At the same time Castro was moving ahead with his revolutionary "reforms" on other fronts. Under labor laws adopted more than twenty years earlier the President had been authorized to "intervene" a business ("temporarily" supersede its management) in order to enforce rulings of the Labor Ministry. Many such "interventions" had been ordered during the inflationary period of World War II, when employers had refused to grant wage increases ordered by the government. The practice had fallen into disuse, however, during the closing years of the Batista administration. In early 1959 Castro revived it with a vengeance, with the difference that *labor disorders were intentionally provoked by the regime* and that once an "intervention" was ordered, *property owners never regained management control.*

This device was used also to expropriate newspaper and other communications media as a means of silencing opposition. The most blatant use of the intervention procedure was against the hundred-year-old *Diario de la Marina,* looked upon by many as the unofficial voice of the Catholic Church. Its courageous editor, José Ignacio Rivero, was outspokenly critical of the new order. This maddened Castro, who cannot stand criticism. To make matters worse, the public was reacting favorably to the *Marina's* stand. Congratulatory messages poured in to the paper, and thousands of new subscriptions were taken out.

At first Castro was fearful of closing down the influential newspaper, but when he learned that Rivero was planning to call for free elections, he moved in. Officials representing the government and the unions showed up at the plant and demanded that the call for elections not be published. When the editors refused, the plant was "intervened," seized forcibly by the regime. This signaled the beginning of the end of freedom of the press in Cuba. A few days later another newspaper, *Prensa Libre,* that had also dared to criticize the new masters was taken over by armed militiamen. From that time onward, Cubans have been fed a constant diet of propaganda.

Several of our clients who had always enjoyed excellent labor relations, including some who had recently negotiated long-term agreements with their unions, were suddenly confronted with wholly unrealistic labor demands, inspired by fanatical Castro agitators aiming at "intervention." Our staff worked hard and late to recapture the lost properties, but our efforts proved hopeless. Arbitrary decisions had superseded all law, including Castro's own supposed laws. When American companies were involved, Embassy staff members had at first cooperated, but without result. As time passed our American clients came to regard Embassy assistance as more harmful than helpful and dispensed with it. For the first time a Cuban government began treating American Embassy officials with demonstrative contempt.

It was in this manner that a number of important businesses and industries passed to government control. An early victim was the Cuban Telephone Company, which was intervened on May 3, 1959. Soon, however, the transparent mask of legality was discarded and the regime began seizing properties at random.

During these early months Castro, hypersensitive to criticism of any sort, appeared to be outraged whenever charges of

Communism were made. He even clashed with the Catholic Church because it dared to charge that his regime was moving toward Communism. But most of the government crises during 1959 were provoked by this issue.

On June 30 another case of this sort developed when the Chief of the Air Force, Major Pedro Díaz Lanz, wrote a letter to President Urrutia charging that Communist elements were carrying out a program of indoctrination in officers' training schools, as indeed they were. He then resigned, defected, and reached Miami in a small boat with his wife. This was a heavy blow to Castro. Major Díaz Lanz had fought with the rebels, transported arms to Castro, and been Castro's personal pilot. To make matters worse from Castro's standpoint, Díaz Lanz turned up on July 14 at a public hearing before the Senate Internal Security Subcommittee; he charged, with supporting evidence, that Castro was a willing tool of international Communism.

The reaction to this development provides an interesting study. Castro, predictably, called Díaz Lanz a traitor, Cuba's Benedict Arnold, and excoriated the Senate Subcommittee for interfering in Cuban affairs. President Eisenhower took an equivocal position when, at a press conference the day after the hearing, he was asked to comment on the charge made by Díaz Lanz. "Now such things are charged," said the President, "and they are not always easy to prove, and the United States has made no such charges." [10]

Most interesting, and perhaps equally predictable, was the manner in which the episode was covered by the free liberal press of the United States. It provides a classic example of how its liberalism often undercuts the responsibility that should accompany its enjoyment of freedom.

Matthews came through with a dispatch from Havana on July 16, prominently featured by *The New York Times*. "This is not a Communist revolution in any sense of the word and

[10] Press conference, July 15, 1959.

there are no Communists in positions of control," he wrote. "The accusations of Major Pedro Díaz Lanz are rejected by virtually all Cubans. It is stated here that before his resignation Major Díaz was removed from high office for incompetence, extravagance and nepotism. . . . Castro is not only not a Communist but *decidedly anti-Communist.*" (Italics added.) His paper followed this up the next day with an editorial complimenting President Eisenhower for declaring that the United States had made no charges against Castro, a fact that it had also pointed out in an editor's note to the Matthews article. Other newspapers presented similar editorials commending the President.

Walter Lippmann, the widely syndicated liberal columnist, joined in the chorus of attack on Díaz Lanz. He underlined the importance of having in Cuba an Ambassador who was in total sympathy with the revolution, but warned that Bonsal would have no chance of succeeding "if Congress is going to rough-house our relations with Cuba" by providing "a platform and loudspeaker for a disaffected Cuban adventurer to denounce the Cuban revolutionists as Communists." [11] Another liberal pundit, Ralph McGill, who was in Cuba at the time, went even further. Like Matthews, he smeared Díaz Lanz, portraying him as a disgruntled soldier-of-fortune who had flown arms in for Castro in the earlier days and had later been involved in "clandestine money-making activities." [12] Other newspapers, among them the *Washington Post*,[13] joined the campaign against the man who had risked his life to warn the American people—with absolute accuracy, as it turned out—of what was to come. The result was that Díaz Lanz's disclosures were rendered valueless.

Outside of the South the editorial columns, and in many cases the news dispatches, of the immense majority of the

[11] Walter Lippmann in the New York *Herald Tribune*, July 23, 1959.
[12] Ralph McGill, editor of the *Atlanta Constitution,* in his column of July 7, 1959.
[13] *Washington Post* editorial of July 16, 1959.

daily newspapers are colored by liberal ideology. Everyone knows that the champions in this respect are the *Washington Post* and *The New York Times*. Even in the South there are the *Atlanta Constitution* and the *Miami Herald*. Few indeed were the American newspapers that permitted their readers intelligently to assess the approaching Communist menace in Cuba. One, to its enduring credit, was the Charleston (S.C.) *News and Courier*.

This is not a case of hindsight revealing belated wisdom. It is a factual account of how the influential liberal segment of the American press handled the first authentic disclosure of Communist penetration in nearby Cuba.

On the very day that the Matthews dispatch attacking Díaz Lanz was published, July 16, Castro turned on Urrutia, the man he had named as provisional President of the Republic. His maneuver had all the earmarks of demagoguery and deceit. He first resigned as Premier and then went on television to denounce the President as a traitor. Urrutia was a colorless but honest conservative provincial judge. He had shown no enthusiasm for new laws imposing the death penalty or for the recently promulgated radical Agrarian Reform Law, and had thus incurred Castro's wrath. As Castro continued his hours-long television performance, crowds gathered outside the Palace shouting, "Down with Urrutia!" The President resigned even before Castro finished speaking, and the "Supreme Chief" then graciously rescinded his own phony resignation. Subsequently Urrutia took refuge in the Argentine Embassy and eventually escaped to the United States. The Presidency was filled by Osvaldo Dorticós Torrado, a Communist.

Matthews of the *Times* came through with a typical explanation for Castro's bizarre performance. The day after the tragicomedy of the "resignation," he claimed that it had been prompted, not by troubles inside Cuba, but *by resentment of American criticism*. "The attacks on him [Castro] in the United States had wounded and injured him," he wrote. The ink on the dispatch was hardly dry when Castro demolished its inverted logic by declaring that he had tried to give up the Premiership because of his quarrel with the President and because Urrutia had spoken unkindly of the Communists. The *Times* withdrew the Matthews analysis from its late edition.

With Dorticós installed, the campaign of hatred against the United States assumed ever larger dimensions. On July 26 Castro called the U.S. "the sworn enemy of all Latin American countries and of the progress of all peoples of the world." [14] A month later he shouted on television that "Cuba is today facing United States imperialism, the rapacious and exploiting imperialism, the bloody and voracious imperialism, which here has lost some of its rapacious claws." [15] No matter how rabid his anti-American tirades, however, there was no dearth of "understanding" Americans in the United States to explain and justify them.

In July, in the face of a mounting depression, income and excise taxes were increased exorbitantly, sales taxes of 20 percent were imposed on such commodities as refrigerators and radios, 30 percent on automobiles costing more than $3,000. In September customs duties were raised from thirty percent to 100 percent, cutting off such American imports as household appliances and automobiles.

The Minister of Finance, Rufo López-Fresquet, had been an active Castro collaborator since 1956. In the autumn of 1958 he had been largely responsible for extorting a million dollars in "war taxes" for Castro in the eastern provinces from producers of sugar, coffee, and other products, as insurance against rebel interference with their businesses. Regarding himself as an "economist," Minister López-Fresquet became a friend of Matthews, Bonsal, and members of what was soon known as the "Castro cell" in the American Embassy. When

14 Phillips, p. 239.
15 *Ibid.*, p. 246.

he resigned thirteen months later, feigning illness, he gave an account of an episode involving me which was almost wholly erroneous and to which I shall refer later in its proper context.

In August 1959, when Castro's wild anti-Americanism and pro-Communist leanings were clearly apparent, an incident involving Dr. Milton Eisenhower took place that in the light of later events appears almost incredible.

The President's brother had just returned from a journey to Soviet Russia with Vice-President Nixon. Tired and wanting several days of rest, he made another of his several trips to Mexico as a guest of the Mexican Government. In Mexico City he stayed with Ambassador Hill,[16] as his house guest. Dr. Eisenhower, who did not speak Spanish, was joined by Wieland, billed as his adviser. Soon after his arrival, Ambassador Hill inquired whether Dr. Eisenhower would be willing to have senior officers of the Embassy brief him on the Embassy's information regarding the Castro-Communist threat in Cuba, and his guest readily agreed. To Hill it seemed a rare opportunity to get his message to the President of the United States, since Milton Eisenhower was still acting as his brother's adviser on Latin American affairs.

The briefing took place in the C-47 plane of the Embassy's Air Attaché, on the way to Mazatlan. Among those present was Raymond F. Leddy, the political affairs counselor of the Embassy, a former official of the FBI and the CIA, and generally regarded as one of the best-informed men in the State Department on Latin America. He had lived as a Foreign Service officer in Cuba, where he had gained an intimate knowledge of the situation there. The Ambassador asked Leddy to prepare his documentation carefully for the briefing. Among his papers Leddy had a reference to dispatch No. 666, dated May 22, 1959, from the American Embassy in Moscow to the

[16] Hearings before the Senate Subcommittee of the Committee on the Judiciary, Part 12, 1961, p. 797.

State Department, identifying Raúl Castro as a Communist. A member of the Embassy staff in Moscow had worked his way into a lecture and had heard the Soviet speaker say that Raúl Castro was "one of us"—a Communist.

The plane was furnished with a divan, with bucket seats at either end. Leddy sat on the divan with Dr. Eisenhower on one side and Wieland on the other. During the briefing, whenever Leddy said, "This Cuban organization is Communist-dominated," or "This Cuban official is a Communist," Wieland would interrupt with, "It is not true!" [17]

Ambassador Hill had been warned by Foreign Service officers that Wieland was not to be trusted on the Cuban issue, and that he (Hill) should be very careful in dealing with him. Annoyed at the interruptions, he finally turned impatiently to Wieland. "I do not recall asking you to be in on this conversation," he said. "Dr. Eisenhower has agreed to listen to a man of integrity and experience in Latin American. What Mr. Leddy is discussing at the moment comes from the joint intelligence report of June 1959 regarding Communist infiltration in Cuba."

The report bore out many of Leddy's contentions. It was obvious to the group that Wieland had not read it; nevertheless he argued that he saw all intelligence reports, and that only a part of them reached Mexico. He knew Castro personally, he declared, and attested that the man was an idealist. "There is no evidence of Communist infiltration in Cuba," he repeated.

After a time Colonel Benoid Glawe, the Air Attaché, came back from the cockpit and joined in the discussion, supporting Leddy's and the Ambassador's point of view. As Leddy was drawing a report from his briefcase, Col. Glawe, provoked by Wieland's continuing opposition, said to him, "You are either a damn fool or a Communist." Tempers flared, whereupon Dr. Eisenhower terminated the briefing, saying he wanted to hear no more about it. Interestingly, this had been a clash between three conservatives on the one hand and the left-wing, liberal

[17] *Ibid.*, p. 798.

Wieland on the other. Dr. Eisenhower, himself a liberal, had failed to reprimand Wieland for his heckling at the briefing.

Wieland had been alone in defending Castro in the plane. He had disagreed, unasked, with every important point raised by Leddy. Subsequently, four witnesses before a Senate Subcommittee vividly recalled under oath the details of the confrontation in the skies over Mexico. It seemed hardly the kind of heated scene that any of its participants would fail to remember. Yet Wieland at first swore that he had no recollection of the whole affair.[18]

A footnote to that lapse of memory was provided by later developments. Early in 1962 Wieland was one of two State Department officials whom President Kennedy defended when they were called possible security risks. The evaluating officer who handled the security study on Wieland and reached an unfavorable conclusion was the Deputy Director of the Office of Security in the State Department, Otto F. Otepka. Asked under oath by the Senate Subcommittee on Security whether he accepted as credible Wieland's claim that he did not recall the discussion in the airplane, Otepka replied: "I think Wieland lied." [19] But Deputy Secretary of State Roger W. Jones testified that he had appraised the "apparent discrepancy" between Wieland's testimony and that of the four other witnesses and had decided the facts in favor of Wieland.[20]

By now, the "Otepka case" having become a *cause célèbre,* it is general knowledge that this official's rigid standards in evaluating security problems was not appreciated by some of his superiors and associates. Wieland was only one of a number of men whose clearance he had attempted to block. His insistence on carrying out his duties as prescribed by official regulations, even when apparent administration favorites were involved, led to his notorious subjection to harassments.

[18] Report of Senate Subcommittee of the Committee on the Judiciary, *The Case of William Wieland,* 1962, p. 124.

[19] *Ibid.,* p. 19.

[20] *Ibid.,* p. 128.

Otepka's telephone was bugged and his office ransacked. Manufactured "evidence" to discredit him was planted in his wastebasket. Several of those engaged in the effort to discredit him perjured themselves before the Subcommittee.[21] Although he had served for nine years and received only highly favorable performance ratings, he was stripped of his security functions and kept on the payroll without meaningful duties while charges against him were supposedly being investigated, year after year. In the end most of the charges were dropped without explanation, but Otepka was rebuked and demoted in rank and pay.[22]

As to Wieland, a three-man interagency panel was appointed to review his case. State Department officials had said that he had at no time been suspended during his review. The panel, however, recommended that Wieland be "restored" to full status as an active senior Foreign Service officer. A Department spokesman was unable to define what lesser degree of status had been implied by the panel's decision that he be "restored" to full status.[23]

In any event the State Department accepted the recommendation of the advisory panel in January 1965, which completely cleared Wieland and closed his case. But the Department's announcement on the decision was deferred until July 18, to coincide with the publication of the highly critical report on Wieland by the Senate Subcommittee.

The State Department verdict against Otepka, signed by Secretary of State Dean Rusk, had been handed to Otepka on December 11, 1967. It directed that he be "severely reprimanded," that his salary be cut by more than $5,000 (about 25%), and that he be assigned to duties which did not involve "security" functions. It was not until eighteen months later, after the election of President Nixon, that Otepka was vindicated. On the recommendation of Senator Everett Dirkson, the President appointed him to the Subversive Activities Control Board (SACB)

21 *National Review Bulletin,* February 20, 1968, p. B30.
22 *The New York Times,* December 13, 1967.
23 *The New York Times,* July 19, 1965.

and, in spite of the strong opposition of Senator Edward Kennedy and *The New York Times,* the Senate confirmed the appointment by a 61-to-28 vote on June 24, 1969.

A final word before dismissing Wieland. In the fall of 1969 a powerful and brilliant book titled *The Ordeal of Otto Otepka,* written by the respected author and journalist William J. Gill, was published. It confirms the references to Otepka which appeared in the first three editions of this book and it adds the following interesting anecdote with respect to Wieland. According to Mr. Gill, Wieland had told Otepka under oath that he had met Fidel Castro only once in his entire life. This had been a very casual meeting, Wieland had said, at a luncheon tendered by former Secretary of State Herter to Castro during the latter's visit to Washington in April 1959, at which thirty other guests were present. But a few weeks after President Kennedy's public defense of Wieland, Otepka happened to spot a newspaper photograph showing Wieland chatting amiably with Castro, so he put his men on the trail. They quickly verified that the picture had been taken at the National Press Club four days *after* Secretary Herter's luncheon. Before the security men finished their investigation they discovered that Wieland had been with Castro at least six times during the latter's brief sojourn in Washington. On one of these occasions, at the Cuban Embassy on April 17, 1959, Castro had been observed slipping off into a private room with his arm wrapped affectionately around Wieland's shoulder. They remained in the room, just the two of them, for more than an hour.

On the basis of this information Otepka recommended to his superiors in the State Department that the Wieland case be reopened but nothing was done and he was sent off to Australia as Consul General.

But let us return to Havana. During the first Castro year men on the American Embassy staff who remained sympathetic to the Cuban leader became known, as I have said, as the

Embassy "Castro cell," although I never heard anyone imply that there were Communists among them. At first they had drawn comfort from the fact that most of those being dispossessed of their property were Cubans—that the expropriations were not directed *exclusively* against Americans. Officials in Washington and in the Embassy who had supported the revolution now had a psychological stake in justifying their mistake. The "agrarian reformer" label became too silly to stick, but they continued doggedly to regard the new dictator as nothing more than a "nationalist." Notwithstanding all that had happened, including the massive blood-letting, they still believed that the policy that would bring the best results, both in Cuba and the rest of Latin America, was one of tolerant "understanding." The leader of this Embassy group was Ambassador Bonsal. Holding a contrary view were a growing number of Embassy officers, headed by Minister Counselor Daniel M. Braddock, the No. 2 man on the staff.

The pro-Castro liberals and anti-Castro conservatives in the Embassy were equally patriotic and intelligent. They were having the same experiences, witnessing the same events, reading the same reports, talking to the same people, and yet they often emerged with diametrically opposite impressions of what was taking place. For the more dedicated liberals the contrast went further than differing interpretations of the same physical facts. Often the facts themselves faded from their field of vision; their minds selected only the impressions which harmonized with their doctrinaire opinions. With the validity of their ideologies at stake, they seemed to shrink from realities and seek refuge in illusory rationalizations. In view of the increasingly evident Communist penetration, a few were beginning to have doubts as to whether their country was pursuing the right policy, but Bonsal was not among these. Most of them still rated Castro as a well-intentioned "nationalist" for whom allowances should be made. One of them referred to Castro as "an inspired patriot."

An ideology involves such a strong commitment to a doctrine

that when reality conflicts with the doctrine it is reality which gives way. Communism involves a total commitment, liberalism is looser. But during 1959 I began to realize that arguing with a confirmed, convinced liberal was as futile as arguing with the many Communists with whom I was dealing. The more sincere he was, the less accessible to facts and reason. Sometimes, it seemed, these Americans actually were swallowing uncritically Castro's fantastic propaganda—including his brutal attacks on their own country. But the Embassy mood was slowly changing. Before the end of 1959 every senior officer had lined up behind Braddock. Fewer and fewer members of the Embassy staff supported Bonsal, who nevertheless clung to his convictions.

On October 3, 1959, government agents swooped down on the Havana offices of the principal oil companies and stole their geology files. Over a period of fourteen years the largest of these—Esso, Standard of California, and Atlantic Refining, all clients of our firm—had invested many millions in search of oil and had drilled a number of deep wells. Although no oil had as yet been found in commercial quantity, the companies had budgeted extensive future programs.

The Castro regime falsely asserted that American companies had discovered large petroleum deposits but had capped their wells, depriving Cuba of an oil-producing industry. Simultaneously, the public utility companies were hit by rate reductions which made profitable operations impossible. And finally, in spite of the deteriorating economy, a labor edict prohibited employers from dismissing workers under any circumstances. These measures destroyed important segments of the Cuban economy.

The attitude of the State Department to all these radical and alarming actions was explained by *The New York Times* on October 24, 1959. "There is no inclination to exert any pressure upon Dr. Castro," it said. "The Department wants to maintain a dignified, big power approach without pressure."

A day later Castro repaid that complacency with another

sharp attack on the United States. Before a large gathering at the Presidential Palace he accused the United States of permitting planes to "take off from its territory to bomb the defenseless population of Havana." It was attempting, he said, to spread terror among the Cuban people "with inhuman, inconceivable fury." Two days later Ambassador Bonsal called on Castro's puppet president to express "deep concern" over the hostility with which the regime was replacing the traditional friendship between the two countries. The President brushed off the complaint, saying that the Ambassador's statement had no foundation.[24]

Another Castro outburst made headlines on October 21, and here again, as in the case of Major Díaz Lanz, the issue was Communism. One of the popular leaders of the rebel forces was Major Hubert Matos. Before joining the Castro movement he had been a school teacher and chaplain of the Masonic Lodge in Santiago. When Castro took over, Matos was named military commander of Camagüey Province. Deeply worried over the Communist infiltration of government, particularly in the armed forces, Matos spoke to Castro about it, supposing that his leader was ignorant of the situation. Later he wrote to Castro in the same vein and with the letter submitted his resignation.

Castro's response was to accuse Matos of being a traitor who was trying to start a new revolution. He falsely linked him to Urrutia and Díaz Lanz in a conspiracy. There had been no conspiracy—Matos simply did not like what he saw happening. Thirty-four of the officers under Matos' command declared their support of his position, but he urged them not to resign. All were arrested along with Major Matos and eventually were tried as counter-revolutionary traitors.

Castro appeared as the principal witness against them. He gave a seven-hour speech, which he arranged to have broadcast

[24] Phillips, p. 120.

by television and radio throughout the island. With a microphone around his neck, and turning his back on the "judges," he harangued the prisoners, witnesses, and audience in the motion picture theater where the trial was being staged. Calling Matos a conspirator and a coward, he admitted that there had been Communists in the rebel army but said that they had fought well and that he saw no reason to expel them now. Major Matos proclaimed his innocence and declared that the testimony of Castro and other witnesses against him was false. He was sentenced to twenty years' imprisonment; most of the other officers drew sentences of two to seven years.

Again the Cuban people were shocked by this action. During the trial, when long-distance calls were made in Havana, the operator would often say, "Matos is *not* a traitor." The only person who attempted to rationalize Castro's vindictive treatment of Matos, as far as I am aware, was Herbert Matthews, who wrote: "By the logic of the Revolution, Hubert Matos was a traitor. Those who condemn the . . . way he was treated had to condemn the Revolution." He admitted that Matos was convicted because he "had watched the growing strength of Communism in the Army with alarm," but explained it as in accord with "the logic of the Revolution." [25]

Not long after this Castro removed two cabinet ministers who had refused to go along with the arrest of Matos. In November he provided proof that Matos' fears had been justified by two other actions. He intervened personally to save the Communists from defeat at a trade union congress, and he named "Che" Guevara, an avowed Communist, to be president of the National Bank.

As Castro ended his first year in power, fear and despair were spreading throughout the island. Patriots who clung to their democratic ideas were being brought, already judged, before the Revolutionary Courts, an institution always actuated by ven-

[25] Matthews, p. 155.

geance. The firing squads were again busy. More than twice as many people had been killed in a single year than during the seventeen years Batista had held power, and thousands had been imprisoned. The educational institutions, from kindergarten up, were being converted into Communist indoctrination centers.

The high hopes generated at the outset had evaporated. In the early months Castro had made a few statements critical of Communism that many of us found it hard to believe any secret Communist would make publicly. But in the later months all indications were that he was veering toward Communism. Those of our lawyers who had worked for him at the start had become disenchanted and returned to us by April. We had had no contact with Castro since August. That was the month when, for the purpose of testing the regime's intentions, I wrote to a prominent American friend criticizing an anti-Castro magazine article and emphasizing the more hopeful aspects of the Cuban scene that should bring progress and peace to the island. The plan was to have a Cuban friend show Castro a translation and observe his reaction. Castro read it carefully, and turned away scornfully without comment. As a result we concluded that the outlook was indeed dark, that probably ruinous decisions had already been taken behind the scenes which would be put on display in 1960. It had been a tongue-in-cheek letter but had served its purpose.

Ambassador Bonsal, once a good friend, had become a virtual stranger. When I ran into him occasionally, I dealt with him as such, answering any questions with the implication that we supported the dictator.

Bonsal's public response to Castro's scurrilous attacks against the United States had always been gentle. Clear indications of Communist encroachment in the regime were either ignored or discounted. He searched for passages in written or spoken attacks which could be interpreted as encouraging. When members of his staff drafted statements answering vicious charges against the United States or its Embassy, he invariably found them too vigorous. They were rewritten in more innocuous language, so as not to give offense.[26] His attitude remained consistently one of out-and-out accommodation.

Bonsal's stance discouraged opposition leaders, who traditionally took their cue from the American Embassy. Nevertheless, underground groups were forming and by the end of 1959 were engaging in sabotage, bombings, and other anti-regime activities that surpassed in scope anything any earlier Chief of State had faced.

We had a premonition that 1960 would be a black year, but we could not conceivably imagine the catastrophic events that would overwhelm us during the next sixteen months.

[26] Paul D. Bethel, Press Attaché on the Embassy staff, has authorized these statements.

CHAPTER THIRTEEN

Castro's Second Year

The growing breach between the United States and Cuba was a source of constant and increasing concern to Dr. Cubas and myself. It occurred to us that perhaps Mrs. Eleanor Roosevelt might be instrumental in helping to heal the breach. I had met her a few years before through her son Elliott, who had lived in Cuba in the early 1950s. If she could be persuaded to visit the island, perhaps to address the American Club, she could stay at my home, and I would arrange to have Castro call on her there.

Castro's line at this time was that he and his regime had nothing against the American people, only against the government. He contended that once an American assumed public office he became a lackey of the "monopolies" and of "Wall Street." Surely, we thought, Mrs. Roosevelt could enlighten him on the fallacies of this childish concept. The possibility, as we discussed it, appeared hopeful enough to justify my going to New York on this mission.

Through Elliott's ready intercession, I met there with his mother. She was gracious as always. Why, she inquired, did I think that she, better than anyone else, could accomplish the purpose I had in mind? I explained that Castro was an egomaniac, devoid of humility, and that in the normal interview he seldom permitted anyone else to do any talking. In her case, because she was a great lady, a fighter for social justice, and the widow of an American President, I felt sure that he would do some listening.

To my distress, our conversation quickly disclosed that Mrs. Roosevelt held the standard, propaganda-fed, distorted idea of conditions in Cuba. She thought that the Cubans had been living for many years in poverty, hunger, and wretchedness, and that this had produced the Communist threat.

That view seemed to me so primitive that I sought to disabuse her. I explained that, contrary to her assumptions, the island had enjoyed one of the highest living standards in the hemisphere. Cuban Communist leaders themselves recognized that poverty is not the deciding factor in the equation of revolution. If it were, the movement would be stronger in at least seventeen countries of Latin America than in Cuba. It would be stronger in Turkey than in Italy, in Saudi Arabia than in Greece. There would be potent Communist movements in Spain and Ireland, both exceedingly poor nations. France, I pointed out, had one of the largest Communist Parties in the world despite its economic prosperity. In short, I argued that Communism is a conspiratorial movement, not a reflex to poverty, and that its leaders *prefer* to take over a relatively wealthy and prospering country like Cuba.

Mrs. Roosevelt remained unconvinced. Perhaps what Cuba really needed, she said at one point, was a "socialist" regime, which Castro might provide. She did not, of course, use the word "socialist" in the same sense as it is used by Communists, to whom it means state ownership and totalitarian control of all human activities, the economy, the press, education, thought, everything. To her presumably it meant what it did to moderate Social-Democratic and Labor Parties in the free world: Government ownership of the principal means of production, if the people so determined in a free election.

Mrs. Roosevelt's false and stubbornly held assumptions about conditions in Cuba and her feeling that the country needed socialism frightened me. Before she came to a decision, which fortunately was negative, I realized that her meeting with Castro would defeat the purpose of restraining him *vis-à-vis* the United States. It was easy to see how he could exploit her naïve political ideas, distorting them for his propaganda through his controlled press and on television.

The experience is worth recounting because, while Mrs. Roosevelt spoke only for herself, she reflected the sentiments of the vastly influential "liberal" community in her country. It helps explain Castro's reckless arrogance in dealing with American rights and interests. He knew that he could count on the wishful-thinking complacency, and even know-nothing support, of powerful segments of the U.S. press and society.

Soon after the start of Castro's second year, on January 10, 1960, Ambassador Bonsal delivered a note to the Cuban Government protesting the confiscation of American-owned property. The U.S. press described it as a strong note. In truth it was weak, and Castro blandly ignored it. On national television ten days later he accused the American Embassy of supporting counter-revolutionary activities![1] That was his oblique answer.

By this time Castro anti-American propaganda was flooding not only Cuba but all of Latin America. To implement this major and always expanding enterprise, Castro established a news and wire service called *Prensa Latina,* which not only supplied all Cuban newspapers but had outlets throughout Latin America. It established bureaus in Washington and New York. Its output was keyed in with the international Communist propaganda network. Tass (the Soviet news agency) and other press agencies behind the Iron Curtain picked up material from *Prensa Latina,* and PL disseminated propaganda from the Communist countries.

Soon thereafter Castro set up another propaganda apparatus, called Imprenta Nacional, a government printing house that turned out immense quantities of books, pamphlets, posters,

[1] R. Hart Phillips, *The Cuban Dilemma* (New York: Ivan Obolensky, Inc., 1962), pp. 145-147.

magazines, etc. Demonstrating that its motivation was not simply "nationalistic," it employed its channels to circulate books and other printed matter from the Soviet Union, Red China, and other Communist sources. One of its offerings was Mao Tse-tung's famous "thoughts" pamphlet; another was "Che" Guevara's treatise on guerrilla warfare.

Nevertheless, Castro could have been easily toppled at the start of 1960 if American diplomats and opinion-makers had not persisted in looking upon him as a misguided nationalist— just a bad boy sowing some wild oats—and condoning his excesses. There were still powerful forces—labor, business, religious, professional—that could have united and overthrown him if they had been given any encouragement by the State Department. But they received not a smidgen of encouragement, and a new era opened on February 4 when Anastas Mikoyan, then Deputy Premier of Foreign and Domestic Commerce of the Soviet Union, arrived in Havana.

More than a year earlier, Mikoyan had visited Washington; Secretary of State John Foster Dulles gave him a dinner party at the F Street Club. There had been fourteen guests, including Mikoyan's son, members of the Soviet Embassy staff, and State Department officials. The younger Mikoyan remarked to Deputy Under Secretary Robert Murphy during the evening that it was "unbelievable" that Dulles should thus be honoring his father.[2] Mikoyan told the Americans present that he was planning a good-will mission to Havana in the hope of setting up trade relations with the Castro regime. The next day Robert Murphy, a conservative, pointed out to his State Department colleagues the likelihood that the "trade mission" might prove to be a cover for subversive operations in Latin America.

[2] Robert Murphy, *Diplomat Among Warriors* (New York: Doubleday & Co., Inc., 1964), p. 442. The author erroneously says Mikoyan first visited Havana in 1958. The F Street Club records show the dinner party as having been given early in 1959.

Mikoyan's visit to Cuba in early 1960 had been preceded by almost a hundred Soviet technicians, who had organized an industrial exhibition at the impressive Palace of Fine Arts in the heart of Havana, constructed during the Batista administration. The exhibits had been brought to Cuba from Mexico in Soviet ships. Castro, his cabinet, and the principal Cuban Communist leaders were at the airport to receive their guests. An army band played the "Internationale" as Mikoyan stepped from the Soviet plane.

The exhibition opened the following day with all those who had welcomed Mikoyan at the airport in attendance. As the formal ceremonies were getting under way, shooting broke out in nearby Parque Central. The police squelched the protesting rioters and Mikoyan started speaking. He attacked the United States, saying that American capitalism was an "antiquated" system, unable to compete with the "planned production" of the U.S.S.R. The previous day Guevara had announced that Cuba did not want foreign investments and that the government would insist on owning 51 percent of all basic industries.[3]

Carmen and I attended the exhibition. I had seen several similar ones abroad, but few Cubans had ever seen anything like it, and they were impressed. There were excellent models of sputnik satellites, with recorded explanations. Television receivers showed beautifully colored scenes of Russia. A model of a TU-114 passenger airplane, described as having a capacity of 225 passengers and a speed of 500 miles an hour, attracted much attention.

Young propagandists circulated among the crowd, feigning discussions on Soviet industrial progress, culture, and the greatness of Soviet civilization. We spotted them immediately as Soviet agents, but it was obvious that most of those who paused to listen did not. In stalls Russian souvenir gadgets were on sale for a few pennies—hammer-and-sickle pins and small red flags.

[3] Phillips, p. 153.

The booths contained an abundance of Communist literature, including biographies of Lenin and Marx. One could learn how to speak Russian for a dime.

The only thing on sale that intrigued us was caviar. Moments later I lost Carmen in the milling crowd and found her at the caviar booth—urging Cubans not to buy. Carmen had always found it difficult to disguise her dislike for anything Communist, in spite of my admonitions that our problem was now one of survival.

When the exhibition closed on February 26, it was announced that 450,000 had paid admission. This probably was no exaggeration, in view of the crowds we had observed. The show had indeed been a success, and we regretted that the United States had never sponsored a comparable undertaking in Cuba.

Except for three or four public appearances, Mikoyan's whereabouts and activities were shrouded in secrecy during the nine days he remained in Cuba. On February 7 he spoke over a national television and radio hookup. Soviet scientific progress, he boasted, had outstripped that of the United States, as proven by the Russian space probe Lunik, which had taken the first pictures of the other side of the moon the year before.

Six days after Mikoyan's arrival the Castro regime and the Soviets signed a five-year commercial agreement under which the U.S.S.R. granted Cuba $100 million of credit to buy Soviet industrial equipment.

When Mikoyan departed on February 13, with a rousing send-off by Castro and his entourage, the police began a mass roundup of anti-Communists. At this time my friend Ruby Phillips, the resident correspondent of *The New York Times* (now often referred to by Cuban exiles as *The New York Tass*), told me that she had been heartened to find that James Reston, who had just visited Havana, agreed with her that Castro was moving toward Communism. She saw in Reston a hope of neutralizing Matthews, who still strongly supported the regime.

Thus was the shadow of the evil Mikoyan first cast on the

Pearl of the Antilles. The events which were taking place so close to the United States seemed unreal to us, almost unbelievable. They often reminded me of the Chinese legend Robert Murphy relates in his splendid book, *Diplomat Among Warriors*. A philosopher dreamed he was a butterfly. The dream had been so vivid that when he awoke he did not know whether he was a man who had dreamed he was a butterfly fluttering among the flowers, or whether he was a butterfly who was now dreaming that he was a man.

Many subsequent events were to recall this sense of unreality. I have in mind, for instance, the occasion, in late 1962, when the Kennedy administration would in effect accept Mikoyan as a mediator to obtain from Castro permission for on-site inspections [4]—the only conclusive assurance that Soviet offensive missiles had really been removed from Cuba. The United States was willing to rely on the man who had been largely responsible for Communist intrusion in Cuba! The result, predictably, was nil.

On March 4, 1960, the French freighter *La Coubre* blew up in Havana harbor while unloading munitions within a few yards of shops and residences. The tremendous explosion killed almost a hundred people and did great property damage.

Castro at once accused the United States of having plotted the destruction. In a frenetic funeral oration at the cemetery he described the United States as "a vulture feeding upon humanity." "We do not have proof," Castro shouted, "but we have a right to believe that they [the Americans] are the guilty ones!" Every Cuban with whom I spoke was convinced that the accident had been caused by careless handling of explosives and, in fact, the Cuban Government never produced the slightest evidence to support its charge. The only support of the sabotage theory came from Matthews, who said he had been shown what appeared to be a detonating device picked up near the dock.[5]

[4] Murphy, p. 443.
[5] Phillips, p. 173.

About this time the extensive and valuable properties of our client, Amadeo Barletta, who represented General Motors in Cuba, were seized. Among these were the newspaper *El Mundo,* which had refused to accept subsidies from Batista, and also the second largest radio-television station in Cuba. The charges against Barletta, a courageous Italian citizen, were completely fictitious, and we worked hard in his defense. Castro was moving from one pretext to another to destroy the free enterprise economy. Barletta's popular son, Amadeo Barletta, Jr., was an American citizen who had served with the United States Army in World War II. Both were widely known and highly regarded. Father and son took refuge in the Italian Embassy and after a few weeks, since an exit permit was not forthcoming, I offered to run them across the Florida Straits from Varadero in my sixteen-foot launch. Fortunately the capable Italian Ambassador arranged their escape in a manner less hazardous than the one I had proposed.

In April 1960 I made a final effort to keep Castro within the Western world. Through Rufo López-Fresquet, the Minister of Finance, I offered to go to Washington at my own expense to negotiate the purchase of arms. We knew that Castro planned a military build-up, and my partner and I reasoned that unless the United States furnished the arms he would turn to the Soviet Union. The Minister was pro-American, married to an American girl whom he had met at Columbia University while a student there. He lost no time in conferring with Castro, who rejected the suggestion scornfully. The experience provoked López-Fresquet's resignation from the Cabinet.

This incident later gave rise to press comment in the United States by seasoned observers of the Cuban scene. They assumed, and the Minister of Finance himself erroneously reported, that I had acted covertly for the U.S. Government. The fact was that the idea was entirely my own, as I tried emphatically to make clear to the Minister at the time. I had not even discussed it with Bonsal, although I had planned to inform him before proceeding to Washington. Its significance was that it confirmed, beyond a doubt, that Castro had already cast his lot with the Soviets prior to April 1960.

By this time the economy of the country was slowing down, visibly and dangerously. The housing program that the government had launched with much ballyhoo had come almost to a halt. Imports from the United States dried up, and government public works projects were abandoned. The dislocation in the economy became apparent to everyone. The organization of state "cooperatives" took the place of the promised redistribution of land to small individual farmers, resulting in rising food costs and unrest. Above all, the Cubans were becoming disillusioned by the growing Communist influence in government. Anti-Castro sentiment was clearly rising.

On April 21, 1960, *The New York Times* published an article in which three journalists expressed their views on the developing Cuban trends. Col. Jules Dubois of the *Chicago Tribune* said that Communists were in control of Cuba and advocated giving Castro "enough rope to hang himself." Joseph Alsop, the syndicated columnist, urged "patience." Matthews said the Castro regime was characterized by "extreme nationalism," but that he saw no signs that the Communists dominated it. He appealed for a more sympathetic understanding of the Revolution, which he said could not be stopped.

At first the peasants and workers had welcomed the measures by which the middle and upper classes were being stripped of their possessions, but now the regime was demanding sacrifices from them too. The workers were asked to make a "voluntary" contribution of 4 percent of their salaries toward an "industrialization" program, and anyone who dared to protest was in danger of reprisals. One after another the labor and social gains which the Cuban worker had achieved through forty years of struggle were being abrogated. All Cuban Presidents, including Batista, had feared and respected the powerful Confederation of Cuban Workers, but now legislation was decreed which deprived the workers of the right to strike. Henceforth labor grievances would be decided by the Labor Minister, and employers would be required to hire workers through the Ministry.

On May 7, 1960 Cuba resumed the diplomatic relations with the Soviet Union that had been broken off in April 1952, shortly after Batista had assumed power. Two days later President Sukarno of Indonesia arrived for a five-day sojourn in Havana and was warmly received by Castro. He had stopped off en route in the United States, where the liberal press reported that he was motivated by the ideals of Washington, Jefferson, and Lincoln—he had said so himself. Shortly after his return to Indonesia he stole property worth more than $2 billion from Dutch owners.

When Cuba began to receive goods from the Soviet Union under the trade agreement of February 1960, in exchange for sugar, the first commodity to arrive was Russian crude oil. Previously the Cuban gasoline consumption had been dependent on the Esso and Shell refineries in Havana and the Texaco refinery in Santiago de Cuba. These refineries had been obtaining crude oil from American and British oil fields in Venezuela. At this time the Cuban Government owed these companies approximately $60 million. Now, in June 1960, "Che" Guevara, who had become President of the National Bank, notified the three refineries that they would have to process the Russian crude. When they contested the arbitrary order, the Castro regime seized the refineries, valued at approximately $140 million, and canceled the Cuban Government's $60-million debt to the companies. In another violent speech Castro declared that he would take all property away from Americans "down to the last nails in their shoes." [6]

On June 30 the regime "intervened" Havana's two leading hotels, the Havana Hilton and the National, accusing them of having failed to develop American tourist travel. Previously it

[6] *Ibid.,* p. 223.

had taken over a number of small hotels and night clubs. We were the lawyers for Hilton and had arranged the local financing for the construction of the $24-million hotel. Everything possible had been done to encourage tourist trade, if only as a matter of self-interest, but Castro told the hotel workers that owing to the "aggressions" of the United States, Cuba had no American tourists. "And these aggressions have only a single purpose," he shouted, "to strangle us economically, create unemployment and hunger in our country." [7] Shortly after the takeover the government did what it had not permitted the hotel owners to do—it cut wages and dismissed the surplus personnel.

For many years the United States had been Cuba's best customer and largest supplier. In 1957, for instance, it bought 58 percent of Cuba's exports, chiefly sugar, and sold Cuba 71 percent of her import requirements. The preferential trade agreement between the two countries was beneficial to both. The price of Cuban sugar in the American market was considerably higher than the world price, since U.S. sugar legislation, through a system of import quotas to certain off-shore producers, controlled competition and managed prices as a protection for American growers.

Fixed sugar quotas were assigned to Puerto Rico, the Philippines, Hawaii, and the Virgin Islands, and Cuba was allotted a percentage of the U.S. consumption not filled by these quotas. In July 1960 Cuba had been authorized to ship to the United States 700,000 tons of sugar during the balance of the year, with the likelihood that this figure would be raised by an additional 165,000 tons. But on July 6, 1960, a year and a half after Castro had come to power, the United States took the first reprisal against Cuba. With Congressional authority, but against the recommendation of Ambassador Bonsal,[8] President Eisenhower closed the door to these shipments. The action repre-

7 *Ibid.,* p. 220.
8 Philip W. Bonsal, "Cuba, Castro and the United States," *Foreign Affairs,* January 1967, p. 273.

sented a loss of Cuban sugar sales to the American market of approximately $113 million.

Castro had been expecting this action for many months and Guevara had taunted the United States to take it, "the sooner the better." Up to this time every step directed against American interests had been represented in a defensive light, as a response to American "aggression." And in July 1960, although Castro at first called the reprisal a "blessing" which would make Cuba "the indisputable master of the world sugar market," [9] his tirades rose to a pitch of hysteria.

Three days after the Cuban sugar quota was cut, Nikita Khrushchev offered to help Castro fight this sanction, adding for good measure that the Soviets would provide "rocket support" if the United States attempted to intervene. President Eisenhower reacted strongly, warning Khrushchev that the United States would not tolerate the establishment of a regime dominated by international Communism in the Western Hemisphere. In spite of this warning, arms from the Communist bloc started pouring into Cuba. An estimated 22,000 tons of armament arrived there between the first of August and the end of October, at which time Castro boasted that he had 250,000 militiamen equipped with Soviet bloc weapons.

In late 1959 and early 1960 the Castro regime, encouraged by the State Department's appeasement policy, had taken fundamental decisions and their consequences would now be seen, in late 1960. Between August 5 and October 14, five edicts were promulgated confiscating all of the remaining important privately owned property, both Cuban and American. The measures, which read like criminal indictments, covered hundreds of concerns, ranging from nationwide public utility services, banks, sugar mills, railroads, and industrial plants of all kinds, to small motion picture theaters.

Since this massive transformation involved far more Cuban

[9] Phillips, p. 225.

than American-owned property, it could not easily be charged to U.S. "aggression." During those nine weeks Cuba's free enterprise system was finally destroyed. The five edicts were the quietus. Our miraculous free market, which produced the order derived from millions of economic decisions made independently of one another in the marketplace, had been replaced by a non-competitive monopolistic society in which freedom would be impossible.

The dynamic competition which had kept things moving, improving, and which had been an economizer as well, was canceled out. The Cubans would now be hearing and stepping to a different drummer. Economic decisions would be made and imposed by a handful of arrogant, inexperienced bureaucrats, dominated by a thirty-one-year-old lawyer who had never had clients and by a doctor who had never had patients. None of us doubted that within a short time the country's economic fabric would be in shreds.

On September 26 Castro descended on New York to address the United Nations. The delegates to the world body were treated to one of his marathon orations, this one lasting four hours, in which he vented his hatred of the United States and expressed his high regard for the Soviet Union and what it represented. He referred to Senator John F. Kennedy, then the Democratic candidate for President, as an "illiterate and ignorant millionaire." [10] Nikita Khrushchev was in New York for this occasion at the UN General Assembly, and the pair embraced while photographers recorded the love affair. Even the State Department now realized that Castro was pro-Communist, at the very least.

One of the greatest humiliations suffered by the United States was the confiscation of the great U.S. Government-owned Nicaro Nickel plant in eastern Cuba.

Nickel is the mineral that makes steel hard and heat-resistant. It is a critical element in the manufacture of armor plate, gun

[10] *Ibid.*, p. 254.

forgings, and airplane engines. Neither the U.S.A. nor the U.S.S.R. produces nickel domestically. During World War II the mineral was in short supply in both countries; the U.S. war-time stockpile never had more than a two-month reserve. In 1960 it was the one Cuban product which both the Americans and Soviets needed most.

The Cuban Nicaro project was conceived two months after Pearl Harbor, when our client, Freeport Sulphur Company, developed a new chemical process for extracting nickel from the low-grade Cuban ore, and Washington approved the financing. Construction was started in 1942, during the Batista regime, and the plant was built on an isolated peninsula in the jungles of Eastern Cuba, when many deadly Nazi U-boats operated in the surrounding waters.

The Nicaro facilities cost the American taxpayers more than $100 million. Eventually the plant produced approximately 10 percent of the nickel of the free world. The success of the project represented one of the great wartime achievements of private American industry. Our firm had been associated with it since before the blueprint stage, when we were consulted by Washington on the most appropriate procedure for acquiring the extensive plant site. Subsequently we devoted close to 40,000 hours of service to the Nicaro project.

On October 24, 1960, the Castro regime confiscated this extraordinarily valuable U.S. Government-owned war industry and placed it at once at the disposal of the Soviet Union. To this day it remains incredible that the United States permitted this action. No imagination is needed to know what would have happened if the situation were in reverse—if a vital war plant built by the Soviet Union on a small island in the Black Sea a hundred miles from Odessa had been stolen and operated for the benefit of the United States.

The Urban Reform Law of October 14, 1960, was no less confiscatory than its agricultural counterpart of May 1959. It was a staggering blow to the large middle class. In Cuba the preferred, almost universal form of investment had always been real estate, either by erecting a building for leasing purposes, often with living quarters reserved for the owner, or by lending funds for home construction against mortgage security.

The "Reform" canceled outright all leases and mortgages, leaving the former owners entitled to only a trifling state pension. Lessees became "potential owners" of the occupied premises. Thereafter they and mortgagees would pay the rent or interest to the state. If they paid punctually, including the real estate taxes (which were now their responsibility), they would become owners after a period of years, depending upon the age of the building. Repairs would also have to be paid by the "potential" owner. The law allowed no flexibility; delinquency meant the loss of all rights.

In the early months of the Castro regime hundreds of thousands of lessees had fallen behind in paying their rent, either because the landlord chose to be lenient or because the courts refused to evict. Now all arrears would have to be paid—the state had become a ruthless landlord. Thousands of tenants refused to sign the government forms that would qualify them as potential owners, feeling that they would be stealing another's property.

Understandably, the Urban Reform Law was generally unpopular. It brought tragedy to all who had invested their life savings in a house or in a mortgage. We knew of countless cases of humble people, including our servants and office workers, who had put every cent they could save into real estate. These people were left with only an insignificant state pension.

The year 1960 was no less a black one for the Cuban legal profession. In addition to the horror of the Revolutionary Court trials, it became necessary to establish many legal actions against the government in the regular courts. Ruthless confiscations had to be contested under threat of being accused of counter-revolutionary activities—a capital offense.

It is a rule of law that in order to establish a claim in the international field for restitution, or compensation for losses, the claimant must first exhaust his local legal remedies. The State Department will not, as a rule, espouse the claim of an American citizen unless he can show that he has no local remedy. Thus, except in the cases where the confiscatory measure itself specified that no appeal could be taken against it, actions against the government had to be carried through all available legal procedures until final negative rulings had been obtained from the Cuban Supreme Court. It was a foregone conclusion that these decisions would be adverse, since the judiciary had been "purged"; nevertheless, they were indispensable in order to lay the groundwork for future legal action after the fall of the Castro regime.

I imagine few lawyers have had the singular experience of having to dispute their own clients' insistent wishes to overpay them for professional services, but that is what happened to us in 1960. Anxious to avoid having their funds fall into Castro's hands, clients often asked us to make from five to ten times the normal charge. In one case I was asked to submit a statement for $100,000 for a job that warranted a fee of $5,000! We pointed out that making charges or receiving fees that could not be justified would undoubtedly be regarded as "counter-revolutionary" actions when government agents later examined the accounts. These suggestions, however, typified the attitude of our clients, especially the American companies, from whom we received only unaffected consideration and kindness during this difficult period.

On October 20, 1960, Washington called Ambassador Bonsal home for consultation, and the American colony in Havana hoped that he would not come back. His policy of unlimited accommodation with the Communist regime, accommodation amounting to appeasement, had been a matter of public knowledge. Yet, throughout his stay in Cuba he enjoyed the support of liberal American journalists and columnists—with one quixotic exception: Herbert Matthews once complained that Bonsal could see only the *American* point of view, that the Cuban point of view made no sense to him! [11]

With the departure of Bonsal, Minister Counsellor Daniel M. Braddock remained in charge of the Embassy. Braddock, whose unassuming looks and manner belied his strength of character, enjoyed the respect of his entire staff. He had made no secret of his disagreement with the "soft" Washington policies that his Ambassador was implementing.

As early as December 1959, during a previous period of several months when he had been in charge, he had informed the Department that he and the country team, which included all the senior officers of the Embassy, were unanimously of the opinion that the United States would be unable to do business with Castro. He had given the reasons that led them to this conclusion, adding, of course, that their finding should be checked with the Ambassador, who might hold different views —as indeed he did. Braddock favored a firm policy line, and one that would put the onus for the break in relations, when it came, on Cuba rather than on the United States.

Later events, of course, confirmed that judgment. Since all efforts by Washington to find a common ground of understanding with the new regime had failed, Braddock felt that further forbearance on its part weakened the confidence and will of all the forces in Cuba opposed to Castro and eroded the respect of other countries in the hemisphere for the United States. From this position he never deviated.

Our American friends and clients hoped, wishfully, that Bonsal's recall would mark a change in American attitudes toward Castro. We were heartened by their faith that their powerful country would not long permit the Communist usurpers to bring ruin to Cuba and to those of its own citizens who had

[11] Herbert L. Matthews, *The Cuban Story* (New York: George Braziller, 1962), pp. 72, 73.

shared their fortunes and lives with us. That hope was never abandoned until after the Missile Crisis, almost three years later.

Because the 1960 Presidential campaign was so important to Cuba's destiny, Carmen and I made a trip to the United States to observe it at first hand. Some of John F. Kennedy's statements on Cuba during 1960 had given us real concern. His trips to Havana in 1957 and 1958 had been "fun" visits, purely social. He had compared the Castro revolution to the American revolution and early in 1960 the author of *Profiles in Courage* had written in *The Strategy of Peace* that Castro was "part of the legacy of Bolívar." [12] He voiced the belief that failure of the United States to give Cuba sufficient aid had paved the way for Communist subversion.

"We used the influence of our government to advance the interests and increase the profits of the private American companies, which dominated the island's economy," he said in a campaign speech in Cincinnati in early October.[13] This, of course, was poppycock. My associates and I know of no instance where U.S. Government influence was sought, or used incorrectly, to advance the interests of American companies or increase their profits. The plain fact was that Cuba had long enjoyed a handsome subsidy on her sales of sugar in the American market and that American capital had contributed enormously to raising the living standard of the Cuban people. These Kennedy statements had amazed us. They sounded remarkably like the very arguments Castro had been advancing for confiscating American properties.

Nevertheless, when on October 19 Richard Nixon came out with a strong anti-Castro statement, saying that a number of steps were planned to "eradicate the cancer in our hemisphere," Senator Kennedy hit back hard the following day. He called

[12] Arthur M. Schlesinger, Jr., *A Thousand Days* (Boston: Houghton Mifflin Company, 1965), p. 224.
[13] *Ibid.*, p. 225.

Nixon's new policy "too little and too late." The Republicans, he said, had ignored repeated warnings and had stood helplessly by while the Russians established a new satellite only ninety miles from American shores. He called the Republican record an "incredible history of blunder, inaction, retreat and failure," adding, "We must attempt to strengthen the non-Batista democratic anti-Castro forces in exile, and in Cuba itself, who offer eventual hope of overthrowing Castro. Thus far these fighters for freedom have had virtually no support from our government." [14]

It was a strong speech and we had no reason for doubting its truth. Watching the television debates and following the speeches, Carmen and I had the feeling that of the two, Kennedy was tougher on Communism and Castro than the Vice President. We were therefore pleased when he won.

We could not know, any more than the electorate did, that strong action had already been initiated. As Nixon would write in the *Reader's Digest* of November 1964,[15] the Eisenhower administration "had been doing exactly what Kennedy seemed to be advocating—supporting and training Cuban exiles so that they could free Cuba from Communist control." Unfortunately for himself, though he had known this for months, the Republican candidate had to keep silent because "this was a top-secret CIA project," known only to the President, himself, and two other Cabinet members. "To protect the security of the program," he could only bite his lip in frustration and allow his adversary to present himself as the stronger champion of American help to the forces of Cuban liberation.

The first Christmas under the Castro regime, the year before, had been called a "Revolutionary Christmas." Santa Claus, who had been almost as much a part of the life of the Cuban child

14 Theodore C. Sorensen, *Kennedy* (New York: Harper & Row, 1965), p. 205.
15 Richard M. Nixon, "Cuba, Castro and John F. Kennedy," *Reader's Digest,* November 5, 1964, p. 288.

as of American youngsters, had been banished as an "imperialist" but, except in the eastern province of Oriente, the people had been gay and had feasted and danced in the streets as in the past. Revolutionary organizations had collected donations, and the usual Christmas packages had been distributed to the poor. In 1960 the situation was changed.

A favorite Christmas decoration in Cuba had been the Nativity, but now it was rarely seen. There was no dancing in the streets, which were patrolled by militiamen and soldiers carrying Czech Tommy guns. There was little food in the marketplace, a small number of chickens and turkeys, a few pigs. Disorders broke out in the markets as people fought over the limited supply. The traditional pears, nuts, figs, dates, and other Christmas luxuries were not to be seen. Across from the newly renamed Habana Libre Hotel, now government-operated, a huge billboard had been erected depicting the birth of Christ in a Cuban *bohio*. The Three Wise Men were painted to resemble Castro, Guevara, and the illiterate Negro Chief of the Army, Major Almeida. The gifts they bore were Agrarian Reform, Urban Reform, and The Year of Education.

Every night during the holiday season bombs exploded in Havana, and there was widespread sabotage. There were reports of torture of arrested people by electrical devices and other sadistic methods. No doubt some of these were exaggerated, but they mirrored the existing uncertainty and fear. Certainly torture and killing under the Castro regime surpassed by far anything that had been known previously. One of my friends told me of a boy he saw lying on a bunk at G-2 headquarters in Miramar, his face so badly beaten that it was unrecognizable. A common form of mental torture was to notify a prisoner that he was to be executed without a trial (as in my own case), but to have the firing squad use blanks.

On the day before Christmas, three hundred Americans arrived in Cuba under the auspices of the Fair Play for Cuba Committee, headed by Carleton Beals. The Committee had received funds from the Castro regime for its organizational activities. There were about a hundred starry-eyed American college students in the group. Two days later the first contingent of Soviet tourists arrived in Cuba.

All the same, as 1960 drew to a close, there was a strong undercurrent of expectancy and hope in Havana, largely because of the outcome of the Presidential election in the United States. Kennedy's campaign oratory against Castro had been balm for our battered spirits. And when I learned from a completely reliable source in late December that the United States was secretly training Cuban exiles, this was the best news of all.

For New Year's Day 1961, the Castro regime planned a huge mass meeting to celebrate the second anniversary of the Revolution. Delegates from Latin America and from all Communist countries had been pouring into Havana for several days at government expense. But on New Year's Eve, one of the largest department stores in Havana, La Epoca, was sabotaged and burned to the ground. Fires broke out in several places at the same time, and as the firemen fought vainly to control them, bombs exploded in other parts of the city. The anti-Castro underground was performing at peak efficiency without endangering the populace. Some of its members raced in cars through the capital, distributing anti-Castro literature.

It was against this background that Castro first displayed his military strength, in a parade on January 2, 1961, which lasted from eleven in the morning until nightfall. There were heavy and medium Soviet tanks, truck-drawn field artillery, rocket launchers, and anti-aircraft and anti-tank guns. The marchers carried machine guns, bazookas, and mortars that had come from the Soviet bloc. It was nightfall when Castro began one of his most hysterical speeches. He called on the American Embassy to reduce its staff to eight members within forty-eight hours. He charged that the Embassy had three hundred officials, of whom 80 percent were FBI and CIA spies. Actually the Embassy at that time had about seventy-five American officials and two hundred Cuban employees. Castro claimed that it was the center of all counter-revolutionary activities against his regime.

"We are going to eliminate all these criminals," he shouted. As he paused to catch his breath, organizers called for chants, much as cheerleaders do at a football game, and the mob echoed the mad slogans. It was amazing to see with what ease human beings could be brought to a pitch of hysteria.

Thus was the United States forced to break diplomatic relations with Cuba. The announcement was made in Washington at 8 P.M. on January 3, 1961.

During January *The New York Times* rendered another service to the Castro-Communist cause. It published a story from Guatemala saying that anti-Castro forces were being trained at a "partly hidden air field in the Cordillera foothills a few miles back from the Pacific." [16] It would have been difficult to render Castro a greater service at that time. He had been predicting an invasion for weeks and had mounted anti-aircraft guns along the Havana waterfront, installed cannons on the hills surrounding the city, and stationed military units at beaches and inlets. But when nothing happened the invasion fever began to die down. Now the *Times* had given him just what he needed.

It was shortly after this that Peru demanded of the United States that it exercise leadership in the fight against Communism. The Peruvian Premier said, "If the United States does not step forward now with dynamic leadership to uproot the unceasing conspiracy of the Soviet Union and Red China on our shores, Latin America is lost . . . as is also the United States." [17]

As the time for the Bay of Pigs invasion drew nearer, sabotage increased. The Hershey sugar mill warehouse and two confiscated Woolworth stores were set afire. On April 14, Cuba's largest department store, El Encanto, was burned to the ground. Throughout the island, towns and cities resounded to explosions as government buildings and plants were bombed. Again the

[16] Phillips, p. 295.
[17] *Ibid.*, p. 312.

night skies reflected the flames of burning cane fields, all symbols of the mounting opposition to Castro and Communism.

And the invasion was coming! We did not know precisely when or where, but it would be soon, and Cuba would again be free.

CHAPTER FOURTEEN

The Mystery of Castro's Communism

By the end of 1960 the Castro regime had confiscated more than $25 billion of privately owned Cuban property and almost $1 billion of property owned by Americans. It had communized Cuba in two years, less than a third of the time it took the Bolsheviks to communize Russia.

The question of when and why Castro embraced Communism remains a topic of endless discussion and dispute among Cubans. It is one which Castro himself is perhaps unable to answer. Never noted for consistency, his public and private utterances may be used to support either of two schools of thought: (1) that he was a secret Communist even before he landed from a small boat on the coast of Oriente province on December 2, 1956, or (2) that he became a Communist months after attaining power in 1959.

One may argue convincingly in support of either theory. Those who hold to the "secret Communist" belief point to Castro's participation in the Communist-inspired Bogotazo of 1948, to the fact that his brother Raúl was known to be a Communist, and to the fact that Fidel Castro associated with Communists in Mexico in 1955–1956, when "Che" Guevara, a known and dedicated Communist, joined his small band of conspirators. But mainly they rely on his own statement of December 22, 1961, which implied that he had purposely concealed having been a Marxist-Leninist while in the Sierra Maestra.

"Of course," he then said, "if we had stopped at the Pico Turquino, when there were very few of us, and said, 'We are Marxists-Leninists,' possibly we would not have been able to get down to the plain. Thus we called it something else; we did not broach the subject; we raised other questions that people understood perfectly." [1]

The second school of thought—that Castro was not a full-fledged Communist when he came to power on January 1, 1959 —is the position of the CIA.[2] Strong arguments may be advanced in support of it. His university classmates in 1948 did not regard him as a Communist at the time. During his imprisonment on the Isle of Pines in 1953–1955 he was not taken to be one. It was during this period that he revised to its later published form his "History Will Absolve Me" speech, originally delivered at his trial in 1953, following the Moncada assault. The pamphlet called for adherence to the 1940 Constitution and for setting up a government "of popular election." It contained no reference to state ownership of property, other than a minor reference to "nationalization" of the American-owned electric power and telephone companies.

When he was first accused of being a Communist, in a Cuban magazine article in July 1959, Castro hit back hard, charging that this was a plot fomented by Batista and the U.S. Embassy. He associated Batista with the Cuban Communist Party, the *Partido Socialista Popular,* pointing to the support it had given Batista in the 1940 Presidential election. The PSP, in fact, had criticized Castro's attack on the Moncada barracks in 1953, referring to it as "putschism" and hence "bourgeois," heroic but

[1] Theodore Draper, *Castroism: Theory and Practice* (New York: Frederick A. Praeger, 1965), p. 17.
[2] On November 5, 1959, more than ten months after Castro came to power, General C. P. Cabell, Deputy Director of the CIA, testified before the Senate Internal Security Subcommittee that the CIA did not believe Castro was a member of the Communist Party.

doctrinally false and futile, and as late as the abortive general strike of April 1958 the PSP blamed its failure on its "unilateral call," issued by Castro "without counting on the rest of the opposition" to Batista.

Castro's "Manifesto of the Sierra Maestra," of July 12, 1957, drafted and signed by him and by two moderates, stated that his rebels were fighting for a "truly free democratic" regime under constitutional government and called for general elections at the end of one year, outlining a ten-point program that included "absolute guarantee of freedom of information, of the . . . press, and of all the individual and political rights guaranteed by the Constitution [of 1940]." The publication of this program was not suppressed by Batista. It was run in Cuba's most popular magazine, *Bohemia*. Furthermore, Castro's public statements from 1956 to 1958 appeared to be increasingly moderate. Almost always he advocated support of the 1940 Constitution. On one occasion he called for recognition of the rights of "free enterprise and invested capital." Even the first draft of an Agrarian Reform Law (Law No. 3 of the Sierra Maestra, dated October 10, 1958) which Castro signed with three colleagues, one of whom was later executed, made no mention of "cooperatives" or "state farms."

Those who contend that Castro was not a Communist when he took power also point to his anti-Communist public statements during the first few months of his regime. Americans heard many such statements, uttered with apparent sincerity, when he visited the United States at the invitation of the American Society of Newspaper Editors in 1959. Prior to addressing the editors on April 15, he spent the morning with members of the Senate and House Foreign Relations Committee. Although it was a closed-door meeting, legislators who were present reported that Castro had expressed opposition to Communism. Most of those who heard him were favorably impressed. One exception was Sen. George Smathers, of Florida, who later predicted that trouble was brewing in the Caribbean area. Another who met with Castro privately on his visit to the United States and sized him up as a dangerous radical, probably under Communist influence, was the late C. D. Jackson, the perceptive publisher of *Life*.

When Castro appeared before the fifteen hundred editors, he again gave the impression that he was a moderate liberal who wanted to give the Cuban people a good government, be a good neighbor, and live up to international agreements. At the end of his talk he was roundly applauded. The following Sunday, on the *Meet the Press* television show, he assured Americans, "I don't agree with Communism." A day later he appeared at a National Press Club luncheon and again denounced Communism. Discussing Khrushchev, he said, "Whatever the nature of dictatorship—class dictator, military dictator, or dictatorship of the oligarchy—we are opposed to it. That is why we are against Communism."

For a short time, a matter of a very few weeks, he continued to talk in this vein. "Communism kills man by wiping out his freedom," he said on April 28, and a month later he referred to Communism as a system which suppresses liberties and sacrifices man. He even accused the Cuban Communists of conspiring with counter-revolutionaries.[3] It is difficult to imagine a true Communist publicly making statements of this nature. A leftist non-Communist, on the other hand, might logically have sought and accepted Communist support in the struggle against the right-wing Batista. With respect to Castro's "confession" of December 22, 1961, that he had concealed his Marxist-Leninist beliefs while "there were very few of us" in the mountains, these theorists argue that he was merely, at that late date, attempting to make his famous "I am a Marxist-Leninist" statement, pronounced *three weeks earlier,* appear to be a logical consequence of the past. Standing alone, they contend, it is not conclusive.

Castro's own account[4] of his "conversion" is that he had al-

[3] Draper, p. 37.
[4] Herbert L. Matthews, *Return to Cuba* (Stanford University: Institute of Hispanic American and Luso-Brazilian Studies, 1964).

ways been *"predisposed"* toward Marxism but did not formally become a Communist until mid-1960, after he had been in power a year and a half. He had entered the University of Havana with ideas influenced by his early upbringing as the son of a landowner, educated by Jesuits, he says. He began reading Marxist literature while there but did not join the Communist Party, although he had radical liberal ideas. He thought of himself as an agitator, a revolutionary who could obtain reforms within the democratic system, and while in the Sierra was still thinking in such "utopian" terms. The pressure of subsequent events, he insists, forced him to choose Marxism. When he came to power his radical ideas split the country into Right and Left. He says he found the Communists to be honest, trained, and loyal, and he needed them. So, according to his own version, he moved into a Marxist-Leninist position in 1960.

This we now know: The disciplined Cuban Communist Party did not approve of Castro's Moncada adventure in 1953. It did not approve of his "invasion" of Cuba in 1956 on the *Granma,* bought with funds provided by ex-President Prío Socarrás. Nor did it approve of his unilateral call for a general strike on April 9, 1958. But in February 1958 it ordered several young Communists to join Castro's forces in the Sierra Maestra. The Communist leader Carlos Rafael Rodríguez himself went into the mountains to offer the Party's support in July, six months later. Presumably there was an alliance at this stage, possibly a fusion.

My own belief is that Castro, known to be a radical, a gangster-type terrorist even during his university days, and vehemently anti-American, was certainly "predisposed" toward Communism long before he came to power, as he himself admits. The pressures which eventually led him formally to embrace Communism, I believe, resided largely in his own character, defined as early as 1948, when he participated in the Colombia uprising. A police official who examined his luggage when he departed for Bogotá on that occasion told my partner that the only evidence lacking of Castro's Communist affiliation was a Party card. Among his effects was a considerable assortment of anti-American and pro-Communist literature.

Eleven years later, lacking balanced judgment, devoid of administrative and economic experience, driven by an abnormal egotism combined with a charismatic ability to sway the masses, little Cuba may have seemed to him too small a stage. He easily visualized himself as the leader of a revolution which would sweep the whole of Latin America.

Toward the end of 1959 Batista had been gone for almost a year, and every conceivable measure had been taken against him and his followers. To provoke a revolution embracing many nations, an exciting and challenging enemy was needed and the logical one, in Castro's mind, was the Colossus of the North. To his profound surprise he had found the United States anything but formidable, and every passing day gave him additional proof that it was politically confused, gullible, and vacillating.

If that was his state of mind, the State Department's pathetic anxiety for an accommodation on almost any terms, and Ambassador Bonsal's humble restraint, both fascinated and encouraged him. In his early months of power, when Castro was feeling his way and moving cautiously, American diplomacy had eagerly, trustingly, accepted his assurances that his methods were evolutionary, not revolutionary. Once he had consolidated his authority and tested his capacity for manipulating the masses, he could visualize himself as Supreme Chief of a history-making continental revolution, unified against the United States as the common enemy. And there was only one place for him to go for support, and that was to the implacable foe of "American imperialism," the Soviet Union. This vision and the process on which it thrived might, it seems to me, have been predicted by those aware of his character and inflated ambitions.

Castro's first all-out public attack on the United States came on October 26, 1959, before a mammoth gathering. The event was carefully staged for maximum propaganda effect. It is my conviction that sometime prior to this date the green light had been flashed by Moscow. He surely would not have cut Cuba's umbilical tie with its great neighbor without advance negotiation and undertakings by the U.S.S.R.

Criticism of the CIA for not having spotted Castro as a Communist before he took over comes, of course, from those who are convinced he was a Communist at the time. This includes most of the Cuban exiles and many Americans in high position.

Castro did not become a subject of real concern to the CIA until he returned to Cuba in December 1956 and holed up in the mountains; actually, not until after the Matthews articles in *The New York Times*. Its agents then began checking with the Catholic hierarchy in both Santiago and Havana. They consulted priests who had taught the boy in the Catholic schools he had attended and they talked to those who had been his University classmates in 1948. Of course, they infiltrated meetings of the 26th of July Movement.

Unfortunately, as we can see it in the perspective of later events, the CIA men who handled the bulk of the investigative work on Castro were doctrinaire liberals. "Progressives" was probably the word they preferred. Almost instinctively they found themselves passionately anti-Batista and therefore, quite illogically, strongly pro-Castro. I write this with profound regret since several were close personal friends, much closer to Carmen and me than Ambassador Earl E. T. Smith and his wife. The motives of these men are not open to question, but their ideological commitments seriously hampered them in their task. In discussing the phenomenon of contemporary liberalism, Prof. James Burnham, in his excellent book, *Suicide of the West*, titled one of his chapters *"Pas d'Ennemi à Gauche."* For broadminded progressives the preferred enemy, when there is a choice, is by definition on the Right.

These able agents, with the most patriotic intentions, eagerly seized upon reports that Castro had been a good Catholic in his boyhood, had regularly attended church and made his confessions. He had once been an altar boy. They found members of the Church hierarchy who ridiculed American concern over the possibility that Castro might be a Communist or even favorable to Communism. They attributed to Batista personal responsibility for police brutality against anti-government terrorists and credited the most extreme accusations against him.

In Santiago American agents talked at length to Vilma Espín, who had just come down from the rebel group in the hills. She was an attractive girl who had studied at the Massachusetts Institute of Technology; she subsequently married Raúl Castro. Speaking in perfect English, she pleaded articulately for American sympathy. Having lived in the United States, she said, she knew the freedom Americans enjoyed and that Fidel and Raúl Castro only wanted for Cubans what the Americans had. She denied vehemently that either of the brothers or "Che" Guevara were Communists. The CIA agents were impressed. Yet a former Executive Director of the CIA has written that Vilma Espín was already known to be a communist when she was studying in the United States! [5]

When Dr. Manuel Urrutia, who later became Castro's puppet President, sought a U.S. visa, he assured a small pro-Castro group in the American Embassy that the Castro Movement was anti-Communist, and they too were impressed. When CIA agents investigated Ernesto "Che" Guevara in Rosario, Argentina, where he was born, his father spoke of the "Che" as a dreamer and idealist who had fought against Perón and had engaged in anti-dictator activities in Colombia and Guatemala, but claimed he was not a Communist.

Earl Smith did not share the views of the CIA agents in Cuba in 1957–1958 and consequently came into sharp, and at times bitter, conflict with them and other pro-Castro members of his

[5] Lyman B. Kirkpatrick, Jr., *The Real CIA* (New York: The Macmillan Company, 1967), p. 169.

staff. He recommended that the CIA agents be replaced. In an "Eyes Only" dispatch to Allen Dulles, Director of the CIA, he urged that an agent be infiltrated into the Castro rebel group in the mountains.[6]

A lawyer's training and experience teaches him to withhold judgment on an individual or organization until he has seen both sides of the coin. The CIA never defends itself and I have therefore been disinclined to condemn it. But surely it must be blamed for having sent into the mountains an agent under cover of being a journalist. This man remained with the group for two or three weeks and upon returning to Washington reported that Castro was an ego-maniac and emotionally unstable but not a Communist. Castro, having had such astounding success with Matthews, would naturally put his best foot forward in the presence of American journalists. He has since said that he wondered at times whether some of them were spies. My partner and I were in close touch with the CIA at the time. If I had been asked, I could have furnished several Cuban boys and girls who would have served as completely trustworthy agents for this vital mission, to remain indefinitely with the rebels, as Smith intended. Others in Havana could have done the same.

There were men in the CIA, including the Chief of the Central American Bureau, who shared Ambassador Smith's apprehensions.[7] The CIA knew there were Communists in the Castro group. It knew of Castro's participation in the Bogotazo in 1948. It knew he was radical, a terrorist and pathologically anti-American. But it chose to emphasize that in its opinion he was not an avowed Communist, and as late as November 5, 1959, more than ten months after Castro had come to power, its Deputy Director testified, "We believe Castro is not a member of the Communist Party, and does not consider himself to be a Com-

[6] Earl E. T. Smith, *The Fourth Floor* (New York: Random House, 1962), p. 35.
[7] *Ibid.*, p. 34.

munist." [8] The FBI, in contrast, had warned the State Department repeatedly since 1948 about Castro and his Communist connections.

In retrospect, the record must show that Ambassador Smith's conservative instincts led him correctly to evaluate the danger of Castro. In substance, semantics and alibis aside, he was right; the liberals around him were wrong.

In the closing days of 1958, very late, CIA Director Allen Dulles finally told President Eisenhower (as I have noted above) that "Communists and extreme radicals" appeared to have penetrated the Castro movement.[9] "If Castro takes over," he said, "they will probably participate in the government." At the same time one of the President's advisers, possibly William D. Pawley, urged that Eisenhower reverse American policy and back Batista as the lesser of two evils. The President was annoyed to have received the CIA report reversing earlier appraisals so belatedly, and he rejected the recommendation.[10]

But whether the CIA was right or wrong in its belief that Castro was not a Communist when he came to power, it seems to me that the point was basically irrelevant. The CIA and the State Department knew of Castro's radicalism, anti-Americanism and Communist leanings as early as 1948, when, at the age of twenty-one, he had agitated against "Yankee imperialism" in Colombia. They knew that in those youthful years, as a student, he had been a member of a terrorist group and had been arrested in connection with one or more political murders. Surely there was no need of "twenty-twenty hindsight," as Ambassador Bonsal sarcastically refers to the vision of those who had the prescience to warn against Castro. *It was folly to clear the path for Castro, in fact deliberately to lift him to power.* There were

[8] *Ibid.,* p. 35.
[9] Dwight D. Eisenhower, *The White House Years: Waging Peace— 1956–1961* (New York: Doubleday & Co., Inc., 1965), p. 521.
[10] *Ibid.,* p. 521.

alternatives short of supporting Batista. Liberal doctrine clings to the conviction that the "non-Communist democratic Left" offers the only solution for the political ills of Latin America. The Washington policy-makers chose to run the risk of trading the pro-American conservative Batista, or even anti-Batista conservatives, for the anti-American radical Castro.

I was privileged to gain an insight into the thinking of one of the master strategists of the Communist takeover of Cuba late one night early in 1960. I believe that what I was told on that occasion provides an explanation as to why Castro threw in his lot with the Communists.

That night I had an interview with Ernesto "Che" Guevara. He was the most powerful man in Cuba next to Castro, and I had been searching for an excuse to see him. Late in the Batista regime Lewis Lapham, President of the Grace Line, had asked me to explore the possibility of making Havana a port of call for the new Grace Liners which would soon be in service. The problem was that stevedores in Havana were among the highest paid port workers in the world. Through their strong union they had been able to raise wages and stretch work to such an extent that port labor costs in Havana had become prohibitive.

New labor practices—especially in connection with bulk freight handling—were essential to attract foreign vessels. Batista liked the project but had been reluctant to pressure the port workers into making the needed concessions and it had been dropped. Now it occurred to me that I could submit the same program to Guevara, who had become President of the Cuban National Bank in November 1959. The announced purpose of my interview was a subterfuge, of course. I knew that he would not approve such a plan, and I did not even check with the Grace people to ascertain if they were still interested. What I really wanted was an opportunity to probe Guevara's political views.

Because of his vital role in Cuban affairs, a few words about

Guevara's background are in order. He was thirty-two years old at the time, and was born in Argentina's second-largest city, Rosario, on June 14, 1928, the first of five children of a well-to-do civil engineer. He obtained a medical degree from the University of Buenos Aires in 1953. The CIA, checking his record, learned that he had engaged in street fights against the Perón regime. Leaving Argentina, he engaged in anti-dictator activities in Colombia and Guatemala; in the latter country he held a minor post with the land reform agency of the Communist-infiltrated government of Arbenz Guzmán, subsequently overthrown in the CIA-inspired uprising of 1954.

While in Guatemala he lived with an attractive, almond-eyed Peruvian girl named Hilda Gadea, an exiled radical. He subsequently rejoined her in Mexico, where they were married in May 1955. Hilda Gadea introduced Guevara to the Castro brothers, who had recently arrived there. Raúl was best man at the wedding. Soon they were joined by other Moncada survivors and exiles, and by Alberto Bayo, a veteran of the Communist-supported Republicans in the Spanish Civil War of 1936–1939. Bayo, an Air Force Captain in the Loyalist army, had commanded the ill-fated Majorcan expedition, which after its defeat had been followed by a mopping-up operation of furious cruelty, with several thousand people massacred by Nationalist (Franco) adherents. Subsequently, in the Tagus River area on the mainland, his men conducted a series of successful guerrilla actions against the Nationalist forces as they gathered to march on Madrid.

Bayo is credited with teaching Guevara and the Castros the rudiments of guerrilla warfare, an art at which Guevara eventually became a master. The group rented a house in Mexico and a ranch in the country, where Bayo conducted a training center for the men under Castro's command. The Mexican police, prodded by Batista's Cuban Embassy, arrested and held the group for about a month, then released them. The police were closing in again in late November 1956, when they set forth to "invade" Cuba in the leaky old *Granma.* Bayo, who died in Cuba in 1967, rated Guevara first among the men he trained.

In Cuba Guevara became the principal strategist of the rebel force. He had the capacity to formulate programs that included details for which Castro had no patience. When Castro digressed in vague theories, it was Guevara who argued forcefully in favor of his carefully planned strategy. During this period he wrote an analysis of guerrilla tactics which was published in 1959 and attained world-wide distribution.

During August and September 1958, Guevara led a bedraggled, hungry, barefooted column of about three hundred into central Las Villas Province. Santa Clara, the provincial capital with the largest fortress in Central Cuba, surrendered to his forces on January 1, 1959, after receiving word that Batista had fled. This marked the only military victory of any substance obtained by the Castroites during the revolution. Fourteen days earlier the U.S. State Department had told Batista to leave Cuba and his flight found the rebels unprepared to take over.

Hilda had followed Guevara to Cuba with their daughter, but she lost her husband to the revolution; the marriage broke up. She was given a job with *Prensa Latina,* Castro's news agency, which began operations in May 1959, and which, incidentally, was organized by an Argentinian friend of Guevara who had worked for Juan Perón's propaganda agency. Guevara's second wife, Aleida March, who had been a school teacher, worked as his secretary. Today she remains in Cuba with her daughter, on a government pension.

According to Guevara's book on guerrilla warfare, indoctrination is the most important element in training new recruits, and it followed that the first organized Communist influence which became apparent in Cuba in 1959 was in the rebel army and in the civilian militia organized by Guevara. He became head of the Department of Instruction of the Armed Forces Ministry, and soon Communists were lecturing in the army camps. It was this sort of indoctrination, in which they saw indubitable proof of the coming Communist domination, that Major Díaz Lanz and Major Hubert Matos opposed and tried in vain to stop.

Much of what I have related here was known to well-informed Cubans by 1960. Everyone looked upon Guevara as a Communist. In fact, when he was appointed president of the Cuban National Bank, a political anecdote which quickly made the rounds had it that at a cabinet meeting Castro had asked, "Which one of you is an *economista?*" Guevara held up his hand. "All right," said Castro, "you are the president of the National Bank." After the meeting Guevara asked Castro why he have given him the appointment. "Didn't you tell me you were an *economista?*" asked Castro. "Oh," said Guevara, "I thought you said '*Comunista*'!"

Guevara was no economist, but Castro trusted him and he became the chief economist figure of the regime. All of his policies were radical in the extreme. In June 1959 he went on a long trip to the Middle and Far East, and on his return he was made Director of the Department of Industrialization within the National Agrarian Reform Institute. Eventually economic decisions would be made by a Central Planning Council, of which Guevara was the most influential member. And he also became the chief architect of the various trade agreements with the Soviet Union and its satellites.

It was with considerable interest, therefore, that I received word that Guevara had given me an appointment. He was a tremendous worker, customarily at his job from about 3 P.M. to 6 A.M., and my interview was scheduled for late at night. I had talked to him briefly on other occasions but never alone. However, I was prepared for the meeting because of dealings I had had previously with Cuban Communist leaders, especially in 1946–1947, when they held Cabinet and Congressional posts and for a time controlled the labor movement. I had found them to be men of financial integrity, highly intelligent, and fanatically devoted to their Marxist beliefs. I was well aware that it would be a futile exercise to adopt a condescending attitude with anyone of Guevara's intellectual stature, and that any attempt at mock revolutionism would evoke only ridicule and contempt.

Guevara's appearance was fascinating. His alert brown eyes and large mustache, framed by a beard and abundant, curly hair, lent an Asiatic cast to his features and made him seem considerably older than his thirty-two years. In the mountains he had permitted his hair to grow to shoulder length but later it had been cut. He wore olive-green fatigues and black boots; his black beret with the major's star hung on a nearby chair. Atop his papers on the desk was his pistol. Although lacking the heartiness that Castro displays, he received me courteously.

As I expected, the Grace Line project was quickly brushed aside. "We are not interested in steamship services with the United States," he said. "We will have other ocean services and American vessels would have nothing to transport." I asked why this should be so. "Because dependence on the American market has enslaved us economically," he replied. But would Cuba not be enslaving herself by depending on the Soviet Union? And what about the preferentially higher prices paid by Americans for Cuban sugar? The Soviets liberate, he said, they do not enslave. The higher sugar prices in the American market, limited by a unilaterally imposed quota, were a fiction, he argued. Once the American quota is eliminated, "and the sooner, the better," Cuba would be master of the world market, able to dictate prices.

An attendant brought black coffee in small cups half filled with sugar, and Guevara offered me an excellent cigar, lighting his own.

"Tell me," he said, "you are the lawyer of the American Embassy, are you not?" No, we were not the Embassy lawyers, but we had done work for departments and agencies of the U.S. Government. "A technical distinction," he commented. "It is the same thing." Then, "Why don't you be smart, Lazo? *We* are the wave of the future. Your imperialist clients promise heaven up there," pointing, "but we offer it here, on earth."

I said I did not understand how the word "imperialism" could be applied to the United States, which had never had colonies. I had always associated the label with the great empires of the past, the British, French, Belgian, etc. No, he said, the United States engages in the most ruthless form of imperialism, which is the economic exploitation of the underdeveloped countries, as had happened in Cuba. The United States, a manufacturing country, did not want the developing countries to produce anything other than the raw materials it needed in order to enrich itself at their expense. "Capitalists use the labor of others exclusively for their own benefit," he said. "That is the essence of capitalism."

Guevara then made a remark that he was to repeat to others later: *The Castro regime and Yankee imperialism are engaged in a death struggle, and we both know that one of the two must die in this fight.*

But the United States is the most powerful country in the world and it does not intend to die, I remarked.

"Yes, my friend," he retorted, "the Americans have guns but they will not use them, even against us, so it is the same as if they had none." He paused for a moment, then summed up: "The fact is, the United States is weak and disoriented."

This conversation, like others, was reported to the Embassy. There was no noticeable effect, not to mention an expression of thanks. The Blind Colossus that is the United States continued to act "weak and disoriented," even when it finally became aware that in Cuba it was squarely up against international Communism.

Guevara's end came eight years later in Bolivia while he was attempting to carry out his and Castro's program of "two . . . three . . . many Vietnams." It is understandable that the project had been launched with confidence, since they were probably under the illusion that they had defeated Batista militarily, and imagined that the Bolivian experience would be similar. But there were differences, some decisive. The Bolivian Indian peasants, traditionally distrustful of the white man, and especially of bearded ones, proved to be even more hostile than the Cuban *montunos*. In Bolivia there was no Herbert Matthews, and, most important of all, the United States *helped* the Bolivian regular army instead of destroying its morale. In Bolivia the American military were permitted to give assistance in training and weaponry, imbuing the Bolivian army with the conviction that it could run down the rebels. The relationship between the Pentagon and the Latin American military establishments has fortunately always been cordial, one of genuine mutual respect. It has been so intimate, in fact, that Arthur M. Schlesinger, Jr., who invariably speaks scornfully of the military and is slick with words, refers to it as an "incestuous" relationship.[11] In hunting down Guevara, one of America's formidable enemies, it paid off.

On October 8, 1967, after a skirmish with government troops, Guevara was shot through both legs and trapped. When captured he identified himself. "I am 'Che' Guevara," he said. "Don't kill me; I am worth more to you alive than dead." The non-commissioned officer in charge of the army detail sent a message to headquarters in La Paz. *"Tenemos a papá,"* it said, *"que hacemos?"* The broad equivalent: "We have captured the big fish, what are your orders?"

At about 10 A.M. the next morning the answer came from President René Barrientos: "Liquidate him." Before drawing lots to see who would kill Guevara, most of the soldiers had themselves photographed with him. Not until about 2 P.M., when one of the men, carrying an M-2, entered the schoolroom where Guevara was being held, did he realize he was about to die. As the soldier pointed the weapon Guevara raised his

[11] Arthur M. Schlesinger, Jr., *A Thousand Days* (Boston: Houghton Mifflin Company, 1965), p. 199.

hands to his mouth in terror, biting down on his fingers in an effort to stifle a scream. A hail of bullets struck him and his body fell against the wall and slumped down. The eyes stared from the dirty bearded face. His body was either cremated or buried in an unmarked grave. From his group only five men escaped into Chile and then back to Cuba. At least ten Cuban Communist guerrillas, including two members of the Central Committee of the Cuban Communist Party, had been killed.

In life Guevara had always been motivated by hatred for the United States. He was a monster of cruelty, utterly ruthless and devoid of any trace of compassion. He always coldly rejected our appeals for the innocent victims of the infamous revolutionary "courts." While in the Sierra Maestra he reveled in presiding over the "trial" and execution of simple, illiterate peasants for being insubordinate, or those suspected of being "defeatists" or informers. Desertions, which were continual, included one of the *Granma* veterans.[12] Desertion was punishable by death upon capture.[13] Youths unable to withstand the rigors of guerrilla life were ordered shot because there were no prison facilities. Of the little band of Castro followers that was arrested by the Mexican police and held for a few weeks before "invading" Cuba in late 1956, Guevara later wrote, "They [the police] committed the error . . . of not killing him [Castro] after making him prisoner." [14]

But according to Communist standards, Ernesto Guevara de la Serna was a man of excellence. In his eulogy on October 18, 1967, Castro called him "a man of spotless conduct . . . a morally superior man . . . of exquisite human sensitivity . . . without a stain." [15] He had been shamelessly murdered, said Castro, by "thugs, oligarchs and mercenaries" who seemed not to be aware of "the repulsiveness of the procedure." Castro criti-

[12] Ernesto "Che" Guevara, *Reminiscences of the Cuban Revolutionary War* (New York: Monthly Review Press, Inc., 1968), pp. 75, 126.
[13] *Ibid.,* p. 108.
[14] *Ibid.,* p. 38.
[15] *Ibid.,* pp. 23, 25.

cized Guevara's "disdain for danger." There was no doubt about his bravery. The Castro brothers had repeatedly begged him not to run unnecessary risks, as they did not.

Castro had played for high stakes in Bolivia, but it proved to be no Cuba, and no Vietnam. Guevara's death was a shattering blow to the Latin America revolutionary movement.

CHAPTER FIFTEEN

The Invasion as Planned

The American military has no peer in the techniques of amphibious landings on a hostile shore. Tens of thousands of American men know about such things, having taken part in the assaults at the Omaha and Utah beaches in Normandy, at Anzio in Italy, and at Iwo Jima, Saipan, Inchon, and elsewhere. Carefully planned and brilliantly executed, these landings gave the American forces victory.

This experience and expertise amounted to a guarantee of swift success in the operation on the shore of Cuba—no less carefully planned.

The geographical setting of the Bay of Pigs invasion is more accurately described as Girón (or Playa Girón, as the Cubans refer to it) since the main body of assault troops disembarked near Girón, a small town of two hundred houses, which had the only good airport in the general area. But whatever name is used for the bay and its environs, the invasion had a catastrophic ending that may well mark one of the turning points in contemporary history.

Had the invasion been allowed to succeed, the first Communist beachhead in the Western Hemisphere would have been liquidated and nine-tenths of the Communist pressure on the other nations of Central and South America would have been removed. There would have been no Missile Crisis eighteen months later. As it turned out, the Soviet Union ended up with a sanctuary in the Carribean that has since been converted into an immensely formidable fortress, honeycombed with underground military installations of unknown power. In the face of this, even the American naval base at Guantanamo is probably useless—neutralized. Soviet weaponry installed in the area surrounding Guantanamo would very likely compel the United States to evacuate the base in a military confrontation between the nuclear giants.

The pernicious consequences of the defeat thus can hardly be overstated. The breathtaking arrogance of the Soviets in converting Cuba into a base for the subversion of Latin America has already stimulated guerrilla warfare in several countries. This in turn has weakened those countries economically, because foreign capital has been withheld or withdrawn and local capital has fled the area. It has spread a pall of fear and uncertainty over the rest of the hemisphere. The impact has been especially great because Cuba was always regarded as the prime example of what happens to a nation that stands close to the United States—geographically, socially, and economically.

Finally there is the moral aspect of the calamity, to which the great majority of Americans are certainly not indifferent. As a result of the Girón fiasco, eight million citizens of a neighboring country traditionally more friendly to the United States than any other in the world have been enslaved by Communism. Its children have been indoctrinated by Marxist teachers for more than ten years. It was Lenin who once repeated this historical truism: "Give me the children and the seeds I sow will never be uprooted." The price of Girón has been high indeed.

Apologists for the Kennedy administration have, of course, sought to play down the political and human costs of the disaster. They have implied, and in some cases said, that Girón was a minor episode. One has written that in later months President Kennedy became grateful that he had learned so much "at so relatively small and temporary a cost." [1] The Presi-

---

[1] Theodore C. Sorensen, *Kennedy* (New York: Harper & Row, 1965), p. 308.

dent's father told his son that the Bay of Pigs "was not a misfortune but a benefit." [2] Some Kennedy apologists have pointed to the fact that the number of men involved and the casualties were small. This reasoning is fallacious. The pivotal significance of a military engagement cannot be measured by the numbers involved or the casualties sustained. At Yorktown, for example, only 262 men were killed or wounded, 186 French and 76 Americans, yet it proved to be a momentous event in the history of North America.

Why and how did this tragic misadventure occur? The confusions which still prevail derive in large part from accounts in their respective books by two men closely identified with the Kennedy administration: Theodore C. Sorensen and Arthur M. Schlesinger, Jr., the first a special adviser to the President in 1961, the second a special assistant.

Both argue that the invasion never had a realistic chance to succeed. They blame the debacle on the Central Intelligence Agency, which developed the original plan, and the Joint Chiefs of Staff, who approved it. They insist, among other things, that the cancellation of a scheduled air strike on the morning of the invasion had little to do with the failure.

Who are these men? The question is a fair one, not only because of their writings on the Bay of Pigs but because one of them, Schlesinger, was an active and voluble member of the group of civilian advisers which emasculated the military plans. Neither of these men has any special knowledge of the military art; both are vociferous liberals; their accounts, presented more than three years after the event, are flatly contrary to the facts on vital points. Because of Schlesinger's involvement in the judgments that brought defeat, his interpretation is in the nature of the case subjective and self-justifying, if only subconsciously.

Sorensen's liberalism might be called hereditary and environ-

[2] Arthur M. Schlesinger, Jr., *A Thousand Days* (Boston: Houghton Mifflin Company, 1965), p. 297.

mental. His father had sailed for Europe on Henry Ford's "Peace Ship" and his mother was accused of pacifism and radicalism during World War I. Young Ted Sorensen registered with his Nebraska draft board as a conscientious objector. He once referred to himself as a "rationally committed liberal," more dedicated and effective than the liberal who is emotionally committed.

Schlesinger, who had once been a speech writer for Adlai Stevenson and remained one of his most zealous partisans, during the Kennedy Administration became the historian-in-residence at the White House, where he had few specific assignments. He was a founder and vice-chairman of the ultra-liberal ADA (Americans for Democratic Action). Kennedy delayed announcement of his appointment until Chester Bowles had been confirmed as Under Secretary of State. "I don't want the Senate to think that I am bringing down the whole ADA," he said.[3]

As a younger man, Schlesinger made little attempt to conceal his opinionated arrogance. Those of whom he disapproved were "idiots," and he publicly labeled them as such. His White House associate, McGeorge Bundy, once said of him, "He's a terribly partisan man, to a degree rarely found in academic life." [4] The conservative New York *Daily News* alluded to the built-in Schlesinger bias in less elegant English: "Junior is an egghead to end all eggheads, so we shudder to think what he may sneak into Kennedy's speeches. . . ."

Schlesinger's version of the Girón tragedy offers an interesting study of the liberal mind at work. Defeats are rationalized into victories. Professional military men, whose meticulously drawn plans were brushed aside on the recommendation of the President's coterie of civilian amateurs, are treated with scorn; the "court historian" refers sarcastically to their uniform, braid, and service ribbons, as if these were somehow dishonorable.

[3] Schlesinger, p. 162.
[4] Victor Lasky, *J.F.K., The Man and the Myth* (New York: Arlington House, Inc., 1966), p. 303.

He once went so far as to say that the United States owed a debt of gratitude to Castro because the bearded dictator had alerted Americans to the dangers of Communism in this hemisphere.[5] Through the magic of such ideological logic, the brutal reality that the Communists hold a beachhead within America's strategic defense periphery is transmuted into a blessing!

Schlesinger's account of the Girón disaster shows little of the intellectual objectivity we have a right to expect from an able historian. The final sentence in his Bay of Pigs chapter reads: "But no one can doubt that failure in Cuba in 1961 contributed to success in Cuba in 1962." Incredibly, it does not occur to him that if the invasion of Cuba in 1961 had been permitted to succeed, there would have been no Missile Crisis in 1962.

I have discussed these men at some length because, in the absence of the official government report on the Bay of Pigs, which has not been released as of this writing, their accounts of the debacle have been accepted throughout the world as authentic. The impact of these accounts is evident in hundreds of articles that have been written on the subject.

What are the facts?

The struggle which led to the failure was waged not in Girón but in Washington. The military action on the Cuban coast could have been shortened or prolonged for a few hours by fortuitous circumstances, but it was doomed to defeat by Washington decisions before the first assault troops had disembarked.

In essence the conflict was between moderate conservatives on the one hand, represented by the CIA and the Joint Chiefs, and the President's civilian advisers on the other—liberals all. Although the fate of Cuba was at stake, no Cuban participated in this critical struggle. Between the contending elements, making the decisions, was the new and youthful President, John F.

[5] Lasky, p. 577.

Kennedy, who has never been accused of lacking either personal courage or intelligence.

To understand how a sound military operation was emasculated by political decisions it is necessary, of course, to have an understanding of the invasion plan as originally conceived.

The decision to help anti-Castro Cubans liberate their homeland was made by President Dwight D. Eisenhower early in 1960. The task was assigned to the CIA. Any plan developed would have to be approved by the President.

By the time of the November 1960 presidential elections a number of tentative plans were under consideration by the CIA, but the Joint Chiefs of Staff as yet had no knowledge of any of them. In fact, no plan was submitted to the Joint Chiefs before January 1961, at least two months after the election. President Eisenhower has said that no tactical or operational plan was even discussed as of the day he turned the Presidency over to Kennedy.

"At no time did I put before anybody anything that could be called a plan," said the former President. "There was no mandate, no commitment by me or anyone in my administration," so that Kennedy could not have felt "he was frozen into any position by me." [6] Among Eisenhower's last words to his successor before the ceremonial drive to the inauguration were, "You people will have to decide what to do about Cuba." And the two men did not speak with each other again for three months, until after the disaster. In spite of this, Schlesinger was later to write, "the Republicans, of course, were a little inhibited by their own role in conceiving the operation. . . ." [7]

Long before the inauguration, four hundred to six hundred Cuban Freedom Fighters were receiving military training in Guatemala, Panama, Florida, Louisiana, and at Fort Meade, twenty miles north of Washington, although the State Depart-

[6] Earl Mazo, "Ike Speaks Out: Bay of Pigs Was All JFK's," *Newsday,* September 10, 1965, p. 51.
[7] Schlesinger, p. 288.

ment wanted all the training to be done outside of the United States. It did not want Cubans trained even at the Jungle Warfare School in Panama. Air drops to the anti-Castro fighters in Cuba's Escambray Mountains were being attempted by Cuban pilots who had been trained by American instructors in planes provided by the U.S. Government.

The morale of the Freedom Fighters was extremely high. Their American instructors exuded confidence, based on the conviction that any enterprise approved by President Eisenhower, and carried out as approved, would not be allowed to fail, even if final victory required the overt support of American troops, ships, and planes. Their confidence at this stage was not misplaced. Eisenhower has said that his country's prestige and power should never be committed unless its Chief Executive was determined to *win*. "There is no alternative," he declared. "Force is a naked, brutal thing in this world. . . . If you are going to use it, you have got to be prepared to go all the way. . . . If our hand had been discovered, then it was more important than ever that we win." [8]

This was the situation that confronted President John F. Kennedy when he entered the White House in January 1961.

The invasion site in the first plan submitted to President Kennedy in February 1961 was not Girón but Trinidad, a city of twenty thousand inhabitants lying almost one hundred miles farther east on the south coast of Cuba, in the foothills of the Escambray Mountains. Trinidad was chosen because it offered a number of substantial advantages. It was one hundred miles farther from Havana, where Castro's troops and armor were known to be concentrated. The local population was known to be strongly anti-Castro. It had a suitable airfield. Most important of all, the site provided an alternative if things went wrong—the invaders could escape into the nearby mountains and conduct prolonged guerrilla operations. The Trinidad invasion site was selected by the CIA and the Joint Chiefs con-

[8] Mazo, p. 51.

curred in the selection. There was no mention of any other site.

The traditional command structure of the United States has been one under which the Commander in Chief sets the primary objectives of combat and leaves to professionals the conduct of operations. In this case, however, Kennedy kept a tight strategic control over the invasion plan. He began to overrule the recommendations of the Joint Chiefs, of whom Eisenhower has said: "These men over decades of devoted service have shown their capabilities, their sense of logic, their understanding of the problems involved in this kind of venture. There is no more expert group in their profession than these men. . . ." [9] But the plans of these men were watered down and then discarded piecemeal. The first of several political decisions which had this effect was made when Kennedy accepted the idea that an amphibious landing at Trinidad would be "too spectacular." He wanted a "quiet landing," and preferably at night.[10]

The reason that impelled the President to make this decision was that U.S. participation in the operation was supposed to be secret, undercover. A landing which had all the earmarks of an invasion mounted by the United States, at a coastal town as large as Trinidad, he was persuaded, would give the whole thing away. He was deeply concerned about world opinion.

Strictly speaking, Trinidad is not a coastal town. Its port of entry, Casilda, on the Caribbean, lies three miles to the south. Casilda is a seaside resort with a population of about fifteen hundred. It has a good beach, far superior to anything adjacent to Girón, and a river that empties into the bay is navigable for small boats almost as far as Trinidad. It offered a completely ideal landing site for the invaders.

Liberal State Department officials have a pathological dread of "world opinion." They do not realize that adverse world opinion subsides quickly in the face of accomplishment; that history never argues long with success but rarely forgives fail-

9 *Ibid.*, p. 50.
10 Schlesinger, p. 242.

ures. The Soviets and the Chinese Communists are entirely indifferent to world opinion. They never bow to adverse publicity or permit it to deter them from policies they consider desirable to themselves. America's staunchest allies are invariably more appalled by a display of weakness resulting in failure. Lyndon Johnson once expressed this idea when he was being warned at a Vietnam briefing by State Department officials that strong military action being contemplated might injure the image of the United States. "You guys are so busy saving my face you are going to lose me my pants!" he said.[11] William F. Buckley, Jr., has expressed the same idea: "I think world opinion is just a paper tiger. When Johnson landed Marines in Santo Domingo everyone expected a lot of shouting and not very much really happened." [12] As Vice President, incidentally, Johnson, although older and wiser than the liberal Frontiersmen who breathlessly invaded Washington in 1961, was seldom consulted or listened to at the time.

The scornful expression "paper tiger" was applied by Chinese Communists to the Franco-American defeat in the Indo-China War and to the stalemate in Korea. In the light of such Western defeats, Peking had no trouble selling Asians the idea that the United States was a "paper tiger," strong in promises, weak in action. Can there be any doubt that the Bay of Pigs calamity, in the measure that it fortified the notion of American inability to use its power without paralyzing inhibitions about world opinion, encouraged the Communist aggressions in Southeast Asia?

But even conceding some importance to world opinion, the fact is that in 1961 U.S. involvement in the invasion project was no secret to anyone, as it never could have been in a free society. In October 1960, six months before the invasion, the *Hispanic-American Report,* a journal published at Stanford University, reported that Cuban Freedom Fighters were being

---

[11] *Time* Essay on World Opinion, May 28, 1965, p. 31.
[12] *Life,* September 17, 1965.

trained at camps in Guatemala. Similar articles had appeared in *La Hora,* a Guatemalan paper, and in November in *The Nation.* On December 22, 1960, the Los Angeles *Mirror* informed its readers of the Guatemalan activities. A representative of the St. Louis *Post-Dispatch* visited Guatemala and confirmed the existence of the camps.

Finally, on January 10, 1961, three months before the invasion, *The New York Times* published a three-column front-page article under the headline U.S. HELPS TRAIN AN ANTI-CASTRO FORCE AT SECRET GUATEMALAN AIR-GROUND BASE. This was illustrated with a map, also on the front page, showing the exact location of the training base. The long article stated that the United States was "assisting the training effort not only with personnel but with matériel and the construction of ground and air facilities." Immediately following was an item reporting that Foreign Minister Raúl Roa of Cuba had accused the United States of training "mercenaries" in Guatemala and of hastily conditioning an airport there with aggressive intentions against Cuba. Four days previously, on January 6, *Time* magazine reported that the CIA was giving financial aid estimated as high as $500,000 monthly to Cuban underground groups.

Many other reports came out of Miami, confirming the invasion buildup. In March 1961, Lyman Kirkpatrick, Executive Director of the CIA, spoke to the Commonwealth Club in San Francisco. Professor Ronald Hilton of Stanford University asked him what he thought of the discovery of the CIA camps in Guatemala. Kirkpatrick answered that he thought it was a bad thing whenever covert CIA activity was discovered, and the press on the West Coast played up what Professor Hilton took to be an acknowledgment that there were CIA camps.

These stories revealed no secrets to Castro. It was all common knowledge. The pretense of secrecy was an exercise in futility. Pierre Salinger, the White House press representative, says that eight days before the invasion the only information Castro did not have was the exact time and place of the invasion. President Kennedy told Salinger, "I can't believe what I am reading! Castro doesn't need agents over here. All he has to do is read our papers. It's all laid out for him." [13] In the weeks before the invasion hardly a day passed without a dispatch in some newspaper or a broadcast over some radio or TV station confirming the invasion prospects. One might therefore conclude that it had become evident, as long as three months before the invasion, that the fear of impairing the U.S. image was no longer a valid consideration. Nevertheless, as will be seen, it continued to be the main argument that influenced the decisions that foredoomed the invasion.

When the President ordered the CIA to find a less conspicuous landing site than Trinidad (in fact, Casilda), the CIA and the Joint Chiefs, after considering a number of alternatives, chose Girón, near the Bay of Pigs. There were excellent reasons for Girón as a second choice. The latest American reconnaissance plane photos showed that there was no concentration of Castro troops in the vicinity, as had also been the case in Trinidad. The air strip at Girón was suitable for B-26 operations. The military men, however, saw that Girón had one big disadvantage. The area was not suited to prolonged guerrilla warfare —if things went wrong there would be no alternative to fall back on. Nevertheless, the fact that the CIA and the Joint Chiefs, though they still preferred Casilda, were willing to accept Girón shows that they believed the operation *as then planned* was very likely to succeed.

The essential element of the invasion plan—called Operation Pluto—was the use of air power. This central fact must be kept well in mind. Castro's small air force of less than thirty operable aircraft was to be destroyed on the ground with a *minimum* of *three* air strikes—not two, as reported by Sorensen and Schlesinger—by the Free Cuban Air Squadron based at Puerto Cabezas, Nicaragua. There were to be two strikes prior to the

[13] Pierre Salinger, *With Kennedy* (New York: Doubleday & Company, Inc., 1966), p. 146.

invasion, with the full squadron of sixteen attacking planes participating, and a third strike to coincide with the landings in Cuba.

The number and timing of the air strikes in the original plan are of the utmost significance in understanding how it was emasculated in the actual operation. The man in charge of the invasion at the CIA, Richard M. Bissell, Jr., has confirmed to me that the plan called for "three air strikes all at full strength." Had the second strike been carried out, he emphasized, it would have caught Castro's Air Force not "in hiding" but "concentrated at the one base known to us." General Cabell, then working with Bissell, informed me that in addition to the three scheduled massive blows there were to be as many more individual sorties as needed to destroy every Castro plane on the ground. Former Vice President Richard Nixon, whose sources of information were certainly unique, has consistently referred to three planned air strikes in speaking or writing about the invasion.[14] Those who persist in referring to two strikes are, knowingly or in honest error, distorting the character of the original plans.

Plainly then, there were to be at least 48 sorties from Nicaragua, and if these were not sufficient to destroy every Castro plane on the ground before the invasion force hit the beaches, additional runs were to be made against the airports. The Americans would replace any planes lost during these strikes. After every Castro plane had been destroyed, and the assault troops had seized the Girón airfield at the beachhead, the Free Cuban Air Squadron would use it as its base of operations. This would eliminate the 1,480-mile flight from Nicaragua to Cuba and back, which took seven hours and allowed the bombers little more than 30 minutes over the target. Thenceforth, with complete control of the air over the entire island, the bombing schedule of the liberating planes, as will be explained, could be

[14] Richard M. Nixon, "Cuba, Castro and John F. Kennedy," *Reader's Digest,* November 1962, p. 290.

expected to bring about Castro's collapse in a very few days.

The first air strike, scheduled for Saturday morning, April 15, had as its sole objective the destruction of as many of Castro's aircraft on the ground as possible. The second strike, scheduled for Sunday morning, April 16, was intended to destroy any remaining aircraft on the ground and to bomb known anti-aircraft and other military installations.

Air strike No. 3, scheduled for Monday, April 17, was to provide final assurance that every Castro plane had been destroyed. As mentioned, additional and repeated strikes would provide extra assurance that the basic and indispensable objective had been accomplished. The third strike would have had the supplementary objective of hitting tank, mobile-gun, and truck concentrations and sinking a gunboat anchored near Cienfuegos. The planes were then to fly support missions over the beachhead, preparatory to using the Girón airport as the base of squadron operations.

Incredibly and in the end fatally, the *minimum forty-eight sorties out of Nicaragua were eventually reduced to eight,* by orders from the White House.

Repeatedly, while in training, Cuban airmen asked their U.S. superiors whether the stripped planes, defenseless from the rear, would not be easy prey for Castro's jets. The answer from the American officer in command was plain and reassuring: "Don't worry about Castro's jet fighters—they won't get into the air." He was echoing the Washington strategists who counted on the complete destruction of the Communist air force on the ground. Operation Pluto, it cannot be too often emphasized, was to be *essentially an air operation.*

The Free Cuban Air Squadron consisted of sixteen B-26 medium bombers, four 4-engine C-54's, and five twin-engine C-46's (the two latter types were unarmed transports to carry paratroopers and supplies). The planes were of World War II and Korean War vintage; the B-26's had been stripped of tail guns to enable them to carry needed fuel for the long flight from

Nicaragua to Cuba and back. U.S. military advisers considered them entirely adequate to the air requirements of Operation Pluto.

The invasion force of which the Air Squadron was a part was known as Brigade 2506 and was composed of 1,443 men. It had been trained at two sites on the south coast of Guatemala by U.S. Army specialists who were veterans of the Korean War and World War II. The name "La Brigada 2506" was chosen by the Cubans because 2506 was the serial number of the first Cuban to die in preparing for the invasion. He was a popular, idealistic young student named Carlos Rafael Santana, who fell into a ravine while on a physical training mission. His death on September 7, 1960, saddened and unified the men in training.

Brigade 2506 was an authentic cross-section of Cuba. It was made up of farmers, fishermen, lawyers, doctors, and bankers. Many of the men were married and had children, and there were several father-and-son pairs. The largest group was composed of students but there were teachers, engineers, mechanics, cattlemen, and clerks. Although the large majority were Catholics, there were also Protestants and some Jews. In addition to 50 full-blooded Negroes, others had some Negro blood. There were about 140 professional soldiers, but most of the men had had no previous military training. Thus the Brigade was composed of men of varying backgrounds, socially, intellectually and politically, with the result that there was some division among them. What united them was their democratic ideals and sense of duty, and their unanimous conviction that the invasion would be successful.

The tragic aspect of "La Brigada," as things turned out, was that its members had a blind faith in the United States. They were certain, to a man, that their American friends would never let them down. In many ways these men were closer to the United States than to any country of Latin America. Their American instructors, to whom the Cubans became deeply attached, were astonished at the fervor which they displayed in the training program, hanging on every spoken word and eagerly grasping every opportunity to improve their military skills.

In back of everything was their certainty that they were dealing with representatives of the world's greatest and most powerful nation, which had always been their friend. Many spoke English and had gone to school in the United States; they knew its history and its record of victory in war. Not one of them conceived the possibility of defeat. And they knew the history of their own country, which taught that small groups of men had often triumphed over large forces. Batista had taken over their government in 1952 with only twenty-five men; Castro himself had started guerrilla activities with only twelve.

Inevitably there were a few trouble-makers. They had confidence in their American instructors but provoked rivalries in the Brigade. During the training period these troublesome Cubans, a total of twelve, were removed from the Brigade and imprisoned by the Americans.

The best estimate of the Brigade was contained in a dispatch from a veteran Marine colonel who had been sent to Guatemala as a special emissary of the President to make a final inspection. It read, in part, as follows:

My observations have increased my confidence in the ability of this force to accomplish not only initial combat missions but also the ultimate objective, the overthrow of Castro. The Brigade and battalion commanders now know all details of the plan and are enthusiastic. These officers are young, vigorous, intelligent, and motivated with a fanatical urge to begin battle. . . . They say they know their people and believe after they have inflicted one serious defeat upon the opposition forces, the latter will melt away from Castro. . . . I share their confidence.

The Brigade is . . . more heavily armed and better equipped in some respects than U.S. infantry units. The men have received . . . more firing experience than U.S. troops would normally receive. I was impressed with the serious attitude of the men. . . . The embarkation was carried out with remarkable smoothness. The Brigade now numbers 1,400; a truly formidable force.

I have also observed the [Brigade] Cuban Air Force carefully. The aircraft are kept with pride and some of the crew are so eager they have already armed their aircraft. [Name deleted] . . . informed me today that he considers the B-26 Squadron equal to the best U.S. Air Force Squadron. *The Brigade officers . . . ask only for continued delivery of supplies* (emphasis added).

This Cuban Air Force is well trained, armed to the teeth, and ready.[15]

When President Kennedy ordered the Joint Chiefs to find a less spectacular landing site than Casilda, Trinidad's port of entry, they of course complied, but only after emphasizing their preference for Casilda and Trinidad in writing to the President, as well as personally whenever the matter was discussed. Once Kennedy had decided against the Casilda-Trinidad operation, however, attention was concentrated on Playa Girón. This was the beginning of a progressive watering-down process.

To the north of the newly selected landing site lies the great Ciénaga de Zapata swamp, extending approximately sixty-five miles from east to west and twenty miles from north to south. Along the shore, however, the soil is hard and rocky, and for about three miles inland the land is smooth and firm. Only three highways, built across the swamp, connect the shoreline with the interior of the island. The enormous swamp of black muck is infested with crocodiles, mosquitoes, and huge black flies.

The invasion plan called for dropping paratroopers along each of the three roads, to cut off any early access to the beachhead. Assault troops were to disembark at three points along forty miles of shoreline, the main force at Playa Girón and

[15] From the magazine article "We Who Tried," *Life,* May 10, 1963, p. 34.

other detachments twenty miles to the northwest and twenty miles to the east. (As things turned out, the invaders did, for a brief time, occupy an area forty miles in width and almost twenty miles inland.) The first landing party would clear the Girón airport runway, while freighters in the invasion fleet unloaded gasoline, bombs, ammunition, and supplies, and put ashore a group of highly trained aircraft mechanics.

With control of the air and operating out of Girón, the Brigade Air Squadron could easily destroy railroad and road bridges, block the few highways leading toward the beachhead, and blast any approaching tanks, trucks, and tractor-drawn artillery. At Matanzas, for instance, where I would soon be held a prisoner with thirty-five hundred other men and women, the only two good highways from Havana leading to the beachhead merge into a single road which runs for a considerable stretch along the bay front, with water on one side and cliffs on the other. To reach the beachhead Castro's tanks and mobile guns, concentrated near Havana, undoubtedly would elect to pass over this single highway. There they could be blasted into a heap of bottleneck wreckage. They would be sitting ducks for an air attack. The only other road from Havana part way to the beachhead was of greatly inferior quality. During the early hours of Tuesday, April 18, we prisoners in Matanzas watched the first column of tanks and armor arriving from Havana and moving slowly, with long pauses, in bumper-to-bumper fashion, toward the point where it would merge with the second column over the single stretch of road.

But this was only the first stage of the invasion, designed to protect the beachhead. The second was to knock out the island's electric power and communications. Without hitting the main power plant in Havana, six undefended transformers located throughout the island could be reduced with machine-gun fire or a single bomb. This would mute 90 to 95 percent of Cuba's radio, telephone, telegraph, and television services. It would paralyze virtually all of the country's industrial plants dependent on electric power.

The supply of water in Cuba, even to the smallest home, is also dependent upon electric power. Knocking out the six transformers would end 90 to 95 percent of the country's water service. Uncontrollable fires would then light the Cuban skies in every town and city from one end of the island to the other.

Under these panic conditions, with industry ground to a halt because of lack of power, with spectacular fires burning in key installations throughout the island owing to lack of water, with Castro unable to talk to the people over the radio or television, and, most important of all, with the knowledge on the part of the populace that the United States was supporting the invasion, *all Cubans agree that the Castro regime would have fallen within a week.*

And this was not all. The invasion plan also provided for immobilizing Castro's tanks, trucks, and tractor-drawn weapons by depriving his army of fuel. Cuba has no native fuel resources. Except for the sugar industry, which burns bagasse, the residue left after grinding sugar cane and extracting the juice, nearly all its fuel needs are met through the importation of crude oil that is refined into gasoline at three principal refineries, two located in the Havana area and one at Santiago.

The Cuban pilots were instructed by their American advisers not to bomb the refinery installations. The most vulnerable part of a refinery is not the processing equipment, as is commonly believed, since refinery designers build the reactors, furnaces, and towers to withstand blasts from accidental explosions, hurricanes and fires. The way to shut down a refinery, the pilots were told, is to hit the main transformers outside the power plants. Without power a refinery is helpless; the motors and pumps do not function; there is no water or light.

Of course, gasoline storage tanks were a preferred target. In addition to the storage tanks adjoining the three refineries there were fifteen major bulk fuel storage installations throughout the island. These, too, were preferred targets. Also, the Cuban pilots had a plan of their own. There were three thousand gasoline service stations scattered island-wide, individually small but collectively significant. The pilots knew the location of every one but, in order to avoid unnecessary bloodshed, planned to destroy only the principal ones, located near Castro's weaponry.

Thus it was a certainty that with complete control of the air and operating out of their nearby air base, the attacking squadron could have knocked out all the refineries and storage facilities at will. None had protection against air attack; all were completely vulnerable. Castro's trucks, tanks, tractor-drawn artillery, and vehicles would soon have been immobilized. The only mobile weaponry would have been that of the invaders, supplied from the beaches.

Conditions inside Cuba in April 1961 presaged an overthrow of the regime. Underground and terrorist activities mounted with each passing day. Bombs exploded in government buildings and industrial plants. Cars loaded with armed rebels often went careening through the streets of Havana, adding to the conviction that the end of the regime was approaching. As I have already said, three days before the invasion the famous El Encanto department store, the largest in Havana, was burned to the ground by saboteurs.

Finally, a hand-picked group of Cuban political leaders was to be flown into Girón to set up a provisional government and to call for recognition and military assistance. It was known that most of the nations of the Caribbean area were ready to respond favorably to such a plea.

The CIA never viewed the operation as one in which the landings would at once touch off a widespread insurrection in a police-state.[16] Its view was that if the beachhead was successfully consolidated, and if Castro's forces were defeated in attacks on the beachhead, and if the Brigade, with command of the air, could supply outlying points, insurrection might occur. At the very least there would be large-scale desertions from Castro's militia. It was also believed that after a few days, fol-

[16] Charles C. V. Murphy, "Cuba, The Record Set Straight," *Fortune*, September 1961.

lowing the recognition of the new government by several Latin American nations and by the United States, Castro would be receptive to a call for a cease-fire, which would be granted on condition that free elections would soon be held.

This was the invasion plan evolved by the CIA, approved by the Joint Chiefs, and improved by the Cuban invaders. It was masterfully conceived, as I would hear Castro himself admit. While Carmen and I were refugees in the Italian Embassy, Castro said in a television broadcast that if the invaders had been able to consolidate their beachhead, the cost in lives to reduce it would have been prohibitive. In truth, he would have had no chance whatever to reduce it.

On April 4th the plan, designed to produce these results, came up for final review at a dramatic meeting in the State Department, over which President Kennedy presided. Among those present were: Secretary of State Dean Rusk; Secretary of the Treasury Douglas Dillon; Senator J. William Fulbright, Chairman of the Senate Foreign Relations Committee; Gen. Lyman Lemnitzer, Chairman of the Joint Chiefs; Adm. Arleigh Burke, Chief of Naval Operations; Allen W. Dulles, Director of the CIA; Gen. Charles P. Cabell, Deputy Director of the CIA; Paul Nitze, Assistant Secretary of Defense; Thomas Mann, Assistant Secretary of State for Latin American Affairs; Presidential assistants McGeorge Bundy, Arthur M. Schlesinger, Jr., and Richard Goodwin; Presidential consultant Adolf Berle; and Richard M. Bissell, of the CIA, charged with supervising Operation Pluto on a day-to-day basis.

Bissell is a modest, unassuming gentleman, with the power to make intelligent decisions. He is a man of quiet manner, with a soft voice, but now he spoke forcefully and lucidly, explaining that the essential element of the proposed operation was the destruction of Castro's small air force on the ground by the three-plus pre-invasion air strikes. This, he said, could be accomplished easily by the Cuban-manned bombers guided by U.S. reconnaissance photographs.

The crowded conference room gave Bissell respectful attention. He was the man mainly responsible for the CIA's share in the extraordinarily successful U.S. reconnaissance satellite program, which had finally opened the closed society of the Soviet Union to U.S. intelligence inspection. Previously he had shared in the development of the amazing U-2 independent Air Squadron, which he eventually commanded.[17] These two scientific achievements were of incalculable importance to the United States. They changed the entire strategic aspect of the world before Kennedy took office. At the time of the Bay of Pigs they had confirmed other intelligence reports that the Soviets had not developed and mounted any intercontinental ballistic missiles (ICBMs). President Kennedy knew that any Soviet threat to support Castro with ICBMs would be an empty threat.

The sole voice raised against Operation Pluto at the meeting was that of Senator Fulbright, who denounced the plan as immoral. Six days earlier he had given the President a memorandum urging a policy of containment to meet the Castro-Communist threat. Remember always, it had concluded, "The Castro regime is a thorn in the flesh; but it is not *a dagger in the heart.*" [18] In view of what developed in the next few days it is significant that Secretary of State Dean Rusk, at that time, did not oppose the plan.

The following day, April 5, President Kennedy made his decision to proceed with Operation Pluto. D-Day was to be Monday, April 17, 1961.

[17] Joseph Alsop, "A Debt Is Owed," *The Hartford Courant,* December 26, 1963.

[18] Schlesinger, p. 251.

CHAPTER SIXTEEN

The Aborted Invasion

There was jubilation in Happy Valley when President Kennedy's "Go Ahead" signal was received there. Happy Valley was the code name of Puerto Cabezas, a coastal town in Nicaragua, where Brigade 2506 had been flown from Guatemala. The movement of the Brigade had taken several days, with the windows of the transport planes covered with tape so that the men, under complete American control, would not know their destination until they landed. On their arrival they found the Brigade Air Squadron awaiting them, together with several cargo vessels.

Morale at Happy Valley remained very high. With word that the invasion had been approved by the President the men worked with new zest, day and night. Often they sang the Cuban national anthem as they gathered for a brief rest.

On Friday morning, April 14, 1961, copies of the invasion plan were distributed to the Cuban officers for the first time:

> Commencing at H-Hour of D-Day, the Brigade is to engage in amphibious and parachute landings, take, occupy and defend beachheads in the area of Cochinos Bay and Playa Girón of the Zapata Swamps in order to establish a base from which ground and air operations against the Castro government of Cuba may be carried out. . . .

The plan, detailed on a large map, seemed superb. Seventy-two tons of arms, ammunition and equipment, sufficient to support 4,000 men, would be unloaded on D-Day. Another 415 tons would be unloaded in the next ten days, and then 530 more, and then 607 tons [1]—there would be "continuing supplies to the beaches." [2] The Castro forces were disorganized, the men were told, and there were none near the invasion site. Castro would have few tanks and no air force.

Nothing was said about U. S. air support, but the Cubans were assured that no Castro planes would be in the air, that Castro's columns would not be able to reach the beachhead because they would be destroyed from the air. No trucks or troops would be able to get through—all the roads would have been bombed. Thousands of gallons of gasoline would be loaded on cargo ships so that the Air Squadron could begin its follow-up missions immediately after the Girón airport had been seized. These missions would destroy the main railway and highway bridges in order to shield the beachhead. There was to be a diversionary landing in the eastern province and a simulated landing in the western province, accomplished with special sound equipment that would give the impression of a great battle being waged. This feature did, in fact, mislead Castro and delay his dispatch of armor to Girón. He knew the invasion was coming—it could not be a strategic surprise—but he did not know when and where.

The Cubans were so impressed that no one asked any questions. As the meeting broke up the men were cheering.

By contrast, there was little enthusiasm in Washington. By April 11, reports indicated that serious disagreements had emerged within the Kennedy administration as to how far the United States should go in helping the Cubans overthrow Castro. They indicated that some of those who had participated

[1] Haynes Johnson, *The Bay of Pigs* (New York: W. W. Norton & Company, 1964), p. 84.

[2] From the article "We Who Tried," *Life,* May 10, 1963, p. 34.

in the April 4th meeting had veered away from their first position.

One of the first critics, we now know, was Chester Bowles, a former partner in a Madison Avenue advertising agency who had become the No. 2 man in the State Department. When Rusk went to a SEATO conference in late March, Bowles, acting in his place, learned of the invasion plan and was horrified. He prepared a memorandum for Rusk, strongly opposing the undertaking, and on his return asked permission to carry his case to the President. Rusk gave Bowles the impression that the project would be cut down, probably into a guerrilla operation, and Bowles was mollified.[3]

Senator Fulbright also gave the President the previously mentioned memorandum that Schlesinger has described as "brilliant." If the invasion were a success, it argued, it would be denounced throughout Latin America and cause trouble at the United Nations. If it seemed to be failing, "we might be tempted to use our own armed force. . . ." Supporting any plan would be equivalent to "the hypocrisy and cynicism for which the United States is constantly denouncing the Soviet Union. . . ." Fulbright strongly urged a policy of containment.[4]

Arthur M. Schlesinger, Jr., had some influence in the Kennedy administration in its initial months. In early February he gave the President a memorandum warning that the invasion plan "would fix a malevolent image of the new administration in the minds of millions."[5] After the April 4th meeting at the State Department he advised Kennedy that he was opposed to the operation. Feeling he had not made his position sufficiently strong, he prepared a memorandum early the next day which foresaw the possibility that if the invasion appeared to be failing and the Cubans called for American armed help, Con-

[3] Arthur M. Schlesinger, Jr., *A Thousand Days* (Boston: Houghton Mifflin Company, 1965), pp. 250, 251.

[4] *Ibid.*, p. 250.

[5] *Ibid.*, p. 240.

gress and other pressures might make it hard to resist the demand to send in the Marines.[6]

"A course of bullying intervention would destroy the new image of the United States," Schlesinger admonished the President. "It is this reawakening world faith in America which is at stake in the Cuban operation."[7] Later Schlesinger would explain his position: "Nothing had been more depressing in the whole series of meetings than to watch a collection of officials, some of them holdovers from the previous administration, contentedly prepare to sacrifice the world's growing faith in the new American President in order to defend interests and pursue objectives *of their own.*"[8] (Emphasis added) He gave the President another memorandum five days after the first, along the same lines.

An April 6 Schlesinger met with Richard Goodwin at breakfast to discuss further efforts to reverse the CIA plan. The youthful Goodwin had been a speech-writer for the President, who designated him to handle Latin America despite the fact that he spoke no Spanish and had spent less than two weeks of his life there. Abrasive and arrogant, Goodwin quickly came into sharp conflict with career officers at the State Department. Later that morning he went to see Rusk to express his opposition.[9] He urged Schlesinger to send Rusk a copy of his memoranda to Kennedy and follow it up with a personal visit, which Schlesinger did the following morning. Rusk subsequently told Schlesinger he (Rusk) had successfully pared down the amphibious assault.[10]

Schlesinger's final contribution to the pre-invasion developments was the preparation of a White Paper on Cuba which included the preposterous statement, "We acknowledge past

[6] *Ibid.,* p. 254.
[7] *Ibid.,* p. 255.
[8] *Ibid.*
[9] *Ibid.,* p. 257.
[10] *Ibid.*

omissions and errors in our relationship to them [the Cubans]." [11] When this document went through the process of inter-departmental clearance, even Edward R. Murrow, then heading the USIA, found it "too racy and liberal." [12] He objected specifically to the confession of omissions and errors. But Schlesinger, taking full advantage of the White House leverage, resisted, and the document emerged virtually intact.

Torn between the opposing factions—the CIA and Joint Chiefs on the one hand, the liberal politicos on the other— President Kennedy wavered. Finally he agreed to further compromises which radically dismembered the original plan. They were made without consulting the CIA or the Joint Chiefs, who, when they learned of them, used every means at their disposal to have them countermanded.

When the Zapata plan had first been submitted to the President he suggested some changes intended to reduce the noise level—such as having the invasion ships unload before dawn. During the superb American record of amphibious operations in the Pacific in World War II, not one assault landing had been attempted at night. Kennedy's military advisers opposed the night landing in this case too. They feared that the submerged, razor-sharp coral reefs on the Cuban coast would pose a serious threat to landing craft at night, making the operation risky, but the President was adamant. After all, "world opinion" had to be taken into account.

The next critical compromise was in air strike No. 1 against Castro's airports, scheduled for dawn Saturday, April 15. The plan called for a strike in full force, using the squadron's sixteen bombers. Here the State Department got into the act, arguing that the attacking group would look too numerous to be consistent with the fiction that the air strike had been mounted solely by defecting Cuban pilots. So, on an order from the White House, the first strike force was whittled down to eight

[11] *Ibid.*, p. 245.
[12] *Ibid.*, p. 246.

planes. This order cut the scheduled forty-eight sorties from Happy Valley to forty.

About a week before the invasion the second of the three planned strikes (scheduled for Sunday, April 16) was canceled entirely. The reason given was the necessity of preserving the "non-involvement image." The President's political advisers also decided that two air strikes (really one-and-a-half) should be sufficient to destroy Castro's planes on the ground. The number of sorties from Happy Valley was now reduced from forty-eight to twenty-four.

These sharply downward revisions greatly alarmed the Joint Chiefs and the CIA men responsible for the operation. They considered recommending that the invasion be canceled. After further review, however, they decided that the third air strike, scheduled for D-Day—Monday, April 17—could be counted on to eliminate the few aircraft Castro would have left. The Communist air force was mostly concentrated at one base near Havana and was under constant surveillance by American reconnaissance planes.

On April 12 uneasiness mounted at the CIA and the Pentagon when President Kennedy stated at his press conference, without consulting any military adviser, that "there will not under any conditions be an intervention in Cuba by U.S. armed forces." The government, he said, would make sure that "there are no Americans involved." This unfortunate statement tied the hands of the United States in advance. A clue to why the President made it may be found in Schlesinger's statement that on April 10 he suggested to Kennedy in still another memorandum that as a "first protection against step-by-step-involvement" the Cuban leaders should be advised that "in no foreseeable circumstance will we send in U.S. troops. . . ."[13]

"Kennedy understood this better than anybody and needed no prodding," added Schlesinger. Pressure also came from Ambassador Adlai Stevenson, who, according to Schlesinger, ex-

[13] *Ibid.*, p. 262.

pressed his misgivings at a White House conference and was assured by the President that "whatever happened, United States armed forces would not be used. . . ." The President's announcement, nailed down when Stevenson quoted it at the United Nations three days later and when Secretary Rusk repeated it at his own press conference on April 17, was to prove a contributing factor to the disaster.

The eight planes authorized to take part in strike No. 1 reached the south coast of Cuba at dawn on Saturday, April 15, on three different courses. Coming in at low altitude, they crossed the island without being picked up on Castro's primitive radar. The attack achieved complete surprise. Three planes hit the field at San Antonio de los Baños; three more struck at Camp Columbia in Havana; two others attacked the airport at Santiago de Cuba. The Free Cuban Squadron lost three planes: one B-26 was hit by anti-aircraft fire, crashed at sea, and both pilots were lost; another, returning toward Nicaragua, made a crash landing on Gran Caymán, a small British island; a third cracked up as it just reached a U.S. base near Key West.

The Cubans and their American supervisors considered the limited strike a success. Castro's air force had been cut in half —but he still had at least two jets, three fast Sea Furies, and two B-26's. The originally scheduled strike No. 2, if it had not been canceled out, no doubt would have finished them off, with No. 3 to follow.

I heard Castro in a televised report to the nation admit that great damage had been done to his air force by this first strike. He boasted, however, that he had immediately ordered a dispersal of the remaining planes. The fact is that American reconnaissance photography, the finest in the world, spotted each remaining plane and reported its exact location to Happy Valley. There was no way Castro could hide a plane. It appeared a certainty that they would be mopped up on the ground by strike No. 3 (still scheduled for takeoff at 1:40 A.M. Monday). But a new, wholly unexpected development in Washington changed the picture.

At 3 P.M. on Sunday, April 16, the B-26 pilots at Happy Valley were called together in the rear of the operations shack. For the next four hours the Monday morning mission was explained in detail by U.S. Intelligence officers, who displayed remarkable aerial photographs taken by the American reconnaissance planes. These photos clearly showed where each Castro plane and anti-aircraft battery was located; tank, gun, and truck concentrations; and a gunboat at anchor off Cienfuegos on the south coast. Again stress was placed on the top-priority objective: *"Destroy every Castro aircraft on the ground!"*

At 7:30 P.M., when individual briefings had been completed, an American adviser named Gregory Bell entered the room. Glancing at a paper in his hand, he told the Cubans that it might not be necessary for them to fly the scheduled Monday mission. Apparently other planes would take care of Castro's aircraft. Nevertheless, the pilots and crew were ordered to stand by until the base confirmed the Washington order. Shortly after midnight Bell returned with confirmation that the third strike had been officially called off. This reduced the scheduled forty-eight sorties from Happy Valley to eight—*the eight that had already been carried out.*

The Cuban pilots realized that some momentous decision had been made in Washington but assumed, naturally, that it was a decision favorable to their cause. Since there was no other Free Cuban Air Squadron, the change of orders, they believed, could mean only that U.S. military aircraft had been assigned to wipe out the remaining Castro planes.

That night all hands were more confident than ever of the success of the invasion.

Their confidence was unjustified. On the preceding day—Saturday, April 15—news of the first air strike against Cuban airfields had brought loud repercussions at the United Nations. Raúl Roa, Castro's Foreign Minister, appeared before the General Assembly's Political Committee and charged that the bombing was the prelude to an invasion planned, financed, and directed by the United States.

As part of Operation Pluto two B-26 bombers, painted to resemble the B-26's in Castro's air force, had flown from Nicaragua directly to Key West and Miami, where the Free Cuban pilots declared that the morning's raid was the work of Castro's own pilots, who, like themselves, were revolting against the Communist regime. My best information, though unverified, is that the idea of this trick originated in the State Department, but it may have originated with the CIA. It had been a last-minute suggestion, designed further to protect the "image" of the United States. The illusion that such a subterfuge could be kept a secret for forty-eight hours, with the UN in session, and failure to weigh the consequences of its exposure, proved to be one of the many political blunders.

When pilot and plane arrived in Miami they were photographed, and the pictures were immediately distributed to the wire services. Stevenson, in his rebuttal of Roa's charges, stated flatly that the raiding planes were Castro's own and that the pilots were defectors. He pointed to the Miami photographs as evidence. He was unaware that a trick was involved; the State Department had decided, for reasons of its own, not to inform him of it.[14] He therefore accepted the story of "defecting" Cuban pilots at face value, rejecting Roa's accusations out of hand with force and eloquence—and stepped into an embarrassing trap.

Roa had no trouble in exploding the story. The B-26 flown to Miami by the "defecting" pilot had a few features which made it recognizably different from Castro's B-26's. The Cuban delegate went on to charge that "mercenaries" hired by the

[14] Johnson, p. 92.

United States were about to bomb Cuba again. Stevenson answered that "steps have been taken to impound the Cuban planes which have landed in Florida, and they will not be permitted to take off for Cuba." [15] The clear implication was that there would be no further air strikes.

In the confusion that followed there is one certainty: when Stevenson learned of the "defecting" pilot trick that had placed him in such a distressing position before the United Nations, he was furious. [16] It has been said that he threatened to resign if any further strikes were launched. When he angrily telephoned Rusk from New York, insisting that further strikes would place the United States in an untenable position internationally, Rusk capitulated. McGeorge Bundy agreed, and together they called the President at Middleburg, Virginia, late Sunday afternoon. The President also agreed and directed that further strikes be canceled. Castro was left in unchallenged possession of the air.

This decision was entirely political. The Kennedy administration had been in office less than three months. Stevenson had twice been a candidate for the presidency and had a considerable liberal following. The support of loyal Stevensonians had helped Kennedy win the big cities in 1960 and provide the microscopic margin that carried him to victory. Stevenson fully expected to be offered the job of Secretary of State in the new administration. Kennedy, however, had questioned Stevenson's capacity for decision and had offered him the United Nations job, which Stevenson at first declined. [17] When Kennedy asked Schlesinger why Stevenson did not want the United Nations job, Schlesinger replied that Stevenson wanted to help shape foreign policy rather than be at the other end of the telephone. But when Rusk was appointed Secretary of State, Stevenson finally accepted

[15] *Ibid.,* p. 93.

[16] Hanson W. Baldwin, "The Cuban Invasion," *The New York Times,* July 31, 1961, p. 3. Also, Stewart Alsop, "The Lessons of the Cuban Disaster," *The Saturday Evening Post,* June 24, 1961, p. 70.

[17] Schlesinger, pp. 138-139.

the Ambassadorship to the UN. Rusk had been a Stevenson supporter in the 1960 campaign and had worked actively in his behalf.

Rusk and Bundy are now the only two who can give an authoritative account of the pressure put on the President through them by Stevenson on April 15 and 16 to cancel further air strikes. However, the *actions* that climaxed the hectic weekend are undeniable. Late Sunday evening, April 16, an order was issued from the White House canceling the final and crucial air strike scheduled for dawn the next morning, D-Day. The order was transmitted to General C. P. Cabell, Deputy Director of the CIA, by presidential aide McGeorge Bundy, who then made a hurried trip to New York to placate Stevenson. Hanson Baldwin, military analyst of *The New York Times,* subsequently expressed the opinion that "the cancellation was apparently the result of representations by Secretary of State Dean Rusk and through him by Mr. Stevenson." [18]

The third strike by the Brigade's Air Squadron, scheduled to coincide with the invasion, could not conceivably have increased any damage to American prestige in world opinion. At that point the cards were down and nothing further could be hidden. The assault troops had to come from somewhere and the attacking planes did too. Whatever "non-involvement" argument could be made for canceling the second air strike did not apply to the third air strike scheduled for Monday. The decision to cancel it was taken for domestic political reasons, to appease one man, Adlai Stevenson.

That decision sealed the doom of the invasion and marked it for certain disaster. For fifteen hundred Cubans already on their way to the Bay of Pigs, it amounted to a sentence of death—or at best, captivity and torture—pronounced by the nation which had mobilized, trained, and sent them on their mission. The supposition that this patently immoral act would somehow enhance that nation's world image surpasses understanding. The

[18] Baldwin, p. 3.

immediate calling off of the invasion might have made some logic; its abandonment to destruction made none.

The cancellation order was a staggering blow to the CIA. Cabell, a U.S. Air Force general with a brilliant combat record, and Bissell, charged with supervising Operation Pluto, instantly recognized the impending catastrophe. They went at once to the State Department.

Secretary Rusk listened to their arguments and pleas but insisted that the political disadvantages of further strikes outweighed any other consideration. The invasion force was at sea and only a few hours from the scheduled landings. Rusk was reminded that the Free Cubans' slow, propeller-driven B-26's were no match for Castro's wasp-like jets, which were still operable. These jets could control the air, sink ships with rockets, and decimate the landing force. The Secretary was unmoved. The political factors must govern, he said, adding that in his opinion the CIA was overstressing the danger of enemy planes.[19]

Rusk had been an infantry reserve officer after graduating from Davidson College in North Carolina. He took part in two campaigns in Burma, rising to be Deputy Chief of Staff for that theater with the rank of colonel. He was released from active duty in February 1946, when he joined the Department of State. Eventually he became its Director of the Office of Special Political Affairs, which later became the Office of United Nations Affairs. In 1949 he became the first Assistant Secretary for United Nations Affairs. Now he supported the Ambassador to the UN in spite of his military experience.

Finally, however, Rusk telephoned President Kennedy, who was still in Middleburg, Virginia.[20] He reported the pleas of the CIA representatives and expressed his own unalterable opposition. The President decided that the cancellation order would stand. Stunned and dismayed, Bissell and Cabell returned to the operations room, where, according to a former Executive

[19] Charles C. V. Murphy, "Cuba: The Record Set Straight," *Fortune,* September 1961, p. 230.

[20] *Ibid.,* p. 230.

Director of the CIA, they were "greeted by an appalled and angry group of officers who described the change in plans with such phrases as 'criminally negligent.' " [21] Cabell complied with the President's order.

That was the order that Gregory Bell confirmed to the pilots of Happy Valley shortly after midnight on Sunday. The men had no way of knowing it but at that instant Cuba's dream of liberation was shattered, and Fidel Castro was handed a smashing victory—about six hours before the first blood was shed at Girón.

Two days before this fatal decision, the ninety-five American advisers of Brigade 2506 said their farewells to their Cuban friends, who so greatly admired them. They were young, tough, experienced war veterans and on parting, Cubans and Americans embraced affectionately. Every American expressed regret that he could not go along. The President of Nicaragua came to the dock to see the troops off. "Bring me a couple of hairs from Castro's beard," he called.

Each battalion had been issued different colored scarves— yellow, white, blue, black, red—and as the ships slowly put out to sea the waving scarves added color to the memorable occasion.

As the invasion fleet, consisting of 5 freighters (Liberty ships) and 2 LCI's (Landing Craft Infantry) moved slowly out, the Cubans saw something that thrilled and heartened them— the U.S. Navy was at hand. The transports had been loaded with meticulous care, under American supervision. Supplies most needed at Girón, which would be unloaded first, were the last to go aboard. "My ship, the *Atlantico*," its radio operator has told me, "was like an immense hardware store. It carried 198 items of armament, including 35 kinds of grenades." The

[21] Lyman B. Kirkpatrick, *The Real CIA* (New York: The Macmillan Company, 1967), p. 198.

freighters were so tightly loaded with high explosives, mines, ammunition, food, medicine, and drums of aviation gasoline that they rode low in the water; the men slept where they could, in lifeboats, on deck, or down below. Smoking was prohibited.

The LCI's, the *Barbara J* and *Blagar,* were radar-equipped and well-armed with .50-caliber anti-aircraft guns. Although ships of this kind had crossed the Atlantic on their own bottoms and were designed to beach and then lower bow gangways for infantry to land, the Navy knew that land-based aircraft could slaughter any landing force before it reached a beachhead. The *Blagar* was the command ship.

As the vessels moved away from Happy Valley on different courses, with orders to rendezvous at "Point Zulu," about fifty miles south of Girón, they were picked up by destroyer escorts. On one occasion a U.S. submarine surfaced and circled one of the transports. The sea was calm, "like a lake."

During the three-day voyage to Point Zulu there was an accident on the *Atlantico.* While some men were practice-firing a .50-caliber machine gun, its mountings tore loose and bullets sprayed the deck. One man was killed and two wounded, one badly shot through the stomach. There was no doctor on board so the master asked the escorting destroyer what he should do. "Come to a complete halt," he was told, and moments later the destroyer drew up alongside, "so quickly and close we thought there would be a collision." American sailors scrambled aboard from a launch. The Cubans lining the rails were astonished at the efficiency of the Americans. The man who had been shot through the stomach was taken to an aircraft carrier, where he underwent an operation and later fully recovered.[22]

The transports arrived at Point Zulu on schedule, between 4 and 5 P.M. on Sunday, April 16, each vessel circling until the entire group had formed. When all had been reunited

---

[22] This account was related to the author by Enrique Rousseau, the Radio Officer of the *Atlantico.*

they were ordered to proceed shoreward as long as they had four fathoms of water. Other vessels proceeding from Viéques Island, an American base near Puerto Rico, joined them.

As the shore, shrouded in darkness, became dimly visible, the lights of Girón "looked like Coney Island." Cuba was never so dark and mysterious to ancient sea-rovers as she seemed that night. On the transports in the hushed tension, one could hear only the rushing water and the throbbing of the ships' engines. About this time a large vessel joined the fleet with a number of small landing craft on board, each of which could carry about fifty men. The fleet carried four medium tanks, about twenty trucks, a bulldozer, a crane, and a trailer with a portable radio station.

At 4 A.M. Monday, after the third strike had been canceled, while frogmen were marking the channels for landing craft through the reefs off Girón, and with some assault troops already ashore, Cabell returned to Rusk to plead for air support from the U.S. carriers lying over the horizon. Among the ships were the aircraft carrier *Essex* and the helicopter landing ship *Boxer,* with destroyer escorts. The *Boxer* had a battalion of a thousand battle-ready Marines aboard, and transports carrying other Marines were in the area. The White House wanted the U.S. ships kept fifty miles away from shore but Admiral Arleigh Burke, in naval jargon, "leaned on his orders," and the vessels drew nearer. Eventually Burke ordered the carrier *Shangri-La* with a third task force into the area.

With Rusk still solidly opposed to providing American support, Cabell himself telephoned President Kennedy in Virginia. The President supported Rusk. The answer, still: No.

So during that fateful night and early morning, with the final air strike canceled and U.S. air support refused, the invasion fleet moved steadily toward catastrophe.

At 10 P.M. Sunday, one of the LCI's led a freighter close in to the beach at Girón. Some 20 miles to the west another LCI escorted a second freighter into the Bay of Pigs. From another vessel appearing out of the night the clank and clash of gears told that landing craft were being lowered. As the noise of landing-craft diesel engines was added to the din, the lights at Girón began to go out. It was the first alert to anyone inside Cuba that the invasion was under way. A single machine gun emplacement on shore opened fire. An LCI quickly wiped it out with its .50-caliber guns. The time was 12:05 A.M., Monday, April 17.

Soon the first assault troops, in spotted camouflage uniforms and with their faces painted black, were leaping ashore and streaking for their objectives. A few boats were ripped apart on submerged coral reefs. Before dawn many of the invaders reached the town of Girón, where they went from house to house reassuring the citizens: "We are Cubans. We have come to liberate Cuba!"

The first stage of the invasion had been spectacularly successful. The three roads across the Cienaga de Zapata swamp had been interdicted by paratroopers. The invaders had control of the Girón airport, the primary objective, and that very morning, they thought, their own bombers would be using it. Scores of militiamen and citizens in the Girón area joined the liberation forces, asking for arms. Five hundred sugar workers gathered together at a nearby mill, prepared to join. The bulk of a Castro militia regiment defected. Within a few hours the victorious forces had control of an area of eight hundred square miles!

Then, to their astonishment and dismay, with most invaders ashore and with others approaching in small boats and still others struggling to unload the freighters, Castro's planes came roaring in, guns and rockets blazing. The Brigade, unbelievably, was defenseless.

By 8 A.M. one freighter, struck by a rocket, had to be beached on a reef in the Bay of Pigs about three hundred yards offshore. The men swam ashore without guns or ammunition. Later a Castro Sea Fury dived out of the sun and made a direct hit with a rocket on a second freighter off the Girón beach. The ship, carrying a precious cargo of anti-tank road mines, ammunition, food, gasoline, and the radio communication trailer, blew up with a tremendous blast and sank quickly. Supplies for the first week's fighting were lost. Near the *Atlantico* a Castro plane was hit and disintegrated in the air, pieces falling on the ship's deck.

But Castro's remaining 2 or 3 jets, 3 Sea Furies, and 2 B-26's commanded the skies. At 3 P.M. the 3 freighters still afloat were ordered by the *Blagar* to leave the invasion area. The medium tanks and a few trucks had been landed before the ships departed, but the withdrawal left the landing forces stranded on the beaches with less than 10 percent of their ammunition and other critically needed equipment. As the Castro troops closed in on them over the highways, they fought desperately and bravely, inflicting heavy losses. A conservative estimate is that about 1,200 of Castro's forces died in battle, an additional 400 later from wounds, and that more than 2,000 were wounded.

The Free Cuban commander on the beach asked repeatedly for air support. By radio he pleaded, "Where is the air cover? Do you back us or quit?" Several times he was told by the American in command on the *Blagar* that air support was coming, and once that air cover would be over the beaches in a matter of minutes.

U.S. Navy jets did in fact fly over the invasion area on several occasions, usually in pairs. When they first appeared, Castro's jets vanished from the air. The invaders on the beaches cheered as the American planes dipped their wings in salute and flew inland. They were sure that the turning point had come. But soon the Navy jets headed out to sea. Castro's planes then returned and brazenly remained over the beachhead during subsequent U.S. flights.

What happened, I later ascertained, was that since Adlai Stevenson, at the UN on Saturday, and Secretary of State Rusk, at his Monday press conference, had repeated with emphasis President Kennedy's earlier statement that U.S. forces would not intervene in any way, Castro assured his pilots that the U.S. Navy jets posed no threat—they were merely "taking photographs." Thus, after their first disappearance from the scene,

Castro's jets renewed their devastating attacks, ignoring the occasional, powerful U.S. jets, which took no part in the fighting at any time.

The Free Cuban Air Squadron, although no match for Castro's jets and Sea Furies, engaged in the unequal contest and lost half its planes the first day. The lumbering B-26's, loaded with 1,500 gallons of gasoline, 8 five-inch rockets, 8 machine guns with 3,000 rounds of ammunition, and 10 bombs weighing 250 pounds each, were easy prey for Castro's jets. One B-26 was shot down from the rear by a Castro jet about 50 miles at sea. The pilots nevertheless continued flying the long seven-hour missions between Nicaragua and the beachheads, even after the task was clearly hopeless. With machine guns and rockets they sprayed the advancing Castro columns and blew up tanks and trucks loaded with militiamen. They sank the gunboat anchored at Cienfuegos and a coast guard cutter approaching Girón beach.

Of the original sixteen bombers, eight were lost and five badly damaged. Ten pilots were killed in the first two days. Only three of the original bombers survived the entire action. Tuesday night American pilots flew additional bombers into the Nicaraguan staging area to replace those lost or damaged. What gave out finally was the Squadron's manpower.

The earliest reports from the Bay of Pigs, reaching Washington over U.S. Navy circuits, confirmed the worst fears of the CIA and the Joint Chiefs. When the President learned of the air squadron's decimation by Castro's jets, and the loss of the two freighters, he again wavered, turning partly away from his political advisers. On Monday afternoon, when it was too late, he countermanded his Sunday evening order forbidding strikes against the Castro airfields. This resulted in a mission dispatched to bomb the San Antonio de los Baños base near Havana on Monday night. But this so-called "air strike," as it later turned out, was in reality no strike at all.

On Tuesday the dispatches reaching Washington grew grimmer by the hour. That evening Bissell realized that his warnings could no longer be disregarded. The impending collapse, he was convinced, armed him for a last effort to save Operation Pluto. He sent word to the President that he must see him urgently.

President Kennedy was holding a reception at the White House for his Cabinet and members of Congress and their wives. But he left the party and joined Bissell in a tense meeting, to which Secretaries Rusk and McNamara, General Lemnitzer, Admiral Burke, McGeorge Bundy, Lyndon Johnson, Schlesinger, and Walt Rostow had been summoned.[23]

Strongly supported by Burke and Lemnitzer, Bissell made an impassioned and fervent appeal for the only thing that could now save the Cuban invasion: use of the U.S. military power available on the ships just over the Caribbean horizon. Rusk and the political advisers opposed him. Secretary of Defense McNamara also opposed the military. The President decided in favor of Rusk and his supporters.

Next Bissell and Burke asked that a detachment of Marines be permitted to go into action. This too was refused. All these proposals, they were reminded, would amount to U.S. "involvement" and lower American prestige in "world opinion."

The last request made by Admiral Burke was for the use of *one* U.S. destroyer, to lay down a barrage on Castro's forces. The President asked, "What if Castro's forces return the fire and hit the destroyer?" Burke answered, emphatically, "Then we'll knock hell out of them!"

The President said that then the U.S. *would* be involved. My informants quote, with obvious admiration, Burke's answer:

"We *are* involved, sir. God damn it, Mr. President, we can't let those boys be slaughtered there!"

The outcome of that meeting was perhaps the most timid compromise of all. The President agreed that Navy planes with their U.S. markings painted out could fly "reconnaissance" over the beaches, but they should not engage in combat and they could fly for one hour only, from 6:30 to 7:30 A.M.! That was the extent of the "support" that was authorized. Although Kennedy knew that the Cubans had been promised continuing supplies to the beaches, betrayal seemed preferable to compromising the American "image" before the rest of the world.

Several accounts have claimed that President Kennedy, in response to the final plea of the CIA and Joint Chiefs, authorized a U.S. "air umbrella" over the invasion perimeter to permit the Free Cuban Squadron to "attack in force." Actually, on Wednesday morning, April 19, of the original thirty-four Cuban B-26 pilots the number able to fly was pitifully small. Yet a final air mission was pieced together in Nicaragua. It was composed of one unarmed C-46 transport plane piloted by two Cubans; two B-26's each piloted by two American instructors; a C-54 piloted by two Americans accompanied by a Cuban; and a B-26 piloted by Gonzalo Herrera, who emerged as one of the many heroes of the Brigade.

The B-26's had orders to attack Castro's heavy artillery that was inflicting losses on the Brigade, and their mission was accomplished. The bombs of all three planes were dropped on their targets. Herrera remained in action for fifty minutes before the Castro jets appeared and attacked the Americans, who challenged them against overwhelming odds. The C-54 had developed engine trouble and was forced to return. The C-46 landed at Girón—the only invader plane to use the airport—and delivered eight hundred pounds of supplies. It picked up Matías Farías, the only wounded Cuban who was nearby, and made it back to the Nicaraguan base. Farías also emerged as one of the many Cuban heroes.

By an incredible mischance the planes from Nicaragua had arrived over the beaches an hour before the U.S. carrier-based jets expected them. The mystery of this mistake remains unsolved. The two B-26's piloted by Americans were shot down. Gonzalo Herrera heard his American comrades vainly calling for carrier support. Their distress signals "Mad Dog Four! May Day! May Day!" brought no response, no help. One landed in

300 DAGGER IN THE HEART

flames at a sugar mill air strip; the other crashed into the sea. Castro, who had always delighted in publicizing American "aggression," made no announcement of the deaths of the Americans. He feared that evidence of U.S. involvement would shatter the morale of his armed forces.

Shortly before 5 P.M. on Wednesday, April 19, the Free Cuban beach commander sent his final message to the American vessels standing off Girón: "I am destroying all my equipment," he said, "I have nothing left to fight with. The enemy tanks are already in my position. Farewell, friends." [24]

By nightfall the fighting on the beaches was over. For three days the men had fought without rest and with little food or water. The promised supplies had never reached them. Now they had run out of ammunition and food. Gathering their remaining strength, the men crawled into the swamps. There some survived for two weeks before they died or were captured. Almost to a man they were killed or taken prisoner. A few put out to sea in tiny fishing boats found along the beach. One of these, with 22 men aboard, drifted for 15 days without food or water. When it was picked up by an American freighter, 178 miles from the Mississippi delta, there were only 12 survivors.

I have talked to two American pilots who flew helplessly over the Cuban beaches as Castro's tanks and forces closed in on the final day. One told me he had cursed his orders; the other said he had cried.

A few of the invaders were picked out of the sea by U.S. Naval vessels. "The Sailors and Marines seemed to be ashamed," one told me. "They tried to be extra nice. If we asked for a cigarette, they gave us the whole pack and when we asked for a light, they gave us a lighter and told us to keep it."

Castro's hawk-like planes, spared by the cancellation of the air strikes, had been in the air constantly. They operated in pairs, while others reloaded and refueled nearby. Flying at

[24] Johnson, pp. 167, 168.

twice the speed of the cumbersome Free Cuban bombers, these jets had turned the tide of battle, just as Burke, Bissell, Cabell, and Lemnitzer had foreseen and forewarned. But Castro's escape had been narrow—only two or three of his planes survived the action.

After the invasion I heard Castro speak of his militia with a peculiar kind of contempt. "They lack discipline and need additional training and indoctrination," he said. But he spoke with great pride of the remnant of his tiny air force, which he said had saved the day.

Why had not the Cuban underground performed up to expectations?

During an early stage of the Brigade's training in Guatemala about sixty men had been chosen to received special training in Panama as saboteurs. Later they were infiltrated into Cuba to help prepare the way for the invaders. In March 1961 there were six main underground groups inside Cuba, each coordinated as a unit and all doing considerable damage. Bombs exploded in factories and other buildings, railway rolling stock was wrecked and bridges destroyed. The great Hershey sugar mill was sabotaged and stores in the heart of Havana burned. But the underground groups operated independently of one another, rivalries existed, and the CIA wished to coordinate their activities under trained leadership.

An underground leader in Cuba who commanded great respect because of his courage, discretion, and resourcefulness, was a tall young activist named Rogelio González Corzo, who went under the cover name of "Francisco." In March the CIA sent Humberto Sori Marín to Cuba on a "unification" mission. Sori Marín had served as Castro's Minister of Agriculture before his defection. He was to meet with Francisco and other group leaders to plan coordinated action under trained leadership, arranging for an orderly distribution of arms, explosives, and incendiary material.

A full-scale meeting was arranged with the utmost precaution for 6 P.M. on March 18, 1961, in a suburb of Havana. Trusted couriers, each unknown to the others, escorted group leaders to the secret meeting place, a yellow building on a quiet street in Miramar, owned and lived in by a retired sugar engineer and his wife.

Betrayed by a Castroite, the building was surrounded, and in one swoop Castro's intelligence network arrested the key figures of the Cuban underground. Their arrest—all were later executed —was a crushing blow to the underground movement, a blow from which it has not yet recovered. These men were also heroes; we know who they were and they will be remembered and honored. Equipment which the various groups expected from the outside never arrived. Contact with the CIA by these groups was lost. The Sori Marín mission was the last of several frustrating CIA efforts to help the underground. Had it been successful, however, the defeat of the Brigade on the beaches would have destroyed its usefulness in any case.

The invasion was over. Castro's boast of how little Cuba had, in three days, defeated mighty Uncle Sam was now heard around the world, relayed triumphantly by Moscow and Peking. U.S. prestige dropped to a new low in Latin America, the Near East, Southeast Asia, and among its European allies. Fidel Castro was raised to the pinnacle of his prestige. The invasion, instead of overthrowing Castro, had entrenched him.

For months there had been no doubt about U.S. involvement, but now it was an involvement in betrayal and failure. The "world opinion" for which the Washington liberals had been so willing to sacrifice national honor now turned sharply against the United States. For those Americans who were aware of what had taken place, and why, sorrow was compounded by humiliation and shame.

CHAPTER SEVENTEEN

Apologists at Work

Public confusion over the Girón defeat has been fostered by misleading and even false statements made by political figures who were close to President Kennedy. Notable among these was his brother Robert F. Kennedy, who served as Attorney General. In an interview published in *U.S. News & World Report* for January 28, 1963, the younger Kennedy said, "There was a flurry at the United Nations and elsewhere. . . . There was supposed to be another attack on the airports on Monday morning [April 17]. The President was called about whether . . . [it] should take place. As there was this stir about the matter, he gave instructions that it should not take place *at that time* . . . And, *in fact, the attack on the airports took place later that day.* [Emphasis added]"

What was the "attack on the airports" that Bobby Kennedy said "took place that day"?

On Monday two Free Cuban bombers were authorized by their American commander to hit the San Antonio airfield, where Castro planes were parked. They were warned, however, to avoid any risk to civilian lives or property. The planes took off from Nicaragua at about 8 P.M. They arrived over the target four hours later, on a moonless night, with both the base and the nearby town blacked out and hidden by a low cloud ceiling. Unable to distinguish the target, the pilots obeyed their orders and returned to Nicaragua *without firing a shot or dropping a bomb!*

To call this "an attack on the airports" and to equate it with the original air strike planned for Monday dawn (and then canceled), which was to have been carried out by sixteen bombers manned by fresh pilots fully briefed with U-2 target photographs before them, is not exactly an exercise in candor. Such word-play with the facts is the more reprehensible because they relate not to a side issue but to the central element in the plan.

Robert Kennedy was a member of the committee appointed by his brother to investigate the fiasco; he helped write the committee's still-secret report. Certainly he had access to all the facts, including those related to the air strikes that were planned and then called off. He must have known that it is not a "fact" that the original Monday attack on the airports "took place later that day," or at any time thereafter.

The investigating committee knew that four American instructors had died in the Girón action, but on January 21, 1963, Attorney General Kennedy said in an interview with David Kraslow of the Knight newspapers that no Americans had died at the Bay of Pigs. The truth was revealed a month later. The authors of *The Invisible Government,* Wise and Ross, relate it: ". . . the story of the four missing Americans . . . . reappeared dramatically on February 25, 1963. On that date Senator Everett McKinley Dirksen . . . revealed that four American fliers had been killed at the Bay of Pigs. He said he had learned this in the course of a one-man inquiry into the Cuban invasion. Dirksen's disclosure was extremely embarrassing for the Kennedy administration."[1] The authors tell how, after Dirksen made this disclosure, newsmen sought out the mother of one of the fliers, who was quoted as having said, "If no Americans were involved, where is my son?"

In the same January interview in which Bobby Kennedy denied that any Americans had been killed in the invasion, he

[1] David Wise and Thomas B. Ross, *The Invisible Government* (New York: Random House, 1964), p. 86.

repeated the line that the "second" planned air strike had been postponed but carried out later. The invasion plan, he said, had been "a bad plan. Victory was never close. . . . We underestimated what a T-33 carrying rockets could do. It wasn't given sufficient thought."

How near was victory?

This is the account of Roberto San Román, one of the Brigade officers, on the manner in which Robert Kennedy and General Maxwell D. Taylor led the questioning by the investigating committee:

> . . . this was a question of Mr. Kennedy—he wanted to know the reaction of the people. They wanted to know if we thought we could have won the battle. What did we need to win the battle? I told them we needed only three or four jet planes, that's what we needed to win. Three or four jet planes that could knock out the little air force that Castro had at that time. I told them I did not know how they [the Americans] could do this to us. Our troops were so good—because they involved people from every class, rich and poor, rebels and soldiers and everybody against the common enemy—and they didn't answer those questions.[2]

Men in public office are as human as the rest of us, subject to all the frailties of man, one of which is the desire to hide their mistakes. It is natural that politicians will use all the power at their command to keep their mistakes from being disclosed. Consider, for example, the case of Adlai Stevenson.

In late 1962, while researching material for this book, I wrote to Ambassador Stevenson from Europe, politely asking what his role had been in the cancellation of the final air strike scheduled for Monday, April 17. The answer came from Elinor Green, Public Affairs Officer of the U.S. Mission to the UN. Mr. Stevenson wished to convey his appreciation for the trouble

[2] Haynes Johnson, *The Bay of Pigs* (New York: W. W. Norton & Company, Inc., 1964), pp. 221-222.

I had taken to check with his office, she said, adding "on behalf of Mr. Stevenson":

> Mr. Stevenson had no information in advance of the Bay of Pigs incident, as he said only last week on a televised interview, and had no hand in any decisions concerning United States actions or inactions. As he stated, in answer to a question on the *Today* show, December 5th. . . . "I wasn't told about the Bay of Pigs in advance, so I couldn't have had any disagreement."

The fact is that Mr. Stevenson was briefed on the invasion plan by the CIA about a week in advance. His close friend Schlesinger eventually told the story:

> Kennedy . . . wished Stevenson to be fully informed, and that nothing said at the UN should be less than the truth, even if it could not be the full truth. . . . In preparation for the debate [on Cuban charges of aggressive American intentions] Tracy Barnes [of the CIA] and I held a long talk with Stevenson on April 8 [9 days before the invasion]. . . . Afterward, when Harlan Cleveland, the Assistant Secretary for International Organization Affairs, Clayton Fritchey of the United States Mission to the UN, and I lunched with Stevenson at the Century, he made it clear that he wholly disapproved of the plan . . . and believed that it would cause infinite trouble.[3]

And what of the Bay of Pigs disaster as described several years after the event by Sorensen and Schlesinger, whose accounts have done so much to formulate world opinion?

Although both admit that the CIA and Joint Chiefs made it crystal clear to all concerned that the destruction of Castro's tiny air force on the ground prior to the invasion was an essential element of the plan, they have nothing but praise for the political meddlers who succeeded in cutting down and making unworkable the military plan formulated by the professionals.

[3] Arthur M. Schlesinger, Jr., *A Thousand Days* (Boston: Houghton Mifflin Company, 1965), p. 271.

Sorensen actually states that Kennedy should have paid *more* attention to his own politically sound instincts and to the politically knowledgeable men who voiced objections, such as Fulbright and Schlesinger! The assurance given the President by the U.S. military that the Brigade could achieve its goals without American participation was a "wild misjudgment." There was no reason to believe that Castro's air force "having survived the first air strike and been *dispersed into hiding,*" [emphasis added] would have been knocked out by the second one. Hence, the President's "postponement" of the last strike "played only a minor role." Even with two more strikes twice as large, the Brigade could not have broken out of its beachhead or survived much longer without substantial help from either American forces or the Cuban people. Sorensen wrote, "Neither was in the cards, and thus a Brigade victory at the Bay of Pigs was never in the cards either."

Thus we have Girón as presented by Presidential Assistant Sorensen!

Schlesinger's account is full of examples of Kennedy's personal courage. Like Sorensen, he writes that "There is certainly nothing to suggest that it [what he calls the second air strike] could possibly have led to the overthrow of the regime." And, like Sorensen, he says Kennedy thought he was approving a plan whereby the invaders, should they fail to hold their beachhead, could melt into the mountains and take up guerrilla warfare. According to Schlesinger, Dulles and Bissell told Kennedy that if worst came to worst and the invaders were beaten on the beaches, they could easily slip away into the mountains. "I don't think we fully realized," the historian ingenuously comments, "that the Escambray Mountains lay eighty miles from the Bay of Pigs, across a hopeless tangle of swamps and jungles." [4]

Here, giving these men the benefit of the doubt, they were probably confusing the Trinidad and the Bay of Pigs plans. The

[4] *Ibid.,* p. 250.

invasion planners have assured me that the President was completely familiar with all details of the terrain. Verbally, with the use of the finest maps that can be made, they explained to him that their preference for Trinidad was based mainly on the fact that at Girón the Brigade had no alternative to fall back on—the distance to the mountains, over a single road blocked by Castro's troops, and with the invaders out of ammunition, food and water, was the distance from New York to Philadelphia.

Schlesinger, in his own defense, once quoted British philosopher Walter Bagehot: "When a historian withholds important facts likely to influence the judgment of his readers, he commits a fraud." [5] Nevertheless, in quoting the final dispatch sent to the President by his special emissary, the Marine colonel who evaluated the Brigade in Guatemala, Schlesinger omits the key sentence: *"They* [the Brigade officers] *ask only for continued delivery of supplies* [to the beaches]." [6]

No supplies were ever delivered.

Six years after Girón another Kennedy apologist, Roger Hilsman, wrote a 582-page book in which he devoted exactly 4 pages to the Bay of Pigs, "a comparatively small disaster." [7] The liberal Hilsman, head of Intelligence in the State Department, followed the Schlesinger-Sorensen line. For him the "experts" were not those in the Pentagon or the CIA. He himself wanted to get into the act, as he had "plenty of people in [my] Bureau" who were experts. He asked Rusk to permit him to put them to work, and his request was denied. He feels, in retrospect, that he should have gone ahead on his own authority; should not have asked "to be permitted to do a study. . . ." The State Department did not play its role "in forcing full weight to be given to political considerations." The operation "had been prepared by the previous administration" and, although

[5] *Time,* December 17, 1965, p. 55.

[6] *Life,* May 10, 1963, p. 34.

[7] Roger Hilsman, *To Move a Nation* (New York: Doubleday & Company, Inc., 1967), pp. 30-34.

Rusk "seems to have made some sort of attempt to get the operation played down," whatever opposition came from him "was neither strong nor clear." According to Hilsman, the "cancellation of the 'second' strike did not doom the Bay of Pigs operation" and "Above all, both the Secretary [Rusk] and the department [of State] *failed to make the case for political considerations that should have been made.*" [Emphasis added] [8] Six years after the sad events, amazingly, he was still ignorant of the plain record that political considerations did prevail, and that as a result of this the military plan was so distorted that in effect it was never put into operation.

And what of the position taken by President John F. Kennedy after the invasion collapse?

The President's first problem, according to Schlesinger, "was to contain the political consequences of the debacle. He moved now with sure instinct. . . ." [9] Kennedy wished to protect himself against partisan attack. Also he wanted to avoid pressure from within the United States for violent retaliation against Castro.[10] Although the Republicans, according to Schlesinger, were inhibited "by their own role in conceiving the operation," Kennedy took no chances.[11] He called in Richard Nixon [whose advice on Cuba was to "find a proper legal cover and . . . go in" [12]] and by the weekend he had talked to Dwight Eisenhower, Nelson Rockefeller, and Barry Goldwater. "Harry S. Truman, being a Democrat, required only the attention of the Vice President."

Among Kennedy's closest advisers there was an instinct for self-preservation, tempting some of them to put out versions of the episode ascribing the debacle to everyone but themselves.

[8] *Ibid.,* p. 34.
[9] Schlesinger, p. 287.
[10] *Ibid.,* p. 287.
[11] *Ibid.,* p. 288.
[12] Richard M. Nixon, "Cuba, Castro and John F. Kennedy," *Reader's Digest,* November 1964, p. 291.

The press was filled with what purported to be inside stories. At an early meeting on Friday, April 21, with Rusk, Bundy, Sorensen, Schlesinger, and others in attendance, the President remarked acidly that the mistakes of the Joint Chiefs were being notably neglected by the press.[13] Nevertheless, as a political device to shut off the continuing criticism, Kennedy decided to accept sole responsibility, and he did so publicly. By taking the full blame upon himself, wrote Sorensen, Kennedy won "the admiration of both career servants and the public, avoiding partisan investigations and attacks, and discouraging further attempts by those involved to leak their versions and accusations." [14]

But the President did not privately concede that he was responsible. He blamed the CIA and the Joint Chiefs, not his political advisers or himself. Schlesinger quotes him as saying, "My God, the bunch of advisers we inherited. . . . Can you imagine being President and leaving behind someone like all those people there?" [15] and "The President said that he could not understand how men like Dulles and Bissell, so intelligent and so experienced, could have been so wrong. . . ." [16] Sorensen adds to the lore of alibis with this Kennedy quotation: "All my life I have known better than to depend on the experts. How could I have been so stupid, to let them go ahead?" [17]

Arthur Krock, the respected journalist, provides some clues to the President's attitude. Krock had been a close and long-time friend of the Kennedy family. As an undergraduate at Harvard, Kennedy had consulted Krock on his senior thesis, *Why England Slept,* which was later published as a book. When Kennedy went to Washington as a member of the House and later as a Senator, the two men met frequently. Later, in his

[13] Schlesinger, p. 289.
[14] Theodore C. Sorensen, *Kennedy* (New York: Harper & Row, 1965), p. 309.
[15] Schlesinger, p. 295.
[16] *Ibid.,* p. 290.
[17] Sorensen, p. 309.

book, *In the Nation: 1932–1966,* Krock wrote that Kennedy's good looks, flashing wit, and mastery of the felicitous phrase were largely responsible for his rise to the Presidency but that "they also explain why he was celebrated for some capacities of leadership he did not possess."

In commenting on Kennedy's handling of Cuba, Krock wrote, "And, after the debacle of the Bay of Pigs expedition that his half-in, half-out support had foreordained, he blamed it on incompetent counsel of the military Chiefs of Staff. Word went out [from the White House] unofficially that the project with the same design had been initiated in the Eisenhower administration. . . . Kennedy's transfer of blame from himself to the Chiefs of Staff for the Bay of Pigs disaster was *leaked to the press* to preserve for him the reputation for resolute leadership he had definitely failed to demonstrate in this instance" [18] [my emphasis].

Arthur Krock's appraisal of Kennedy's leadership is interesting in the light of a ringing statement that appears in the book he helped Kennedy write, *Why England Slept:* "We cannot tell anyone to keep out of our hemisphere unless our armaments and the people behind those armaments are prepared to back up the command, even to the ultimate point of going to war. . . . If we debate, if we question, if we hesitate, it will be too late."

The reaction in the Kennedy family was curious. The President's father, as I have said, believed the experience had been beneficial. His brother, the Attorney General, is reported to have told the President emotionally, "They can't do this to *you*—those black-bearded Commies can't do this to *you!*" [19]

But they did, and nothing can alter the fact that instead of overthrowing Castro, the invasion failure had tightened his grip on the country; that instead of protecting the image of the United States before world opinion, it had subjected the country

[18] Arthur Krock, *In the Nation: 1932–1966* (New York: McGraw-Hill Book Company, 1967), pp. 321-325.

[19] *National Review,* May 2, 1967, p. 479.

to worldwide scorn. No one believed the shrill Peking claims that America was a "paper tiger," but everyone believed that it behaved like one.

When the debating, questioning and hesitating ended in the Girón disaster, Herbert L. Matthews made a comment entirely in character: "Thank the Lord," he wrote, "for the United States and for Cuba that the invasion of April 17, 1961 failed!"

The Bay of Pigs defeat was wholly self-inflicted in Washington. Kennedy told the truth when he publicly accepted responsibility. He had turned from the old, conservative pros— the CIA and the military—to the new political liberal overseers he had brought into the government. They were the ones who knocked out the battle plan. He had ignored the professionals, assuming that they could not accomplish a simple task for which a life-time of experience had qualified them.

The heroism of the beleaguered Cuban Brigade had been rewarded by betrayal, defeat, death for many of them, long and cruel imprisonment for the rest. The Cuban people and the Latin American nations, bound to Cuba by thousands of subtle ties of race and culture, were left with feelings of astonishment and disillusionment, and in many cases despair. They had always admired the United States as strong, rich, generous —but where was its sense of honor and the capacity of its leaders?

The mistake of the Cuban fighters for liberation was that they thought too highly of the United States. They believed to the end that it would not let them down. But it did, and the Communist threat in the American hemisphere could now be dated "Before Girón" and "After Girón."

CHAPTER EIGHTEEN

Lives for Sale

In 1797 Napoleon called on the United States for a large gift to France, to be disguised as a loan. The American Minister to Paris at the time, Charles Cotesworth Pinckney, refused, with an assertion of principle that became a patriotic slogan: "Millions for defense, but not one cent for tribute!"

A few years later Thomas Jefferson sent a small naval force "to the shores of Tripoli," as the Marine hymn has it, to put an end to another form of tribute. The Barbary Coast pirates were demanding money from nations whose ships sailed the nearby waters. President Jefferson believed that fighting the pirates would be more honorable and less expensive than bribing them.

In 1961–1962 President Kennedy decided to buy off Fidel Castro. In the course of the prolonged bargaining the American people were misled and deceived, as were some of those Americans called on to participate in the pay-off. The negotiations and fund-raising processes, moreover, were so confused and at times inept that the ordeal of more than a thousand Cuban prisoners was protracted to nearly twenty months.

It all started with a speech by Castro on May 17, 1961, exactly one month after the invasion. He demanded tribute: "an indemnity for partial damage caused to the nation by the invasion," in the form of five hundred bulldozers of the "Caterpillar type, not with rubber tires, no." In return for these, he he promised that the Bay of Pigs captives would be released.

This offer set in motion forces whose strange cross-currents caused the United States to pay more than twice what Castro originally demanded. He asked for tractors worth $28 million [1] and ended up getting goods which had an ultimate cost of $55.9 million, not counting shipping costs,[2] plus almost $3 million in cash.

Two days after Castro called for the ransom, President Kennedy telephoned Dr. Milton Eisenhower. He explained that Castro was sending to the United States a delegation of 10 prisoners, selected from among the 1,199 members of Brigade 2506 captured at the Bay of Pigs, and asked whether Dr. Eisenhower would serve on a committee to deal with them. While the United States felt a moral obligation to obtain the release of the prisoners, the President said, the government could not deal with the Cubans directly because diplomatic relations had been severed. To get around this technicality he proposed the formation of a committee of private citizens to raise money to buy the tractors. Mrs. Franklin D. Roosevelt and Walter Reuther had agreed to serve and the President hoped Dr. Eisenhower and another Republican would also serve, to make the committee bipartisan. The fourth member would be Joseph Dodge, former Director of the Bureau of the Budget in the Eisenhower Administration.[3]

President Kennedy told Dr. Eisenhower that he would explain publicly the next day that the decision to negotiate with Castro was governmental and the committee's only responsibility was to raise the funds. This was never done.

Criticism of the proposed negotiations arose immediately after the committee's formation was announced. On May 22, Senator Homer Capehart said he thought that the negotiations would be illegal unless "directly authorized by the President."

[1] Haynes Johnson, *The Bay of Pigs* (New York: W. W. Norton & Company, Inc., 1964), p. 242.

[2] Milton S. Eisenhower, *The Wine Is Bitter* (New York: Doubleday and Company, Inc., 1963), p. 296.

[3] *Ibid.*, pp. 274-277.

And if he did authorize them, the Senator declared, it would constitute "an unforgivable sin," adding that "we will become the laughing stock of the entire world." [4] Senator Styles Bridges said, "How much more humiliation and disdain must be taken from the Communist dictator?" [5] Senator Barry Goldwater said that if the United States sent tractors to Castro, American prestige "would sink even lower." [6] Senator George E. Smathers compared Castro's offer to "the cold offer of one million Jews in return for 10,000 trucks which Adolph Eichmann made 16 years ago. . . ." [7] Doubtless it was the barrage of such criticism that led the President to back away from his promise to Dr. Eisenhower to tell the American people that the decision to negotiate with Castro was the government's.

Castro consistently adhered to his original position. In succeeding statements he continued to demand five hundred bulldozers, Caterpillar type, and he repeated that he was seeking "indemnification" for wrongs committed by the United States. When the State Department issued a release to the effect that "the United States would give its most attentive consideration to the issuance of appropriate permits for the export of bulldozers for Cuba, for the rescue of the prisoners," Castro was furious. He resented having the negotiations interpreted as an exchange instead of as an indemnification.

The committee itself was divided. The two Republicans, Dr. Eisenhower and Mr. Dodge, felt that private citizens should not meddle in foreign affairs without explicit government authorization.[8] They feared that it would be a violation of the Logan Act, which forbids private negotiations with foreign governments. Eleanor Roosevelt and Walter Reuther had no such qualms. They were willing to go along with the white lie that all phases of the negotiations were private. At one point Mrs.

[4] Johnson, p. 232.
[5] *Ibid.*
[6] *Ibid.,* p. 233.
[7] Eisenhower, p. 277.
[8] *Ibid.,* p. 276.

Roosevelt went so far as to say that the committee had been functioning before Mr. Kennedy became involved.[9]

The committee met for the first time on Monday, May 22. Mrs. Roosevelt was named Honorary Chairman. The twenty-nine-year-old Richard Goodwin, the President's principal adviser on Latin America, was present and assured the committee that the Treasury would arrange for tax exemptions on gifts,[10] and for transportation of the prisoners when they were liberated. At 1 P.M. ten prisoners arrived at the Statler Hilton Hotel in Washington to meet with the committee. Their spokesman made it clear that Castro expected five hundred bulldozers, Caterpillar type, and that he was irritated by the use of such words as "trade" and "exchange," because he was demanding "indemnification." The prisoners were given a letter stating that the committee would undertake to raise funds for five hundred agricultural tractors. It also offered to send a committee of agricultural experts to Havana to work out the details, and it reported this to Castro by cable.

On Wednesday, May 24, the President finally issued a statement. It said the government was not and could not be a party to the negotiations, adding, "But when private citizens seek to alleviate suffering in other lands—this government must not interfere with their humanitarian efforts." The government, he said, was "putting forward neither obstacles nor assistance to the wholly private effort." Any contribution would be wholly tax deductible, he explained, as for any charitable organization.

Dr. Eisenhower later wrote: "I now realized, in chilling clarity, that the President intended to maintain the fiction that all aspects of the case, from negotiation to critical decisions, from raising funds to actually freeing the citizens, were private."

The "vitriolic and unrelenting criticism" continued and on June 2, in an effort to placate its critics, the committee cabled Castro that it was willing to make available 500 farm tractors

[9] *Ibid.*, p. 284.
[10] *Ibid.*, p. 277.

worth about 3 million dollars.[11] It set a time limit—12 o'clock noon on June 7—"so that we may know that you are prepared to carry out the proposal you made on May 17, 1961."[12] It offered to send an agricultural delegation to Havana.

Castro replied on June 6. His position remained consistent with his original offer. He said that the committee knew exactly the amount and type of indemnification being claimed, since it had received precise information from the delegation of prisoners. He had suggested that Mrs. Roosevelt or Dr. Eisenhower come to Cuba, but agreed, nevertheless, to meet with the agricultural experts, who arrived in Havana on June 13. Out of their conversations came the suggestion from Castro that if the committee could not meet his demands for five hundred bulldozers ("big tractors"), he would accept the equivalent in cash and credits. If it were to be cash only, he placed a value of twenty-eight million dollars on the five hundred bulldozers. The experts returned to the United States on June 15.

In the meantime, Congressional opposition increased. "We were beset by ridicule and misunderstanding of our motives," Dr. Eisenhower would write. "My frustration . . . was almost overwhelming." Mortimer M. Caplin, Commissioner of the Bureau of Internal Revenue, indicated that he had issued no ruling on tax exemptions and that he would probably consult Congress before reaching a decision.

Dr. Eisenhower then wrote President Kennedy what he himself has called "the bitterest letter I have ever written." The public should have been told from the first and "should even now be told . . . that only the fund-raising was private," and that the rest of the transaction, involving foreign policy decisions, was governmental. He was opposed to continuing the negotiations. Reuther wanted to continue.

The mail to Senators and Representatives was running at least four-to-one against the deal. Dr. Eisenhower's office esti-

[11] *Ibid.,* p. 290.
[12] Johnson, p. 238.

mated that only one letter in ten had a good word to say about the committee's efforts. He described the first three weeks of his work as "a virtual nightmare." He and Dodge began to wonder if the committee could raise even three million dollars. Governor Paul Fannin of Arizona expressed the hope that the people of his state would "not contribute a dime."

As for Castro's position, Dr. Eisenhower described it in this way: "We had found ourselves in verbal combat with a most unscrupulous rascal, adept at dirty tricks and in-fighting. Castro responded to our genuine expressions of humanitarian concern with nothing but ranting lies and deceitful propaganda. . . . It soon became clear, to me at least, that Castro would not negotiate in good faith."

On June 23 Castro cabled a rejection of the offer of farm tractors: "Your committee lies when it states that Cuba has changed its original proposal. . . ." In this he was on solid ground. In his speech on May 17, and in all subsequent statements, he had made it clear that his proposal was based on an admission of responsibility by the United States and that he would accept only Caterpillar-type bulldozers. When the committee dissolved itself in late June, President Kennedy placed the entire blame on Castro. At a press conference he said, "The committee did everything conceivable for the purpose of showing its good faith, but Mr. Castro has not accepted."

The prisoners could have been released in June of 1961 for $28 million in tractors or in cash and credit. But they were doomed to another year and a half in prison, and in the end the ransom price was more than doubled.

What of the ordeal of the 1,199 survivors of Brigade 2506 who had been literally abandoned by the United States and permitted to run out of ammunition on the beaches?

Following the collapse of the invasion they were first taken to the recently constructed Sports Palace in the center of Havana. There they remained for several weeks, some of them wounded, all covered with the dirt and mud of battle. They were not permitted to bathe or shave. For twenty-one hours a day they were forced to sit on small chairs; from 3 A.M. to 6 A.M. they were permitted to lie on the floor. Their captors played on their bitterness at having been betrayed and abandoned. All the prisoners were certain they faced execution.

During these weeks Castro arranged to put a group of carefully selected prisoners before a panel on a nationally broadcast TV program. Carmen and I watched the cruel exhibition while we were at the Italian Embassy. The performance continued for four nights. Some of the thirty-seven who appeared, in a state of exhaustion, testified as Castro wished—but not all of them. "If you have so many people on your side, why don't you hold elections?" one prisoner asked an interrogator. When another was asked why he joined the Brigade he replied, "Because I want in my country the restoration of the 1940 Constitution, with a democratic government, a free press, and elections." Thirty underground Cuban activists were with us in the Italian Embassy; we all applauded, and some cheered the courage of these men.

The most memorable performance was that of Felipe Rivero, a thirty-seven-year-old prisoner, a member of a wealthy and aristocratic family. When privately questioned beforehand he had deliberately feigned cowardice in order to qualify for the TV appearance. During his long interrogation on the air, each of the ten panel members tried to get Rivero to admit that the Brigade was composed of mercenaries, American lackeys, men from wealthy families, and murderers. "If you think I am going to attack my comrades because I am on the point of being shot," he said, "you are wrong." There were many laborers in the Brigade, Rivero said, and all of its members had been guided by patriotic ideals. "You will understand that at this moment the most that I can feel about being executed is sadness for my family, but it is not a thing that makes me afraid or terrifies me." After his eventual release Rivero was arrested and imprisoned in the United States for anti-Castro activities! The big show at the Sports Palace came on April 26 when

Castro, standing in the center of the amphitheater, gloated over the humiliation of his defeated enemies and stressed the duplicity of the United States, which, he said, had trained them for a year and then abandoned them on the beaches.

One of the prisoners asked, "Dr. Castro, are you a Communist?" and Castro turned away without answering. Speaking of the liberties Negroes enjoyed under his regime, he said that they were even permitted to go swimming in private pools with white men. He singled out one of the prisoners: "You, Negro, what are you doing here?" The prisoner replied quietly that he had no complex about his race. "I have always been among white people, and I have always been a brother to them. And I did not come here to go swimming."

The treatment of the prisoners varied in accordance with the vicissitudes of the ransom negotiations. Four days before Castro's first offer to release them in exchange for bulldozers, the men were transferred at night to an uncompleted Naval Hospital, where they slept twenty in a room on the floor and were given soap, a tremendous improvement. But on July 17, a few days after the Tractors for Freedom Committee dissolved, they were moved again, at night, to the Castillo del Príncipe, a Spanish fortification completed in 1794. Here they were to spend eighteen months.

The Brigade leaders were at first taken to the worst cells, deep in the prison, damp and dark and infested with rats and cockroaches. Above them, in the upper galleries, common criminals and mental cases were confined. The toilet was an uncovered hole in the middle of the floor. Later the leaders were transferred to four large cells, known as the *leoneras* (lion dens), where four hundred Brigade prisoners were crowded in. There was one hole in the floor for each hundred men. Hepatitis and dysentery swept the Brigade. Five prisoners were executed, nine sent to the infamous Isle of Pines prison with thirty-year sentences. Several became mental cases; one attempted suicide. But out of their degradation came an even deeper hatred for Castro and Communism.

The harshest treatment was reserved for Manuel Artime, the only one in the Brigade who had dealt with the Americans in preparing the invasion. He had been captured after fourteen days in the swamps, his mouth so swollen that he could not talk. "You are the son-of-a-bitch who caused us the most trouble," he was told. He could die in two ways, slowly and miserably or, if he cooperated with his captors, with a bullet "but like a hero."

He was taken to a room where he was strapped into a chair, with his hands tied behind him. Spotlights were turned on his face so that he could not see his interrogators. He was questioned for three days without sleep. When he lost consciousness ice water was dashed in his face. He remembers two voices, one gentle and the other loud and harsh. Twice he was told he was about to be shot. A pistol muzzle was placed in his mouth, the second time against his temple. Artime kept repeating that he did not know anything and would not sign anything.

Finally it ended. When Artime regained consciousness he was lying on the floor, untied. Someone kicked his shoulder. "Get up, you son-of-a-bitch, we are going to take you to the *laguito*." This was a small lake, about four blocks from our home in Country Club Park, where my friend Pelayo Cuervo had been murdered and dumped beside the road. In the car he was offered "a last chance." A gun was put against his head and he was told that at the count of four he would be shot. When he repeated that he didn't know anything, the gun was put away, and Artime was taken to the Sports Palace and left alone in a cell.

On March 22, 1962, when they had been in captivity almost a year, the Cuban Government announced that the prisoners would be tried as war criminals. It was the only such mass trial in Cuban history. It began on a Thursday morning, March 29. The men were brought into the courtyard of Príncipe Castle Prison and seated there, facing a five-man tribunal presided over by Augusto Martínez Sánchez, the Minister of Labor, one of Castro's top-ranking officials. (Later, on December 8, 1964,

Martínez Sánchez would shoot himself after having been dismissed from office.)

The government expected that the trial would provide a propaganda extravaganza, with the prisoners denouncing the United States, and television cameras were installed to record the event. The prisoners decided among themselves, however, that they would refuse to answer questions. Their honor had been assailed; they had been called cowards and mercenaries. Their situation was hopeless in any case, they believed, and they chose to die like men of honor.

The trial started when a witness stood at a microphone in front of the prisoners and began berating the Brigade. The "yellow worms" had behaved like cowards in the fighting in April, he said, and now they were trying to pretend they were brave. He singled out the Brigade commander, José Pérez San Román, charging that he was so cowardly that when captured he had signed several papers and documents. The witness then read slowly from a statement assailing the United States; he claimed San Román had written it to Castro. When he finished, Martínez Sánchez called San Román to come forward. He was asked what he had to say.

"In the name of all the Brigade," San Román stated, "I refuse to accept the defense counsel who has been imposed on us by the government. We don't want anyone to defend us. We don't need any defense." He was asked what he had to say about his letter to Castro. "I did not write that letter," said San Román. "It is a good falsification, but it is not mine."

At the end of the first day the government announced that the prisoners had "confessed their crimes." On the second day another of the Brigade leaders was shown a typewritten statement alleged to have been made by him, denouncing the United States. It said that he now repented but that at the time of the invasion they had been puppets of the United States. When the witness had finished reading the statement the leader exclaimed, "This is a complete lie!" Laughter and catcalls, directed against the judges, came from the ranks of the Brigade.

Other prisoners were confronted with statements that they were alleged to have made, and all but two denied them. One of the two referred bitterly to the Tractors for Freedom Committee negotiations. He admitted that the United States had trained the Brigade in Guatemala and then landed them in Cuba, but he added that he could never support Communism and that he was an enemy of the regime. The second man, who was regarded within the Brigade as a Judas, blamed the United States for everything that had happened.

The conduct of the prisoners throughout the trial was magnificent. They had not only fought bravely in combat but now, with only two exceptions, they refused to criticize the United States!

When news of the mass trial was reported in Miami, a brother of San Román, one of the Brigade members who had escaped, collected five hundred dollars from Cubans and went to Washington with two other members of the Brigade to see Attorney General Robert Kennedy, who assured them, "We are going to do everything we can." While the trial was under way the State Department urged Latin American embassies to appeal to Castro to spare the lives of the men. Several countries complied, among them Brazil.

Cuban exiles meanwhile had organized a "Cuban Families Committee," which hoped to raise the twenty-eight million dollars that Castro had demanded. The most active participant was Alvaro Sánchez, Jr., who later became the most active Cuban negotiator. On April 7, with four other committee members, Sánchez cabled Castro that the committee was in a position to negotiate. Sánchez had been told by a representative of the State Department that he could count on twenty-eight million dollars in foodstuffs.

During the night of Sunday, April 8, Castro visited the prisoners and spoke to one of the leaders. He had come to announce the tribunal's verdict, namely that the prisoners were guilty but that the Revolution had spared their lives and sentenced them to thirty-year prison terms. Because they were so valuable to the Yankees, however, he was asking a ransom of $500,000 each for the three leaders. The rest of the Brigade would be divided into three groups; in the first, each man's freedom could be bought for $25,000; in the second $50,000; and in the third group, $100,000. The total ransom price was thus $62 million, $6 million more than *twice* what he had first demanded. Later that day Castro announced the verdict publicly and cabled Alvaro Sánchez, authorizing him to come to Cuba and begin negotiations.

Sánchez and three other members of the committee arrived in Havana on April 10, 1962, and shortly thereafter met with Castro, who began by reviewing the negotiations from the time of his original proposal on May 17, 1961, when he had asked for 500 bulldozers and then had agreed to equipment of equal value. "The Americans offered me five hundred ridiculous toy tractors worth a little over three million dollars," he scoffed. "As a result, eleven months have gone by." He said he would permit the most seriously wounded prisoners to go back to the United States when the committee had deposited their ransom, totalling $2,925,000, in the Royal Bank of Canada.

On April 18, 1962, members of the Cuban Families Committee met with Robert Kennedy, who said that it was going to be difficult to raise the ransom, because the government could not contribute money that would go to Castro.[13] He advised the Cubans to organize an aggressive fund-raising campaign and to obtain the services of a professional organization. And he suggested that they try to get Castro to accept food and medicine instead of cash. He also recommended that they try to form a committee of prominent citizens. The Cuban Families Committee opened an office at 527 Madison Avenue, New York City, and went to work. Its members wrote countless letters and made endless solicitations. On April 21 they got an

[13] *Ibid.*, p. 291.

excellent publicity break when Ed Sullivan interviewed several of the prisoners on his TV show. But during the eight months that the committee worked, it was unable to raise even a half-million dollars.

Sánchez went back to see the Attorney General, who suggested that they get in touch with James Donovan, a lawyer who had become a public figure in 1957 when he defended Rudolph Abel, indicted as a top Soviet espionage agent in the United States. Later, in 1962, Donovan was chosen by the United States to negotiate the exchange in West Berlin of Abel for the U-2 pilot, Francis Gary Powers. Donovan agreed to represent the committee without payment.

On June 26 the Families Committee announced a list of fifty-two sponsors, men and women prominent in the arts, business, education, labor, and religion. Among them were Princess Lee Radziwill, Jacqueline Kennedy's sister; Richard Cardinal Cushing, Roman Catholic Archbishop of Boston; the Right Rev. James A. Pike, Protestant Episcopal Bishop of California; James A. Farley; and General Lucius D. Clay. A day or two later a reporter asked President Kennedy at a press conference whether he approved of public subscriptions for ransoming the prisoners. He replied: "I certainly sympathize with the basic desire, which is to get a good many hundreds of young men out of prison whose only interest was in freeing their country." Donovan, meeting with Robert Kennedy for the first time on July 2 at the Justice Department, was assured that the mission was in the national interest and that any negotiations wih Castro would not be a violation of the Logan Act.

On August 30, Donovan, Sánchez, and another Cuban, Dr. Ernesto Freyre, flew to Havana. That same day Donovan met with the Attorney General of the Cuban Government. Donovan conceded from the outset that the planned action would be an "indemnification." The next day, accompanied by the two Cubans, he met with Castro. The Cuban tribunal had imposed a ransom of $62 million in cash. Donovan had to persuade

Castro to agree to accept the ransom in some other form.[14] After four hours Castro agreed to give consideration to three main proposals: 1) The negotiations would be independent of the earlier negotiation with the Cuban Families Committee when a cash indemnification of $2,925,000 had been pledged for the freedom of 60 wounded prisoners; 2) the payment for the remaining prisoners would be accepted in food products and medicines; 3) the value of these products in the world market would be equal to the indemnification imposed when the prisoners were sentenced.[15]

The following day there was another meeting with Castro, who agreed to the three proposals and said that his government would prepare a list of acceptable products. The next day Donovan returned to the United States. Shortly thereafter, the Cubans, who had remained in Havana, received a list of food products and were told that a list of medical products would follow. It was estimated that at least thirty ships would be required to transport the goods to Cuba. Later, in the United States, this estimate was increased to sixty-eight ships.

At this time Donovan accepted the Democratic nomination to oppose incumbent Jacob Javits for the U.S. Senate. He returned to Havana on October 3, and met with Castro the following day at Varadero.

As though dictating terms to a defeated country, Castro informed Donovan that he would take drugs and medicine in place of food but that he wanted them at wholesale prices. He demanded banking guarantees to assure the payment of the ransom, two letters of credit with the Royal Bank of Canada, one covering the $2,925,000 for the 60 wounded prisoners and the other covering drugs and medicines. Donovan told Castro he would receive drugs, medicines and surgical equipment at a 60 percent discount; that the insurance, packing, and transportation charges would be borne by the Families Committee;

[14] *Ibid.*, p. 312.
[15] *Ibid.*, p. 313.

that baby food would be included in the shipment; and that the banking arrangements would guarantee completion of payment in six to nine months. As an indication of good faith, a first shipment of 20 percent of the total goods would be made immediately by air before any prisoners were released.[16]

But even these concessions did not satisfy the Cuban dictator. He complained that the wholesale prices published in the catalogues of the drug companies were too high and insisted that they be reduced by 35 percent. To back up his demand he showed list prices from Japan, Poland, and Italy, prices that were lower on the world market than those of the United States.

At this point the Missile Crisis of October 1962 occurred, but the negotiations were held open.

Toward the end of November a meeting at the Waldorf-Astoria in New York, attended by Robert Kennedy and representatives of the Cuban Families Committee, set in motion a series of interdepartmental activities in Washington of a nature and scope without historical precedent. The Justice Department became the nerve center and command post for "Project X," the ransom operation. Robert Kennedy instructed Assistant Attorney General Louis F. Oberdorfer to devote his full time to it. Additional desks and telephones were installed in his office. Private attorneys were brought in to assist Justice Department lawyers. During December more than 344 long-distance calls were placed; 42 trips were made between Washington, New York, and Florida; and nearly 900 hours of overtime were recorded.

At the offices of the Internal Revenue Service a staff of twelve was set up to be on continuous call to answer questions and issue rulings in connection with Project X.

On November 30, 1962, an important high-level meeting took place at the Justice Department, attended by officials of

[16] *Ibid.,* pp. 316-317.

the State Department, the CIA, and the Internal Revenue Service, as well as by top Justice Department aides to the Attorney General. It was agreed that a study of the tax angles involved should be made and a memorandum prepared for submission to Robert Kennedy on Monday, December 3. It was realized that some drug companies might gain a tax "windfall" by making charitable contributions and that they would demand maximum protection from legislative and public criticism; moreover, they would object to having price mark-ups exposed in the transaction.[17]

Armed with the memorandum, Robert Kennedy called on the President and before noon on Monday received the green light to proceed. The next day he met with Donovan in Washington. To forestall public criticism, the Red Cross was called in and asked to serve as a cover, permitting the operation to be conducted in its name. In actuality, of course, all major plans and decisions were made in the Justice Department.

Now it became necessary to approach the drug and food companies, and this posed a delicate and embarrassing problem for the Kennedy brothers, whose relationships with big business were anything but cordial.

Earlier in 1962, when the steel industry announced an increase in prices, President Kennedy had made a remark in private which somehow reached the press. "My father always told me," he had said, "that all businessmen were sons-of-bitches, but I never believed it until now." In an attempt to limit the impact of the words, he told a press conference that his father's comment referred only to steel men. But privately, according to Arthur Schlesinger, the President told him and Adlai Stevenson, "They *are* a bunch of bastards—and I'm saying this on my own now, not just because my father told it to me." [18]

Now the President and his brother had to appeal to "the

[17] *Ibid.*, pp. 323-324.

[18] Arthur M. Schlesinger, Jr., *A Thousand Days* (Boston: Houghton Mifflin Company, 1965), p. 636.

bunch of bastards," to extricate them from one of the consequences of the Bay of Pigs blunders. The drug industry in particular felt no love for the Administration, having been hard
hit by a Senate investigation of its high prices.

On December 7, 1962, Robert Kennedy met with officials of
the Pharmaceutical Medical Association. He told them that although the Bay of Pigs invasion had been launched under his
brother's orders, the plan had been started during the Eisenhower Administration.[19] The United States had a moral obligation to get the prisoners out, he said, but could not conduct
negotiations directly with Castro because this would be "mis-
understood." The prisoners were in poor condition, and some
of them might soon die. The list of drugs Castro wanted had
been received, and none was considered strategic. Two days
later he gave the same talk to a group of baby food manufacturers.

Castro had prepared a 327-page list (typed and single-
spaced), specifying the brand name, manufacturer, quality and
dollar value of each item demanded. Favorable tax and anti-
trust rulings were issued. All gifts were not only tax deductible
but had a two-year carry-forward credit.[20] The Commerce Department issued drug and food export licenses. The Immigration
service, the CIA and the Air Force began arranging to receive
the prisoners in Florida. Clearances were issued by the Civil
Aeronautics Board and the Interstate Commerce Commission to
permit contributions of surface and air transportation to haul
the products to Florida. When some members of Congress objected to dealing with Castro at a time when the United States
was asking other countries to cut off trade with Cuba, the White
House explained that Donovan was acting as a private attorney
on behalf of the Cuban Families Committee, and was merely

[19] David Wise and Thomas B. Ross, *The Invisible Government* (New
York: Random House, 1964), p. 282.
[20] James B. Donovan, *Challenges* (New York: Atheneum, 1967),
p. 93.

keeping the President informed. It refused to say whether any government funds would be used.[21]

The goal was to obtain the release of the prisoners by Christmas, which was less than three weeks off, and of course it would take several months to deliver the drug-food ransom. Although the first agreed-upon down payment of 20 percent of the ransom was "sweetened" by about $500,000 in products, Castro now demanded a bank guarantee that the balance of his extortions would be paid in full.[22] Deputy Attorney General Katzenbach (later Under Secretary of State) flew to Montreal to negotiate the guarantee with the Royal Bank of Canada, which insisted on formal guarantees by American banks. Katzenbach then flew to New York and made these arrangements. The Continental Insurance Company issued a $53 million performance bond.

On December 21 Donovan and Castro signed a Memorandum of Agreement in Havana, but Castro made further conditions. He wanted his own people to inspect the drugs, and three Cuban Red Cross officials were secretly flown to Miami for the purpose. Every precaution was taken to keep the press from becoming aware of their presence.

But Castro was still not satisfied! After four plane-loads of prisoners had landed in Florida on Sunday, December 23, he demanded payment by 3 P.M. Monday, December 24, of the $2,925,000 that had been pledged as ransom for 60 wounded prisoners released the previous April.[23] Robert Kennedy was contacted at 5 A.M. that day. The Attorney General called Richard Cardinal Cushing, Archbishop of Boston, and obtained a pledge of $1 million. He then called General Lucius Clay, who borrowed the remaining $1,925,000 on his own signature. Castro insisted on proof that the cash had been deposited in Montreal, and he was finally given this assurance late in the after-

[21] Wise and Ross, p. 280.
[22] Johnson, pp. 328, 329, 332.
[23] *Ibid.*, pp. 338, 339.

noon at the Canadian Consul's office.[24] Every Castro demand had been met, and on Christmas Eve, 1962, the last of the Cuban prisoners touched down in Florida.

A transaction of such proportions could not be entirely hidden, but some aspects which were particularly vulnerable politically were carefully concealed. One was any direct contribution by the U.S. Government. Thus, beginning a few days after the prisoner release, when the Department of Agriculture began delivering dried milk and shortening to the Red Cross for shipment to Cuba, a cover was needed. Eventually Agriculture contributed thirty-five million pounds of surplus food to the prisoner ransom—fifteen million pounds of dried milk and twenty million pounds of shortening.

The dried milk and shortening cost the government $5,655,-000 [25] when it was bought from producers under the farm price-support program, and the government normally uses the price paid producers when it calculates the value of surplus food contributions to charity. In this case, however, seeking to minimize the donation to Castro, it figured its contribution at slightly less than $2 million, the price the milk and shortening might have brought in the world market.

Furthermore, the Agriculture Department announced on January 8, 1963, that "the Red Cross had indicated that the Cuban Families Committee expects to raise funds to reimburse the department." [26] It was saying that the government would receive cash for the surplus food. The fact is that by then the Committee had become inactive, with no chance whatsoever of raising $2 million—over the eight months of its existence, as already noted, it had not been able to raise even $500,000.

This is the way the matter was finally handled: The Union Carbide Company had contributed two million dollars worth of

[24] *Ibid.*, p. 340.
[25] Wise and Ross, p. 286.
[26] *Ibid.*, p. 286.

a bug-killer toward the ransom. The Commerce Department ruled that the insecticide would be of strategic value to Castro by helping his crops. The Red Cross accepted the insecticide and turned it over to the Agency for International Development, which sent it to India, Pakistan, and Algeria, and Agriculture accepted this as repayment for the milk and shortening. These were the "funds" that Agriculture had announced would be raised by the Cuban Families Committee "to reimburse the department."

President Kennedy, it will be recalled, had announced on May 24, 1961, that the government was not and could not be a party to the negotiations, but would not "interfere" with the humanitarian efforts of private citizens. *Actually, at least fourteen branches of the U.S. Government participated in the ransom.*[27]

It has been conservatively estimated that it cost the government $29,793,000 to extricate itself from the prisoner dilemma, including a $20 million tax loss, according to an estimate of Mitchell Rogovin of the Internal Revenue Service.

The drug and food companies came out well. All their demands were met. They were not required to disclose their cost and mark-up data to secure tax deductions, and in many cases the tax benefit granted (52 percent of their wholesale prices) exceeded their production costs, so that the transaction resulted in a profit. And the drug industry in particular drew satisfaction from having had the Kennedy brothers come begging for their cooperation.

Donovan, the experienced lawyer, and Alvaro Sánchez, the Cuban negotiator, performed admirably. Donovan obtained the release of more than thirty Americans held in Cuban jails, including three CIA men. More than five thousand members of the families of the prisoners were permitted to depart on the Red Cross ships. When Donovan insisted, as late as June 1963, that

[27] *Ibid.*

he was "a private citizen acting on behalf of the Cuban Families Committee," he was adhering to the position he had agreed to take at the outset. The prisoners who survived the Girón debacle were released and reunited with their families, and for this all patriotic Cubans are profoundly grateful.

Castro came out far better than he had dared hope at first. The ransom he exacted was more than twice what he had originally requested. Among his friends he ridiculed the United States as it met each of his arrogant demands. In June 1963 all thirteen Republican members of the House Foreign Affairs Committee called for an investigation, but the Democrats were in control of the Committee and nothing happened.

There had been alternatives. On April 20, 1961—three days after the Girón invasion—President Kennedy asked Richard Nixon to come to the White House. In answer to the President's question, "What would you do now in Cuba?" Nixon replied, "I would find a proper legal cover and go in," and he cited three legal justifications for such action. He added that if the President moved affirmatively, he would support him publicly *"to the hilt" and urge all other Republicans to do likewise.*[28]

What suffered in the ransoming of the Bay of Pigs prisoners was the prestige of the United States.

---

[28] Richard M. Nixon, "Cuba, Castro and John F. Kennedy," *Reader's Digest,* November 1964.

CHAPTER NINETEEN

Missiles in Cuba

On October 22, 1962 President Kennedy made his celebrated report to the American people on the Soviet nuclear buildup in Cuba. My wife and I were in Madrid at the time. We were with a small group of distinguished Americans that night in the penthouse apartment of our good friends Mr. and Mrs. Kenneth Crosby, atop the tallest building in the Spanish capital.

Not a word was spoken as we listened to the President tell of Soviet duplicity that had brought the nations of North and South America within range of Soviet nuclear missiles. Approvingly we heard him confront Khrushchev with the damning facts and tell the world that "in an area well known to have a special and historical relationship to the United States and the nations of the Western Hemisphere . . . this sudden, clandestine decision to station strategic weapons for the first time outside Soviet soil, is a deliberately provocative and unjustified change in the status quo which cannot be accepted by this country, if our courage and our commitments are ever to be trusted again by either friend or foe."

One of us made a note of the steps Kennedy said he had directed to counter the Soviet threat. There was to be a quarantine of all offensive military equipment under shipment to Cuba. Surveillance of the military buildup in Cuba had been stepped up, and U.S. armed forces were ready to move if military preparations continued. The Soviet Union was put on notice that any missile launched from Cuba against any nation in the Western

Hemisphere would be considered an attack by the U.S.S.R., calling for "a full retaliatory response upon the Soviet Union." The U.S. Naval Base at Guantanamo Bay had been reinforced and dependents evacuated; the Organization of American States had been called to consider necessary action; the United Nations had been asked to call an emergency meeting of the Security Council; and, finally, the President called on Khrushchev to "halt and eliminate this clandestine, reckless and provocative threat to world peace."

Addressing himself to the people of Cuba, the President said he and the American people had "watched with deep sorrow how your nationalist revolution was betrayed—and how your fatherland fell under foreign domination." He expressed the hope that in time this would change and that the Cubans would be "truly free." To his fellow Americans the President addressed a call for courage. He warned of grave hazards ahead and reminded them that "the cost of freedom is always high" but said that Americans had always been willing to pay it.

He ended with this stirring peroration:

"Our goal is not the victory of might, but the vindication of right; not peace at the expense of freedom, but both peace *and* freedom, here in this hemisphere, and, we hope, around the world. God willing, that goal will be achieved."

These were brave words (later I learned that the chief author had been Ted Sorensen), and at the conclusion we remained silent as we weighed the sobering implications of the message we had heard. My feeling, I recall, was one of relief. This sounded like a different John F. Kennedy from the man who had been responsible for the fiasco of the Bay of Pigs. At last he seemed to have become aware of the Communist menace in Cuba and the threat it posed to the hemisphere. He was apparently prepared to eliminate the cancer. Certainly the Soviets had given him a perfect opportunity to do it. One who was not impressed was Carmen, my wife. *"Palabras,"* she said, *"nada más,* you will see."

And as days passed and events unfolded she proved to be

right. Evidently John F. Kennedy had not changed at all since the Bay of Pigs. Here again he demonstrated the same lamentable tendency to vacillate and back away from hard decisions. Once more he took his guidance from many of those who had been so profoundly wrong about the Bay of Pigs, the failure of which had led to the new crisis. Indeed, he operated with almost the same cast, with the notable exception of Arthur M. Schlesinger, Jr. Once again he adopted a course of action opposed by his country's best military experts.

The end result of the Missile Crisis was to give Communism a sanctuary in Cuba, with a guarantee from the President himself that no attempt would be made to dislodge it. Nor was that all that was to come from what some have called "Kennedy's finest hour."

Those who heard Kennedy's historic October 22 speech were under the impression that the youthful President was bravely standing up to a nuclear giant capable of inflicting terrible damage and loss of life on the United States. This was not the case. In October 1962 the military power of the United States was incomparably superior to that of the Soviet Union and, equally important, both Kennedy and Khrushchev knew this to be a fact. The advantage of this immense power superiority could have been lost or lessened if Khrushchev had been in a position to bluff. He was not in that position. Both men *knew* that Kennedy *held all the trump cards.*

How did Kennedy and Khrushchev acquire information of such critical importance, and why, knowing the enormous military imbalance in favor of the United States, did Khrushchev attempt to mount nuclear missiles in Cuba?

The remarkable story of how the closed society of the Soviet Union was opened to American intelligence goes back to the summer of 1954, when one of President Eisenhower's advisory agencies, the Killian Committee on Surprise Attack, suggested building a reconnaissance plane of the U-2 type. The recommendation brought together a three-star team composed of the brilliant Kelly Johnson of Lockheed Aviation, E. H. Land of the Polaroid Company, and Richard M. Bissell, Jr., of the CIA.[1]

The plane and its phenomenal photographic equipment proved to be a marvel of design and engineering. It carried so much scientific paraphernalia that it could not be burdened with landing gear. It was launched from another plane and landed by skidding in on a reinforced belly, with the tips of its wings bent down, like an outrigger canoe. The plane could fly at heights of almost 14 miles and its cameras, aimed through seven portholes in the belly, could photograph a strip of earth 125 miles wide and 3,000 miles long. Less than 1,000 gallons of fuel could carry it 4,000 miles. The definition of its photographs was amazing. A newspaper headline photographed at an altitude of eight miles was legible.

Starting in 1956, and until Francis Gary Powers was shot down over the Urals on May 1, 1960, the American reconnaissance planes flew over Russia for four years.[2] They brought back priceless data on Soviet airfields, aircraft, missiles, missile testing and training, special weapons storage, submarine production, atomic production, and aircraft deployment. The independent U-2 air force was placed under the command of Richard M. Bissell, Jr., Deputy Director of the CIA.

The success of the plane was so great that it stimulated the development of the U-3, which has become the present SR-71, and of a reconnaissance satellite, and an all-out secret effort to build such a satellite began.[3] The first of these new orbiting spybirds was launched in August 1960, only three months after Powers had been downed and the U-2's had ceased their flights over Soviet Russia. There was thus only a brief lapse in the aerial inspection operations. They continued to confirm that the Soviets had not deployed and mounted intercontinental

[1] Joseph Alsop, "A Debt Is Owed," *The Hartford Courant,* December 26, 1963.

[2] David Wise and Thomas B. Ross, *The Invisible Government* (New York: Random House, 1964), p. 122.

[3] Alsop, "A Debt Is Owed," December 26, 1963.

ballistic missiles (ICBMs),[4] which they were entirely capable of producing.

By January 1961, the United States had begun putting into orbits no higher than one hundred to three hundred miles a whole series of the cigar-shaped reconnaissance satellites known as the SAMOS, combining the initials of Satellite And Missile Observation System. The new spy-birds were orbited almost perpendicular to the equator, which meant that, with the earth's motion, at least once a day every point on its surface would come within range of their cameras. While one camera aimed at the earth below, another was synchronized to shoot the stars above, so that the picture of the earth could be exactly oriented. Some of the cameras pointed straight down, others obliquely forward, to give various views of a target. Still other cameras swept from side to side, taking panoramic photographs of airfields or of entire cities.[5]

The satellites took pictures only on command from the ground. Some models carried a television system that permitted ground operators to take a quick look to determine what areas required special attention. Closeups with a more powerful lens could then be ordered for the next orbital pass. The film capsule could be ejected, also on command from the ground, and parachuted down to a chosen spot in the Pacific, where planes equipped with special devices snatched it out of the air. If a capsule was not picked up within a given time, a plug dissolved and the capsule sank. The sphere of operation for the U-2 plane was approximately fifteen miles above the earth. Higher than that was the domain of the unmanned reconnaissance satellites. This amazing system permitted the United States to identify every military installation on earth, and by repeating the picture coverage, to keep abreast of changes that were taking place.

A basic element of the new science of aerial photography was

[4] James Burnham, *The War We Are In* (New York: Arlington House, 1967), p. 21.
[5] *The New York Times Magazine,* "The Camera Keeps Watch on the World," April 3, 1966, pp. 27, 54.

the training and development by U.S. military services of experts in the interpretation of the remarkable blown-up photographs. For instance, a good photo interpreter could determine the relative economic status of a family from a photograph taken by a satellite a hundred miles overhead. He could describe the construction of the house, the relative age of the community, and even see whether it had a telephone system.

During the Cuban Missile Crisis a photograph showed the fin of a missile protruding from under a canvas cover. The dimensions of this fin were calculated in relation to the gauge of a railroad in the same picture. The canvas-covered object was thereupon identified as a Soviet intermediate-range ballistic missile (IRBM), since the measurements of the fin matched those of the fins of an IRBM photographed on the ground during a May Day parade in Moscow. The measurements of *that* photograph had been determined by relating it to a known yardstick —the bricks in Red Square.[6] Again, during the Cuban Missile Crisis, a U-2 picture revealed a very small shadow in a forest, but another picture taken a few seconds later showed no such shadow. The conclusion was correctly drawn that the trees were hiding a missile site's rotating radar antenna.

The great achievement of American aerial reconnaissance was the confirmation of information the CIA was receiving through many conventional intelligence sources. One of these, for example, was Colonel Oleg Penkovskiy, a senior officer of the Soviet military intelligence and a graduate of the Soviet staff college and of the Missile Academy. Over a period of years Penkovskiy furnished priceless information to the West. He was on the friendliest terms with the Chief of Soviet military intelligence and with prominent Soviet generals and political leaders. Until his arrest on October 22, 1962, six days before Khrushchev agreed to dismantle the missile sites in Cuba, Penkovskiy reported on the development and testing of Russian missiles. While Khrushchev was threatening the West with

[6] *Ibid.*, p. 56.

a shower of missiles, Penkovskiy was able to report that the big ones were still on the drawing boards. The smaller missiles, he said, deviated several hundred kilometers in their tests and in some cases had hit inhabited areas.

"In short, Khrushchev often brags about things we do not have," he reported.[7] He worried over the possibility that the West might take Khrushchev's boasts at face value and he urged the United States to take a firm stand. At the time of the Bay of Pigs he reported that members of the Soviet General Staff were all of the opinion that Kennedy had as much right to help the Cuban patriots as the Soviets had when they "helped" the Hungarians. This opinion, he said, was also often expressed by ordinary citizens on street-cars in Moscow.

Penkovskiy was executed on May 16, 1963. He is reported to have been betrayed by the British intelligence agent Harold A. R. (Kim) Philby, who served the Soviets for thirty years. Penkovskiy died because he believed in the traditions of the Western World.

In the fall of 1961 a decision was reached in Washington to let the Soviets know that there had been an intelligence breakthrough.[8] Roswell Gilpatric, Deputy Secretary of Defense, was chosen to handle the assignment. He did so in an address delivered at Hot Springs, Virginia, on October 21, 1961, a year before the Missile Crisis. He disclosed that there was in fact a dramatically wide "missile gap," but that it was *in favor of the United States.*

Gilpatric said that the United States possessed six hundred intercontinental heavy bombers and many more medium bombers that could reach Soviet targets by refueling in flight. In addition, it had "dozens" of intercontinental ballistic missiles (ICBMs) and six Polaris submarines at sea, each carrying six-

[7] Oleg Penkovskiy, *The Penkovskiy Papers* (New York: Doubleday & Company, Inc., 1965), p. 323.

[8] Roger Hilsman, *To Move a Nation* (New York: Doubleday & Company, Inc., 1967), p. 163.

teen missiles. The missiles carried by a single Polaris submarine had more destructive power than all the bombs dropped by both sides during World War II. "The total number of our nuclear delivery vehicles," Gilpatric said, "tactical as well as strategic, is in the *tens of thousands;* and, of course, we have more than one warhead for each vehicle." (In military jargon the expression "nuclear delivery vehicles" includes aircraft, missiles, submarines, and artillery.) Then the Deputy Secretary of Defense spoke these portentous words: "Their Iron Curtain is not so impenetrable as to force us to accept at face value the Kremlin's boasts."

The all-important news that there had been an intelligence breakthrough was conveyed to the Soviets in a number of other ways in the weeks that followed. The United States briefed its allies and deliberately included countries that it knew were penetrated by Soviet spies.[9] In this way Soviet intelligence channels received confirmation of the message openly conveyed by Gilpatric.

A year later, at the time of the Cuban Missile Crisis, the magnitude of American superiority had increased. Instead of "dozens" of ICBMs, the United States had almost two hundred [10] and there were eight Polaris and more hunter submarines at sea. Although the Communists never disclose their military statistics, it is known that the U.S.S.R. was still very weak. Its incipient ICBM system was a "soft" system, not buried deep in the ground and protected by steel and concrete, as was that of the United States. The Soviets had no second-strike capability, since the United States had virtually all of the Soviet launching pads plotted. Khrushchev knew that the United States was capable of blackening all important Russian military installations and centers of population in two or three hours, while his own nuclear potential posed no remotely comparable threat to America.

[9] *Ibid.,* p. 163.
[10] *Bulletin of the Atomic Scientists,* February 1963, p. 9.

Why then did the Soviet leader pursue his audacious plan to mount missiles in Cuba?

The answer is that Khrushchev had long since come to the conclusion that Kennedy's lack of experience and his tendency to temporize could be safely exploited. He had noted that the President had shied away from using any of his great power to liquidate Castro, though Castro must have been as repugnant to the Americans as the Nagy regime in Hungary had been to the Russians. He had undoubtedly drawn conclusions from the manner in which Kennedy had stood aside when the Berlin Wall was erected and from his less than adroit handling of the situation in Laos, which ended in that unfortunate country's bogus "neutralization."

Khrushchev had had an excellent opportunity to appraise Kennedy personally when they met at the Vienna conference in June 1961. There the Soviet Chairman prodded and bullied the American President over the Bay of Pigs failure, and twitted him for abandoning Brigade 2506 on the beaches without ammunition, supplies or reinforcements, and Kennedy had confessed personal responsibility for the failure.

James Reston talked to Kennedy at the American Embassy in Vienna ten minutes after his meeting with Khrushchev and found him "shaken and angry." The President said enough to convince Reston that "Khrushchev had studied the events of the Bay of Pigs; he would have understood if Kennedy had left Castro alone or destroyed him; but when Kennedy was rash enough to strike at Cuba but not bold enough to finish the job, Khrushchev decided he was dealing with an inexperienced young leader who could be intimidated and blackmailed. The Communist decision to put offensive missiles into Cuba was the final gamble of this assumption." [11]

But Reston, then an associate editor and now the executive editor of *The New York Times,* goes further. He thinks he has the answer to the question that puzzles so many Americans—

[11] *The New York Times Magazine,* November 15, 1964.

how their country became involved in a ground war in Southeast Asia. In an article published in his newspaper on January 18, 1966, he wrote that Kennedy had told him he thought Khrushchev had decided that "anyone who was stupid enough to get involved in that situation [the Bay of Pigs] was immature, and anyone who didn't see it all the way through was timid and therefore could be bluffed." According to Reston, Kennedy then said that it was necessary to take steps to make American power "credible" to the Russians. Hence the military budget was increased, the Rainbow Division was sent to West Germany, and the war in Vietnam was intensified, "not because the situation on the ground demanded it in Vietnam" but because Kennedy "wanted to prove a diplomatic point, not a military point. . . . That, I think," Mr. Reston adds, "is where we began to get off the track."

Another reason for the apparent imprudence of moving Soviet missiles into Cuba was undoubtedly Khrushchev's conviction, as he told the poet Robert Frost in Moscow, that the democracies were "too liberal to fight."

In any case, although Arthur Schlesinger, Jr., has described the President and his brother as making careful decisions "under the most unimaginable conditions of pressure and panic," [12] it is clear that there was no reason to make any significant concessions to the Communists during the October 1962 Missile Crisis. Nevertheless, during the ten days of the crisis and the ensuing settlement, President Kennedy backed away from one position after another; he not only gave the Soviets a guaranteed sanctuary in Cuba but made other major concessions, as will be seen.

In tracing the events in the following two chapters, it will be interesting and significant to observe the sharply different reactions of the few conservatives who occupied high-level positions, as against the large group of liberals who participated. The conservatives called for strong action to eliminate the threat

[12] *The New York Times,* May 8, 1968, p. 33.

posed by Khrushchev's nuclear blackmail. The liberals opposed steps that they felt might provoke or humiliate the Soviets. It was, in short, a repetition of the Washington scene at the time of the Bay of Pigs discussions, and the dialogue ended in another defeat for the United States and in a soul-shattering blow to the Cuban people.

CHAPTER TWENTY

What Led to the Crisis

The first Soviet arms arrived in Cuba in the early summer of 1960, and by late October Castro was able to boast that he had a militia of 250,000, equipped with weapons supplied by the Communist bloc. Early in 1962 there appeared to be a lull in arms shipments, but they started again in mid-summer, when American naval reconnaissance planes spotted a steady stream of ships heading for Cuba from Soviet ports in the Baltic and Black Seas.[1]

Much of this maritime traffic docked at Mariel, a deep water port on the north coast, thirty-five miles west of Havana. CIA agents reported that Cubans living near Mariel harbor had been forced to evacuate their homes and that Soviet sentries guarded the docks while others unloaded the ships. High fences were erected to hide these activities, which were carried out at night, while night convoys moved equipment out to remote wooded areas, from which the population had also been evacuated.[2]

In a State Department press briefing on August 24, Roger Hilsman, in charge of State Department Intelligence, explained that the Soviet bloc ships streaming into Cuba were carrying electronic gear and construction equipment that apparently

[1] Roger Hilsman, *To Move a Nation* (New York: Doubleday & Company, Inc., 1967), p. 170.

[2] Elie Abel, *The Missile Crisis* (New York: J. B. Lippincott Company, 1966), p. 16. Also Hilsman, p. 165.

would go into coastal and air defenses. He conceded that three to five thousand Soviet "technicians" had also arrived but explained that they were not organized into combat units and were not in uniform. He assumed that their function was to install defensive equipment being imported and to teach the Cubans how to operate it.[3]

During early September Cuban political leaders and anti-Castro groups in the U.S. published paid press announcements reporting the arrival of Soviet troops and the construction of missile pads in Cuba.

On September 12 an experienced CIA subagent in Cuba saw a middle-of-the-night convoy proceeding in a westerly direction from Mariel. It included exceptionally long trailers carrying a sixty-foot tubular object concealed by canvas, which he sketched. Surface-to-air anti-aircraft missiles (SAMs) were only thirty feet long, half the length of the missile that the CIA agent had seen and reported.[4] In quick succession additional intelligence reports indicated that there were other surface-to-surface missiles in Cuba. A second long-trailer convoy was observed heading west by another professional CIA agent on September 17,[5] and three days later a Cuban refugee gave an accurate and detailed description of construction work under way at Remedios, in central Cuba, that he had seen a few days earlier. This clearly seemed to be one of the buildings the Soviets intended to use for nuclear launching and storage. Concrete installations were required for launching the two-thousand-mile intermediate-range ballistic missiles (IRBMs), whereas the thousand-mile medium-range ballistic missiles (MRBMs) could be fired from vehicles.

In late September another report from a CIA agent told of Castro's private pilot having boasted that Cuba no longer feared the United States because it had acquired long-range missiles.[6]

---

[3] Hilsman, p. 170.
[4] *Ibid.*, pp. 174, 186.
[5] *Ibid.*, p. 175.
[6] *Ibid.*, p. 175.

Also, U.S. naval reconnaissance planes spotted Soviet ships with exceedingly long hatches riding high in the water, indicating a low weight but high volume cargo. These were the vessels that carried the sixty-foot missiles to Cuba.

The night convoys proceeding over the Cuban roads were observed by thousands of Cubans, and it was not long before more information was reaching the United States. Literally hundreds of Cubans reported to CIA agents in Florida that they had seen *cohetes* (missiles) being transported through the countryside during September 1962.[7] When these reports appeared to arouse little interest and no action on the part of the administration, some of the refugees approached well-known Republicans, among them Senator Kenneth B. Keating of New York.

By October 2 the CIA knew that eighty-five shiploads had arrived at Mariel and a few other similarly protected Cuban ports, that fifteen sites had been prepared for SAMs, and that about four thousand five hundred Soviet military technicians were then in Cuba.[8] Nevertheless, as Roger Hilsman has stated, "all through late September and early October there was a determination [in the government] to move slowly and deliberately."

John A. McCone, Director of the CIA, a Republican and a conservative businessman, had no inclination to move "slowly and deliberately." He felt certain that the Soviet military build-up in Cuba was the first stage of a plan to introduce *offensive* Soviet missiles there, and on August 22, 1962, shortly before leaving for Seattle to be married, he presented his arguments to President Kennedy, and also to the Secretary of the Treasury, Douglas Dillon.[9]

McCone's logic was impeccable. He reasoned that the Soviets would not be so naïve as to believe that anti-aircraft missiles could protect Cuba against an invasion from the United States.

[7] *Ibid.*, p. 174.
[8] *Ibid.*, p. 176.
[9] Abel, pp. 17, 18.

The SAMs were being installed, he was certain, to protect something else—offensive missiles trained on the United States.[10] The Soviets had not done this in Poland and Hungary, he argued, because they did not trust the Poles and Hungarians, who might have turned them around and used the U.S.S.R. as their target. But the medium or intermediate range missiles in Cuba could not reach the Soviet Union.

President Kennedy was not impressed; he accepted the State Department view that the Soviets would never have the audacity to introduce ballistic missiles into Cuba. Its reasoning was that they were cautious on nuclear matters, had never positioned such weapons outside the U.S.S.R., and would certainly not do so in the Caribbean.

This comforting concept was shattered by Senator Keating in a series of ten speeches, between August 31 and October 1, warning the Kennedy administration of the danger of the Soviet military buildup. On one occasion he said that he had been able to confirm from completely reliable sources that six intermediate range ballistic missile sites were under construction. This later proved to be correct, except that the six sites then under construction were for medium-range missiles. The Soviet plan called for four IRBM sites to be added later.

The administration either denied or ridiculed the Keating reports, accusing him of peddling refugee rumors. But the public was becoming alarmed. When Senator Barry Goldwater and other Republicans began to prod the administration, and concerned citizens started questioning its "do nothing" policy, it fell into a semantic trap. It attempted to make a distinction between "offensive" and "defensive" weapons in Cuba.

The situation was the reverse of what it had been in 1960, when Kennedy had been the leader of the "outs." Then, he had hit hard at Richard Nixon for not standing firm in Cuba. "If you can't stand up to Castro, how can you be expected to stand up to Khrushchev?" he had asked in an address on October 15,

[10] *Ibid.*, p. 18.

1960. "The transformation of Cuba into a Communist base of operations a few minutes from our coast by jet plane, missile or submarine . . . is an incredibly dangerous development to have been permitted by our Republican policy-makers."

By 1962 it was understandable that Kennedy should have been sensitive about Cuba. Making a campaign speech in New Haven on October 17, he had been confronted with a sign calling for "More Courage, Less Profile," and there were many other symptoms of growing public dissatisfaction with his handling of the Cuban situation.

Anxious to refute embarrassing charges of weakness or softness, with the off-year elections only a few weeks away, the administration used the various channels open to it to reassure the public that all was well. On October 3, Under Secretary of State George W. Ball told a Congressional committee that the equipment arriving in Cuba did not offer offensive capabilities against the United States. "Our intelligence is very good and very hard," [11] he said.

Eleven days later, on October 14, McGeorge Bundy appeared on television, on ABC's *Issues and Answers* program, and flatly denied that the Soviets had any offensive weapons in Cuba. He was questioned about the administration's "defensive" interpretation of military installations in Cuba. Wasn't it possible that these could be converted into offensive weapons virtually overnight? "Well," said Bundy, "I don't myself think that there is any present—I *know* there is no present evidence, and I think there is no present likelihood that the Cubans and the Cuban government and the Soviet government would in combination attempt to install a major offensive capability." [12]

This was the closest adviser to the President of the United States speaking! He was the man who had the last word with the President after all briefings by the CIA and the military had been completed. Furthermore, he was the key member of

[11] Hilsman, p. 176.
[12] *Ibid.*, p. 180.

a top-secret committee known as the Special Group, the other members of which were Secretary of Defense McNamara, Gilpatric, U. Alexis Johnson (Deputy Under Secretary of State for Political Affairs), and McCone.[13] This committee was the hidden power center of the intelligence community, its existence known to only a handful of men. It met about once a week to make crucial decisions too sensitive to be entrusted to the National Security Council (NSC) or the United States Intelligence Board (USIB).

On September 19 the USIB had met at the State Department to review the Soviet arms buildup in Cuba and prepare what became known as the "September Estimate." Such Estimates are statements of what is going to happen in any given area, projected as far as possible into the future. During the twelve days preceding the September 19 meeting McCone (then in Europe) cabled his deputy on four occasions stressing the strong indications that the buildup presaged the introduction of offensive ballistic missiles. And when he learned that the Board nevertheless had reached the conclusion that the Soviets would not introduce offensive missiles in Cuba, he strongly urged in a further dispatch that it reconsider and reverse its findings.[14] The record of the CIA and of its Director during this critical period is above reproach.

In brushing aside the CIA warnings, the Kennedy administration relied to a very large extent on assurances it was receiving from the Kremlin that the Russians meant no harm. On September 4 the Soviet Ambassador in Washington, Anatoly Dobrynin, had called on Attorney General Robert F. Kennedy with a message from Khrushchev. The Chairman wanted the message passed along to the President by his brother and no one else. It was a promise that the Soviets would create no trouble for the United States during the election campaign. Robert Kennedy at once reported to the President, and the two brothers

[13] David Wise and Thomas B. Ross, *The Invisible Government* (New York: Random House, 1964), p. 260.
[14] Abel, pp. 23, 24.

prepared a public statement that was released the same day. "There is no evidence," it said, "of any organized combat force in Cuba from any Soviet bloc country; of military bases provided to Russia; . . . of the presence of offensive ground-to-ground missiles; or of other significant offensive capability, either in Cuban hands or under Soviet direction and guidance. Were it to be otherwise the gravest issues would arise." [15]

Four days later the Kremlin came through with a new disclaimer. "There was no need," it said, "for the Soviet Union to shift its weapons for the repulsion of aggression, for a retaliatory blow, to any other country, for instance to Cuba." The official statement said that Soviet nuclear weapons were so powerful that there was no need for sites beyond the U.S.S.R. Actually, the Soviets had few if any ICBMs mounted.[16]

At his news conference on September 13 President Kennedy again assured the country that the arms shipments to Cuba "do not constitute a serious threat to any part of the hemisphere." If they did, he said, or if Cuba should ever attempt to export its aggressive purposes, "then this country will do whatever must be done to protect its own security and that of its allies."

Although the specific U-2 planes involved had always operated under the control of the CIA, their flight schedules were determined by a small, top-secret group dominated by civilians, known as the Committee on Overhead Reconnaissance (COMOR), which usually met in McGeorge Bundy's office at the White House.[17] Until late August the schedule had called for two flights a month, but with the discovery of the first SAM installations it was stepped up. The SAMs had a slant range of twenty-five miles and were therefore effective against high-flying planes. Between August 29 and October 7, seven U-2's were dispatched over Cuba. In addition to the flight on August 29, others took place on September 5, 17, 26, and 29, and October

[15] *Ibid.*, pp. 19, 20.
[16] James Burnham, *The War We Are In* (New York: Arlington House, 1967), p. 21.
[17] Abel, p. 25.

5 and 7. All but the September 5 flight, however, were limited to the portion of Cuba lying east of Havana. The reason for this was that COMOR knew that the main activity in deploying the SAMs was *west* of Havana, and it feared that a U-2 over that area might be shot down!

When McCone returned from Europe he was astonished to find that western Cuba had not been flown over for a full month, and he reacted immediately, recommending that the entire island be photographed at once, *especially* the area *west* of Havana. This recommendation was made on October 4, but five days elapsed before COMOR approved the new flight plan. Then there was a delay of another five days when Secretary McNamara insisted that the U-2 squadron be placed under the jurisdiction of the Air Force, under his control.[18]

The CIA very strongly opposed this change, arguing that intelligence was *its* business, that it had the trained pilots and the experience and its own control center. It had controlled the U-2 squadron since its inception. It made a fervent appeal to the White House to continue the organizational efficiency of the U-2 operations. Bundy, however, supported McNamara. Two regular Air Force majors, Rudolph Anderson, Jr., and Richard S. Heyser, were then assigned to make a sweep over western Cuba in a U-2 plane, with which they first had to familiarize themselves.

The main photographic target was an installation near the town of San Cristóbal, west of Havana, where the CIA had reports that SAMs had been placed at corners of a trapezoidal pattern similar to missile installations that Gary Powers and others had photographed in the Soviet Union.

The Anderson-Heyser flight, made on October 14, was uneventful. No ground fire was encountered, and when their plane skidded into its landing with the wings folded down at the tips to prevent ground looping, their film magazines were transferred to a waiting jet that streaked to Washington.

[18] *Ibid.*, p. 27.

The developed film showed a clearing in the woods with missile erectors, launchers, and transporters, all inside a quadrilateral pattern of two parallel and two non-parallel sides. A SAM had been installed at each corner. The pattern was exactly similar to missile sites photographed in the Soviet Union.[19] McCone's warning could no longer be ignored. The negative September Estimate of the United States Intelligence Board would now have to be discarded, as McCone had urged. Those who had clung to the theory that the Soviets would not put missiles into Cuba now became convinced they had been wrong. The Kennedy administration finally realized that the Kremlin had lied. The Missile Crisis was on.

A tragic footnote to the discovery on October 14 by the Anderson-Heyser team of the first missiles deployed by the U.S.S.R. in the Western Hemisphere records the death of the valiant Anderson two weeks later during the Crisis. The group of Presidential advisers that became known as the ExCom had decided that if a U-2 were shot down over Cuba, the American response should be to destroy the responsible SAM site. If a second U-2 were shot down, all SAM installations in Cuba were to be destroyed. Khrushchev had informed Kennedy that the missiles were controlled by Soviet officers, not by Cubans. "Therefore," he had said, "any accidental use of them whatsoever to the detriment of the United States is excluded."

At about 10 o'clock on the morning of October 27, Major Anderson was shot down and killed. Backing away from what his Executive Committee had decided, Kennedy ordered that there be no response.

As matters approached a climax, the Soviets continued to draw a veil of deception over the buildup. On October 13, Soviet Ambassador Dobrynin assured both Robert Kennedy and Chester Bowles that the Soviet Union had no offensive

[19] *Ibid.,* pp. 28, 29. Also Hilsman, p. 180.

weapons in Cuba. The following day, the very day that the missile bases were being photographed in Cuba, Khrushchev met in Moscow with U.S. Ambassador Foy Kohler and assured him in his most jovial manner that he had nothing but good will for the United States. He asked the Ambassador to let the President know that, with an election coming up, he intended to cause Kennedy no embarrassment. And on October 18, when all the evidence was in, Foreign Minister Andrei Gromyko spent two hours in the White House giving President Kennedy the same lying assurances that Khrushchev had given Ambassador Kohler four days earlier.

The Soviet used maximum duplicity to the end—to achieve surprise and to obtain maximum gains.

McGeorge Bundy received the news of the missile erectors spotted by the U-2 flights at 8:30 P.M. on October 15, the very day after he had stated on national TV that there was no existing evidence or likelihood that the Soviets would mount offensive weapons in Cuba. He was the usual channel to the President, and he decided to inform him the next morning. This was done at 8 A.M., and Kennedy instructed Bundy to call a meeting for 11:45 that morning, giving him the names of the men he wanted present: Vice President Johnson; Secretary of State Rusk; McNamara; Robert Kennedy; Gen. Maxwell Taylor; Gen. Marshall S. Carter (McCone's deputy, since the CIA Director was out of town); Roswell Gilpatric; George Ball; Edwin Martin, Assistant Secretary of State for Inter-American Affairs; Sorensen; Douglas Dillon, Secretary of the Treasury; Charles Bohlen, who had just been appointed Ambassador to France; Kenneth O'Donnell, the President's appointments secretary; and Bundy himself. This was the group, with a few additions, that later became known as the Executive Committee of the National Security Council (ExCom). Among the notable omissions were Hilsman, Schlesinger, and Adlai Stevenson, although the latter was destined to attend some of the meetings.

Stevenson had arrived in Washington from New York that

morning, and he first heard about the missiles that afternoon from Kennedy himself. He was alarmed when Kennedy mentioned that an air strike had been suggested, and urged caution. The best course, he felt, was to go to the United Nations.[20] Dean Acheson later joined the group at the President's request, and since Bohlen was about to leave for his new post in Paris, Llewellyn Thompson, who had just returned from Moscow, took his place. When McCone returned to Washington from the West Coast, where he had been summoned because of a death in his family, he joined the group, as did Paul Nitze, an Assistant Secretary of Defense.

The "hardliners" in the ExCom included McCone, Dillon, the few military men who were consulted, and, curiously, Acheson. The leaders of the liberal group advocating caution were McNamara, Robert Kennedy, Bundy, Ball and Gilpatric. As the conversations developed during various meetings held on each of the succeeding days, five major plans emerged, each with several variants. One was to take out the missiles with a swift military strike; the second was invasion by sea and air; the third was blockade; the fourth was to move through diplomatic and political channels, preferably the United Nations. The fifth was to do nothing at all.

The President telephoned a Republican friend in New York, John J. McCloy, who had served under various Democratic presidents. McCloy, who was about to leave on a business trip to Europe, recommended drastic action.[21]

With one exception, everyone realized that to do nothing about the missiles in Cuba would be by far the most dangerous course. The one dissenter, amazingly, was the Secretary of Defense. In spite of intelligence reports, fully confirmed by the American reconnaissance satellites, that the Soviets had little capability of launching a missile attack from Soviet soil, McNamara argued that they already possessed ICBMs and that

20 Abel, p. 49.
21 *Ibid.*, p. 45.

whatever happened in Cuba they would go on building more. The only military effect of the missiles in Cuba, he argued, would be to reduce America's warning time. He dismissed the idea that the Russians had sneaked missiles into Cuba in order to close the missile gap. "A missile is a missile," he said. "It makes no difference whether you are killed by a missile fired from the Soviet Union or from Cuba." Incredible though it may seem, *McNamara's instinctive initial "do nothing" reaction has been fully established. In this he stood almost alone.*[22]

When others objected that a policy of inaction would make Khrushchev look like a winner to the entire world, McNamara sharply disagreed. Paul Nitze, one of McNamara's Assistant Secretaries, had the courage to oppose his superior.[23] He pointed out that the warning time of a sudden missile attack would be cut from fifteen minutes to one or two and that the strategic bomber force of the U.S. could be largely destroyed by such a sudden attack. But the Secretary of Defense held to his position for several days, the lone advocate of a "do nothing" policy.

At a later time McNamara would refer to the Missile Crisis as "the most satisfying episode of my life." His attitudes during that episode furnish an insight into the mental processes of the man who headed the military establishment of the world's most powerful nation for seven crucial years. During that period the U.S.S.R. made astonishing progress toward overtaking the U.S. in missile weaponry. Shortly after McNamara took office, it was customary to speak of American nuclear superiority in terms of 5-to-1 or 4-to-1. When he relinquished office in 1968, he was suggesting that the U.S. forego superiority and accept parity with the Soviet Union; this by then, in fact, appeared well on the way to achievement.

The political-strategic philosophy that rejects American su-

[22] Hilsman, pp. 195, 197.
[23] Abel, p. 52.

periority in favor of parity has been propagated by many influential men within and outside the U.S. government. But its acceptance by McNamara is among the elements that made him one of the most controversial figures in recent American history. Hanson W. Baldwin, the well-known *New York Times* military editor, has written: "Secretary McNamara is the first Secretary of Defense who has attempted to define the potential enemy's policies and strategies as well as our own. This dangerous arrogance—dangerous to the U.S.—matches his periodic propensity, sometimes likened to occasional columns by Walter Lippmann, for arguing with impeccable logic [and] complete precision, from one false premise to a false conclusion."

Within the scope of this narrative it is worth noting that McNamara's behavior in the Missile Crisis commended itself to the Soviets. When they spoke of the "madmen" of the Pentagon they pointedly excepted the Secretary of Defense; they looked upon him as an intelligent and sophisticated spokesman for the "realist" camp. In refusing to share this appraisal, Baldwin had the solid backing of virtually all American military experts.

The ExCom meetings took place in George Ball's conference room at the State Department. Some were called for specific times, but as a rule they continued through the day and into the night in a confused and disorganized fashion, with members coming and going at random. Secretary of State Rusk should have presided, but his noncommittal attitude, as in the early Bay of Pigs discussions, opened the way for Robert Kennedy to become the discussion leader.[24]

The President himself seldom attended these early meetings, at which Bobby Kennedy's custom of barking sharp questions and commands annoyed some of the older men. He was generally regarded as the "Assistant President," and he seemed so

[24] *Ibid.,* pp. 57, 58.

to consider himself. One participant said, "We all knew little brother was watching and keeping a little list of where everyone stood." When George Ball argued against an air strike, Kennedy backed him. He spoke of Pearl Harbor, saying his brother was not going to be the Tojo of the 1960s. He feared an invasion would have to follow an air strike and that many innocent people would be killed.

The experience of Dean Acheson and Robert Kennedy in the discussions has been related in fascinating detail by the highly regarded TV news correspondent Elie Abel. The elderly statesman certainly had soft spots in his early career, but he has become, through long experience and at an incalculable cost to the Free World, a "hard liner" in dealing with Communism. Robert Kennedy, thirty-two years his junior, came into conflict with him by following a soft approach.

Acheson took the position that to compare the Missile Crisis to Pearl Harbor was patently absurd. The Monroe Doctrine had been a warning to the world for many years that the United States would not tolerate an aggressive European power in the Americas. Congress and the President had specifically warned the Soviets in the clearest language that the United States would act if they installed offensive weapons in Cuba. Acheson specifically recalled the Presidential warnings of September 4 and 13 and the recent Joint Congressional Resolution of October 3, in which the United States expressed its determination "to prevent in Cuba the creation or use of an externally supported military capability endangering the security of the United States." The security of the United States was now at stake, Acheson emphasized, and the entire free world would understand if the country moved forcefully to protect itself. The Soviets had provided the perfect opportunity to get rid of Castro and Communism, as well as to force removal of the missiles. "We had the thumbscrew on Khrushchev," Acheson later said, "and we should have given it another turn every day. The Russians had no business being in Cuba in the first place."

But Robert Kennedy challenged Acheson, asserting that his brother simply could not order an air strike. Once again, as in the Bay of Pigs meetings, he raised the specter of "world opinion," and he spoke of the ideals and convictions of the American people. An air strike, he feared, would irreparably damage America's image in the world.

It was these meetings that gave currency to the labels of "hawk" and "dove." Some of the participants, notably Dean Rusk, were described as "dawks" and "hoves" because of their ambiguous position. It was the Bay of Pigs all over again, although here the presence of uniformed representatives of the military was limited to General Maxwell Taylor, whose participation in the discussions remains unclear. The conservatives advocated a military strike, and the liberals backed away. Some of those involved wavered from one position to another, while others held to their convictions.

One who never wavered was Adlai Stevenson. It may have been just happenstance, but Stevenson and Acheson never confronted one another in the conference room. And this was just as well since, according to Elie Abel, they despised one another, Acheson having long regarded Stevenson as indecisive, soft, and fuzzy-minded, and Stevenson looking upon Acheson as a warhawk.

On Thursday night, October 18, a decision was reached in favor of a blockade. The military found it impossible to accept the wisdom of this decision. The following morning the Joint Chiefs of Staff met with the President and argued for half an hour in favor of an air strike or an invasion.[25] This annoyed the President because it delayed his departure for Cleveland, where he was to make a campaign speech, but he heard them out. When he informed them that he had made up his mind, the Joint Chiefs, in the usual military tradition, assured the President that his orders would be carried out to the best of

[25] *Ibid.*, p. 83.

their ability. When the President said to Admiral George W. Anderson, Chief of Naval Operations, "This will be up to the Navy," Anderson replied, "Mr. President, the Navy will not let you down." General Curtis LeMay, Chief of Staff of the Air Force, was assigned responsibility for all reconnaissance activities.

By the evening of Friday, October 19, Acheson decided to stop attending the ExCom meetings. He was not in the government and did not wish to take part in working out plans for the blockade he had opposed. He went off to his farm in Maryland and did not return the next day.

That night Sorensen started working on the President's speech. The conservatives, however, were not happy. They continued to argue that a heaven-sent opportunity had been afforded to get rid of Castro and Communism in Cuba. The blockade, if effective, would prevent the delivery of more missiles or bombers, but what about those that were already in Cuba? It was known that 42 MRBMs were being prepared for launching, and the IL-28 bombers were being assembled.[26] Sorensen dropped his work on the speech and joined the Committee, protesting that a decision had been reached and that the discussion should not be reopened. McNamara strongly supported him. Then, at the suggestion of the State Department, the blockade was called a "defensive quarantine," on the theory that it would give less offense to the Soviets.[27] There was some discussion as to whether petroleum should be barred by the blockade but McNamara opposed this, and his view prevailed.

On Saturday morning, October 20, Kennedy broke off his campaigning and returned to Washington with the explanation that he had a slight respiratory infection and temperature. He met with the ExCom in the Oval Room of the White House in what proved to be a bitter session. Rusk had prepared a memorandum giving seven reasons for choosing the "quaran-

[26] Arthur M. Schlesinger, Jr., *A Thousand Days* (Boston: Houghton Mifflin Company, 1965), p. 815.
[27] Hilsman, p. 205.

tine" over the air strike, the chief of them being that an air strike would be irreversible.[28] Predictably, McNamara supported him.

At this point Adlai Stevenson, who had come in late from New York, came up with several incredible proposals. Although the CIA had reported that twenty-eight launching pads were under construction and that the first thousand-mile MRBM could be ready for firing in a few hours, Stevenson advocated a *diplomatic* approach to the U.S.S.R. He also proposed that the United States abandon the great naval base at Guantanamo Bay as part of an agreement with the U.S.S.R. to neutralize and guarantee the territorial integrity of Cuba. Rationalizing this proposal, he said that the base was of little value in any case.

Then Stevenson brought Turkey into the discussion. Calling attention to the American Jupiter bases in that country, he argued that people would ask why it was right for the U.S. to have bases in Turkey but wrong for the Russians to have them in Cuba. President Kennedy, he said, should consider offering to remove the Jupiter bases in exchange for the removal of the Soviet missiles from Cuba.[29] McCone and Dillon bitterly and sharply attacked Stevenson, who nevertheless held his ground. The President rejected the suggestions, although the one having to do with the dismantling of the Turkish bases obviously had made a deep impression upon him.

Stevenson's position at this meeting so frightened most of those present that even the Kennedy brothers decided he lacked the toughness necessary to deal with the Soviets at the United Nations.[30] John McCloy was therefore asked to return from Europe to work with and watch over Stevenson at the United Nations. Instead of abandoning the Guantanamo Naval Base, orders were given to reinforce it.

It was no secret that Adlai Stevenson had wanted to be Sec-

[28] Abel, p. 93.
[29] *Ibid.*, pp. 94-96.
[30] *Ibid.*, p. 96.

retary of State and had chafed at being on the "wrong end of a telephone" in New York, being told what to do. Eric Sevareid has written, "In particular, he could not bear having certain White House and State Department people whom he regarded as mere youngsters telling him what to do." [31]

Stevenson's later performance with McCloy's help at the United Nations, however, was creditable. On one occasion he sharply questioned Russian Ambassador Zorin on the introduction of missiles into Cuba, demanding to know whether he denied that they were being placed there: "Yes or no? Don't wait for the translation. Yes or no?"

Khrushchev did not like this and told Stevenson so when he visited Moscow the following summer to see the limited nuclear test ban treaty signed. "What has happened to you, Stevenson, since you started working for the United States government? We don't like to be interrogated like a criminal in the dock." Stevenson related this incident a few months before his death, and expressed regret that the Kremlin leaders no longer considered him "objective."

It was the October 20 meeting of the ExCom that gave rise to the charge that "Adlai wanted a Munich."

The President's speech was set for 7 P.M. Monday. By Sunday the press had a fairly complete idea of what was happening, and the President telephoned the publishers of the *Washington Post* and *The New York Times,* asking them not to give the story away in the Monday morning editions. McNamara made a similar plea to the publisher of the New York *Herald Tribune.* All complied except the *Times,* which ran a front-page story on Monday saying that there was an air of crisis and tension in the capital and that the President was expected to go on television in the next day or two to remove the veil of secrecy. The Navy and Marine Corps were staging a powerful show of force,

[31] Eric Sevareid, "The Final Troubled Hours of Adlai Stevenson," *Look,* November 30, 1965, p. 86.

not far from Cuba, it said, "which has been the site of a large Communist buildup in recent weeks." There was speculation in Washington, the *Times* reported, that there had been "a new development in Cuba" that could not be disclosed as yet.

It had been decided that America's principal allies should be advised of the developing crisis in advance and that Dean Acheson was the best man to tell de Gaulle. Rusk called his former chief Saturday night, October 20, and asked if he would fly to Paris. The final decision was not the one Acheson had favored, he explained, but in spite of this the President wanted him to tell de Gaulle. On Sunday Acheson flew to London, where he was met at the airport by Ambassador Bruce and where he dropped off a set of aerial photographs, one security man and one photo interpreter. Bruce was to take the evidence to Macmillan the following morning. Acheson then continued to France, landing a little after midnight. At 2:30 P.M. he reached Paris, where he received a call from Kennedy asking him to go on to Germany after seeing de Gaulle.

The meeting between Acheson and the President of France, which took place late Monday afternoon, October 22, is of historical interest. De Gaulle had never forgotten that at the time of the German occupation of France, Roosevelt and Churchill had ignored and humiliated him. Since that time, he believed, Washington, through its intimate relations with weak British governments, had shown that it did not consider de Gaulle worthy of its confidence. Now de Gaulle had become one of the giants of his time. He had ended the Algerian War, made the franc a hard currency, balanced the budget, almost doubled social security allowances, greatly increased his country's gold reserves, and in general had made France a rich, stable country for the first time in many years, with a sense of pride in its future. But he did not have much love for the "Anglo-Saxons."

According to Elie Abel, de Gaulle opened the conversation by saying that the occasion presumably was one of importance,

since Kennedy had done him the honor of sending so distinguished an emissary. He asked Acheson whether he had come
to consult him or to inform him. When Acheson said he had
come to inform, de Gaulle commented that this was quite
all right since he favored independent decisions. When Acheson
completed his report de Gaulle said Kennedy had done exactly
what *he* would have done, that he had no other choice. "You
may tell your President," he said, "that France will support
him." When the two men finally turned to the photographic
evidence, de Gaulle inquired from what altitude the pictures
had been taken. From 14 miles, he was told. *"C'est formidable,"*
he said, and repeated, *"C'est vraiment formidable."* De Gaulle
had never seen such amazing photography. Using a magnifying
glass the old soldier picked out four different types of Soviet
fighter planes on the Cuban airfields.[32]

The conversation turned to possible counter-actions Khrushchev might take in Berlin, Turkey, and elsewhere, but de
Gaulle brushed these possibilities aside. "If there is a war,
France will be with you. But there will be no war." He questioned whether the quarantine would be sufficient, as Adenauer
would later. According to Elie Abel, de Gaulle asked Acheson
why, in his opinion, the Russians had put missiles into Cuba,
and Acheson said that the answer *might not be flattering to his
own government.* The Russians had perhaps been led to believe
they could get away with the audacious plan. De Gaulle agreed.
Khrushchev, of course, did not question the power of the United
States. What he questioned was Kennedy's ability to use it
intelligently.

On Monday, October 22, the group of Presidential advisers
was formally organized into an Executive Committee of the National Security Council and instructed to meet with the President at ten o'clock each morning in the cabinet room. On the
same day the President met with Congressional leaders, who

---

[32] Abel, p. 113.

had been hastily summoned to Washington. At the briefing one of the most respected leaders of the Democratic Party, Senator Richard B. Russell of Georgia, criticized the blockade plan as being a half-way measure.[33] Even Senator Fulbright of Arkansas, Chairman of the Foreign Relations Committee, called for an invasion. Fulbright later explained that he had recommended invasion of Cuba because he felt that a blockade, which would involve a forceable confrontation with Russian ships, would be more dangerous than an invasion that would put American soldiers against Cubans and allow the Russians in Cuba to stand aside.

Most of the Congressional leaders felt that the blockade would be ineffective in achieving what should have been accomplished; they felt that the time had arrived to get rid of Castro. The meeting lasted more than an hour, and it left the President in what one of his aides has described as "a smoldering rage." [34]

The President also consulted the British Ambassador, David Ormsby Gore, who is now Lord Harlech. He presented the various alternatives: air strike, invasion, blockade, or a diplomatic move through the United Nations. McNamara's "do nothing" recommendation had been discarded. The Ambassador said that the reaction in England to an air strike would be unfavorable; he preferred the blockade. Pleased, a smiling President told the Ambassador that this was what the United States was going to do. Later the British Ambassador was to offer a suggestion as to how the U.S. Navy should tactically conduct the blockade, and, establishing a historical precedent, an American President would gratefully receive the advice and act upon it immediately,

---

[33] Years later, in an interview in *U.S. News & World Report,* Senator Russell said of the Missile Crisis: "It's very unfortunate we didn't go ahead then and clean up Castro and the Communists and the missiles all at one time when we had a reason for doing it. I think it would have had a very salutary effect all over the world and probably would have avoided a number of Vietnams in the future. . . . I begged the President on bended knee to go ahead and wind up that Cuban episode while we had a reason for doing it."

[34] Abel, pp. 119, 120.

although it was considered imprudent by Admiral Anderson, Chief of Naval Operations, and by Admiral Robert Dennison, the Commander in Chief of the Atlantic Fleet.

After his meeting with the President, Ormsby Gore sent a long report to the British Prime Minister. If the British Government was not formally consulted, it certainly became the first of America's allies to be completely informed, lending support to de Gaulle's opinion that France was usually relegated to a secondary position by Washington.

The stage was now set for the momentous "eyeball to eyeball" confrontation with Khrushchev. Only the few representatives of the military and the CIA, together with two or three civilian Presidential advisers, had given serious thought to the fact that the Kennedy administration had been offered, for the *second* time, a glowing opportunity to eliminate the Communist beachhead in the Western Hemisphere.

CHAPTER TWENTY-ONE

Anticlimax

The Soviet Union's military weakness *vis-à-vis* the United States at that juncture was not recognized by the general public, and the press and electronic media overran with panicky talk about a nuclear showdown. Many people therefore expected that Moscow would react to President Kennedy's tough speech of October 22, 1962, by sealing off Berlin, bombing American missile bases in Turkey, or ordering Soviet submarines to protect Soviet vessels running the American blockade.

But the hours slipped by, and the Kremlin did nothing. Not until the next morning was there any sign of response, and this was merely an official statement transmitted by Tass calling the blockade a violation of international law and repeating that the missiles in Cuba were defensive. As for Khrushchev, his customary bluster vanished and he began to show unmistakable symptoms of fear.

Admiral George W. Anderson, Chief of Naval Operations, was given charge of the "quarantine" by the President; Anderson designated as the blockade line a great arc extending eight hundred miles out from Cuba, beyond the reach of MIG fighters and IL-28 Soviet bombers based there. He ordered the closing off of the five navigable channels through which vessels could approach Cuba from the mid-Atlantic. He assigned a task force of nineteen destroyers and cruisers to this duty, including the flagship of the Second Fleet of the Atlantic Command. About twenty-five Soviet vessels heading for Cuba had been spotted by Navy reconnaissance planes. The position and speed of each was plotted on a large wall chart in the Navy Command Center at the Pentagon and the White House was kept fully informed.

On the evening of October 23, President Kennedy had another meeting at the White House with British Ambassador Ormsby Gore, who expressed concern over the unfavorable reaction of the British newspapers, most of which were calling the blockade an act of war that could lead to nuclear annihilation. The Ambassador suggested that the U-2 photographs showing the Russian missile sites be published the following day, and this suggestion was followed.[1] While they were talking Robert Kennedy walked into the room and said he had just come from a meeting with Dobrynin. He reported having found the Soviet Ambassador tired and shaken and said he had told him, rather bitterly, that it had been largely on the strength of his false assurances that the President had assured the American people that there was no danger from Cuba. Dobrynin, according to Robert Kennedy, kept repeating that, so far as he knew, there were no missiles in Cuba that could reach the United States.

It was at this meeting that the British Ambassador made his recommendation for an important modification in the tactical blockade plan of the U.S. Navy: That the arc be drawn much closer to Cuba, to give Khrushchev more time to consider his plans. Kennedy agreed immediately and called McNamara, telling him to give the Navy these instructions.[2]

The President also was worried that there might be some shooting, and issued orders that vessels approaching the interception arc should not be boarded, but merely followed and kept in view. No ships were to be intercepted without specific

[1] Elie Abel, *The Missile Crisis* (New York: J. B. Lippincott Company, 1966), p. 138.
[2] Arthur M. Schlesinger, Jr., *A Thousand Days* (Boston: Houghton Mifflin Company, 1965), p. 818.

instructions in each case from the White House,[3] and this order was relayed immediately to the naval forces through regular command channels. However, to make certain that the instructions were understood, McNamara decided to call on Admiral Anderson in the Navy Command Center in the Pentagon. Accompanied by his deputy, Gilpatric, he went to the Navy Flag Plot at about ten o'clock on the night of Wednesday, October 24.[4]

Admiral Anderson was concerned over the order to draw much closer to Cuba the great arc the Navy had laid out as the line at which Soviet ships would be intercepted. McNamara explained that the concession was a political decision,[5] to give the Soviets time to determine their course of action, but Anderson said he saw no reason to risk American lives and ships by bringing them within range of the MIGs and bombers. McNamara did not apprise the Admiral that the order was British-inspired.

Those who heard the conversation between McNamara and Anderson say it is unlikely that any civilian head of the American military establishment has ever addressed the ranking officer of the U.S. Navy in a more arrogant and insulting manner. Spotting a marker on a chart, indicating an American ship at a considerable distance from the blockade arc, McNamara demanded to know what it was doing there. Anderson did not reply immediately, as there were thirty men in the room and the answer involved information of a highly classified nature. A little later he drew McNamara aside and told him that the ship was "sitting on top" of a Soviet submarine.[6] There were six Russian submarines in the Atlantic at the time, all of which had been spotted by the U.S. Navy.

[3] Abel, p. 154. Also, Roger Hilsman, *To Move a Nation* (New York: Doubleday & Company, Inc., 1967), p. 215.
[4] Abel, p. 154.
[5] *Ibid.*, p. 155.
[6] *Ibid.*, pp. 154, 155.

Although in October 1962 the American Navy did not yet have the anti-submarine rocket (ASROC), it had emphasized anti-submarine warfare and had developed and improved several detection devices and new weapons which permitted it to detect and follow enemy submarines and force them to the surface. The ASROC, which came later, is able to blast a rocket from under the water to the surface and through the sky until near the target. The rocket then releases a torpedo or nuclear depth charge by parachute. After falling into the water the depth charge explodes, or the torpedo homes-in on its victim, as would a conventional torpedo.[7]

American Naval Intelligence knew when each Soviet submarine left a Baltic or Black Sea port, when it passed into the Mediterranean and out into the Atlantic, and the Navy knew the general position of each Soviet undersea ship in the Atlantic. U.S. anti-submarine forces were able to track them and bring them to the surface if necessary, and since none of the Soviet subs had nuclear missile capability, they posed no threat to American centers of population. They were, of course, a serious threat to naval and merchant vessels in the Atlantic.

McNamara sharply asked Anderson how the Navy planned to intercept vessels in the blockade zone. The answer was that each ship had on board a carefully prepared blockade manual that had been evolved continuously from the earliest days of the U.S. Navy. But this was different, McNamara insisted; this was a political and not a military confrontation. The President did not want to push Khrushchev to extremes and therefore did not want any Russians shot; nor did he want to humiliate them. The purpose of the blockade was to persuade Khrushchev to draw back without retaliating.

The Secretary of Defense called for full details. He asked whether there was a Russian-speaking officer on each blockading vessel, and Anderson said he personally was not sure but that orders had been issued for each ship to have one. "Then

[7] Life Science Library, *Ships*, 1965. Time Inc., p. 133.

find out," McNamara snapped.[8] The fact was that the Navy had anticipated this requirement and had assigned Annapolis language instructors to blockade duty. At one point McNamara asked Anderson what he would do if a Soviet ship captain refused to answer questions about his cargo. Anderson replied that all such details were covered by the manual carried on each ship.

"I don't give a damn what John Paul Jones would have done," McNamara exploded, "I want to know what *you* are going to do now."[9] Anderson had not mentioned John Paul Jones. He tried hard to control himself and he did. The conversation came to a close when he said lightly and smilingly to McNamara, "Now, Mr. Secretary, if you and your deputy will go back to your offices, the Navy will run the blockade."[10] Without replying McNamara and Gilpatric stalked out of the room. However, that was not the end of it. Later, presumably on McNamara's demand, Admiral Anderson was not reappointed at the close of his two-year term in July 1963. And after he had testified under oath before a Senate Committee investigating the award of the TFX (F-111) contract, the Public Affairs officers of the Department of Defense told the story of the "Incident in Flag Plot." They attributed Anderson's non-reappointment to the poor performance of the Navy during the Missile Crisis. In truth, the Navy's performance had been superb.

Not only did the President order that there was to be no boarding attempt without his specific approval, he personally checked the way in which the blockade was being conducted. On Thursday, twenty-two hours after the blockade became effective, a Soviet tanker was permitted to pass through after reporting by radio that she carried only petroleum. A half-hour later an East German passenger ship was permitted to go through the blockade. Before the quarantine was terminated,

8 Abel, p. 155.
9 *Ibid.*, p. 156.
10 *Ibid.*, p. 156.

after being in force for twenty-seven days, fifty-five vessels were allowed to breach the blockade arc. Of these, nineteen were Soviet merchant ships; six were vessels of other Communist-bloc countries; twenty-three ships were registered in other countries but sailing under Soviet-bloc charters; and seven belonged to friendly countries.[11]

During the blockade, only a single ship was boarded. Kennedy had decided that, in order to give minimum offense to the Russians, the first ship to be boarded should be a dry cargo ship of neutral registry. It proved to be an American-built Liberty ship, the *Marucla,* Panamanian-owned but of Lebanese registry, and bound for Cuba under Soviet charter. The *Marucla* was sighted at about 10:30 P.M. Thursday night, October 26, by an American destroyer, the *John R. Pierce,* which was later joined by another destroyer. The two destroyers trailed her at a distance of two miles. Talking with the skipper by radio, they found he was entirely willing to cooperate.

At 7 o'clock the next morning one of the destroyers signaled, "You should have to; stop at once." A boat was lowered over the destroyer's side, and the *Marucla* dropped a ladder over her side. The destroyer was able to reassure a jittery Washington at 7:50 A.M.: "Party aboard *Marucla.* Cooperation good. No difficulties expected." After the ship's records and the contents of one hold had been examined, the *Marucla* was allowed to sail on. By pure coincidence, the destroyer that made the headlines with its action in placing a boarding party on the *Marucla* was the *Joseph P. Kennedy, Jr.,* named for the President's brother.

Meanwhile Khrushchev was showing increasing signs of fear. One of the earliest was Moscow's eager reply to a peace appeal put out by Bertrand Russell, the British peer who still performs prodigiously for peace when Communist interests are at stake. The Earl had sent his appeal to both Kennedy and Khrushchev:

[11] *Ibid.,* pp. 172, 210.

"The question of war and peace is so vital." Moscow replied on October 24, "that we consider useful a top-level meeting [in order] to do everything [possible] to remove the danger of unleashing a thermonuclear war." Kennedy's answer was more appropriate. The matter was being discussed in the United Nations, he said, and added, "I think your attention might well be directed to the burglars rather than to those who have caught the burglars."

Another indication of Soviet alarm came on the same day from London. There Dr. Stephen Thomas Ward, an osteopath who later became notorious in the Christine Keeler sex scandal, was approached by his friend the Naval attaché of the Soviet Embassy, Captain Eugene Ivanov, who suggested that the British immediately call a summit conference in London. The Russian said he could guarantee Khrushchev's acceptance of such an invitation and added that the U.S.S.R. was prepared to turn back all ships carrying arms to Cuba and to discuss the removal of missiles already installed there.

Ward had many influential friends, and he went to work. He gave the Resident Clerk at the Foreign Office an account of his conversation with Ivanov, and this was passed on to the Permanent Under Secretary at the Foreign Office. In reporting this incident to the Commons later, Prime Minister Macmillan quoted Ivanov as having told Ward "that the Soviet Government looked to the United Kingdom as their one hope of conciliation."

On the same afternoon, October 24, Khrushchev sent for an American businessman who was visiting in Moscow, William Knox, the president of Westinghouse International, who had once been a neighbor of Dean Rusk in a New York City suburb. When Knox arrived for the unsolicited appointment, he found Khrushchev in a state of exhaustion, appearing not to have slept all night. The Chairman's aim was to get a message to Kennedy through a private channel, and he regaled Knox with peasant jokes and anecdotes. The details of this conversation have never been published but the astonished Knox left Moscow the next day and delivered the message to Washington. Khrushchev at about the same time chose to pay a well-publicized call on the American singer Jerome Hines, after his Moscow concert. These various actions led Averell Harriman to conclude, according to Schlesinger, that Khrushchev's behavior was that of a man "who was begging for our help to get off the hook."

By Thursday, October 25, twelve of the twenty-five Russian vessels had turned back from Cuba, and the Soviets had taken no action in Berlin, Turkey, or elsewhere. The ships that had turned around were presumably those carrying missiles. On the same day the British Ambassador in Prague reported that the Russian leaders there were "damned scared." They needed a way out, he declared. And also on the same day the Soviet *chargé d'affaires* in London, V. A. Loginov, requested and was accorded an interview by the Foreign Secretary. He expressed the hope that Her Majesty's Government would do all in its power to avert developments in Cuba which could push the world to the brink of a military catastrophe. Meanwhile several members of the Soviet Embassy were making approaches to various diplomatic missions in London, and again Ward, the versatile osteopath, arranged for Ivanov to call on a cooperative member of Parliament. The Russian repeated his suggestion that Britain appeal for an urgent summit conference to be held in London. This conversation was reported to the Foreign Office, and later Ward himself delivered the same message there.

The previous day U Thant, Secretary General of the United Nations, had appealed to the Russians to suspend arms shipments to Cuba and to the Americans to call off the quarantine for two or three weeks to open the way for negotiations. In his reply to Thant, Kennedy gave assurances of the American desire for a peaceful solution and said Stevenson was prepared to discuss the matter with him. Khrushchev's reply the same day was even more specific and affirmative. "I welcome your initiative," he said. "I declare that I agree with your proposal, which accords with the interests of peace." And on Friday, October 26, V. A. Zorin, the Soviet Ambassador to the UN, was assuring other UN diplomats that the U.S.S.R. would not fall into the American "trap" of retaliatory action in Berlin.

In addition to these and many other probes by the Soviets, seeking a way out of their dilemma, there were ten communications that passed between Moscow and Washington, five each way.[12] Several of these have not as yet been published. One, which will be described later, was a long, rambling communication from Khrushchev. An ExCom member who saw it is reported to have said that Khrushchev must have been either "tight or scared" when he wrote it.[13]

It will be recalled that one of Adlai Stevenson's suggestions at the ExCom meeting of October 20 was that the United States should give up its Jupiter missile bases in Turkey in exchange for Khrushchev's bases in Cuba. By a strange coincidence, Walter Lippmann got the same idea and presented it in a column that appeared in the *Washington Post* and elsewhere throughout the country on October 25. Like Stevenson, he argued that the U.S. missile base in Turkey was all but obsolete, the Soviet base in Cuba was also of little military value, and "the two bases could be dismantled without altering the world balance of power." The fact was that the American missiles in Turkey, Italy and England had just become operative.

Ambassador Dobrynin evidently came to the conclusion that this was a trial balloon floated by the White House, and on October 27, two days after the Stevenson-Lippmann proposal appeared in print, Khrushchev officially and formally called for dismantling of the Turkish bases.

Although no more missiles were coming into Cuba, the Russians were losing no time in speeding to completion the installa-

[12] *Ibid.*, p. 202.
[13] *Ibid.*, p. 182.

tion of those already on the island. This was apparent from continuing photo surveillance. Realizing that time was running out, the conservatives again urged an air strike. The missiles could be ready to fire in a matter of hours, and the only safe course was to eliminate them before they could strike at the United States, or enable the Kremlin to blackmail the United States with the threat of a strike. McNamara agitatedly opposed this, and the President backed him. If further action were needed, McNamara declared, the next step should be a tightening of the blockade, perhaps by adding petroleum, oil, and lubricants to the contraband list, a step the military had urged from the outset.

Certain events of Friday, October 26, led to an extraordinary development, unprecedented in American diplomatic history. It resulted in the violation of the Kennedy pledge, announced April 20, 1961, three days after the Bay of Pigs invasion, that the United States would never abandon Cuba to Communism. It also made a mockery of the message Kennedy had addressed to the Cubans in his Missile Crisis speech only four days earlier, when he said the American people had watched with deep sorrow when their fatherland fell under foreign domination, and expressed the hope that Cubans would be "truly free."

At about 1:30 P.M. John Scali, an American Broadcasting System reporter assigned to the State Department, received an urgent telephone call from a Russian acquaintance named Alexander S. Fomin, who was one of several Soviet Embassy counselors. Fomin wanted Scali to meet him in ten minutes for lunch, saying it was of the greatest importance. When Scali arrived at the rendezvous Fomin appeared to be highly excited. Would the State Department, he asked, be willing to settle the Cuban crisis if the missile sites were dismantled under UN supervision and the United States pledged itself not to invade Cuba? Fomin explained that if Stevenson would approach Zorin at the UN, he would find the Soviet Ambassador to be interested.

Scali hurried back to the State Department office of Roger Hilsman, to report this astonishing, informal, unofficial inquiry. Hilsman contacted Rusk, who communicated with the White House. Rusk then asked that the television man be brought to his office, where he handed Scali a single sheet of paper on which he had written in his own handwriting the message Scali was to give the Russians: "I have reason to believe that the USG [United States Government] sees real possibilities in this and supposes that representatives of the two governments could work this matter out with U Thant and with each other. My impression is, however, that time is very urgent." [14]

At 7:30 P.M. Scali met with Fomin again, this time in the coffee shop of the Statler Hilton Hotel, a block away from the Soviet Embassy. "Are you absolutely certain this comes from the highest sources?" Fomin asked. Upon receiving this assurance he rushed off, saying he must communicate with the highest authorities in Moscow. In his hurry he dropped a five-dollar bill on the table for a thirty-five-cent check. The Russian Embassy had received an affirmative answer from the White House within six hours of the time it submitted the extraordinary proposal.

A day or two later Fomin met with Scali again and told him, "I have been instructed to thank you and to tell you that the information you supplied was very valuable to the Chairman [Khrushchev] in helping him to make up his mind quickly." [15]

In researching this almost incredible story I have not been able to uncover the slightest evidence that Kennedy, Rusk, or any other American official considered, discussed, or even mentioned the welfare of Cuba. At this moment in history the President and his advisers, concerned solely about the missiles, agreed to abandon more than seven million Cubans to Communism and to give the Soviet Union a sanctuary 90 miles from the shores of the United States! This marked, after 139 years,

[14] *Ibid.,* p. 177.
[15] Hilsman, p. 224.

the death knell of the Monroe Doctrine, which President Cleveland had said "cannot become obsolete while our Republic endures."

About two hours after the Scali-Fomin episode, the already mentioned long and disordered communication from Khrushchev started coming into the State Department for the President. It has never been published, but several who have seen it say it showed signs of great alarm. Elie Abel has written that even in paraphrase it read like "the nightmare outcry of a frightened man." The time had come, the Soviet boss said in the still-secret letter, to stop the drift toward war, the horrors of which he described. He appealed to Kennedy as a "military man" to understand that missiles were only a means of extermination, and that unless they were backed by troops they could not be offensive. He repeated that ships then en route to Cuba carried no weapons at all. Passions should be controlled on both sides; relations should be normalized. He was prepared to enter into the negotiations U Thant had proposed. They should each stop pulling at the ends of a rope in which a knot of war had been tied. He was ready to take measures to untie the knot.

The missiles had been sent to Cuba to defend the country against invasion, Khrushchev added. If the President would publicly give assurance that the United States would not attack Cuba *or permit others to attack,* the motive for having missiles in Cuba would be removed. And if Kennedy would then withdraw the American fleet, the entire situation would be normalized.

In the State Department there was jubilation. Secretary Rusk consulted Acheson, who was not impressed. Acheson is reported to have said later, "We were too eager to make an agreement with the Russians."

As the days had passed and the Kennedy administration showed by its actions and inactions that it was anxious not to provoke the U.S.S.R., Khrushchev's alarm apparently subsided, but on Saturday, October 27, an incident occurred that again raised the temperature in Moscow and undoubtedly induced Khrushchev to bring the crisis to an end, as some of those close to President Kennedy subsequently admitted. But this salutary experience was unintentional and, in fact, seemed to frighten the White House as much as it did the Kremlin.

An American U-2 on a routine air sampling mission from Alaska to the North Pole chose the wrong star to guide it on its return flight and strayed over the Chokut Peninsula of the Soviet Union. Soviet planes rose to meet it and American planes took off from Alaska to help escort it back. The lost plane was asking for directions—in the clear—and there was no encounter, but there is reason to believe that Khrushchev viewed the flight as possibly a final reconnaissance preparatory to a nuclear attack.

It was Hilsman, "out of breath and shaky," according to his own account, who excitedly gave the President the news of the off-course American plane. Kennedy's reaction was interesting. With an ironic laugh he said, "There is always some so-and-so who doesn't get the word," [16] and he later apologized to Khrushchev, saying that he would "see to it that every precaution is taken to prevent a reoccurrence."

An episode that may also have had an influence on Khrushchev took place when Lincoln White, the official State Department spokesman, announced that work was continuing on the missile sites in Cuba and quoted from a Presidential speech that "further action will be justified" if such work did not stop. Kennedy was furious, feeling that White had been unnecessarily provocative. He called the Secretary of State, the Assistant Secretary for Public Affairs, and finally Lincoln White himself, using the kind of language he was accustomed to use on such occasions.[17] Some of his advisers, however, felt that the incident

[16] *Ibid.*, p. 221.
[17] *Ibid.*, pp. 213, 214.

had been beneficial, that it led the Soviets to believe the President should be taken seriously.

It was also on October 27 that Radio Moscow began broadcasting another Khrushchev letter addressed to Kennedy. It suggested that the American bases in Turkey be evacuated in exchange for the withdrawal of Russian missiles from Cuba. (This proposal, it will be recalled, originated in the United States with Adlai Stevenson and Walter Lippmann.)

Schlesinger had first heard of the Missile Crisis late on Friday, October 19, from Stevenson, who had always admired Schlesinger's facility of expression and now asked him to help prepare the speech he would have to make early in the week at the Security Council of the United Nations. The following day, Schlesinger met with the President, Rusk, Robert Kennedy, and others, to go over the draft. The President struck out a passage that threatened an American air strike if the missile buildup in Cuba continued. Schlesinger reports a remark by Robert Kennedy, who drew him aside and said, "We're counting on you to watch things in New York. . . . We will have to make a deal at the end, but we must stand absolutely firm now. Concessions must come at the end of the negotiations, not at the beginning." [18]

When the second Khrushchev communication was announced over Radio Moscow on Saturday, October 27, the liberal members of ExCom began discussing ingenious ways to remove the Turkish missiles without seeming to accept Khrushchev's terms.[19] They felt that a grateful United States could afford to pay a considerable price if the Russians would stop their Cuban buildup at once; this new concession could be masked as part of an offer to relax tensions between NATO and the Warsaw Pact.[20]

[18] Schlesinger, p. 811.
[19] Abel, p. 194.
[20] *Ibid.*, p. 194.

After the ExCom meeting there was a private conversation between the President, Rusk, and McNamara, and the President then assigned Gilpatric to spend the afternoon in Bundy's office at the White House with State Department and military assistants, writing a "scenario" for the early removal of all Jupiter missiles from Turkey and, presumably, from Italy and England as well. Judging from the partial disclosure of the messages which passed between Washington and Moscow, Khrushchev had not even mentioned the American bases in Italy and England. Evidently they were thrown in as a bonus. Gilpatric's scenario was to be ready for an ExCom session at nine o'clock the same evening, and the White House that afternoon issued a statement that read in part, "As to proposals concerning the security of nations outside this hemisphere, the United States and its allies have long taken the initiative in seeking properly inspected arms limitations, on both sides. These efforts can continue as soon as the present Soviet-created threat is ended."

In his excellent book *America Is in Danger* [21] General Curtis E. LeMay, former member of the Joint Chiefs and first commander of the Strategic Air Command, says that the United States had provided IRBMs to Europe because the Soviets have at least 750 intermediate and medium range nuclear ballistic missiles in place, with a range of up to 2,500 miles. Thors and Jupiters were mounted at great cost: sixty in England, thirty in Italy, and fifteen in Turkey. "These IRBMs," writes General LeMay, "became operational just before the Cuban Missile Crisis in 1962, but after the crisis was resolved, the United States dismantled its entire IRBM operation in Europe. . . . Nothing is left of the extremely expensive complex of Thors and Jupiters." The reason given at the time was that the American IRBMs were obsolete. "I did not accept the explanation that the missiles had become obsolete so quickly," says General LeMay, "nor did any other military man I know." An-

---

[21] Curtis E. LeMay, *America Is in Danger* (New York: Funk & Wagnalls, 1968).

other military expert remarked acidly that the cement in the American missile bases in Europe was hardly dry when the politicians ordered them dismantled.[22] "The precipitous action smacked of a deal," says LeMay, and if it was a deal "we definitely came out on the short end of the bargain in a confrontation which has been hailed as a great American diplomatic victory." [23]

In the first three editions of this book I wrote that the question as to whether the decision reached at the White House on Saturday, October 27, 1962 (to remove the newly mounted American missiles from Europe) had been "passed along" to the Kremlin would have to remain a secret that only future revelations could clear. Since then Robert Kennedy's posthumous book, *Thirteen Days,* has been published. In it he confirms that he communicated the decision to the Soviet Ambassador in Washington (pp. 108-109).

The removal of the American Jupiters from Turkey and Italy must be viewed in the larger context of Mediterranean power balance. Since the eighteenth century Russia had been trying to extend its influence into the Western *mare nostrum.* After World War II, Stalin vainly sought naval bases in the colonies of defeated Italy. But by 1968 the power equation in that sea was changing. The U.S.S.R. at this writing maintains a regular Mediterranean fleet of forty to forty-five ships, which use Syrian and Egyptian bases and may soon be using facilities in South Arabia and Algeria as well. According to a statement made by Hanson W. Baldwin, the renowned naval authority, to the author on October 8, 1969, the U.S. Sixth Fleet in the Mediterranean then varied between fifteen and more than sixty ships. It was still stronger than the Soviet fleet because of its aircraft carriers and Polaris submarines; yet the Russians were moving up. Their intrusion was not due only, or even mainly, to the closing down

[22] *Ibid.*
[23] *Ibid.,* p. 200.

by the United States of its Turkish and Italian missile bases. The biggest Soviet step forward came as a result of the six-day Arab-Israeli war in 1967, which made the Arab belligerents wholly dependent on Soviet Russia militarily, politically and economically. The new threat to the Sixth Fleet comes from the Soviet thrust toward the airfields and air facilities on the north coast of Africa. Using Egyptian facilities, their bombers already cover the eastern Mediterranean and the loss to the United States of air facilities in Libya, coupled with the use by the Soviets of Algerian facilities, would be a tremendous factor in swinging the balance of power against the West, with strategic consequences of enormous importance. Now the Soviets are calling for the *extrusion* of the American Sixth Fleet from the Mediterranean! At the same time, Turkey is quietly asking for a reduction in the American garrison.

Who will say that the removal of the U.S. missile bases from Italy and Turkey seven years earlier—without revealing to the American people that it was part of the Missile Crisis settlement —did not signal the turning point against the West in this crucial area?

The acceptance of the Russian proposal that the United States pledge itself not to invade Cuba was drafted by Robert Kennedy with the assistance of Sorensen and dispatched to Khrushchev at 8:05 P.M. Saturday, October 27.[24] It said that if work ceased on the offensive missile bases in Cuba and the weapons system were rendered inoperable "under effective UN arrangements," American representatives in New York could work out with U Thant and the Soviet representative "an arrangement for a *permanent* solution to the Cuban problem along the lines suggested in your letter of October 26" [Emphasis added]. The United States would "remove promptly the quarantine measures now in effect and . . . give assurances against an invasion of

[24] Abel, p. 197.

Cuba." The President added, "I am confident that other nations of the Western Hemisphere would be prepared to do likewise." The United States would also "work toward a more general arrangement regarding 'other armaments' as proposed in your second letter, which you made public."

Those on the inside were aware that the "other armaments" included the missile bases in Turkey, and probably in Italy and in England, but this was not made clear to the public. On the previous day the White House had eagerly agreed to the "no invasion" formula, even before the Russians had formally proposed it, and now came the formal acceptance—including a confident prediction that "other nations of the Western Hemisphere" would give a similar "no invasion" pledge.[25] *President Kennedy was not authorized to commit other nations and, in fact, none of them ever gave the U.S.S.R. such a pledge.*

On Sunday morning, October 28, at approximately nine o'clock Washington time, Radio Moscow broadcast the answer. It announced that orders had been given to dismantle the missile bases. Khrushchev added, "I regard with respect and trust the statement you made in your message of 27 October, 1962, that there would be no attack, no invasion of Cuba, and not only on the part of the United States, but also of other nations of the Western Hemisphere, as you said in your message."

Did the United States give the Soviets a secret commitment that it would *prevent* an invasion of Cuba if other nations attempted one? This question has been raised through the years and seems justified by the wording of Khrushchev's reply. But no clearcut answer has been provided by Washington.

There remained, of course, the vital problem of arranging for on-site inspection in Cuba. The CIA and the military took the position that only physical on-site inspection would provide complete confirmation that the Soviet missile threat had ended,

[25] *Ibid.,* p. 194-198.

ANTICLIMAX

and President Kennedy agreed. The first step in conducting a preliminary inspection was taken immediately. C-130 transport planes were ordered to be painted white with UN markings, and Canada agreed to supply the pilots. Four administration officials, including White House, State Department, and Air Force representatives, proceeded to New York to talk to Stevenson. The UN Ambassador took a negative attitude; he did not think Thant could be persuaded to act so quickly. He said he would not talk tough to Thant and, in fact, Thant refused to move until he had what he regarded as proper authority.[26] He met with Castro and the Cuban President on October 30 and 31 in Havana.

Castro, who had been almost completely ignored throughout the crisis, had just broadcast an arrogant demand that the blockade and all economic pressures be suspended, as well as harassments and raids by exile commando groups. He also demanded American withdrawal from Guantanamo Bay. When Thant arrived in Havana he did far more to save Castro's face and restore his prestige than Khrushchev had done. My stenographic transcript of the conversation shows that Thant started off by criticizing the United States for having established the blockade: "an extremely unusual thing, a very unusual act, except in times of war," he said. This, Thant went on, is what he had told the Security Council, and his view had been shared by the forty-five countries that had met with him. On at least ten occasions he told Castro that in his view a UN inspection team would violate the sovereignty of Cuba.

When Castro asserted that the United States was trying to humiliate Cuba, Thant replied that he was "completely in agreement . . . that the proposed action of the UN involved the invasion of the rights of a member state." Throughout the interview Thant's attitude was abjectly apologetic. He gave the impression that he was performing a distasteful duty for the

[26] *Ibid.*, p. 206.

United States instead of trying to implement an agreement reached by both the U.S. and the U.S.S.R. He never once mentioned the U.S.S.R.

Then, amazingly, the United States accepted as its next emissary the wily Anastas Mikoyan, the Soviet official who had been largely responsible for providing arms to Castro! The mission was, of course, doomed to failure. As though this were not enough, the administration made still another concession obviously dangerous to the security of the United States. Disregarding the warnings of military and intelligence experts, *it settled for high-altitude flight inspection* instead of the on-site plan. U.S. Intelligence chiefs now concede that surface-to-surface missiles could be secreted in Cuban caves and in highly sophisticated underground installations.

Thus ended the 1962 Missile Crisis. The American people had been led to believe that they had faced a danger of awesome proportions. Secretary Rusk said a misstep could have meant the "incineration of the North American continent." Schlesinger described Kennedy's performance as "a combination of toughness and restraint, of will, nerve and wisdom, so brilliantly controlled, so matchlessly calibrated, that [it] dazzled the world." Small wonder that the outcome was regarded by a misinformed public as an American victory.

But was it?

The accounts of the crisis did not make clear that it was a *power* confrontation, that the power of the U.S.A. was *incomparably superior* to that of the U.S.S.R., and that *the leaders of both nations knew this to be a fact.* The United States, it is worth repeating, could have erased every important Soviet military installation and population center in two or three hours, while the strike capability of the U.S.S.R. was negligible. Although Kennedy held the trump cards, he granted the Communist Empire a privileged sanctuary in the Caribbean by means of the "no invasion" pledge. Apologists for the White

House deal argue that the pledge was conditional and that the conditions have not been fulfilled, but it has remained intact now for eight years—the "permanent solution" guaranteed by the White House.

The Soviets regard the pledge as binding, and the United States acts as if it were binding. On January 16, 1964, in Red Square and with Castro standing behind him, Khrushchev said, "The understanding with the United States administration is still valid and we honor our pledge [not to mount rockets] as long as [it] is observed." As late as July 11, 1967, in a broadcast nationally televised in the United States, Khrushchev said, "We took our bombers and rockets away in exchange for President Kennedy's promise not to invade Cuba." He added, "After President Kennedy's death, President Johnson, who took over, assured us that he would stick to the promises made by President Kennedy."

What about additional secret American commitments?

In an interview published in December 1966 Castro said that the United States made concessions "about which not a word has been said. . . . One day perhaps it will be known that the United States made some other concessions in relation to the October crisis besides those that were made public. It was not an agreement in accordance with protocol. It was an agreement that took place by letter and through diplomatic contacts."

Following the crisis, orders went out from the White House to arrest anti-Castro activists in the United States and confiscate their weapons and vessels, and this has been the fate of the Cuban Freedom Fighters ever since. Sorensen put it this way: "He [the President] asked that precautions be taken to prevent Cuban exiles from upsetting the agreement. . . ."

Why has Congressional leadership not forced the disclosure of all communications that passed between Washington and Moscow at the time of the Crisis, as well as any pledges given by Robert Kennedy to Ambassador Dobrynin in Washington or by Adlai Stevenson to Ambassador Zorin at the United Nations?

According to the columnists Robert S. Allen and Paul Scott, aides of Secretary Rusk have said that he opposes release of the Kennedy-Khrushchev exchange because the contents "would anger and excite anti-Castro groups in this country" and "cause embarrassment to officials who participated in the correspondence." But surely the American people deserve to know to what extent the security of their country has been impaired, and the Cuban people want to know what kind of a deed to their country Washington has given to Communist Russia.

Is the security of the United States and the hemisphere threatened?

It is not difficult to imagine the fascination with which the Kremlin has studied the map of the Caribbean—America's Mediterranean. Because of the narrow straits that separate Cuba from its neighbors, the nation that dominates it commands the sea approaches to the Mississippi Valley, the Panama Canal, Mexico, Central America, and the north coast of South America. Giving the Soviets a privileged sanctuary in Cuba is equivalent to converting a strategic island inside the final defense perimeter of the United States into a Trojan Horse. Cuba has already become a fortress of unknown power, and it is an incalculably valuable asset to the Soviet Union as that country thrusts toward world maritime dominance.

The maritime program of the U.S.S.R. has expanded amazingly. Moscow plans to have acquired the largest merchant fleet in the world in the next decade. While the United States has been losing merchant fleet tonnage, Russia has been adding about 500,000 tons yearly. It has the world's second largest navy and the world's largest submarine fleet. It is laying down aircraft carriers and developing marine commandos, essential to conventional warfare along maritime peripheries. It already operates the world's largest and most modern fishing fleet, keyed, as are all Communist projects, to political-economic purposes, and equipped with radar, electronic, sonar, and sound-ranging equipment. Soviet fishing trawlers show up wherever the U.S. Navy goes. As of this writing the U.S.S.R. has more naval vessels in the Mediterranean than the United States.

With a Caribbean outpost Russian vessels can avoid the long trip home for repairing and refueling. Scores of excellent Cuban harbors provide the needed havens. Nipe Bay alone is large enough to serve as an anchorage for the combined navies of every nation in the world. Located on the north coast of the eastern province, it is superior to the U.S. Guantanamo Naval Base. About eleven miles from east to west and seven miles long, its entrance is only half a mile wide and has a depth of twenty-eight fathoms. In outline it resembles the famous harbor of Sydney in New South Wales. Within sight, on a nearby peninsula, stands the great Nicaro Nickel plant, built by the American taxpayer at a cost of over $100 million and now operated for the benefit of the Soviets.

So Khrushchev knew where he was going when he probed for a "no invasion" pledge in October 1962, and President Kennedy knew, to some extent at least, what he was doing when he handed Cuba over. Schlesinger quotes him as saying, "They will attack us on the ground that we had a chance to get rid of Castro and, instead of doing so, ended up by guaranteeing him against invasion. . . . But the military are mad . . . it's lucky for us we have McNamara over there."

In 1968 McNamara, after resigning his Defense post, publicly and extravagantly praised Robert Kennedy—who was by then a Senator and seeking his party's nomination for the Presidency —for his role in the Missile Crisis. As the realities of the 1962 settlement become more widely understood, this friendly praise may well appear unintentionally ironic.

The performance of Dean Acheson and his subsequent equivocal views offer an interesting study. A statement he had made three years before he became Secretary of State for President Truman marked him as being soft on Communism. He was a liberal. Here is what he said:

> "Never in the past has there been any place on the globe where the vital interests of the American and the Russian people have clashed or even been antagonistic. And there is no objective reason to suppose that there should now, or in the future, ever be such a place. We understand and agree with them that to have friendly governments along her borders is essential . . . for the peace of the world."

A month later President Truman called on Chiang Kai-shek, who throughout his life had opposed Communism, to accept Communists into his government. It became the policy of the United States to withhold aid from Chiang unless he formed a coalition with Chinese Communists. In January 1949, the month that Acheson became Secretary of State, Tientsin and Peipin fell to the Reds, who had already occupied Mukden and captured Manchuria. That same month Congressman John F. Kennedy, in an address at Salem, Mass., sharply criticized America's policy in Asia. "It has reaped the whirlwind," he said. A month later Acheson suggested to Truman that supplies which were being loaded in ships in Hawaii and San Francisco for the Chiang Kai-shek government "be dramatically stopped, as a move toward peace." But six months after Acheson became Secretary of State the State Department issued a White Paper disclaiming responsibility for the debacle in China!

Five months later, on January 12, 1950, Acheson announced publicly that Korea was outside the American defense perimeter, and that the United States would not give aid to Formosa. And five months after that, on June 25, 1950, as if in response to this announcement, the North Koreans invaded South Korea spearheaded by 100 Russian tanks and with Russian arms, opening a war that many believe never should have been fought and in which 157,530 Americans were killed or wounded.

More than twenty years have passed since Acheson became Secretary of State and his views have changed. He knows now that the United States is confronted throughout the world by a ruthless, incompatible ideological power, the basic principles of which have not changed in half a century. *In the interim China, with one-fourth the population of the world, has been lost.*

But let us return to the 1962 Missile Crisis. Acheson had strongly urged President Kennedy to liquidate the Communist outpost in Cuba and, although this advice was rejected, he is nevertheless entitled to the highest marks for advocating it. One wonders, however, where the explanation lies for his extraordinarily equivocal position in the aftermath of the settlement.

On the very day, a Sunday, that Radio Moscow announced acceptance of the Kennedy "no invasion" pledge, Acheson wrote President Kennedy what Sorensen has described as a letter "which praised in superlative terms his handling of the crisis," a letter in which Acheson himself says he praised Kennedy for his "leadership, firmness and judgment." And in a letter to me dated February 1, 1968, he expressed "great respect" for the performance of the President during the crisis.

But in the February 1969 issue of *Esquire* magazine Acheson published an article revealing radically different views. In it he writes critically of Robert Kennedy's posthumous book, *Thirteen Days*. Its title: "Dean Acheson's Version of Robert Kennedy's Version of the Cuban Missile Affair"—with the sub-title: "Homage to Plain Dumb Luck."

Acheson challenges Robert Kennedy's contention that to take military action would have been "a Pearl Harbor in reverse." He says this is to "obfuscate rather than clarify" the issue "by a thoroughly false . . . analogy." As between the choice of destroying the missiles or pressuring for their removal by a naval blockade, he describes the former as "the necessary and only effective method . . ." In his mind the blockade created greater dangers. He agreed with de Gaulle and Adenauer that a "blockade was a method of keeping things out, not getting things out."

When McNamara receded from his "do nothing" stance to the next softest position, the blockade, arguing that "it would leave us in control of events," Acheson felt otherwise. He believed "the blockade left our opponents in control of events" and that the Secretary's argument was "unworthy" of his "analytical mind." The decision to resort to a blockade "was a decision to postpone the issue" while the nuclear weapons were being made operable. He calls the ExCom meetings "repetitive, leaderless, and a waste of time" and says that on October 19 "I asked to be excused from further attendance."

In referring to Robert Kennedy's statement that on one occasion, when there was almost unanimous agreement that the U.S. had to attack the next morning and that the President had said, "We won't attack tomorrow. We shall try again," Acheson writes that what Kennedy tried again was another postponement of action while the Soviet work on the missiles drove on. "It was a gamble to the point of recklessness," he says, a "hundred-to-one shot." Hence the subtitle: "Homage to plain dumb luck."

Robert Kennedy's remark that Dean Rusk "had other duties and responsibilities during this period and frequently could not attend our meetings" provokes sharp comment. What other duties and responsibilities could have been "half so important as those they displaced"? The ExCom "should have been under the direction of the head of Government or his chief Secretary of State and his military advisers," according to Acheson. But the main advice reached the President through his brother "out of a leaderless uninhibited group, many of whom had little knowledge in either the military or diplomatic field." And finally: "This is not the way the National Security Council operated at any time during which I was officially connected with it; nor, I submit, the way it should operate."

Thus we have Acheson's final appraisal of the Missile Crisis! How account for his adulatory letter to the President six years earlier? Can it be, as some have suggested, that the installation of a Republican administration in Washington in January 1969 was the catalyst that induced the change?

The law firm which Dean Acheson heads, Covington & Burling, is one of Washington's oldest, largest and most prestigious firms. I have handled some of its Cuban work and know it well. It occupies the top four floors of a building across Lafayette Park from the White House. It represents corporations, trade associations and individuals before Federal administrative agencies such as the Internal Revenue Service and the regulatory commissions. Typical of its clients are the tobacco manufacturers who are fighting Federal regulation of cigarette advertising and the manufacturer of a pharmaceutical preparation, Geritol, which has been struggling for ten years with the Federal Trade Commission over allegedly deceptive advertising. But it is no reflection on the Acheson firm that it should seek to establish a cordial relationship with the new Republican bureaucracy. My firm occupied a relatively similar position in Havana and we always strove to maintain a good relationship with every Cuban government, whether we liked it or not. Nor can I subscribe to the suggestion that this was the principal consideration that led Dean Acheson eventually to speak candidly about the Missile Crisis. But whatever his reasons for so doing, I welcome his contribution to the historical record.

Was honor forsaken?

On April 20, 1961, three days after the Bay of Pigs invasion, President Kennedy addressed a group of newspaper editors at the White House. In referring to the invaders who had determined that Cuba must not be abandoned to the Communists, he said, "And we do not intend to abandon it either." But eighteen months later he *did* abandon Cuba to Communism.

In the same address Kennedy said, "If the nations of this hemisphere should fail to meet their commitments against outside Communist penetration—then I want it clearly understood that this government will not hesitate in meeting its primary obligations, which are to the security of our nation." Eighteen months later Kennedy told Khrushchev that he was confident that those hemisphere nations would join the United States in giving assurances that "outside Communist penetration" would not be disturbed!

In the same address Kennedy spoke of the reign of terror in Cuba, of the police state and its use of mass terror to prevent free dissent. "We must build a hemisphere," he said, "where freedom can flourish; and where any free nation under outside attack of any kind can be assured that all our resources stand ready to respond to any request for assistance." But eighteen months later he regarded his more than seven million Cuban neighbors as expendable and delivered them into Communist enslavement.

No, the solution of the Missile Crisis was far from the grandiose achievement it has been acclaimed as being. There is no foundation for the belief, hardened into legend, that it was "Kennedy's Finest Hour." On the contrary, it may well prove to have been a defeat and a calamity for the United States and Latin America, and therefore for the Free World.

One who never equivocated was Richard Nixon. He correctly said that the same group of advisers who stayed the President's hand at the Bay of Pigs persuaded him to back away from a strong course of action in the Missile Crisis. He wrote, "They enabled the United States to pull defeat out of the jaws of victory." [27]

For the Cuban people, who have always been staunch allies and genuine friends of the United States, the settlement was a soul-shattering blow.

[27] Richard M. Nixon, "Cuba, Castro and John F. Kennedy," *Reader's Digest*, November 1964.

CHAPTER TWENTY-TWO

The Cost

Under the banners of a self-righteous "liberalism," the American Government made a series of policy choices with respect to Cuba that can be fairly called "decisions for disaster." They began with the deliberate raising of Fidel Castro to supreme power. There followed the sabotage of an invasion by Cuban Freedom Fighters that had been approved, prepared, and mounted by Washington itself. The climax was a settlement of the Missile Crisis that guaranteed a protected sanctuary for Communism, without time limit and without consent by other nations directly concerned.

These unhappy decisions have imposed costs too staggering to be treated adequately in a limited space. I can only suggest their magnitude. Because today's world is shrunken and intermeshed, misfortunes in one segment are reflected everywhere else. The exacerbated troubles and perils on the American continents affect the destinies of all mankind.

A large part of the price of the American errors is being paid by the nations of Latin America, especially those in the Caribbean area. They must live with the fact that the "no invasion" guarantee has enabled Soviet Russia and its associates to convert Cuba into a powerful base, sophisticated and effective, for subverting the hemisphere, not excepting the United States. The annulment of the Monroe Doctrine is breeding fear and doubt where there had been a large measure of confidence. In

March 1968, for instance, the President of Argentina told several hundred of the highest officials of that country that Latin America could no longer rely on the United States for protection against Communist aggression. The United States, he pointed out, had failed to come to grips with the Red penetration of Cuba and had narrowly averted a similar defeat in the Dominican Republic; Latin America would have to follow a go-it-alone policy for its own defense and security.

Cuba has become a multi-sided center for preparing Communist leaders and activists: experts in sabotage, terrorism and espionage; orators and agitators; specialists in handling unconventional arms and electronic equipment. Thousands of young men are brought from Latin American countries for training as guerrillas. Already imbued with the Communist mystique, they are professionally indoctrinated and assigned targets for sabotage (principally United States installations); given the names of known or suspected homosexuals among members of home-town police and army units who might be vulnerable to blackmail for subversive purposes; informed of possible tax irregularities among business and industrial leaders with the presumed connivance of bureaucrats. Then they are infiltrated back into their homelands by Red Cuba's fishing fleet.

Their purpose—working with the local Communist Party, backed by agents from Cuba and other countries—is to exploit student and labor conflicts and social problems, and to create disorder by provoking violence. They apply tested techniques for driving the authorities to rigorous law enforcement and the use of police measures, in order that they may label their government as "dictatorial" and impute to the authorities sole blame for the weakening of the democratic structure.

Cuba, in short, has become the protected staging area for Communist propaganda directed against the entire hemisphere. Printed matter on a vast scale—magazines, books, pamphlets of every variety, presenting the Communist ideology and assailing established institutions—is produced in Cuba; motion pictures are made and exported; international festivals and congresses are staged. The volume of propaganda, radiated to the entire hemisphere by radio and news media in several languages and dialects, is constantly enlarged, aggravating existing racial problems and fomenting new tensions. It even plays a calculated role in the incitement of riots in U.S. cities. Everywhere the objective is to undermine democratic systems and destroy elements of stability.

When Khrushchev exacted the sweeping "no invasion" pledge from President Kennedy in October 1962, he struck a mighty blow at the foundations of society in the Americas. But, for the present at least, the main costs of the decisions for disaster are being paid by the almost eight million Cubans subjected to Communism; paid in servitude, suffering, and death. *Their martyrdom should weigh as a burden on the conscience of America.*

Cuba today is a totalitarian state, in many respects as repressive as Soviet Russia was under Stalin. Castro has made his country as shabby, unproductive, police- and censor-ridden as any nation behind the Iron Curtain—all in less than a decade.

Havana, formerly one of the most beautiful cities of the Western Hemisphere, is now drab and sleazy. The *supermercados,* drug stores, and cafes still function there and elsewhere on the island, but they are tarnished and dirty, and half empty of merchandise. Streets and roads are littered with automobiles and buses in various stages of disrepair, and gasoline is strictly rationed. Machines in factories break down chronically, absenteeism runs as high as 30 percent, and the regime has to resort to various species of forced labor to keep the economy limping along.

The conversion of a free enterprise system into a monolithic noncompetitive "socialist" economy by an arrogant and inexperienced lawyer has produced chaos. With each passing month the flow of foodstuffs to the cities and towns slows down, while weary housewives stretch in queues from shop doors, awaiting rationed goods. Even Castro's Soviet allies, who have to subsidize his incompetence and bungling, grumble at the way their bearded puppet has mismanaged what was once a flourishing and expanding economy.

The only commodities plentiful in Cuba today are "Hate America" propaganda and promises of a better future. Brought to power by propaganda, Castro continues to use it without let-up. Cubans are incessantly exhorted and harangued to work harder, to love Fidel and the new Cuba he has fashioned, and to hate the "imperialist Yankees." But the people have become disillusioned with the slogans and the failures of the regime. Despite the risks, more and more of them are no longer remaining silent over the shortages and the endless calls for ever greater sacrifice.

Castro is no longer getting the kind of favorable reportage that Herbert Matthews used to provide in *The New York Times*. Too many of the crimes of the dictatorship have become known; too many personal experiences under the terror have been recounted by fugitives. But the regime still obtains considerable "objective reporting"—a euphemism for reports slanted in Castro's favor—in the outside press and on the air. The dictatorship sees to it that only liberal journalists and commentators visit Cuba. In issuing visas, it favors newsmen and writers with little knowledge of what the country was like before it became a Communist outpost.

Most of the dispatches and books read by Americans concede "difficulties," even discontents, but proclaim that the people are better off than in the past. They seem determined to find historical alibis for obvious political oppressions and economic evils of the present. The motivation for this brand of apologetics under the guise of reporting is often ideological, but in the main it stems from simple ignorance; sometimes it is a combination of both.

The lamentable practice of comparing present-day Cuba with the Cuba that supposedly was, has been followed even by James Reston of *The New York Times*. An article he wrote about an automobile trip he took from Havana to Santiago along the

Central Highway on July 23, 1967, provides an example. He took note of the miserably poor houses and other squalors but affirmed that life was much better than it had been a decade ago. "Then there was no continuous paved road from Havana to Santiago, or so it is said. . . ." But every Cuban and hundreds of thousands of Americans know that the Central Highway was constructed between 1927 and 1931 and served as the back-bone of the Cuban highway system for more than a third of a century before Reston's journey. He recently discussed Cuban women in a manner that was, if possible, even more distant from the realities. Castro had "liberated" the women, he told his readers, adding the gratuitous insult that prior to Castro the women of Cuba were "ninnies."

The truth is that Castro has degraded and humiliated the Cuban woman. As in Soviet Russia, women in Cuba now do arduous manual labor. By December 1967, Castro had 196,000 women doing servile agricultural work in the fields. This was a "gain" of almost 100,000 over his female work force in 1965, and he has plans for further "liberation." The government has announced that by 1970 it expects to have 500,000 women employed in field work, and to help meet this goal it is constructing additional camps to accommodate between 300,000 and 500,000 of both sexes. Selection will be made by its G-2—the Cuban Gestapo—on the basis of political unreliability. Cuban women have never before swung the machete in the blistering sun and the sudden torrential showers that convert the cane fields into seas of mud.

This kind of liberation is more than matched by the way in which Castro has "liberated" Cuban women from morality. The regime itself admits that illegitimacy, abortion, and divorce rates have risen dramtically.

A revealing reference to moral debasement under the Castro regime appears, curiously enough, in *Castro's Cuba, Cuba's Fidel,* an adulatory book written by Lee Lockwood, an admirer of the dictator. The author carried a tape recorder and camera to Cuba and spent seven days and nights taking pictures of

Castro and recording his words. Subsequently, since he judged Lockwood's heart to be in the right place, Castro enabled him to visit some of his prison camps. In the course of the marathon interview Lockwood raised the subject of prostitution. Castro explained that changes were being made in sexual relations but these presented problems, in view "of certain traditions derived from Spanish customs, which are stricter in this aspect than, for example, Anglo-Saxon traditions."

Castro, however, was tackling the problem boldly and obviously breaking down some of those religious and moral traditions. One shocking device is a government-run chain of *posadas,* "where couples go to make love, no questions asked," as Lockwood put it. This enterprise is flourishing; Lockwood could report that there are at least two or three dozen in Havana alone. Because of economies possible under "socialism," the Revolutionary Government rents rooms for only 2.65 pesos (about 66 cents in U.S. values) for the first three hours and 50 centavos (about 12 cents) an hour thereafter. So popular in this nationalized recreation that some nights, according to Lockwood, "there is often a long line waiting for rooms in front of some *posadas,* at times extending a block or two down the street." This is the kind of scene never witnessed in the "dark" pre-Castro era. Posadas existed, but such activities were clandestine and discreet.

In the nation's economy the picture is gloomy and growing gloomier. Time after time Castro has proclaimed grandiose economic plans, always with tremendous fanfare, and invariably his big ideas have flopped. Cubans cannot openly ridicule his performnce, but the vast majority now regard the man as a charlatan. Only the most gullible continue to take his plans and promises seriously.

The most conspicuous failure was probably his blueprint for industrializing Cuba. He started on this tack in mid-1961, when he openly proclaimed that he was a Marxist-Leninist and that Cuba was to be a socialist state. Declaring the United States to be Cuba's enemy, he said it was necessary to liberate Cuba from the capitalist yoke so that native industry and agriculture would be free to seek their own high levels of development. In this program he had the help of the late Ernesto "Che" Guevara, unquestionably Castro's superior in the field of economics. The pair had the enthusiastic cooperation of various Communist nations.

The Soviets promised one hundred million dollars for a steel industry, electric plants, and an oil refinery. Czechoslovakia promised an automobile factory, and China said it would provide sixty million dollars for twenty-four different factories. From Romania, Bulgaria, Poland, and East Germany came offers of forty-two more factories. With all these production facilities in the offing, a campaign was launched to prepare the public for breaking off Cuba's traditional trade ties with the United States.[1]

The industrialization plan proved infantile. Wildly unrealistic goals were set and announced with sloganized ballyhoo. Boasts were made that by 1965 Cuba would be the most highly industrialized country in Latin America, leading all others in the production of electric energy, steel, cement, tractors, and refined oil. Guevara declared that within nine or ten years Cuba would have the highest living standard in Latin America, and Castro joined in with the prediction that Cuba's economy would grow at a rate of 10 to 14 percent from 1962 to 1965.

Instead, the economy declined at the rate of 15 to 20 percent annually. Productivity per industrial worker dropped 23 percent in a single year (1962–1963), and by mid-1963 the Cuban economy was a shambles. There were plenty of reasons for this. Stolen machines always run less well than they did for the owners who worked to acquire them. Much of the new Communist machinery could not function because of a lack of buildings to house it, a lack of technicians to operate it, and a lack of spare

[1] Ernesto "Che" Guevara, *Cuba Socialista,* March 1962, p. 30. Also Theodore Draper, *Castroism: Theory and Practice* (New York: Frederick A. Praeger, 1965), p. 143.

parts. In the humid climate, the equipment deteriorated on the piers. In addition, Castro and Guevara had overlooked the simple fact that to make a finished product one must have raw materials. And when they started shopping for raw materials they were amazed to find that in many cases these cost almost as much as the finished products previously imported from the United States.

A balance-of-payments crisis developed when the Soviet bloc demanded an accounting. Moscow complained about Cuban waste, disorganization, and unwillingness to work. Guevara finally acknowledged "two fundamental errors," namely "the declaration of war on sugar" and the push for factories "without thinking of the raw materials for them." [2] Castro began to criticize his own people, calling them "bums" and "parasites." By the end of 1964 he publicly conceded that the machinery he had received was functioning at only 50 percent of capacity.

In the meantime, since the Cuban economy had formerly been geared to the American economy, and American replacement parts no longer were available, much of Cuba's own machinery was stalled. A black market developed in which a few illicit speculators, thriving on shortages and chaos, made fortunes by importing American spare parts and tools from middlemen in Europe. These were brought to Cuba by way of Casablanca, Rostock, or Singapore—a slow and expensive process. A set of used piston rings cost 90 pesos (about $22) on the black market.

And what happened to the agricultural sector of the economy?

For 150 years sugar cane had spread throughout Cuba because nature had endowed the island with exactly the right conditions of rainfall, sunshine, and soil to make it the lowest-cost sugar producing area in the world. But contrary to the propaganda legend, pre-Castro Cuba was by no means a one-crop

[2] Guevara, *Revolución,* August 21, 1963.

country. There had been a strong trend toward diversification; less land was being used for sugar and more for other crops. As far back as 1953, according to a publication of the U.S. Department of Commerce, Cuba had developed an export surplus in such commodities as corn, winter vegetables, citrus fruits, and coffee, and was self-sufficient in beef, fresh pork, poultry, fresh milk, condensed and powdered milk, cheese, and butter. Rice and beans had registered substantial gains. In May 1962 another U.S. Government publication, *Agricultural and Food Situation in Cuba,* stated: "When the present government [Castro's] assumed power, the Cubans were among the better-fed peoples of the world."

Castro chose to make the sugar industry his main target, "declaring war against it," as Guevara put it. In lengthy harangues he depicted it as the embodiment of all the horrors of capitalism, and a means through which the United States exploited Cuban workers in mammoth American-owned mills and on farms. As a weapon against "exploitation," he called for diversification of crops and less emphasis on sugar.

I have pointed out that in the sugar industry the trend prior to the advent of Castro had been strongly away from American-owned mills. During the 19 years preceding 1958, the sugar processed by Cuban-owned mills had increased almost 300 percent and constituted by far the larger part of the crop. Furthermore, in 1958 Cuba had the smallest average farm size of any country in the Americas—140 acres.

Castro confiscated the larger farms first, but when the small farmers attempted to sell their products at market prices rather than hand them over to the government at the much lower official prices, he seized their lands too. Following the precedent of Soviet agriculture in Stalin's time, the farmers retaliated with their best weapon—they produced only enough for their own needs. In 1962 the newly formed "cooperatives," in which the farmers had been promised a share of the profits, were swallowed up by the *granjas del pueblo* (state farms), where the farmers received only a low fixed wage.

Production plummeted. The last sugar crop which the government had not restricted in the pre-Castro era had been that of 1952, when Cuba produced within 36,000 of 8 million short tons. Under Castro the sugar crops were all unrestricted, but in 1962, four years after he took power, the crop dropped to 4.8 million tons. Before the Castro period the United States had bought Cuban sugar and paid a better price for it than Cuba could get in the world market. But Soviet Russia does things differently. It buys the sugar, not for cash but for goods and services at prices set by the U.S.S.R. itself and heavily weighted in its own favor.

On returning from a trip to Moscow in May 1963, Castro announced a new agrarian reform. His "war" on sugar was called off—henceforth Cuba would specialize in what she was best suited by nature to raise. By 1970, he predicted, the country would be producing 10 million tons of sugar annually. He ordered a comeback of "monoculture." *It had taken a Communist revolution to restore sugar to the place it had held in the bad old days of American economic domination.*

The following year, 1964, when sugar prices in the world market hit 13.2 cents a pound, the highest in forty-three years, the Cuban crop declined still further, to 3.8 million tons. Since then the Communist regime has kept production figures secret; though it has moved large segments of the population into the cane fields under conditions of slave labor, there has been little improvement in output.

Plans for harvesting the 1970 sugar crop indicate the desperate situation Castro now faces. Under private ownership, the sugar mills normally begin to grind in late December or early January of each year, because the sucrose content of cane is highest in February and March (almost 13 percent of the cane's weight). The harvesting of the 1970 crop, however, was started prematurely in mid-1969, when the sucrose content runs as low as 9 percent. Pressed, Castro sent into the fields a labor force consisting of militia, paid at the rate of 7 pesos, or less than two U.S. dollars, a month: yes, *less than two dollars a month.* Also working the fields were many thousands of political prisoners, who were paid nothing at all; thousands of industrial workers, who received agricultural wages that were sharply lower than their industrial pay; and massive "volunteer" labor battalions, recruited throughout the country. Among the latter were several hundred thousand "liberated" women.

By now Castro admits that at the time he seized power he was not well informed about Cuba's foreign trade. Unfortunately for Cuba and the Cubans, it took four calamitous years to teach him that the country depends on exports, mostly sugar, to pay for many of the things it needs; that sugar has always been Cuba's "money crop"; and that Cuba cannot get something for nothing, even under "socialism." As Theodore Draper has pointed out, this was perhaps the most expensive course in elementary economics ever given.

During the Castro years the rice crop yield has fallen 18 percent, the yield of corn 40 percent, and of sorghum 50 percent. The quality of tobacco has worsened catastrophically, and the drop in fresh milk production has produced consternation.

At this writing the supply of food available for Cubans varies from month to month. Occasionally it is augmented by imports from Iron Curtain countries. But the over-all trend is downward. Toward the end of 1967 butter was no longer available, nor could chickens or fish be purchased. Except for infants and the aged, milk could be bought only on a doctor's prescription. Coffee was restricted to one and a half ounces a week. Rice, an important staple in the Cuban diet, was limited to three pounds, or twelve cups, a month per person. Meat was doled out, a quarter-pound a week—what Americans consume in a single hamburger. The weekly ration of beans was six ounces, and each person was allowed a pound of potatoes a week. Even the lowly *malanga,* which resembles the potato, once thrown into market baskets *gratis,* is now rationed. Early in 1968 the regime began rationing bread. Queues begin to form at grocery stores at 4 A.M., hours before opening time, and too frequently supplies are exhausted long before closing time at 6 P.M.

Economic distress is just one of the many causes of discontent, bordering on despair. In Cuba today there is a form of passive civil war between the rulers and the people. It is reflected in work slowdowns, low productivity, poor quality of farm and industrial commodities—and by the sand that is often found in gears. It is reflected, too, in the dream of escape that obsesses so many Cubans. Despite all obstacles, 600,000 men and women have fled the country, leaving behind everything but the clothes on their backs. Among other things, this has deprived the island of a substantial percentage of its technical and professional brains and skills.

The proportion of those Cubans against the Communist regime has been estimated by knowledgeable enemies of the system at 85 to 90 percent. Obviously, this is not the kind of phenomenon that can be "proved" or measured. But having studied all available data and interviewed the best informed escapees, I can only confirm that the malcontents are an overwhelming majority of the population.

Labor certainly has no reason to love the Castroites. Here again there is a parallel with what has happened in Europe's Iron Curtain countries. The trade unions have become little more than a branch of the totalitarian government. All the great gains labor had made before the advent of Communism were lost during Castro's first years in power. At the end of 1963 the screws were tightened on workers by the imposition of "wage scales and work norms." Wages were fixed according to eight categories. Three-quarters of all workers were graded to earn from 85 to 115 pesos monthly (about $21 to $30 U.S., according to the present black market rate of exchange). All wages were predicated on the fulfillment of "norms," or standards of production, a familiar Soviet practice. If a worker failed to reach his norm, his wage was reduced by the percentage it dropped below the norm. If he exceeded the norm, his wage was increased by only half the percentage of excess. Thus the penalty was double the reward.

Despite its harshness, the system has not worked as expected. On October 30, 1964 the frustrated Fidel Castro admitted in a speech that Cubans had worked more and better before the revolution. He blamed it on the "rigor" of the capitalist system; the private owner, he said, did not "throw away his money or manage his business badly." [3]

On October 3, 1964 came the "Law of Labor Justice." Punishable offenses ranged from lateness, absenteeism, delinquency, and lack of respect for superiors, to fraud and damage to equipment. Penalties ranged from wage deductions, starting at 15 percent for periods up to four months, to permanent deprivation of the right to gainful employment anywhere. "Work councils" were set up to enforce the tougher rules. Members of these councils were elected for three-year terms in every work center employing twenty-five or more people. To qualify, they had to display "a good socialist attitude toward work." In this way trade union officials were placed in the position of punishing workers instead of defending their interests. The Labor Minister justified the measure on the grounds that "labor discipline has weakened extraordinarily, while absenteeism has reached extraordinary proportions." [4] Six days after the election of the work councils, the Minister shot himself.

As in all Communist countries, Cuba looks upon religion as an enemy of socialism, and since Cuba is essentially a Catholic country the Catholic Church has suffered grievously. All Catholic educational institutions, hospitals, asylums, and social centers have been confiscated. For example, the Catholic University of St. Thomas of Villanova, Marianao, has been closed for

[3] Draper, p. 184.
[4] *Ibid.*, p. 185.

seven years and is at present used as a storehouse. The large chapel of the *Colegio de Belén* is being used for secular activities, occasionally functioning as a night club. Religious services have frequently been interrupted; members of the Catholic hierarchy have been vilified, and some have been arrested. The Cardinal Archbishop of Havana, His Eminence Manuel Cardinal Arteaga, sought asylum in the Argentine Embassy and died in asylum at the Papal Nunciatura. Before Castro there were 1,000 priests and 2,700 nuns in Cuba. Now there are fewer than 125 priests, and about 100 nuns.

Castro had been unequivocally on record against forced military service. "We will not establish military service because it should not be compulsory to be a soldier." [5] But on July 27, 1963, he called for compulsory military service to fight "the parasitical element, the potential *lumpen* [bums] of tomorrow." Actually, his purpose was to build up a cheap militarized labor corps; recruits cut cane and do other hard work for a few pennies a day. Heading these labor battalions is Raúl Castro, the army chief.

One of the saddest consequences of the Bay of Pigs and of the Missile Crisis is that the new generation in Cuba is being systematically indoctrinated with the idea that the United States is the embodiment of everything evil and eventually must be destroyed. The youth of Cuba are taught hatred and violence. The whole life of the country is saturated by anti-American propaganda, and the job is done with typical Communist thoroughness. The gutter press, the three Havana television stations and five radio stations pour half-truths and whole lies into Cuban homes every hour of every day. The unvarying Communist line calls for struggle against the Yankee devils and their "puppet" nations of Latin America. Textbooks from kinder-

[5] *Revolución,* January 14, 1959.

garten up, and history books in particular, have been revised and distorted to conform to authorized "truths," another name for official lies. Total censorship of reading matter makes a mockery of any improvement in literacy.

To spread hatred of the United States throughout Latin America and to stir up wars of "national liberation," Castro recently placed in operation a 150,000-watt radio station, said to be three times as powerful as any single radio station operating in the United States. Located in Oriente province, and built under the direction of Czech engineers, it is capable of extending its radio tentacles throughout Latin America and of jamming more than 70 U.S. stations. Five more such stations are under construction. Obviously these facilities, which are in addition to 134 commercial stations for domestic use, are enormously costly for a country experiencing serious economic trouble, but Communism does not count the cost where its campaigns of political subversion are involved.

One of Cuba's greatest problems is housing. The shortage of living accommodations is so extreme that engaged couples often have to wait two and three years to get married. To build the desperately needed homes would require great quantities of cement, among other things, and most of the nation's supply is being diverted to build vast underground installations, storage facilities, and connecting tunnels.

The grimmest aspect of Communist Cuba is the domination of the individual person's daily life by the CDR, the "Committee for the Defense of the Revolution." This highly personalized espionage system is geared into the country's judicial system; it supplies a constant source of victims for Castro's execution walls, prisons, prison camps, and labor battalions.

The CDR operates in every block of every town and village. It issues ration books, doles out milk for children, and recruits boys and girls for the militia. Its most important function is to spy on everyone and make sure that anyone harboring "counter-revolutionary" sentiments is promptly reported. The opportunities for local persecution are, of course, limitless. One cannot change his residence or transport so much as a stick of furniture to a new apartment without the knowledge and consent of the CDR. That special tool of tyranny, the informer, is the CDR's mainstay, and Cubans, like Russians and Chinese, have come to know the anguish of denunciation by close friends and relatives, and even by their children. They are aware that their most casual conversations, their mail, their telephone calls may be monitored and bring the panic of the after-midnight knock on the door.

The unfortunates who are arrested come up against a legal system that is a brutal machine of punitive compulsion. A law decreed on March 13, 1963 prescribes imprisonment of from twenty to thirty years for stealing as little as one hundred pesos (about $25 U.S.), and the death penalty if the accused was in uniform. Revolutionary courts composed of trustworthy Communists are required to pass sentence within seventy-two hours.

The harsh efficiency of these courts may be judged from the way in which they have jammed the prisons and prison camps with men and women whose only real crime was that they could not or would not adjust to the Communist way of life. No one knows the exact number of political prisoners, and Castro has not permitted the International Red Cross or any other organization to inspect his prisons and labor camps. The lowest estimate comes from Lee Lockwood. In his book, which Castro himself reviewed and corrected, he says that Castro told him that there were approximately twenty thousand "politicals" in custody and that the number was increasing. Without question this figure is a lie; estimates by knowledgeable exiles are several times higher. Some refugees insist that the inmates of prisons and punitive camps come to hundreds of thousands.

I have in my possession an official list of the number of political prisoners as of April 1967, stolen from the Ministry of the Interior and brought to the United States. It shows 69,315 political prisoners in more than 100 jails, prisons, and prison camps. Lockwood remarks that the 20,000 political prisoners Castro acknowledges "would be equivalent to having 600,000 in jail for political reasons in the United States." But on the basis of the government's figure of 69,315, the U.S. equivalent would be almost 2 million Americans in jail for political reasons!

Castro's labor camps have all the characteristics of those in other totalitarian countries, including the barbed-wire fences and verminous barracks. Physical punishment is common, along with the spiritual insult of Communist indoctrination. Significantly, as Lockwood puts it, "the majority of the internees are not, as one might assume, men of urban backgrounds, but *campesinos*—peasants of the mountains and outlying rural areas." He goes on to say that a high percentage of the prisoners were jailed for trivial "errors," and that many appeared to have been the victims of overzealous revolutionary tribunals that, in the aftermath of the Bay of Pigs invasion, meted out "justice" with a vindictive severity recalling the Reign of Terror in France.

In the prisons the food consists of watery coffee, bread, rice and beans, and for dinner usually thin soup and macaroni. Dysentery and hepatitis are rampant. After a few weeks the prisoners become gaunt from hunger, the skin tight on their skulls. They are not allowed to exercise; they receive no mail, packages, or visitors. In the labor camps conditions are better. Prisoners live behind barbed wire, of course, rise at five in the morning, have at least three hours of indoctrination five days a week, and spend the rest of their days at forced labor in the fields—but at least they are permitted to visit their families once every forty-five days. These conditions are a matter of common knowledge throughout Cuba.

All of this concerns the living. The dead must also be counted as part of the cost of the lost invasion of April 1961 and the no-invasion pledge given by President Kennedy eighteen months later.

In the fall of 1967 I talked to an old friend who had just come out of Cuba. He has always been a man of few words and given to understatement, but he reported to me that the prevailing belief in Havana was that by mid-1967, more than 15,000 men had been put to death by the regime. Fewer than 1,000, he recalled, met violent deaths during the almost seven years Batista last controlled the Cuban government, among both the government and non-government forces and including the Castro revolutionary activities of 1957–58.

Batista has been criticized for many things and some of the criticism is justified. But even so-called "dictatorships" are relative in their oppressions. Who would defend Hitler on the ground that the last Kaiser was a tyrant? No self-respecting expert in the field of Russian scholarship can fail to note that Tsarist absolutism, for all its faults, was benign in contrast to the Soviet police-state.

Not in defense of Batista but in defense of historical fact, it must be acknowledged that his rule was benevolent and "welfarist" in comparison to Castro terror. There are no political or other freedoms in Cuba today except on Castro's terms. Whatever the basis of measurement, the pre-Castro past was infinitely more attractive than the Communist present. Had it not been interrupted by the Castro tragedy, the consistent progress in industry and agriculture, science and education, would unquestionably have put Cuba far ahead of where it was even in 1958 and incomparably better off than it is today. And the population would have been spared the miseries, the physical and spiritual degradations, inseparable from Communism in practice. They would have been spared the thousands of lives snuffed out by Castro, the tortures in prisons, the wretchedness of slave labor camps.

When we read about those killed in Red Cuba, we think in terms of men riddled by firing squads. But there has been a continuing toll of life, thousands in the aggregate, among the men, women, and children trying to escape from the prison-island. The able columnist and former U.S. Ambassador to Switzerland, Henry J. Taylor, recently offered a chilling glimpse of this calamity. In a column he titled "Carnage Off Key West," he wrote in part:

> Each day the Coast Guard sends into Castro's patrol belt two Grumman Albatross planes and at least one cutter. With this limited allotment, they have brought to safety more than 800 small craft escaping from Cuba. But all too often they find pathetic little boats carrying the bodies of men, women and children riddled by machine gun bullets. . . .
> The records of the Miami Cuban Refugee Center (of the Department of Health, Education and Welfare) show 10,000 arrivals in 1,002 small boats since June 1961, a figure which becomes about 12,000 by including those not registered with the Center. It has been estimated that for every one who wins freedom three die. Forty thousand men, women and children: 12,000 alive, 35,000 corpses! This is the awful arithmetic on the nearby island that the United States swore to defend.

Some liberal American pundits try to persuade themselves and their readers that Cuba has gained in national dignity, arguing that it is no longer dependent on foreign capital, no longer "semi-colonial." They manage to slur over the obvious fact that Red Cuba is completely dependent, economically and politically, on foreign nations—namely the Communist bloc.

In any case, the "colonial" issue is irrelevant. All young industrial societies have relied upon capital and technical help from advanced societies. The United States in the last century drew heavily on foreign capital, from Great Britain in particular. America and other industrialized nations, including the U.S.S.R. itself, take pride today in providing capital and know-how to new and undeveloped countries; those countries welcome the help. Now and always, economically young nations **have used tax benefits** and other incentives to attract foreign capital investments. The Communist jargon about colonial and semi-colonial "exploitation" should not be permitted to cloud our minds on the realities of this subject.

I have been reproved on occasion for failing to find "something good" in the Castro dispensation. I can only reply, in all honesty, that I have been unable to discover any virtue or achievement to justify a system guilty of such major and fiendish sins. I feel deeply about the gruesome fate of the country and the people I learned to love and admire in four decades of living and working in Cuba.

Even things that we normally consider good have been perverted for evil purposes. Education has been misused by Castro to disseminate lies and to instill hatred of the United States; to condition his followers, especially the young, to the task of overthrowing U.S. democracy along with the societies of Latin American countries. It has been misused to sow hatred for religion and contempt for humane and spiritual values and traditions.

No Cuban can support the Castro regime except on the basis of a privileged position of self-interest, youthful delusion, inertia —or fear. It cannot be supported by genuine faith, since even those who had nothing to lose have learned that nothing plus nothing is still nothing. In the population at large there are thousands of pockets of passionate hatred for the man who has shed so much blood and dishonored his own promises, while ripping to shreds the economic fabric of the country.

This then is the Cuban scene behind the protective shield of the Kennedy no-invasion pledge, and it will worsen with the passage of time.

The Kennedy-Johnson administrations were, of course, unwilling to admit their share of responsibility for the degradation of their Cuban neighbors. The State Department argues that the no-invasion pledge was conditioned on a promise of on-site inspection to provide assurance that the missiles had been removed. Refusal to permit such inspection, it reasons, makes the Kennedy pledge "inoperative," and *The New York Times* supports this argument editorially.

The Soviet answer to this *de jure* reasoning is that the United States accepted a modification of the agreement when it settled for high-level air inspection in return for a promise that its planes would not be shot down. As a consequence, says Moscow, when the ground-to-air missiles in Cuba were turned over to Cuban crews, it obtained a pledge from Castro not to shoot down the American U-2's. And Khrushchev added that when Johnson took over from Kennedy, he recognized the validity of the Kennedy pledge.

It is indisputable that an agreement exists *de facto,* and that the *realities* of the situation are the only aspects that interest those who are suffering and dying in Cuba. Castro has confirmed that the agreement not to invade "exists *de facto,*" adding, "and I can say to you that even more agreements exist besides, about which not a word has ever been said."

Such secret agreements may well refer to the harassment of Cuban exiles. During his Presidential campaign in 1960, John F. Kennedy criticized the Republicans for not giving more help to the Cuban "fighters for freedom," but immediately following the Missile Crisis settlement he ordered that they be arrested and their vessels and weapons confiscated, calling their raids ineffective. Everyone who has lived in Cuba is familiar with the importance of any action that symbolizes the spirit of counter-revolution, and they know of the sacrifices that Cubans in exile are ready to make for their country. Kennedy's order sent a chill of dismay through the hearts of the Cuban patriots. To them it meant not a hands-off policy but *American intervention to protect Castro and the Soviet forces in Cuba.*

Behind the protective shield of the Kennedy no-invasion pledge, the best brains of the Communist Empire meet secretly and openly to conspire and plot the destruction of democracy in the Western Hemisphere. In January 1966 about five hundred delegates from seventy-nine Communist parties and "liberation fronts" in Latin America, Africa, and Asia met in Havana. Known as the Tricontinental Conference, it was dominated by the thirty-four-man Soviet delegation, whose leader, Sharaf R. Rashidov, announced that it "had come to this conference to promote in every conceivable way . . . our common struggle against imperialism." A "Permanent Committee of Assistance to Movements at War with Imperialism" was set up with headquarters in Havana, its purpose to synchronize and promote armed revolution throughout Latin America. The Conference pledged moral, political and material support for this objective. Secretary of State Rusk noted that at the close of the Conference the Latin American delegates "had left Havana with their suitcases bulging with money for the intensification of subversive movements."

The failure of the United States to react to this momentous threat at its very threshold is part of the cost of the Missile Crisis and the Bay of Pigs. Four years earlier Kennedy had announced at a press conference that "If Cuba should ever attempt to export its aggressive purposes by force or the threat of force against any nation in this hemisphere . . . this country will do whatever must be done to protect its own security and that of its allies." The statement proved to be meaningless.

The terrible losses, defeats, and withdrawals continued unabated in spite of the fact that experience has taught that appeasement of would-be aggressors operates to bring on the wars it is designed to prevent. The Bay of Pigs and the Missile Crisis showed that dictators construe pacifism as moral weakness. They then take more gambles and increase their aggression. Winston Churchill expressed this idea when he wrote after World War II:

> Still, if you will not fight for the right when you can
> easily win without bloodshed; if you will not fight when
> your victory will be sure and not too costly; you may

come to the moment when you will have to fight with all the odds against you and only a precarious chance for survival. There may be a worse case. You may have to fight when there is no hope of victory, because it is better to perish than to live as slaves.

CHAPTER TWENTY-THREE

The Root of the Tragedy

If my story were to end here, it would be little more than an account of the principal events of Cuba's tragic decade. We would not have identified the cause of the disasters. It is not enough to name those chiefly to blame and to label them "liberals." Nearly all of them are intelligent and well-meaning men.

What motivated them? How account for their actions?

These are questions I have pondered since my escape from Cuba. If logical and convincing answers can be found, we will have arrived at something of importance—the cause of the tragedy.

My search for the answers, I soon learned, was complicated by the fact that the contemporary liberal differs radically from the "old" liberal whom I knew so well and with whom I identified nearly fifty years ago. The liberals of my youth, when I was living and working in the United States, were nationalistic and patriotic. There were few pacifists or semi-pacifists among them. Then, as now, they wanted their country to be right. But in any critical struggle their country came first, even if they believed it might not be right. *They wanted the United States to win.*

This no longer holds true. Most liberals today, if they feel their country to be wrong, prefer that it lose out. There can be no doubt that, for good or ill, the present-day liberal is more internationalist, less patriotic, more inclined to pacifism than the liberal of several decades back. He is likely to rate the survival of mankind above the survival of American civilization or even the survival of the United States. Essentially he has renounced patriotism for ideology.

An ideology, as I understand it, is a habit of thinking and feeling so ingrained and compulsive that it functions independently of reality. It involves such a strong commitment to a doctrine that if empirical truth conflicts with dogma, it is truth that becomes distorted.

A striking example of the extent to which doctrinal thinking may blot out reality remains etched in my memory. It was a conversation I had in early 1965 with Dr. Milton Eisenhower, the distinguished former President of Johns Hopkins University, whose character and dedication to noble causes have never been open to question.

Dr. Eisenhower's book, *The Wine Is Bitter,* published in 1963, contained some wild misstatements about conditions in Cuba under Batista. In my view it is possibly the worst book on Latin America published in the last quarter-century. He wrote, for example: "Every person wanting an export permit, every foreigner who purchased property in Cuba . . . paid tribute." My law firm obtained export permits covering Cuban products worth a great many millions of dollars and supervised the purchase of property in Cuba that also ran into many millions. No "tribute" (graft) was paid in any instance.

Astonished at such statements by a man of Dr. Eisenhower's reputation, I asked for and obtained an appointment with him. To start the conversation, I asked when he had last been in Cuba. *He had never been there,* Dr. Eisenhower replied. *He did not even speak our language.*

A day or two before our meeting, President Johnson had ordered the Marines into the Dominican Republic, and our talk turned at once to that event. The intervention had "horrified" him, Dr. Eisenhower told me. It might have been justified to save lives, but never for a "political" purpose, as he felt was the case in this instance. There would be riots and anti-American demonstrations throughout Latin America, he was sure. The President had violated the "sacred" hemispheric policy of non-intervention, and this could only serve the cause of Communism.

There are many men, including high State Department officials, who count Dr. Eisenhower among those primarily responsible for bringing Castro to power; as his brother's adviser on Latin American affairs he was the man through whom Wieland and Rubottom had a short-cut to the White House. *American political intervention had delivered Cuba to Communism.* Now, six years later, though known Communists had a dominant role in the Dominican rebellion, Dr. Eisenhower still clung to his conviction that the best hope for resolving the political ills of Latin America rests with what he termed "democratic central groups," what other liberals call the "non-Communist democratic Left." The Cuban experience had taught him nothing. It conflicted with liberal doctrine, and it was the ideology that remained unimpaired.

Subsequent events proved Dr. Eisenhower wrong on all counts. The Foreign Ministers of the OAS voted to support the intervention in the Dominican Republic. No noticeable anti-American manifestations occurred in Latin America. Brazil, Paraguay, Honduras, Nicaragua, and Costa Rica sent military contingents; a Brazilian general assumed command of the inter-American force. Order was restored and honest elections were held. The Dominicans overwhelmingly rejected the leftist anti-American Juan Bosch. Castro and the Communists suffered a setback, and President Johnson was vindicated.

Had Dr. Eisenhower been as influential in determining policy in 1965 as he was in 1958, there is a strong likelihood that we would now have *three* Caribbean countries in the Communist camp; Haiti, occupying the same island as the Dominican Republic, undoubtedly also would have fallen.

Within the context of this book it is neither necessary nor

possible to attempt an analysis of contemporary liberal ideology as a whole, but to understand the motivations of those policy-makers in Washington chiefly responsible for the Cuban tragedies, it is indispensable to underline a few basic characteristics of liberal thinking as it affects Cuban and Latin American issues.

1. *All liberals unite in the belief that their main enemy is to the Right, never to the Left.* Pas d'ennemi à gauche.

To topple a rightist regime, liberals call for boycotts, embargoes, the end of tourism and of cultural contacts, and the support of revolutionary opposition. They denounce aid to or compromise with reactionary—to them fascist—governments as dishonorable appeasement. Often they justify war itself if that becomes necessary to bring the regime down.

But their response to leftist regimes and to Communism is gentler. Here they call for an *increase* in cultural exchange, an expansion of trade and of tourism, and a search for areas of common interest. Thus, there can be no dialogue with Franco, for Franco is a man of the Right. Tito, however, is generously provided with money, goods, and food, because Tito is of the Left. *Over a fifteen-year period* (1945–1960) *the United States gave more foreign aid to Tito's Communist Yugoslavia,* with a population of about nineteen million, *than to all of Latin America put together,* which then had a population of about two hundred million.[1] "Foreign Aid" is not "aid," it is a *political* instrument.

In Cuba the enemy, for liberal American officials and the liberal press, was Batista, although he was pro-American, had always voted at the United Nations with the United States, had given the Pentagon every military facility, and had welcomed

---

[1] Arthur M. Schlesinger, Jr., *A Thousand Days* (Boston: Houghton Mifflin Company, 1965), p. 172.

and protected American trade and business. Because Batista was a conservative and a man of the Right. Castro, on the other hand, although known to be anti-American, a radical terrorist, and under Communist influence, was judged by the liberals to be worthy of support, one with whom they could cooperate, for whose violent nature and hatred of the United States generous allowances should be made. Castro was a man of the Left. For the liberals the enemy too often is not the Communist, but the anti-Communist; not a Khrushchev or a Mao, but a Chiang Kai-shek.

Nine months after Castro had declared himself a Marxist-Leninist, the ADA *World,* official organ of the ultra-liberal Americans for Democratic Action, strongly objected to any armed action against him or unilateral economic sanctions against his regime.[2] At the same time it was calling for economic and political sanctions against South Africa and Portugal![3] This double-thinking is standard for such groups. Without exception liberal opinion has favored, in its early stages, every revolution during the present century that seemed to come from the Left and to be aimed against the Right, including the Russian and Chinese Communist revolutions.[4]

Over the years Americans for Democratic Action has condemned the Spanish regime and supported anti-Franco opposition. Its program, adopted at the annual ADA conventions, has never asked for support of the people enslaved by Communism in their struggles for liberation, whether in Russia, China, Eastern Europe, or Cuba.[5] It has recommended diplomatic recognition and United Nations membership for Mao Tse-tung and withdrawal of recognition of Chiang Kai-shek. It

[2] James Burnham, *Suicide of the West* (New York: The John Day Company, 1964), p. 211.

[3] *Ibid.,* p. 211.

[4] *Ibid.,* p. 211.

[5] *Ibid.,* p. 209.

calls for an attitude of "understanding of legitimate aspirations" of the Soviet Union and urges that Washington continue both negotiation and conciliation with the Soviet totalitarian state.[6]

2. *Modern liberalism always favors discussion, negotiation, and compromise as the only rational and acceptable method of settling disputes. It rejects the use of coercion and force.*

The majority of liberals are either moderate or absolute pacifists, and therefore are against both war and warriors, except when it comes to canceling out the far Right. They find it difficult to reconcile themselves to the use of force, or to handle it realistically. Among other things, American liberals have an obsessive fear that the use of their nation's power will offend world opinion.

But, human nature being what it is, there are often clashes that cannot be resolved by discussion and compromise. Force has always been a normal and natural ingredient of every human society—for the maintenance of internal order and protection against external threat—and this will continue to be the reality. But since this is a pessimistic view of human affairs, it does not harmonize with the wishful thinking of most liberals. They shy away as much and as long as possible from the application of force, and when its use becomes unavoidable, they plan it badly and apply it erratically.

Their tendency is to employ power as an instrument of bluff. An example of this, if James Reston of *The New York Times* correctly reports a conversation with President Kennedy, is the manner in which the United States became militarily involved in Southeast Asia. Kennedy, according to Reston, said that it was necessary to make American power "credible" to the Russians, so the war in Vietnam was intensified, "not because the situation

---

[6] *Ibid.*, p. 209.

on the ground demanded it" but because the President "wanted to prove a diplomatic point, not a military point." [7]

Internally, when minority groups resort to violence to attain their objectives, liberals try to avoid using counter-force. And when the conduct of a minority group reaches limits that provoke the use of counter-force and some demonstrators get hurt, it is the police and the authorities who are termed the aggressors. In external relations, similarly, liberals seldom apply the right amount of force at the right time.

The classic example of this, of course, is Cuba. The way in which the force available to the United States was mishandled at the Bay of Pigs is utterly beyond comprehension. President Kennedy, under the influence of his liberal mentors, *used just enough force to assure the worst possible result from every conceivable point of view.* It hardly need be added that men who understand force and its functions would have brought to bear all the power needed to guarantee victory.

Dr. Milton Eisenhower has referred to the Bay of Pigs debacle in these terms: "In the long history of the United States, this was our worst planned, most capriciously managed action—and our most humiliating defeat." He is wrong. The operation was skillfully planned by professionals but later wrecked by liberal amateurs. Besides, there would have been no Bay of Pigs if the State Department (under Dr. Eisenhower's influence) had not ousted Batista and opened the road for Castro.

During the 1962 Missile Crisis, American power was again mishandled. The armed forces were ordered to back away from a confrontation on land and on sea. The Communists succeeded in nullifying the vitally important understanding for on-site inspection. Soviet troops and technicians remained on the island. The Castro dictatorship emerged *strengthened* by the no-invasion pledge. All the American IRBMs in Europe confronting the Soviets (in England, Italy and Turkey) were withdrawn. The public was given to understand at the time that these mis-

[7] *The New York Times,* January 18, 1966.

siles were obsolete but no less an authority than General Curtis LeMay now reveals that they had just become operational. "They should have been left in place," he says.[8]

The fact is that, although it enjoyed tremendous power superiority, the United States failed even to maintain the *status quo ante*. In his address on October 22, 1962 President Kennedy said that the greater risk lay in *not* acting—that strong action involved the *lesser risk*. But in the ensuing days he followed policies of risk avoidance. To the adversary his restraint suggested fear, weakness, and ineptness. At home it widened the gap between word and deed, and in the end weakened the hemisphere by strengthening Castro.

Liberals had a greater voice in international policy during the Kennedy administration than in any previous government of the United States. Certainly theirs was the dominant influence in shaping American policy with respect to Cuba. Invariably their advice produced decisions for disaster.

3. *Liberal ideology favors "democracy" everywhere, at all times, and is unable to acknowledge the possibility that some other type of rule may be suitable for a developing nation, unless it be some form of leftist totalitarianism.*

Liberalism has a passion for political and social innovation and reform, and if the changes do not come rapidly, it favors revolution to bring them about. In Latin America it looks with distaste on the traditional *caudillo*.

Any Washington policy-maker who adheres to these views, I am convinced, is not qualified to deal with Latin American affairs. As underlined in the Foreword of this book, the political structure of Latin America is rooted in a past that goes back almost six centuries and does not lend itself to rapid innovation. It goes back to the earliest days of the great explorations, when

[8] Curtis E. LeMay, *America Is in Danger* (New York: Funk & Wagnalls, 1968), p. 140.

Columbus established the first colonial government in the West Indies and had the title of Governor, appointing all officers and distributing land and natives to his fellow countrymen.

During this long period there evolved a traditional society composed of four principal elements: A strong chief of state; the military establishment; the Church; and the educated class, which includes the so-called "oligarchs." *If any of these four basic ingredients of society are destroyed or greatly weakened, a churning social disturbance results,* and unless some strong personality, usually a military figure or *caudillo,* steps in to pick up the pieces, the Communists will take over and impose their dictatorship, since their apparatus is there and always ready to fill a power vacuum.[9]

From the educated class and "oligarchs" come the teachers and technicians, the political, industrial and business leaders, the entrepreneurs. They want progress for their countries but they feel that the transition to a better life for the masses should be orderly, not disruptive, and that the maintenance of political stability is the indispensable condition for attaining it.

Most of the millions of men and women who hope and strive for social, economic and political progress for their countries want "democracy," but they know it can be achieved only from *within,* that its attainment is basically a personal and spiritual problem, one that the people of each country must painstakingly solve for themselves.

The basic issue, therefore, is not whether a government is democratic and representative or whether it is dictatorial and authoritarian. It is whether a government, so long as it is not totalitarian, *can hold a society together sufficiently to make possible the gradual transition to a better life for the masses.*[10]

[9] This conviction is lucidly reiterated in James Burnham's *Suicide of the West,* p. 282.
[10] John Paton Davies, Jr., *Foreign and Other Affairs* (New York: W. W. Norton & Company, Inc., 1964), p. 57.

An example of the liberal passion for reform in Latin America, geared to theory rather than practical considerations, is the Alliance for Progress, Washington's answer to Castro in 1961. Under this scheme the United States offered to put up twenty billion dollars if the Latin Americans contributed eighty billion—and turned virtually everything upside down in their countries. Although the program was openly hostile to the propertied classes and the military who rule most of Latin America, these were expected to be good sports and yield to American concepts of reform of a magnitude and at a pace that could have been accomplished only through bloody social revolutions and with great risk of Communist takeovers. In some countries the reforms demanded by Washington amounted to incitement of revolution, which scared off the private capital on which the Alliance had counted to contribute to the growth process.

The end result was that no waves of reform swept the hemisphere. As originally conceived, the program would have been resisted by the native establishments with violence if necessary. Kennedy and his advisers were astonished to discover that the Latin Americans persisted in being themselves, determined to defend their way of life against Communism in their own fashion. Eventually Washington learned that the Alliance, so consistent with liberal theory as originally conceived, had a serious flaw: *It couldn't work!* It learned, too, that the plan was resented as paternalistic. Whether it has taken the lessons to heart—in a realization that no one in Washington is wise enough to manipulate traditional societies south of the Rio Grande—remains to be seen.

The rulers of Latin America were entirely right in rejecting this naïve, self-righteous, and basically misinformed foreign proposal to weaken or destroy their societies. They recognized that any short-range program of this nature, if implemented, was more apt to hasten than to prevent the Communist conquest of Latin America. Who would question that the rulers of Latin America know their own people?

*   *   *   *   *   *

More than eight years have passed since I waited to be finished off by a Castro firing squad. But because the Girón invasion was then under way, presumably under American management, I was supremely confident it would succeed. I took it for granted that my impending death was a small part of the price for the certain liberation of our country.

It all turned out differently. I evaded death—but Cuba remained in chains. I made a vow to devote my remaining years to finding out *why* the Bay of Pigs undertaking failed. For this inquiry I had some advantages. More than most exiles, I had personal contacts with both American and Cuban men of affairs, inside and outside of government circles, and I have found them for the most part willing and even eager to help me get at the facts. Necessarily, my explorations took me far beyond the Bay of Pigs—backward to the primary disaster of Castro's achievement of total power, and forward to the Missile Crisis and other events since 1961.

This book is the fulfillment of that long-ago pledge. Its conclusions will be rejected out of hand by doctrinaire liberals whose opinions derive from ideological fixations; they are normally immune to fact. There are no arguments to dislodge firm ideological commitments. But even know-nothing liberals must confront some truths that are not in the least theoretical, if only to explain them away. They cannot wholly shut their minds to the sharp decline of the prestige of the United States in the Western Hemisphere following the Girón calamity and the Missile Crisis retreat, or to the obvious dangers of a Communist bastion off the shores of their country.

Cuba is outward quiescent at this writing, but no one can deny that it is America's most critical arena of confrontation with Communism. The island nation is not under enemy threat, as is South Vietnam. *It is in enemy hands.* It is not on the other side of the globe but *inside America's ultimate defense periph-*

ery. Which is more vital to the security of the United States, Vietnam or Cuba? And which should be easier to handle, *given the will to do so?*

The caves, the underground installations, the airfields, and the harbors of Cuba pose a military threat of unknown potential to neighboring countries, including the United States. Equally important, Cuba remains a source of political infection for the entire hemisphere—even the streets and campuses of American communities—an infection expressed in violence and contempt for law and order. *The mere survival of the Castro regime is an element of incalculable importance in the world equation.* The successful defiance of the United States from a stronghold in its own back yard produces an image of Communist invincibility and American weakness, which in turn encourages further anti-American campaigns.

There is uncertainty as to whether nuclear missiles are secreted below the surface of Cuba, but there is no uncertainty about the massive Soviet military presence there. The continued forbearance of Washington, its failure to cancel out the threat and immunize the center of a debilitating infection, raises significant and inescapable questions about American policy.

Does the United States simply have no master plan for ridding its "Mediterranean" of Communism? Is it merely drifting and improvising on this crucial front? Has Cuba been accepted as a permanent bastion of Communism—part of the Communist "peace zone" closed to American "interference," while the "war zone" (the Free World) remains open to the waging of phony "wars of liberation"? The Cuban people know only that during the Kennedy and Johnson administrations the United States, far from firming up its stand on Cuba, softened it, loosening travel restrictions, and, most ominously of all, using its power to *prevent* anti-Castro activities.

One other question inevitably comes up: Can it be that in the settlement of the Missile Crisis, Khrushchev extracted from President Kennedy commitments about which, according to Castro, "not a word has been said"? The State Department denies any such commitments. To make the denials credible, however, some explanations appear to be in order.

Why have the ten communications that passed between Kennedy and Khrushchev not been made public? Is it because, as two responsible American journalists have written, Secretary Rusk fears that the contents would "cause embarrassment to officials who participated in the correspondence" and also would "anger and excite anti-Castro groups in this country"? Clearly the only way to remove the deepening doubts and apprehensions on this score is by releasing the entire exchange of letters.

A forthright American commitment to Cuban liberation by Cubans—without interference by either the United States or Soviet Russia—would change the whole political climate in the Caribbean. And the elimination of the Castro government would remove at least 90 percent of the Communist and other subversive pressures in Latin America. If a choice has to be made in the United States as to where to take a firm stand, surely Cuba is the logical place. That is where the nations face each other most ominously and conspicuously, and that is thus far the Kremlin's weakest and America's strongest front.

Yet, aside from occasional U-2 overflights and half-way economic measures, Washington refrains from employing any of the several means at its disposal to restore and bolster freedom in the Caribbean.

A firm policy would demand a reassertion of the Monroe Doctrine, coupled with a credible determination that Soviet troops and "technicians" be repatriated. Through every possible channel the United States should assist and arm the underground inside Cuba and freedom fighters outside, encouraging sabotage and raids and the establishment of bases for Cuban rebels outside United States territory. It should quarantine Cuba against the importation of weapons, even if defined as defensive, and against shipments of petroleum. American sanctions on shipping should apply to all vessels of any line that uses a single ship in the Cuban trade. The United States could call for public support of a Radio Free Cuba and launch other major propaganda efforts. Finally, it could organize a Latin America Treaty Organization (LATO) outside the OAS, composed of nations prepared to join a task force patterned after NATO. LATO could then help generate task forces for eventual use in support of an internal Cuban liberation movement.

I submit that these are moderate and reasonable options, when compared to what the Soviets would do if the circumstances were reversed; that is to say, if the United States had planted a military sanctuary in the Black Sea, their "Mediterranean," within a few minutes' flight from Soviet shores. There seems to me no doubt that the Russians would have wiped out the threat in a matter of hours. They are never deterred by "world opinion," but act on a rational calculation of the odds.

The present stance of the United States with respect to Cuba is *less* than a "do nothing" policy. It employs its power to *prevent* anti-Castro organization and activity in the Caribbean. Theodore Sorensen has written that immediately following the Missile Crisis President Kennedy ordered that precautions be taken to prevent Cuban exiles from upsetting "the agreement." [11] What agreement? The agreement to remove the missiles and lift the blockade? How could exiles upset such an agreement? Or was the reference to a secret agreement to protect the Communist regime in Cuba?

One man who knew the answer to these disturbing questions was Robert F. Kennedy, but there are others. Surely the time is ripe for these to take the American people, and their traditional friends, the Cuban people, into their confidence.

Against this background of doubt and vacillation, the chiefs

[11] Theodore C. Sorensen, *Kennedy* (New York: Harper & Row, 1965), p. 717.

of state and most influential leaders in Latin America have observed the conduct of the United States in the Caribbean with an increasingly jaundiced eye. Not long ago President Onganía of Argentina informed his cabinet and a group of national leaders that in view of what has happened in the Caribbean their country can no longer look to the United States for support in the struggle against the Communist Empire. And it is no secret that Onganía and President Costa e Silva of Brazil are planning to rescue neighboring countries if they should fall to Communism, by joint military action independent of American participation and without necessarily informing Washington in advance. These are symptoms of hemisphere sentiment that cannot, in the context of the Communist challenge, be ignored or shrugged off by the most powerful nation in the world.

*   *   *   *   *   *

Whither Cuba?

There is no real margin for doubt that one day Cuba will be free. Washington policies will hasten or delay its liberation, but they cannot prevent it. Regardless of any secret Washington-Moscow understanding on the issue, the Cubans are certain to throw off the yoke of Castro and Communism.

Many reasons lead me to this rock-bottom conviction, some of which may not be spelled out in print. But the basic, all-embracing reason is that the Cubans love their country with a profound love, a love of the land, their good earth, and their traditional way of life. We exiles give unstinting thanks to the American people for their generous hospitality. Here we have found open doors, open hands, and open hearts. But no Cuban ever forgets that he is bound by ties of the deepest affection to his homeland, and no day passes when he does not long for home.

One day, perhaps in the noonday sun in a crowded plaza, Castro will be canceled out by a bullet, a knife, or a bomb. Or perhaps, as in the case of Hungary, the people will simply take to the streets.

Because the Hungarian revolution of 1956 was crushed by a

Soviet invasion, it is not generally realized that it was completely successful within its own frontiers. Western journalists and diplomats had believed, until the moment of the uprising, that all elements of potential revolt had been liquidated. The army had been thoroughly indoctrinated; a large proportion of its officers were Communist Party members. The former middle class had ceased to exist, and youth had been indoctrinated by Leninist-Marxists teachers. On the surface everything was peaceful, and by way of clinching guarantee, Soviet forces were stationed in the country.

The explosion that came notwithstanding was unexpected and spontaneous, unplanned and unled. Yet there have been few modern precedents of a revolution that triumphed so overwhelmingly so quickly. Within three days the power had passed to the people. The workers and farmers, the remnants of the middle class, and even the armed forces joined the rebellion almost at once. A large portion of the ruling Party itself went over to the citizenry. The Soviet Union, unable to depend on its military forces already on the scene, had to withdraw them and replace them with more dependable divisions. The revolution was crushed, but from outside, by a foreign invader.

Hungary taught the lesson that revolution against a totalitarian state is possible. The larger the army and militia, the closer it is to the people; the more it is likely to share their despairs and aspirations. The size of Castro's armed forces will not necessarily save the dictatorship and may, indeed, play a decisive role in its overthrow.

Most knowledgeable Cubans agree that the liquidation of Castro will be followed by a swift degeneration and collapse of his regime. But the eruption may well come before he is eliminated. When it does, everyone will say that what seemed "impossible" had in truth been "inevitable." The future political leaders will then emerge from the prisons and from among returned exiles.

Because the people have suffered so long and so grievously under totalitarianism, the pendulum of Cuban history assuredly will swing in the opposite direction—toward free institutions and traditional cooperation with neighboring countries. The island will once again join the family of free nations, to become one of the most beautiful, most prosperous and safest countries in the hemisphere.

Then the Cuban people will seek to restore their historic friendship with the American people. When restored, it must be a friendship based on mutual respect and the Cuban people will only respect the United States when it has political leaders who are capable of acting firmly and courageously in pursuit of their country's enlightened self-interest, which almost always serves the general interest.

Index

3-9-98
Phillip Jason